Introduction to International Development Cooperation

Introduction to International Development Cooperation

Issues and Actors in the Global Arena

Changrok Soh | Kyungyon Moon

Korea University Press

Korea University Press
82-2-3290-4230 (Tel.) 82-2-923-6311 (Fax)
http://www.kupress.com kupress@korea.ac.kr
145, Anam-Ro, Seongbuk-Gu, Seoul, 02841 Korea

Published August 2021

ISBN 979-11-91161-73-1 93320

PRINTED IN REPUBLIC OF KOREA

Introduction

Any students interested in understanding current international affairs are sure to encounter the issue of development assistance, which has emerged as an important global issue. With more than a billion people living on less than a dollar a day and 8 million people dying each year due to poverty and poverty-related diseases, many agree that the problem of global poverty is a moral challenge for all mankind. Over the last several decades, millions of dollars have flowed into developing countries in efforts to alleviate poverty, but the results have been disappointing. Beginning with the Marshall Plan, the United States' initiative to resuscitate Europe following the end of World War II, humanitarian and development assistance has evolved into the primary means to eradicate global poverty. The question remains: can this profound goal be reached?

Theoretically speaking, the eradication of poverty is not an unachievable goal. Rich countries have vast resources and advanced technology at their disposal. They possess enough resources to provide aid to impoverished poor countries. Although there were fluctuations in aid flows to developing countries over the last decades, the interest in alleviating global poverty has continued to increase. More than ever before, the rich are trying to help the poor. However, despite decades of persistent efforts, global poverty continues to exist and many countries continue to suffer from a lack of food, water, proper healthcare and technology. The process of development assistance, as well as poverty eradication, is not as clear-cut as it may seem. This book tries to understand the underlying reasons and the global efforts to achieve this attainable, yet challenging, goal.

The objectives of this book are threefold. It is essential to first understand why the issues of poverty and foreign aid have emerged as a global agenda and how and why these relationships between the rich and the poor have developed. In this sense, the first step is to trace the evolution of foreign aid from its beginnings in the aftermath of World War II to better understand the historical contours of donor and recipient relationships. Second, we seek to assess global efforts made by the international community during the 50-year history of development aid and identify challenges for the Post-2015 era. The international community has improved aid practices but there are still many obstacles to achieving global goals and eradicating global poverty. Last but not least, we recognize that the boundaries of development aid have expanded to include a wide range of complex issues and practices as well as the participation by multiple actors. We also emphasize the importance of constructing a global governance framework and aid architecture that encourages cooperative networking among multiple actors for increased aid effectiveness in the future.

Chapter Overviews

Chapter 1 examines development assistance from the perspectives of various theories of international relations. These theories offer diverse explanations as to why states provide aid. The traditional state-centric approach assumes that the state is the main actor in the global arena and that aid reflects its national interests. However, non-traditional perspectives recognize the emergence of new actors within the global community. They question traditional analyses that concentrated solely upon state actors and attempt to understand today's structural transformations.

Chapter 2 provides an overview of the history and institutionalization of development aid. The original purpose for providing foreign aid was to reconstruct war-torn countries. Over the years, however, the objectives and mandates of development assistance have increasingly focused on the importance of providing assistance to impoverished countries. An analysis of the historical context of development aid sheds light on the purposes and motives driving donor countries to provide development assistance. Another important goal of this chapter is to explore international efforts to institutionalize development aid by the establishment of the OECD Development Assistance Committee (DAC). The efforts of the international community to promote effective aid are presented to provide an understanding of the complications that exist in the development assistance arena. The chapter also discusses efforts to eradicate poverty through the Millennium Development Goals (MDGs). The MDGs signify that poverty alleviation has become the ultimate goal of the international development community. Finally, the chapter covers the recent dialogue and global efforts to replace the MDGs under the Post-2015 regime.

In Chapter 3, we examine the meaning and influence of official development assistance (ODA) as global public goods for poverty alleviation. For this, the chapter seeks to give a concrete definition of the concept of ODA, details its significance, and gives success stories of poverty reduction. It covers the stories of Botswana, Indonesia, South Korea, Mozambique, and Tanzania. The chapter also studies the role of major OECD DAC countries in poverty alleviation and the patterns and characteristics of their ODA, including France, Germany, Japan, the United States, Sweden, and European Union. In addition, the chapter reviews the issues related to emerging donors, such as China, India, and Russia.

Chapter 4 examines different channels of aid from bilateral and multilateral aid to multi-bi aid. Brief cases of bilateral donors illustrate different behaviors amongst donor countries and various examples of multilateral aid donors are introduced to demonstrate how multilateral aid donors are not limited in size or scope. This chapter also recognizes that both bilateral and multilateral aid donors can provide benefits to development aid and also identifies the challenges of promoting aid effectiveness. It examines the different characteristics and advantages and disadvantages of bilateral, multilateral and multi-bi aid. In particular, the last part of the chapter seeks to overcome the challenge of aid harmonization in international development cooperation among these different levels of aid.

Chapter 5 discusses the increasingly influential role of NGOs in development assistance. First, it reviews differing definitions of NGOs. Second, case studies of several NGOs are presented to provide examples of how NGOs can assist developing countries. The chapter next examines how transnational networks are exploited by NGOs in order to maximize their influence on state, civil society, and the international community. Last, the chapter looks at the dynamics of NGO operations. How and when do NGOs exert this influence on state development policies?

Chapter 6 is devoted to private sector participation and considers the relationship between Foreign Direct Investment (FDI) and ODA. The participation of the private sector is highlighted as another critical aspect of development assistance. The second part of this chapter presents cases of countries that have been able to successfully use aid to achieve economic growth and development. These success stories in developing countries demonstrate the potential for development assistance in promoting economic growth and development. Non-conventional cases of aid are also examined to illustrate the diverse aid practices of different countries. As capital in the form of private investments can stimulate economic growth in a developing country, we explore the relationship between capital flows into poor countries and poverty reduction. We also consider the possibility of implementing a governance framework to encourage public-private participation. Public Private Partnerships (PPP) have been advanced to promote collective efforts between the public and private sector. The different options of development assistance available to the private sector will also be explored.

Chapter 7 emphasizes the importance of aid effectiveness. It underlines the importance of increasing aid effectiveness as essential to the international community's efforts in achieving poverty eradication. This chapter explains international efforts to increase effectiveness in aid. It covers a series of international conferences from Rome to Accra and discusses the results of these conferences, focusing on the evolution of the aid effectiveness paradigm in the international aid community. Then, the chapter looks at the most recent conference and agenda on aid effectiveness, which is the 4th Busan High Level Forum on Development Effectiveness held in 2011.

Chapter 8 discusses aid planning and monitoring. It first examines the process of aid planning, which is the selection and combination of differing aid type (project and program aid), conditionality (tied and untied aid), and resource (grant and loan). An example of this is the development of the logical mechanism of project design matrix (PDM). The second part of this chapter explains the differing types and methods of aid as well as various types of projects and programs. A comparison of tied aid to untied aid is provided, and the difference between grants and loans is discussed. The chapter concludes with a discussion of the monitoring and evaluation of aid.

Chapter 9 revolves around the relationship between poverty, security and human rights. Pro-poor growth, defined as growth that maximizes the income gains of the poor, is an essential element of poverty reduction. The focal point of this chapter is to provide explanations of concepts of poverty, security, human rights, and their relationships. These concepts are all interrelated. Human security, unlike traditional state-centric conceptualizations of security, puts particular emphasis on the importance of individual security. It is within the context of human security that poverty alleviation gains further importance; namely, suffering from poverty is a direct violation of human rights. This chapter emphasizes the need for a rights-based approach to development.

Chapter 10 is devoted to sustainable development and green growth. Sustainable development is envisioned as a form of development that meets the needs of the present without compromising the abilities of future generations to meet their own needs. Of the three pillars of sustainable development, social, economic and environmental development, this chapter concentrates on environmental sustainability. Throughout the history of environmental aid the developed countries of the North have clashed with the developing countries of the South. Both sides debated over who are to blame for environmental problems and how these problems should be resolved. These issues can be understood by examining the historical developments of environmental aid. The chapter also discusses current issues such as transboundary air pollution, ozone depletion, climate change, toxic waste, loss of biodiversity, desertification, and deforestation. Environmental aid, or aid that aims to resolve environmental challenges, plays a critical role in achieving environmental sustainability.

Chapter 11 examines development assistance to promote trade in developing countries. Development theories emphasize the importance of production and capacity building for manufacturing, which enables a country to earn and accumulate surplus resources and profits for economic and social development. As a result, the international community has focused on aid to promote and empower the trade capability of developing countries under the approach of aid for trade (AfT). This chapter looks into the operational mechanism of AfT and introduces some successful cases. It also examines major players and policies in this type of aid.

Chapter 12 is devoted to policy coherence for development (PCD) and its application to aid effectiveness. PCD covers different levels of coherence issues between aid and non-aid policies, between donors, between donor and recipient countries, and between recipients. The chapter first discusses the evolution of PCD and examines how this approach is used in the area of development assistance. Secondly, the chapter looks into the working mechanisms of the PCD approach and how it is applied to development policies and practices. The last part of this chapter examines how PCD is used in Peer Review and provides an evaluation of major donor countries.

Chapter 13 recognizes the importance of strengthening partnerships to resolve the fragmentation that exists between multiple actors in development assistance. The role of developing strategies to implement aid projects is left to recipient countries, whereas the evaluations are conducted by donors. In order to strengthen partnerships between donor and recipient countries, it is necessary for both parties to participate throughout the entire development aid process. The chapter also tackles the limitation of the DAC in coordinating the activities of recipient and donor countries to increase cooperation and strengthen partnerships. In this chapter, we also propose a global governance framework designed to promote collaboration among the multiple actors involved in development assistance and, most importantly, to help achieve the goal of global poverty eradication. While global partnerships have been emphasized within the international development community, this chapter proposes that global partnerships and networks are not adequately addressing the extensive diversity that exists in development activities. In this chapter, we propose the construction of an aid regime and emphasize the importance of global networks that can take us towards a new multilateralism.

Chapter 14 introduces international norms and lessons learned from the experience and practice of development cooperation. It first examines the 12 lessons drawn from the Peer Review, which is an informal evaluation of OECD DAC donors' aid policies and practices. Second, the chapter reviews the initiative of Good Humanitarian Donorship, which was introduced by the Swedish government in 2003 and endorsed by 17 donor countries. Including the efforts of non-state actors, this chapter introduces the Code of Conduct for the International Red Cross and Red Crescent Movement and NGOs in Disaster Relief, which was agreed upon by eight of the largest disaster response agencies in 1994. It also examines the Sphere Project, which is a voluntary initiative that brings a wide range of humanitarian agencies together around a common aim to improve the quality of humanitarian assistance and the accountability of humanitarian actors to their constituents, donors and affected populations. Finally, the chapter looks at the case of Better Aid, which is an open forum for NGO development effectiveness.

Table of Contents

Chapter 6. NGOs in International Development Cooperation

Chapter 7. Private Sector & Public-Private Partnership (PPP)

Chapter 8. Aid Effectiveness

Chapter 9. Poverty, Security and Human Rights

Chapter 10. Sustainable Development and Green Growth

Chapter 11. Aid for Trade (AfT)

Chapter 1

Theoretical Perspectives of Foreign Aid[1]

> *"The history of aid-giving has been one of competing pressures swinging the pendulum back and forth between the motivation of altruism, solidarity, poverty and need on the one hand, and the motivation of different forms of self-interest on the other."*[2]

The motives for individual countries to provide aid are diverse and complex. Traditional theories of international relations argue that aid giving simply revolves around a desire to promote national interest, particularly by augmenting the donor country's political power or increasing its economic benefits. Realists put the state at the center of their analysis and see international relations as a process of state competition and collaboration under a structure of anarchy. Since foreign aid is a component of a state's foreign policy, they argue that it is impossible to understand foreign aid without considering the role of national interests.

Some may argue that human beings possess a humanitarian side, motivating them to help the poor. But, in the case of official foreign aid, considerations of morality or humanitarianism are not very persuasive. It is necessary to explain state actions as arising through political calculations of national interest. From this perspective, foreign aid is provided under the belief that donors can achieve economic benefits by enlarging the economic pie, assisting development of newly emerging markets, or finding potential sites to secure natural resources. In the long term, these economic benefits can be translated into political power.

This national interest approach to official foreign aid was a staple of the Cold War period, when both the US and USSR competitively provided aid to their allies in order to expand their political and economic power. With the collapse of the USSR and the demise of the bipolar structure of world politics, this competitive aid-giving was no longer necessary. As a result, many scholars of traditional theo-

1 Some parts of this chapter are revised from Changrok Soh, "Theoretical Considerations Why Countries Provide Development Aid," *Journal of International Politics*, vol. 15, no. 1 (2010): 191-218.

2 Roger C. Riddell, *Does Foreign Aid Really Work?* (London: Oxford University Press, 2007), 92.

ries, realists in particular, predicted that foreign aid would decrease after the end of the Cold War.

However, the emergence of a rapidly changing global environment after the end of the Cold War has required new perspectives to explain the new state of the world, especially the transformation of the relationships between states. Contrary to realists' predictions, foreign aid from advanced countries to less developed countries has steadily increased during the 21st century. New perspectives are also necessary to understand what should be done for the future. How is it possible to explain these trends that contradict traditional understandings of international relations? What happened during this period? What are the theoretical perspectives that can explain this phenomenon?

New perspectives for foreign aid are necessary in an era of new globalization. These are needed, not only to provide a proper explanation for increases in Official Development Assistance (ODA), but also to provide sound policy options for creating a more humane and just global society.

1.1 Traditional Perspectives

While individuals might have some altruistic reasons for providing aid, foreign aid provided by the state, particularly official development assistance, is a political decision that uses public funds. Thus, the context for understanding aid provided by individual persons differs from that of government-funded development assistance, and must be recognized as such.

The political dimensions of development assistance are multidimensional and must be separately understood from the perspectives of both donor and recipient countries. In the case of donors, political considerations are central to the decision making process. Before a government allocates funds to ODA, it must be approved within the domestic political sphere. For ODA efforts to continue on a long-term basis, public awareness and support are also necessary. This is especially true since the funds allocated to development assistance come from the pockets of taxpayers. In this case the decision-making process of any government is complex and difficult because these budgetary choices have serious financial and political consequences. Since the amount of capital that a national government possesses is limited, governments must consciously balance the welfare of their citizens with those of a foreign country.

All decisions for allocating national budget to development aid goes through this process. Even if the provision of aid to developing countries to promote economic development appears to be based on truly altruistic beliefs, further considerations must be made to identify whether this aid has been provided to achieve implicit political interests. It is rare that a state actor will provide aid for "truly" altruistic reasons, or that states will act without considering the impact of their behavior on their domestic economy or populations.

Development aid forms relationships between and among nation states. Developed or advanced countries provide aid to developing countries; thus, development assistance has increased transactions between countries. ODA, which comprises the majority of all development assistance, is a core mechanism in promoting relations among different nation states. In this regard, development assistance has become an important issue of international relations.

Riddell(2007) argues that there are eight main clusters of motives in fluencing donor decisions to allocate aid: ① to help emergency needs; ② to assist recipients achieve their development goals; ③ to show solidarity; ④ to further their own political interests; ⑤ to help promote donor-country commercial interests; ⑥ because of historical relationship; ⑦ to provide global public goods, and ⑧ to promote human rights in recipient countries.[3] All of these donor motives have been explained through the concept of national interest and can be understood through the perspectives of traditional theories of international relations. The following sections will discuss three of the major traditional theories: realist, liberal, and Marxist.

Realist Views

Realist views of international relations are prevalent and influential. This theory emphasizes the strategic purpose of aid. Traditionally, international relations perspectives have concentrated on interpreting state interactions and behaviors to protect national security. The core responsibility of each individual state was to maintain the status quo, nationally and internationally, while serving its own interests. According to realists, the state's core interest in self-protection can explain global patterns of development assistance. Bilateral assistance protects national security interests of donor states while

3 *Ibid.*

multilateral aid enhances the stability of the international system as a whole, thereby increasing the stability and security enjoyed by all states.[4]

According to realist views from Hans Morgenthau to George Liska, aid is a tool for enhancing national power. For them, foreign aid is a policy tool. Viewing foreign aid as just another part of foreign policy was a result of the Cold War, when competition among the great powers included a struggle for influence in developing regions. Foreign aid was seen as a key weapon because it facilitated the possibility of influencing the decision of Third World countries to align with one side or the other. For realists, this political choice is what donors buy when they give assistance to developing countries. The existence of foreign aid is justified as a policy tool because there are interests beyond national borders that cannot be secured through military might. Foreign aid is also able to garner more support than could be achieved through traditional methods of diplomacy. Without foreign aid, donor countries may not be able to receive any such support at all.[5]

Hans Morgenthau

In the article "A Political Theory of Foreign Aid," Morgenthau develops a typology of foreign aid. He identifies five policy aims ranging from military, prestige, humanitarian, economic, and subsistence. This typology seeks to organize the complexity of policies that are labeled 'foreign aid.' Attached to these there are two more types of strategies used for exercising influence: propaganda and bribes. Although most of the identified types of foreign aid policy are political, humanitarian foreign aid is less so, which in spite of being understood as non-political, receives a political function when it is set within a political context.[6]

The main challenge in the realist approach is that it refutes the existence of a goal of helping countries develop and by doing so, it fails to construct a theoretical framework that would allow such a policy goal to be accomplished. Realism also does not acknowledge

4 S. Tisch and M.B. Wallace, *Dilemmas of Development Assistance, The What, Why and Who of Foreign Aid* (Boulder: Westview Press, 1994).

5 Hans Morgenthau, "A Political Theory of Foreign Aid," *The American Political Science Review*, vol. 50, no. 2 (1962): 301.

6 *Ibid.*

the possibility of utilizing foreign aid to promote economic development. Realists believe that the term, 'aid for economic development,' is merely a label masking a policy tool that states employ in their fight for power and supremacy.

Realists have recognized foreign aid as an instrument of political power. This interpretation of aid is founded on realist views of national interest oriented behaviors of individual nation states. Realism identifies states as rational actors that actively seek to increase national security and thus ensure their survival. As such, states struggle to accumulate power, measured as both military and economic capabilities. This leads to the use of aid as a tool to influence other states. Another important aspect of realist thought is that since the 'real' objective of providing aid is the donor state's interests, the actual impact of this aid on the poor is purely incidental.

Liberal Views

Unlike realists, liberals see the development of foreign countries as essential for the future of capitalism because it can help create global stability. While realists do not even accept the idea of sponsoring development, liberals admit that moral vision, values, and ideas may constitute the basis for donor involvement in poor countries.

Lumsdaine draws directly on idealist theory by arguing that the postwar period was a vindication of the Wilsonian vision.[7] An unprecedented degree of official consensus has been reached in what Lunsdaine regards as the practice of development managing to rally support from the developing countries. In Lunsdaine's words, "those who wanted more aid wanted aid divorced from national interests."[8] In contrast to Morgenthau's understanding of aid, and contrary to his advice, the liberal position not only grants an important role to values but takes a step even further by creating the expectation of successful development processes. It is not enough to give aid; the aid must also have a positive outcome.

Liberal internationalists perceive aid as a response by states to collaborate in addressing problems coming from the acceleration of globalization and interdependence. In other words, it is a collective effort to expand the stock of international public goods. If realist views are based on competition in order to achieve national inter-

7 D. H. Lumsdaine, *Moral Vision in International Politics: The Foreign Aid Regime, 1949-1989* (Princeton: Princeton University Press, 1993), 280.

8 *Ibid.*

ests, liberal internationalists accept the possibility of military and humanitarian interventions of sovereignty to pursue liberal objectives. In contrast to realists, liberal internationalists maintain that relations founded on power politics can be avoided through the intervention of multilateral institutions like the UN. They envision a liberal world order that promotes global democracy and democratic peace among states through free trade and interlocking liberal economic and political systems.

While idealists and liberal internationalists maintain their idealistic visions, more recent strains of liberalism, so called neo-liberal institutionalism, has deviated from many traditional tenets. Neo-liberal institutionalism accepts many assumptions found in realism, particularly the belief that the nation state is a unitary and rational actor bent on pursuing national interests. Neo-liberals also agree with realists that anarchy is an important international structure that influences the behaviors of national states.

Robert Keohane

Differences between realists and liberal institutionalists can be found in discussions of cooperation among nation states. While neo-realists believe that cooperation among nation states is extremely difficult due to relative gain concerns, neo-liberals see the possibility of cooperation emphasizing absolute gains.[9] Whereas realists think that states focus on relative gains and the potential for conflict, neoliberal institutionalists assume that states put priority on absolute gains and cooperation. Neo-liberals also emphasize the ability of institutions and regimes to promote cooperation. Cooperation is more likely with the development of institutions because institutions reduce transaction costs and provide information that is normally scarce in conditions of anarchy. Keohane(1988) argues that "institutions are described by neoliberals as persistent and connected by sets of rules (formal or informal) that prescribe behavioral roles, constrain activity, and shape expectations."[10]

According to this view, individual donor countries can cooperatively increase their foreign aid because it contributes to increasing

9 Ian Clark, *Globalization and International Relations Theory* (Oxford, New York: Oxford University Press, 1999).

10 Robert Keohane, "International Institutions: Two Approaches," *International Studies Quarterly*, vol. 32, no. 4 (1988): 383.

the total size of the economic pie that will eventually benefit their economies in the long run. Alongside states, international institutions can perform a key role of reducing uncertainty and transaction costs, which will cause foreign aid to also increase.

Liberals are troubled when they face development failures in recipient countries. The underlying assumption of all international development aid activities is that aid will benefit developing countries and reduce poverty, i.e. to make the pie larger. However, as there is no concrete evidence that foreign aid actually promotes development, the economic benefits of foreign aid to recipient countries has been the focus of debate. Some studies criticize aid, saying it is harmful or counterproductive in reducing poverty. The relationship between economic growth and ODA has also been an issue of debate, with the literature attempting to identify factors that indicate aid effectiveness such as economic growth, infant mortality rates, composition of government spending, or the influence of aid quality on governance.[11] It is widely accepted that ODA assists in promoting the economic growth of developing countries but the conditions for aid to be beneficial are still a focus of discussion.

Research by economists at the World Bank found the relationship between foreign aid and good policy to be positive.[12] Aid boosts economic growth, if countries have reasonable economic policies. Further studies also supported the view that aid's impact on growth was contingent on the policies of recipient countries. Aid would work better in countries with better policy regimes. However, a greater number of studies found that aid works in countries irrespective of the quality of the policy regime.[13] Following these studies, it was argued that weak governance with corruption and bad policies had improved in developing countries, and that donors should be selective in providing more aid to countries that had sound economic policies.

11 See arguments by Peter Boone, "Politics and the Effectiveness of Foreign Aid," *European Economic Review*, vol. 40, Issue 2 (1996): 289-329; Tarhan Feyzioglu, Vinaya Swaroop and Min Zhu, "A Panel Data Analysis of the Fungibility of Foreign Aid," *The World Bank Economic Review*, vol. 12, no. 1 (1998): 29-58; Craig Burnside and David Dollar, "Aid, the Incentive Regime, and Poverty Reduction," The World Bank Development Research Group, *Macroeconomics and Growth* (June 1998) ALL; Stephen Knack, "Aid Dependence and the Quality of Governance: Cross-Country Empirical Tests," *Southern Economic Journal*, vol. 68, no. 2 (2001): 310-329.

12 Craig Burnside and David Dollar, "Aid, Policies and Growth," *American Economic Review*, vol. 90, no. 4 (2008).

13 Mark McGillivray, *Is aid Effective?* (Helsinki: WIDER, 2004).

Marxist Views

According to Marxist thought, the shape of society is determined by its underlying material conditions. In this context, material conditions are the relationships that people enter into in order to fulfill their basic needs. The idea of exploitation is core to understanding Marxist ideas, which is emphasized by Marx as an inherent element of capitalist production. An important distinction is made between labor and labor-power. The latter can become a commodity under capitalism, allowing the employer to buy or sell labor-power. The Marxist critique of aid emphasizes how it acts as a tool for dominant states at the center of the world to control and exploit developing countries. This view is further supported by the quantity of aid that is actually tied to donor countries, since the underlying rational behind tied aid is that donor countries hope to provide domestic incentive through providing foreign assistance.

Immanuel Wallerstein

Several streams of IR theories have been influenced by Marx's thinking. As Robert Wood argues, the neo-Marxist tradition sees aid to be "a set of practices designed to ensure the worldwide expansion of capitalism."[14] Donor's policies of disbursing aid are connected to the recipient's capacity to follow the principles of a market economy. Rather than perceiving foreign aid as a right for developing countries, donors perceive it as a privilege and therefore conditionality appears justified. Hayter takes this view a step further. In her view, aid is a "concession by the imperialist powers."[15] This concession is made with the sole purpose of enabling them to continue their exploitation of the semi-colonial countries, just as reforms are done in capitalist countries by exploiting classes relinquished to the minimum necessary to retain their essential interests. World system theory sees foreign aid as the underlying structure of world capitalism that works to expand the basic infrastructure and institutions of capital circulation that foster unequal accumulation and constrain the development path of recipients to a subordinate role in the world system.

14 Robert E. Wood, *From Marshall Plan to Debt Crises: Foreign Aid and Development Choices in the World Economy* (Berkeley: University of California Press, 1972).

15 T. Hayter, *Aid as Imperialism* (Baltimore: Penguin Books, 1972), 9.

1.2 Non-Traditional Perspectives

While realism, liberalism and Marxism each bring unique perspectives to international relations and explain foreign aid in different ways, they are all considered traditional state-centric perspectives because they focus on the state as a rational actor and national interest as a motivation of foreign aid. Unlike these traditional perspectives, post-positivist theories try to find new explanations for foreign aid. Two theories will be introduced- social constructivism and critical theory. Social constructivism shows that because national interests are not fixed, they can be changed and reconstructed through the interaction of actors. Critical theory, a very diverse body of theoretical thinking, is making important contributions in that it argues that actors other than nation states should be considered and emphasizes a bottom-up process of norm-making.

Social Constructivism

While scholars such as Stephen Browne have written that the expansion of aid has been due primarily to geopolitical, commercial and other interests and not by altruism,[16] other scholars such as David Lumsdaine have argued "foreign aid cannot be explained on the basis of the economic and political interests of the donor countries alone, and any satisfactory explanation must give a central place to the influence of humanitarian and egalitarian convictions upon aid donors."[17] Social constructivists argue that the national interests of donors have been changing and the relationship between donors and recipients has been modified by this emphasis on humanitarianism and egalitarianism.

Alexander Wendt

Constructivist theory rejects the neo-realist assumption that the state of anarchy which is the lack of a higher authority or government is a structural condition inherent in world politics. Rather, it argues, in Alexander Wendt's words, "Anarchy is what states make of it."[18] In other words, anarchy is a structural fact

16 Stephen Browne, *Aid and Influence: Do Donors Help or Hinder?* (London: Earthscan, 2006), 9.

17 David Lumsdaine, *Moral Vision in International Politics: The Foreign Aid Regime 1949-1989* (Princeton: Princeton University Press, 1993), 29.

18 Alexander Wendt, "Anarchy is What States Make of It," *International Organization*, vol. 46, no. 2 (1992): 391-425.

only because states have historically chosen to make it so. Anarchy is not a natural fact but a social fact arising from changing rules or norms governing the interaction of states. If anarchy was created by the interplay of states and the state system, it can also be uncreated. Thus, constructivists argue that it is possible to change the anarchic nature of world politics by changing the nature of the interactions that sustain it.

Thus, for constructivists, national interest is endogenous, not exogenously given. Depending on changes in ideas and identities, not only will a state's interest change but even the nature of the international structure. New developments in the post-Cold War era, such as new interactions among states, emerging issues such as the environment, human rights, and humanitarian disasters, all contributed to changes in the concept of national interest. This is not to say that individuals and states spontaneously became more altruistic and humanitarian in the post-Cold War era, but new environments and changing characteristics of the interactions among diverse actors have created new patterns and identities in the relationships.

Lancaster(2006) emphasizes the impact of domestic politics in donor countries on aid-giving, especially the imperative of governments gaining domestic support for annual aid expenditures, the creation and professionalization of aid agencies, and the rise of development-oriented NGOs, which created a domestic constituency for aid's development purpose.[19] While different characteristics of domestic politics in each donor country have led to different ways of aid giving, there are general trends in global society towards more aid-giving and the development of new international norms in development assistance. The idea that governments of rich countries should provide concessional resources to improve human conditions in poor countries did not exist in the 1950s when foreign aid was first distributed, but by the 21st century it is widely accepted.

Among international relations theories, social constructivism was developed in response to neorealist and neoliberal institutionalist thought. For example, social constructivism analyzes a key realist concept, power politics, as being socially constructed, and maintains that it is possible for the concept to change through social and human interaction. Constructivism is based on two core ideas, that the structure of human association is determined primarily

---

19 Carol Lancaster, *Foreign Aid: Diplomacy, Development, Domestic Politics* (Chicago: The Chicago University Press, 2006), 5.

through shared ideas rather than material forces and that the identities and interests of actors are constructed and formulated through these ideas. Therefore, constructivism perceives emerging norms that rich countries should help poor countries to better their qualities of life.

Critical Theories

Critical theories, or post-positivist approaches of international relations, oppose fundamental assumptions that nation states are major actors and that national sovereignty is a major norm of international relations. Post-positivism is an umbrella term for a variety of theories that are loosely similar but also have importance differences. Unfortunately, none of these theories have produced a substantial contribution to the understanding of foreign aid.

One of the few attempts was Hattori, who looked at foreign aid as a 'form of giving.' Hattori connects foreign aid with Bourdieu's 'symbolic domination'- "a practice that signals and euphemizes social hierarchies." To him, foreign aid appears to play a crucial role at the systemic level, as symbolic practices that "have not only helped to maintain order in the post-war states system but have done so in a way that has avoided the more standard recourse to violence or coercive means: the pervasive hierarchy between the industrialized states and their former colonies...was naturalized by a practice of extending and accepting gifts."[20]

Critical theories are generally blamed for their incapacity to provide practical alternatives. Their critiques are valuable because they raise awareness of the underlying structures of power existing within certain practices, such as aid giving, or within structures, such as the international system. These perspectives could be crucial for envisioning and building new practices of foreign aid. Even though his work is not related to foreign aid issues, Robert Cox suggested that 'bottom-up' approaches are the means to break out of the trap of social hierarchies at systemic level. The current 'top-down' structure with dominance by the 'hegemonic bloc' of dominant states, international institutions, and capitals would never lead to positive changes of system.[21] He calls for active participation

20 T. Hattori, "Reconceptualizing Foreign Aid," *Review of International Political Economy*, vol. 8, no. 4 (2002): 649.

21 Gill and Law (1989) and Black and McKenna (1995) portray a neo-Gramscian perspective where the aid regime becomes a "hegemonic consensus" among the main actors of the international community. These are donor agencies, transnational capital, and the international

by the bottom of global society in re-writing global structures.

Robert W. Cox

Robert W. Cox, one of the most important theorists in critical theory, noted that "theory is always for someone and for some purpose...all theories have a perspective. (And) perspectives derive from a position in time and space, specifically social and political times and space. Theories are reflecting social and political time and space and when and where the theory was invented. No theory has permanent truth beyond time and space."[22] With these words, he emphasized that political theory cannot be separated with the historical context surrounding the particular theory: in that sense, he also criticized the formal methodology used in social science, the scientific method. In addition, his great works is a problem solving theory that serves as a guide to addressing the problems posed within the terms of the particular perspective that was the point of departure. The general aim here is to make these relationships and institutions work properly by dealing with particular sources of trouble.

Unlike the problem solving theory, critical theory takes its purpose as to appraise the very framework for action, or problematic, which problem-solving theory accepts as its parameters. It does not take institutions and social power relations for granted, but calls them into question by concerning itself with their origins and how and whether they might be in the process of changing. The general aim here is to understand the processes of change in which both the parts and whole are involved.[23]

Thus, critical theory contains problem-solving theories within it, but contains them in the form of identifiable ideologies, thereby pointing to their conservative consequences and not to their usefulness as guides to action. The aims of critical theory are just as practical as those of the problem-solving theory. It approaches practice from a perspective that transcends that of the existing order, which the problem-solving theory takes as its starting point.

---

financial institutions.

22 Robert W. Cox, "Critical political economy," in *International Political Economy: Understanding Global Disorder*, ed. Bjorn Hettine (London: Zed Books, 1995), 31.

23 Robert W. Cox, "Social Forces, States, and World Orders: Beyond International Relations Theory," in *Approaches to World Order*, ed. Robert W. Cox and Timothy J. Sinclair (New York: Cambridge University Press, 1996), 88-90.

While many scholars use the term "global governance" these days, critical theory has used this term with its own meanings. Global governance means the procedures and practices that exist at the international or regional level for the management of political, economic and social affairs. One hypothetical form of governance can be conceived as having a hierarchical form of coordination whether centralized (unitary) or decentralized (federal). The other form of coordination would be non-hierarchical, or multilateral.[24]

While global government may not be achievable under present conditions, using multilateral entities in the quest for an ideal of global governance is nevertheless considered worthwhile, especially if some progress is being made in the living conditions of people across the globe. Global governance arrangements can be conceived as the use of the existing historical structure of world order to address the problems faced by, and meet the demands of, states and civil society. Therefore, the way to promote genuine global governance is first to recognize the existence of various actors in international relations and make more explicit the diverse coexisting ontologies. This can be done through exercising empathetic understanding, or the ability to get inside the mind of the other while retaining one's own identity.

The next step is the search for common ground among the various inter-subjectivities. These movements and identification from below will give more challenges to the state actor and international politics. It also provides a formula for pluralizing international organizations to become a main actor for global governance.

1.3 Governance for Global Public Goods

In this chapter, various theoretical perspectives on foreign aid were discussed. No one theory can adequately explain this 21st century change and paradigm shift. Traditional state-centric approaches reflect a vision of the world in which states are the main actors in international relations. Since the late 1980s, constructivism was introduced as a critique to state-centric theories and argued that the interests and identities of the actors of international relations are not exogenous and taken for granted. It argued that the structure

24 Robert W. Cox, "Introduction," in *The New Realism*, ed. Robert W. Cox (London: Macmillan for the UN University Press, 1997), 16.

and norms of international society are socially constructed, and both can be changed through social interactions among the actors. New structures lead to new state policies that can be coordinated on the basis of generalized principles of conduct. Critical theory on the other hand targets state centrism and raises the possibility of people's power or "community-based movements" in international politics. In this context, governance implies the participation of all the actors and a high degree of democratization at the multilateral level. Until now, global governance has been viewed primarily as a pattern of intergovernmental relationships, but it must now be understood as also involving non-governmental organizations, citizens' movements, multinational corporations, and the global market.

More attention needs to be paid to critical theorist terminology, such as "bottom up multilateralism" or "new multilateralism." This new or emerging multilateralism is an attempt to "reconstitute civil societies and political authorities on a global scale, building a system of global governance from the bottom up."[25] New multilateralism offers a challenge to existing multilateralism not only because it entails institutional transformation, but also because it represents a different set of interests. This concept of new multilateralism is comparable with old or existing dominant forms of multilateralism outlined by John Ruggie, which he defines as "an institutional form that coordinates relations among three or more states on the basis of generalized principles of conduct."[26] Before the 1980s, the IMF, World Bank, and the GATT actions were indicative of this state-centric form of multilateralism. These organizations were dominated by member states, had little institutionalized connection to civil societies within member states, and were intent upon generalizing a particular set of principles.

By applying the concept of global governance to development assistance, it is possible to create and promote a network for organizing and harmonizing the existing fragmented aid efforts. Global cooperation will increase aid effectiveness for poverty relief and eradication. The roles of different actors must be well coordinated in order to minimize overlap and waste of resources. While there is no sovereign authority within the global aid architecture, a well-

25 *Ibid*, 27.

26 John Gerald Ruggie, "Multilateralism: The Anatomy of an Institution," in *Multilateralism Matters: The Theory and Praxis of an Institutional Form*, ed. John Gerald Ruggie (New York: Columbia University Press, 1993), 11.

coordinated division of labor in international development and cooperation will minimize inefficiencies. For this, the diverse development actors need to be well inter-connected and interdependent, with effective collective action aimed at maximizing interactions. This can start from increasing the recognition among different actors of the mutual gains that they can derive from cooperative efforts. It is also possible to create a governance framework that relies on distinctive roles for diverse actors, with each organization contributing its unique strengths and advantages to increasing the effectiveness of overseas development aid.

Chapter 1. Review Discussion Questions

1. How do political and economic considerations influence donor motivations for providing aid? What kind of considerations do donor countries make before selecting recipient partner countries?
2. How do traditional international relations theorists understand donor motivations for providing aid to developing countries?
3. Identify how critical theorists explain development assistance.
4. Which theory best explains development assistance in the current international order and why? What are some further considerations that should be taken into account to better understand state actors and foreign aid?

Chapter 2

Evolution of Aid: Origin and History

> *"The motives of donor nations for providing foreign aid have evolved over time.... This aid, which focused on creating markets for the United States by reducing poverty and increasing production in developing countries, also concentrated on diminishing the threat of communism by helping countries prosper under capitalism. These dual goals—humanitarian and strategic—continue to exist in the agency's foreign aid goals to [develop] the markets of the future...[and] partnerships with countries committed to enabling the private sector investment that is the basis of sustained economic growth to open new markets for American goods."*[1]

The Westphalian order is built on the principle of state sovereignty over a bounded territory and population. Ideas of foreign aid were subversive in this order since intervening in the form of foreign aid was perceived as a violation of a state's sovereign power. In short, foreign assistance was perceived as a threat against state power and states neither offered nor desired foreign aid.

The first acts of foreign aid were motivated by self-interest. Donor countries were not pursuing altruistic values but were focused on expanding their imperialistic power or influencing colonial countries. Today, however, globalization has changed the world order. Now the international community is not limited to the actions of state actors, but diverse non-state actors have emerged as well. These new actors are creating patterns of complex relationships. With these changes in the international order it was increasingly recognized that state power was not absolute. States came to realize that some of their counterparts were incapable of protecting their own citizens and needed outside assistance. These ideas are now the foundation for foreign aid.

Despite the short fifty year history of modern foreign aid, there have been many developments and changes to how and why countries provide foreign aid. The structures and conditions of the international community have strongly influenced trends in the practice

1 Subhayu Bandyopadhyay and E. Katarina Vermann, "Donor Motives for Foreign Aid," *Federal Reserve Bank of St. Louis REVIEW*, July/August (2013): 327.

of ODA. Historically, development assistance has been evaluated or conceptualized according to the motives of the countries giving the aid. Although commonly accepted today, development aid concentrating on poverty alleviation and enhancing human wellbeing is a recent phenomenon. In the early years, aid was used to assist countries struggling to rebuild their national economies from the destruction of war.

2.1 Evolution of Foreign Aid

The first instances of foreign aid occurred at the beginning of the 20th century. Non-administrative aid was provided to British colonies through the 1929 Colonial Act and the Colonial Development and Welfare Acts of the 1940s while French aid to its colonies expanded rapidly in the 1940s.[2] While it is evident that aid existed in the years before the Truman Doctrine or the Marshall Plan, the aid provided by governments was typically limited to their colonies and served to reinforce imperialist ambitions. This colonial aid is distinguished from what is commonly considered modern overseas aid, which dates from the period after World War II.

The idea of foreign aid emerged from the international society of the time. In the 1940s, the International Labor Office (ILO) argued for aid funds to raise living standards in poor countries and the United Nations Relief and Rehabilitation Administration (UNRRA) received funds from more than forty countries to help provide food, medicine, agricultural, and industrial goods to more than fifty recipient countries. The founding documents of the United Nations provided further support. The UN Charter committed all countries to work for the promotion of higher living standards, full employment and economic and social progress and development through cooperation. In addition, the Universal Declaration of Human Rights stated the right to a standard living for the wellbeing of individuals.[3]

Following the two world wars and the development of international organizations, the United States recognized the significance of providing foreign aid to struggling countries. In 1947, the Truman Doctrine[4] reoriented US foreign policy by stipulating that it

2 Roger C. Riddell, *Does Foreign Aid Really Work?* (London: Oxford University Press, 2007), 24.

3 *Ibid.*

4 The Truman Doctrine was the outcome of a speech delivered by President Truman to Congress on March 12, 1947. Truman voiced his concern regarding the British government

would provide political, military and economic assistance to all democratic nations under threat from external or internal authoritarian forces.

This was a direct challenge to authoritarianism and the Truman Doctrine became "the policy of the United States to support free peoples who are resisting attempted subjugation by armed minorities or outside pressures."[5] These acts stemmed from the belief of President Truman that the US could no longer allow the forcible expansion of Soviet totalitarianism into free, independent nations. In essence, the Truman Doctrine was a foreign policy tool whereby foreign aid was used to encourage an expansion of democratic values and the containment of Soviet communist beliefs.

In 1949, President Truman called for a new program to share US scientific advances and industrial progress with underdeveloped countries. This was later developed into the Point Four Program,[6] which provided scientific and technical assistance, including hundreds of US experts, to Latin American, Asian, Middle Eastern, and African nations. The Point Four Program was part of a new foreign policy to contain threats from the Soviet Union. It was also believed that US technical expertise could foster economic development and capital investment opportunities. Critics, however, pointed to the Point Four Program as a new form of imperialism designed to cajole Third World nations into increasing their natural resource production for the benefit of Western industries.[7]

The modern era of aid giving began with these American foreign assistance efforts. In the aftermath of a devastating world war, the US became the main provider of assistance to European countries that were struggling to rebuild. The US continued to emphasize the importance of foreign assistance and later pressured Japan and Europe to provide aid as well. However, these countries had different

announcement that it would withdraw military and economic support to the Greek government, which was engaged in a civil war against the Greek Communist Party. It was possible that Soviet Union support for the Greek Communists could ultimately influence Greek policy. Other foreign policy problems emerged in 1946, making it difficult to achieve any durable post-war rapprochement with the Soviet Union. In light of these conditions, during his speech, President Truman requested $400,000,000 worth of aid to Greek and Turkish Governments and support the dispatch of American civilian and military personnel and equipment to the region.

5 Quote taken from the Truman Doctrine.

6 The Point Four Program received its name from being the fourth point in Truman's inaugural address.

7 Willard L. Thorp, "The Objectives of Point Four," *Annals of the American Academy of Political and Social Science*, vol. 268, no. 1(1950): 22-26.

motives from the US in providing aid. Within Europe for example, Britain and France provided increasing amounts of assistance for their colonies in Africa, Asia and the Caribbean, but neither country desired to continue assistance after the colonies declared independence. In the case of Japan, its aid was a form of reparation payments largely restricted to Asia. For Japan, aid was also seen as a means of securing access to vital raw materials and export markets.

The US had two motives in providing aid to Europe. First, American policymakers wanted to assist in the reconstruction of European countries destroyed by the war. Second, they wanted to protect the US economy from the possible recurrence of the Great Depression. The Marshall Plan is largely recognized as a pivotal point in the history of US foreign assistance and a predecessor institution for the current US Agency for International Development (USAID).

Marshall Plan

US Secretary of State, George Marshall, proposed a four-year program to provide foreign assistance to seventeen different European countries struggling to reconstruct their nations after World War II. His proposal was instituted at the Paris Economic Conference in July 1947, dispensing over $13 billion between 1948 and 1951.[8] It aimed to restore economic stability, facilitate foreign trade, and to contain Communist ideas. A key concern of the Americans after the war was a recurrence of the economic recession of the 1930s. The idea was that the Marshall Plan, by re-creating demand in European economies, would eventually increase prosperity in the US by promoting exports. Indeed, the American economy flourished as European recipients spent money that was received through the Marshall Plan on US-produced food and manufactured goods.

The Marshall Plan was officially termed the European Recovery Program (ERP) and was approved by the United States Congress in the Economic Cooperation Act of April 1948. The legislation that established the Marshall Plan was the Foreign Assistance Act. With the exception of Spain, which was under the dictatorship of Franco, and West Germany, which was under Allied occupation, most European countries outside of the Soviet bloc were members of the plan. In total, the Marshall Plan ran for three years, with payments made to European countries in annual installments. Most assistance was made in the form of grants to avoid transfer problems that were

8 It is estimated that $13 billion in 1950s would be about $100 billion at 2003 prices.

caused by American loans in the interwar period. The Economic Cooperation Agency (ECA), a US board operating in Europe, was in charge of distribution of funds to recipient countries and its allocation to key sectors.

The Marshall Plan was the major US aid program for post-war Europe. An important element of the Marshall Plan was that it identified the inconsistencies and limitations of previous aid programs. The Truman administration wanted to increase the efficiency of existing aid programs and to devise a unifying concept. The Marshall Plan concentrated on systematically centralizing the previous aid programs and focused on policies that liberalized trade and payments within Europe.

The Marshall Plan led to the creation of the Organization for European Economic Co-operation (OEEC).[9] The mandate of the OEEC was to continue work on a joint recovery program and to supervise the distribution of aid. Within the United States, the Marshall Plan helped solidify the development of US foreign assistance policy and the establishment of USAID in 1961 by President Kennedy.

April 3, 1948, US President Harry Truman signed into law the Foreign Assistance Act, commonly known as the Marshall Plan

9 In 1961 the OEEC became the OECD.

Today, the Marshall Plan is widely recognized as the first successful case of foreign assistance. It is credited with restoring food supplies, opening bottleneck industries, and the reconstruction of capital equipment and housing stocks within devastated economies of Western Europe. Nonetheless, there was awareness that bilateral arrangements alone were inadequate. The Marshall Plan and US Foreign Assistance policy were pivotal steps in the earliest stage of foreign assistance but concerns with instability in the world economy led to discussions to create multilateral international financial institutions. During the United Nations Monetary and Financial Conference, the US and Great Britain proposed the establishment of two key institutions which came to be recognized as the Bretton Woods Twins – the International Monetary Fund (IMF) and the World Bank (WB).

Table 2.1 Key Dates for the Marshall Plan[10]

March 12, 1947	The "Truman Doctrine," outlined in a presidential speech to Congress, makes it US policy to protect nations threatened by communism.
June 5, 1947	In a Harvard commencement speech, Secretary of State George C. Marshall calls for an American plan to help Europe recover from World War II.
June 19, 1947	The British and French foreign ministers issue a joint communiqué inviting twenty-two European nations to send representatives to Paris to draw up a cooperative recovery plan.
July 12, 1947	The Conference of European Economic Cooperation, which became the Committee of European Economic Cooperation (CEEC), meets in Paris. The Soviet Union declines to attend and pressures Czechoslovakia, Poland, and Hungary into staying away.
September 1947	The CEEC submits its report estimating needs and the cost of the European Recovery Program (ERP) over four years. It provides for the establishment of the Organization for European Economic Cooperation (OEEC) to coordinate the program from the European side.

10 United States Library of Congress, "For European Recovery: The Fiftieth Anniversary of the Marshall Plan," http://www.loc.gov/exhibits/marshall/mars.html, last visited December 2008.

February 1948	A Soviet-backed communist coup occurs in Czechoslovakia
April 2, 1948	Congress passes the Economic Cooperation Act that authorizes the Marshall Plan. President Truman signs it the next day.
April 1948	Paul Hoffman of Studebaker Corporation is appointed Administrator of the Economic Cooperation Agency (ECA), the temporary American agency created to implement the plan. Averell Harriman is appointed special representative of the ECA in Europe.
April 15, 1948	First official meeting of the OEEC held in Paris to determine national needs prior to passage of appropriations bill by U.S. Congress.
June 30, 1949	The Federal Republic of Germany officially enters the OEEC in the second year of the program.
December 31, 1951	The ERP ends six months early because of the escalation of the Korean War, which had begun in June 1950. Transfer of funds from the US to Europe had totaled $13.3 billion.
July 5, 1972	In a Harvard commencement speech, West German chancellor Willy Brandt announces creation of the German Marshall Fund to thank the US for its assistance.

Table 2.2 Historical Timeline of US Foreign Assistance

March 31, 1942	Institute of Inter-American Affairs formally established — first technical assistance by United States.
November 9, 1943	Agreement signed to furnish aid to war-ravaged countries through UN Relief and Rehabilitation Administration.
December 27, 1945	International Monetary Fund (IMF) and International Bank for Reconstruction and Development (World Bank) formed.
May 15, 1947	Congress approves economic and military aid to Greece and Turkey.
June 5, 1947	Secretary of State Marshall's speech voices US interest in rebuilding European economies.

April 3, 1948	Truman signs Economic Cooperation Act (Marshall Plan) creating Economic Cooperation Administration.
January 20, 1949	President Truman's Point IV inauguration speech.
June 1, 1950	Act for International Development (Point IV) creates authority for Technical Cooperation Administration.
June 30, 1950	Termination of Marshall Plan.
October 31, 1951	Mutual Security Act of 1951 unites military and economic programs and technical assistance, Mutual Security Agency established.
July 10, 1954	Public Law 480 authorizes sale and use of US surplus food for economic development.
March 1, 1961	Peace Corps created.
March 13, 1961	President Kennedy calls on people of hemisphere to join in an Alliance for Progress
September 4, 1961	Foreign Assistance Act passed, reorganized US foreign assistance programs including separating military and non-military aid, and combines International Cooperation Administration, Development Loan Fund and other US assistance functions.
November 4, 1961	President John F. Kennedy established US Agency for International Development (USAID), the first US foreign assistance organization with primary emphasis on long-term economic and social development assistance efforts. USAID was distinguished from previous organizations because it could offer direct support to developing nations and was free from political and military functions.

The Bretton Woods System: IMF and World Bank Group

In the 1940s, the United States and Great Britain proposed the creation of international financial institutions to stabilize exchange rates and boost international trade. In 1944, the United Nations Monetary and Financial Conference was held in Bretton Woods, New Hampshire, during the first three weeks of July. Forty-four countries participated in the conference. Delegates understood the importance of international finance and trade in promoting peace and prosperity. The delegates also discussed the postwar recovery of Europe. The world economy had experienced unstable currency exchange rates in the previous decade and more countries were relying on restrictive trade policies.

This meeting resulted in the creation of the Bretton Woods Agreement, which established a postwar international monetary system of convertible currencies, fixed exchange rates and promoted free trade. To facilitate the goals set forth in the agreement two international institutions were created: the International Monetary Fund (IMF) and the International Bank for Reconstruction and Development (IBRD), today widely known as the World Bank (WB).

The Bretton Woods system sought to benefit all economies by expanding international trade and stabilizing exchange rates to avoid the kind of beggar-thy-neighbor policies that had been prevalent in the 1930s. The IMF, IBRD and the International Trade Organization were realized through the Bretton Woods Agreement. However, the US Congress would not endorse the International Trade Organization, and it was later replaced with the General Agreement on Tariffs and Trade (GATT). These efforts have developed today to become what is known as the World Trade Organization (WTO).

The IMF and WB are known as the Bretton Woods Twins. The IMF seeks to maintain an orderly system of exchange rates and balance of payments between nations. The IMF was founded on the belief that all countries share an interest in a stable system of exchange rates and the basic rules governing international monetary transactions need to be agreed upon by the international commu-

Bretton Woods Monetary Conference, July 1-22, 1944

nity. There was a consensus that broad international action was necessary to maintain an international monetary system, which would serve to underpin international trade. It was to this end that a permanent international body was established with powers and resources available to perform these tasks at the Bretton Woods conference.

Compared to the IMF, the World Bank is primarily a development institution that functions as a vital source of financial and technical assistance to developing countries around the world. It is made up of two unique development institutions owned by the 187 member countries: the IBRD and the International Development Association (IDA). The IBRD aims to reduce poverty in middle income and creditworthy poorer countries, while the IDA concentrates its efforts on the world's poorest countries. The WB provides low interest loans, interest free credits and grants to developing countries for various purposes, including investments in education, health, public administration, infrastructure, financial and private sector development, agriculture, environmental and natural resource management.[11]

Box 2.1 GATT-WTO

The main objective of the GATT-WTO system has been the liberalization of international trade. This was attained by reductions of tariffs, quotas, subsidies, provision of frameworks for negotiation and dispute resolution.

After the end of World War II, multilateral negotiations took place to create an international trade system and an entity called the International Trade Organization (ITO) was proposed. However, confronted with political opposition from several countries, the ITO was not established. What was created instead was a treaty, the General Agreement on Tariffs and Trade (GATT), which established a set of rules on tariffs. Formed in 1947, the GATT lasted until the World Trade Organization (WTO) supplanted it.

The historical development of the GATT was marked by a series of eight trade rounds. Among these rounds, the first five trade rounds took the form of "parallel" bilateral negotiations, where each country negotiated pair-wise with a number of countries at once. The sixth agreement, the so-called Kennedy Round involved an across-the-

11 www.worldbank.org, last visited December 2010.

board 50% tariff reduction by the major industrial countries. The Tokyo Round reduced tariffs with a more complex formula than was used in the Kennedy Round.[12] The most recent round, the Uruguay Round, reduced tariff rates imposed by advanced countries almost 40%. It was during this round that the WTO was created, incorporating the basic logic of the GATT system. The WTO provides rulings for settling international trade disputes.

Institutionalization of Aid

Following the modernization of aid, the 1940-50s saw the birth of several important international institutions aimed at encouraging countries to provide aid. A core issue in the 1960s was the problem of economic distribution. In 1959, the concept of the North-South divide was first introduced. This term referred to the inconsistent development of countries. Countries in the northern hemisphere were developing at a faster pace while countries in the southern hemisphere were struggling to develop their economies. To address this issue, the first UN Development Decade was launched by the General Assembly in December 1961.

The North-South divide, however, is used as a loose term and is not limited to geographical location. The North consists of developed countries with advanced economies, such as Australia, and the South comprises countries that are less developed. It was after Willy Brandt used this terminology within the Brandt Commission Report in the 1980s that the concept became popular.

The General Assembly asked member states to intensify efforts to accelerate progress for creating self-sustaining economic growth and social advancement in developing countries. Developed countries pursued policies designed to enable participation of developing countries within the world trade market and to increase flows of developmental resources, with the aim of stimulating the flow of private capital to developing countries. Despite these efforts, the growth rate of developed economies accelerated further in the 1960s and the gap between the developed and less developed regions of the world widened. Two thirds of the world's population living in less developed countries possessed less than one-sixth of

12 Paul Krugman, *International Economics: Theory and Policy* (Boston: Addison Wesley, 2003), 238.

the world's income while five-sixths was left to the developed third of the population.

During the 1950s, the United States was the dominant donor of foreign assistance and its influence continued into the 1960s as the US contributed to infrastructural development in various countries. The 1960s were also an important period for the history of development assistance since it was during this time that the main donor countries, the US, France, Germany and Japan, established aid administrations agencies. Furthermore, in 1961, the United Nations declared that the following ten years would constitute the first UN Development Decade and identified a 1% target for aid donors, including private investments.

Following the creation of the Development Assistance Committee (DAC), core definitions of development assistance terms were established, including Official Development Assistance (ODA), as well as distinguishing between government level support from other official flows (OOF) and between officially supported resource flows or private sources of grants and loans. The establishment of new multilateral aid organizations and institutions were prevalent in the 1960s and occurred in parallel with efforts by individual states to formally establish governmental aid programs.

United Nations Development Program

The United Nations was created on October 24, 1945, as a joint commitment of the fifty original members to collaborate their efforts to avoid another world war. It was organized under six main organs, the General Assembly, the Security Council, the Economic and Social Council (ECOSOC), the Trusteeship Council, the International Court of Justice, and the Secretariat, all dedicated to the preservation of world peace.

The United Nations Development Program (UNDP) is the world's largest source of multilateral grant assistance. It has a budget of $1 billion. The UNDP aims to promote economic growth and higher standards of living by supporting projects in agriculture, health, housing, public administration, industry, trade and other fields. It works directly with 166 countries and assists them to develop local capacity. It was established in 1965 by the General Assembly as a result of the merging of the United Nations Expanded Program of Technical Assistance (1949) and the United Nations Special Fund (1958). Today, it focuses on four main areas: democratic governance, poverty reduction and achievement of the

MDGs, crisis prevention and recovery, and environment and energy for sustainable development.

The UNDP has a unique development indicator, the Human Development Index. The index identifies people as the center of development and ranks countries by measuring human development on the basis of life expectancy, education, and basic purchasing power while also allowing effective cross-national comparisons. An annual report, the Human Development Report, provides updated rankings of countries by health, sanitation, the treatment of women, and other aspects of human experience. Human Development Indices for countries are further categorized and ranked into High Human Development, Medium Human Development, and Low Human Development. In 2008, out of a total of 179 countries, 75 countries had attained a place in the High Human Development category and 26 were classified as Low Human Development.

Table 2.3 Human Development Index Rankings (2010)

Very High Human Development		Low Human Development	
1. Norway	6. Liechtenstein	160. Mail	165. Mozambique
2. Australia	7. Netherlands	161. Burkina Faso	166. Burundi
3. New Zealand	8. Canada	162. Liberia	167. Niger
4. United States	9. Sweden	163. Chad	168. Congo
5. Ireland	10. Germany	164. Guinea-Bissau	169. Zimbabwe

2.2 From OEEC DAG to OECD DAC

The Development Assistance Committee (DAC), originally known as the Development Assistance Group (DAG), is a part of the Organization for Economic Cooperation and Development (OECD). It was founded in 1960 by leading donor countries to promote aid from donor governments. The original members of the DAG included Belgium, Canada, France, Germany, Italy, Portugal, the United Kingdom, the United States and the Commission of the European Economic Community. Although not founding members, Japan and the Netherlands joined the DAG in 1960. In 1961, DAG was reconstituted as DAC and within the OECD Secretariat a new Development Department (DD) was created, consisting of two branches: the Development Finance Branch[13] and the Technical Co-

13 The "Development Finance Branch," later becomes the Development Assistance Directorate

operation Branch.

The DAC concentrates on how international development cooperation can contribute to improving the capacity of developing countries to participate in the global economy and the capacity of individuals to overcome poverty and participate fully in their societies. The DAC group of donors has continuously set targets for aid, and in 1964 members accepted a target of 1% of external resources to be transferred to poor countries. However, this amount included foreign direct investment, which was difficult for governments to control. This difficulty triggered discussions on how to separate official aid from other flows with a specific target for official aid.

Following its initial conceptualizations in 1969, the DAC revised its definition of Official Development Assistance (ODA) in 1972. It set an overall financial target for each DAC member's ODA program at 84% grants and special term recommendations for the least developed countries. This definition set by the DAC in 1972 is still applicable today. The DAC has developed into a key forum for major donors to work together to increase the effectiveness of their aid to support sustainable development. It has continued its efforts to promote development assistance and aid effectiveness.

There are currently twenty nine members of the DAC. The DAC ratified South Korea as a new member state in 2010. In 2013, Iceland, Czech Republic, Slovak Republic, Poland, and Slovenia also became member states.

Table 2.4 DAC Members and Dates of Membership

Country	Year	Country	Year
Australia	1961	Switzerland	1968
Belgium	1961	New Zealand	1973
Canada	1961	Finland	1975
European Union	1961	Ireland	1985
France	1961	Spain	1991
Germany	1961	Portugal	1991
Italy	1961	Luxembourg	1992
Japan	1961	Greece	1999
Netherlands	1961	Republic of Korea	2010
United Kingdom	1961	Czech Republic	2013
United States	1961	Iceland	2013

(DAD) (1969) and the Development Cooperation Directorate (DCD) (1975).

Norway	1962	Poland	2013
Denmark	1963	Slovak Republic	2013
Sweden	1965	Slovenia	2013
Austria	1966	-	-

Understanding aid as a concept means that it is necessary to inquire more closely into the purposes behind these flows of money and goods. The purpose of aid, or the intent of a donor, has been studied since the advent of development assistance. These purposes have been characterized as falling into one of four categories: diplomatic, developmental, humanitarian relief and commercial.[14] Even within the context of aid for the purpose of development, however, there have been discussions of how aid can actually promote development. In the earliest stage of foreign aid, such as the Marshall Plan, these flows were used to provide assistance to reconstruct developed economies that were torn apart because of war. Later on, however, aid was used in countries that were economically undeveloped.

Due to globalization and an increasing awareness of interconnectedness, the Brandt Commission recognized the reciprocal relationship between the North and South. For long-term economic prosperity, developed countries were as dependent on the development of the South as the South was on the North.[15] New focus was placed on understanding the underlying purpose of aid. The DAC's definition covers three dimensions of this purpose: the sector of destination, the form or type of aid, and the policy objective(s) of aid.[16] In general terms aid provided by the DAC has been defined as aiming to contribute to human welfare and development in poor countries.[17]

In 1977, the DAC High Level Meeting adopted a "Statement of Development Cooperation for Economic Growth and Meeting Basic Human Needs." The statement emphasized the concern of member countries that basic human needs are not a substitute but

---

14 Carol Lancaster, *Foreign Aid Diplomacy, Development, Domestic Politics* (Chicago: Chicago University Press, 2006).

15 See The Brandt Commission Papers (New York: Independent Bureau for International Development issues, 1980)

16 See definition of Purpose of Aid, http://www.oecd.org/glossary/0,3414,en_2649_33721_1965693_1_1_1_1,00.html#1965422.

17 Roger C. Riddell, *Does Foreign Aid Really Work?* (New York: Oxford University Press, 2007).

an essential component of economic growth. The basic needs approach is not concentrated on welfare or charity but is productivity-oriented and seeks self-generating development in partnership with recipient countries. Partnership not only emphasizes the importance of understanding local contexts in providing assistance but also acknowledges the need for local ownership and responsibility to promote sustainable development.

The Twenty-Five Years of Development Cooperation (1985) was published by the DAC on its 25th anniversary in an attempt to trace major volume and policy developments and the importance of assessing the effectiveness of aid. The report concluded that aid, accompanied by growing exports to OECD countries, has been a major factor contributing to the gains of many developing economies, especially those experiencing fast-paced economic and social growth.

Pearson Commission

At the start of the 1960s, aggregate official aid grew to over 0.5% of Gross National Income (GNI). The first drop in the total flow of official aid was in 1968 and by 1970, the level of aid provided by developed countries had dropped to 0.33% of GNI. There were diverse reasons for this decrease, including domestic problems, balance of payment difficulties, or even criticisms from the public. President Robert McNamara of the World Bank set up a commission under the chairmanship of former Canadian Prime Minister Lester Pearson in an attempt to revive interest in development aid (1969). Pearson was a former diplomat and Nobel Peace Prize winner who had played an active role in UN affairs. The Pearson Commission set out to study the consequences and results of the first 20 years of official development as well as to clarify the errors and propose policies for the future. On September 15, 1969, the Commission on International Development, widely known as the Pearson Commission, delivered its final report, *Partners in Development*. The Pearson report continues to be relevant for development assistance today.

Pearson Commission on International Development

The Commission's report provided a comprehensive view of development as a complex set of domestic and external factors, including trade, aid, and investment. It called for an elaborate aid strategy to attack decreasing foreign aid contributions by major donor countries. It also identified several important contributions of assistance on the economic development of less developed countries. It found that the role of aid had been critical in areas of savings and imports and was an essential risk absorber for industrial and agricultural enterprises.

The Pearson Commission emphasized the importance of partnerships. It found that to achieve self-sustaining growth in developing countries, increased flows of international aid were necessary and that actions of both donor and recipient countries should be scrutinized. It proposed increasing the proportion of multilateral aid rather than the practice of bilateral aid, which was prevalent at the time. The Commission observed that bilateral aid was often dispensed primarily to gain political favors, for strategic purposes or to promote donors' exports and political ideologies. Also, donors perceived aid as a means to stimulate a second industrial revolution in developing countries but often overlooked the need to ensure food, economic and social security.

To increase actual flows of aid, the Commission called for a refinement of the previous 1% target to 0.7% official aid of GNI by 1975, but the rate should amount to 1% of total aid. It also acknowledged that increasing the efficiency of aid should be a future objective for aid donors. The Pearson report also presented a recommendation to developed countries that they set a target of contributing 0.7% of GNI to ODA. This was the goal later identified by the Millennium Development Goals (MDGs) at the Millennium Summit in 2000. The goal of setting aside 0.7% of donors' national income for ODA is presently the best-known target for development aid and has a long history. The World Council of Churches initially proposed a target of 1% of donor countries' income in 1958. By 1968, this target had been subscribed to by all DAC members.

A separate sub-target for official flows was also discussed. Dutch economist Jan Tinbergen, the 1969 Nobel Prize winner for Economics, estimated the capital inflows that developing economies needed to achieve desirable growth rates. He proposed a target for official flows, both concessional and non-concessional, of 0.75% of GNP, to be achieved by 1972. Some developed countries accepted this target goal but did not agree with the timeline for implementation. The Pearson Commission built on the 0.7% target for official flows, but since the non-concessional component of these flows was repayable, its net volume was small. In the Commission's report it proposed that ODA "be raised to 0.70% of donor GNP by 1975, and in no case later than 1980."[18]

The Pearson Commission's 0.7% target was formally recognized in 1970 when the UN General Assembly adopted a resolution that stated "each economically advanced country will progressively increase its official development assistance to developing countries and will exert its best efforts to reach a minimum net amount of 0.7% of its gross national product at market prices."

UN Development Decades

The first UN Development Decade began in 1961 with calls on member states to intensify efforts to mobilize support for measures required to accelerate progress toward self-sustaining economic growth and social advancement in developing countries. The objective was a minimum annual growth rate of 5% in aggregate national income by the end of the decade. The General Assembly recommended international capital and assistance to developing countries at about 1% of the combined national incomes of economically advanced countries. Unfortunately, at the end of the first UN Development Decade in 1970, the attainment of a 5% growth rate in developing countries was not achieved. The total domestic product of developing countries grew by 4.6% in the period from 1960-67, but the increase in per capita gross product was a mere 2%. The first UN Development Decade helped force recognition that a framework of international development strategy was necessary.

Following the first UN Development Decade, the General Assembly adopted a resolution calling for a new international development strategy for the 1970s, which became known as the second UN Development Decade. This strategy aimed to promote sustained economic growth, particularly in developing countries, to ensure a higher standard of living and narrow the gap between developed and developing countries. It also identified assistance from developed countries as critical for developing nations to achieve economic growth.

The objectives set for the second UN Development Decade were an average annual rate of growth in the gross domestic product of the developing countries of at least 6%, which translated into an

18 See Pearson Commission Report (1969). http://unesdoc.unesco.org/images/0005/000567/056743eo.pdf

average annual expansion of 4% in agricultural output and 8% in manufacturing output. In addition to raw economic targets, the General Assembly further identified the importance of an equitable distribution of income and wealth, social justice, and the efficiency of production. Efficient production would be achieved by targeting employment levels, income security, environment safeguards, and measures to expand and improve facilities for education, health, nutrition, housing and social welfare.[19]

The third UN Development Decade was initiated on January 1, 1981. Governments pledged to fulfill their commitments to establish a new international economic order based on justice and equity. The objectives for accelerated development in developing countries included a 7% average annual rate of growth of GDP; a 7.5% annual rate of expansion of exports and an 8% annual rate of expansion of imports of goods and services; an increase in gross domestic savings to reach about 24% of GDP by 1990; a rapid and substantial increase in ODA to reach or surpass the target of 0.7% of GNI; a 4% annual rate of expansion of agricultural production; and a 9% annual rate of expansion of manufacturing output. In addition, the strategy included diverse policy measures targeting international trade, industrialization, food and agriculture, financial resources for development, international monetary and financial issues, science and technology for development, energy, transportation, environment, human settlements, disaster relief, social development as well as technical cooperation.

Despite the comprehensive strategy set out in the third UN Development Decade, the 1980s was a challenging period for many developing countries. Only a few countries, such as Norway, the Netherlands, Denmark, Sweden and France, met the UN target for providing 0.7% of GNI as ODA. During this period the gap between developed and developing countries grew wider as overall growth in developing countries decreased to 3% annually, compared to 5.5% in the 1960s. There was also a dramatic increase in the number of countries categorized by the General Assembly as least developed. Whereas there were twenty four least developed countries in 1972, by 1991 this number grew to 47.

In 1990, it was recommended by the Second United Nations

19 Encyclopedia of the nations, "Economic and Social Development - Second un development decade," http://www.nationsencyclopedia.com/United-Nations/Economic-and-Social-Development-SECOND-UN-DEVELOPMENT-DECADE.html, last visited December 2008.

Conference on the Least Developed countries to set special targets for ODA to these particular countries. The General Assembly encouraged developed countries to reach or surpass these targets and recommended developing countries to raise their rate of industrialization by 8 to 10% and increase annual food production by 4%. Eight goals were set forth to achieve sustainable development:

- Stand by the commitment made in 1986 to halt and reverse protectionism
- Liberalize trade and improve developing countries' access to all markets by reducing or removing tariff barriers
- Free up trade in tropical products and products based on natural resources
- Bring trade in textiles under the normal rules of GATT
- Substantially reduce agricultural subsidies and other protective policies
- Implement and improve the generalized system of preferences under which some developing countries' exports are admitted to industrialized countries at reduced rates or duty-free
- Ensure that regional economic arrangements and trade blocs conform with GATT rules
- Make sure that GATT contracting parties adhere strictly to the agreement's rules and principles

Brandt Commission

The report by the Independent Commission on International Development Issues, widely known as the Brandt Report after the chairman of the commission, was the most comprehensive analysis of international development to date. With hopes to contribute to the development of worldwide moral values and emphasizing priorities for change in "Peace, Justice, Jobs," the report illustrated the best way for governments to realistically move forward to reduce the growing economic disparity between rich and poor countries, overcome world hunger, mass misery, and alarming disparities in living conditions.

The commission broadly grouped developing countries as those occupying the southern hemisphere and developed countries as those in the northern hemisphere. It distinguished between the heavily concentrated wealth in the North to the relative impoverishment of the South. The South continued to struggle with poverty despite its large populations. The Brandt Report identified a need to transfer resources to the South in order to revive the world economy but discarded the assumption that rich countries simply had to supply aid to the developing world. Instead, the Brandt Commission proposed a restructuring of the global economy to encourage participation of developing countries and so strengthen the ties between the developed and developing countries.

According to the Brandt Commission, development should not be restricted to economic and industrial growth. The purpose of development is to enable poor nations to realize self-fulfillment. Recommended priorities included:

- Alleviation of hunger, malnutrition and extreme poverty, particularly across Africa and Asia
- Improvement of conditions for, and removal of constraints to trade in agricultural and other commodities produced in LICs
- Reform of the international monetary system to stabilize exchange rates, with greater provision of Special Drawing Rights for poorer nations; World Bank and regional banks should sizably increase their lending capacities
- Donors must commit their ODA and development assistance on a predictable, long-term basis; as repeatedly emphasized, all development proceeds slowly, and aid projects of short duration often do more harm than good
- An international energy strategy that encourages rigorous conservation and cooperative development of alternative renewable resources
- A systematic program for long-term international food security[20]

An important aspect emphasized within this report was the principal of mutual interest. It serves the interests of both rich and poor countries to empower developing countries to participate within the global economy. It demonstrated that trading with the South accounts for a large share of jobs in the North and also keeps prices affordable for consumers and that media reports circulating fears of competition from growing industries in the South were unsubstantiated. The report also points out that protectionism restricts the South's access to markets that can lead to an inflationary impact on the North. Facilitating trade between the North and South was beneficial for both sides by significantly expanding world trade, supporting growth in developing countries, increasing

20 International Development Research Centre, "From Pearson to Johannesburg," http://www.idrc.ca/en/ev-114186-201-1-DO_TOPIC.html, last visited December 2008.

growth and employment for the North, and stabilizing the financial markets of both.

2.3 New Objectives of Aid

With the collapse of the Soviet Union in 1991, momentous changes occurred in the international order. The Soviet Union was broken up into fifteen independent countries and former socialist regimes in Eastern Europe started a painful transformation into liberalized free markets. As the threat from the Soviet Union evaporated, the new international order that replaced Cold War bipolarity was structured by the unilateralism of US power and a corresponding expansion of democratic values and norms. The practices of aid-giving were strongly influenced by this change in the international order.

During the 1990s, there was an attempt to 'rediscover' the relationship between poverty and aid. The primary purpose of development aid was the direct alleviation of poverty. Official aid agencies reinforced the link between aid and poverty alleviation as a counter to the notion of 'aid dependency.' Aid dependency was a concept that emerged in the 1990s, positing that too much aid was detrimental to development. It was feared that a surplus of aid would encourage recipients to depend on aid as a source of finance, thereby discouraging the expansion of domestically created revenue and self-sustaining development.[21]

New motivations for providing aid emerged with these changing conditions, including the promotion of economic and political transactions, addressing global problems, democracy promotion, and managing conflict.[22] It was necessary for former socialist countries to draft new constitutions and reform their political and economic structures. In some cases aid was also needed to support privatization of state-owned enterprises. With the spread of democratization and the liberalization of markets, reforming the economic structures of socialist countries required assistance from countries with free market economies.

Aid to address global problems

The 1990s was a period of widespread globalization. There was also

21 Roger C. Riddell, *Does Foreign Aid Really Work?* (New York: Oxford University Press, 2007).

22 Carol Lancaster, *Foreign Aid Diplomacy, Development, Domestic Politics* (Chicago: Chicago University Press, 2006).

a growing awareness of the dire effects of various global problems. The interconnectedness among countries was revealed in challenges that affected multiple countries on a global scope. For example, many concerns in the 1990s were related to environmental issues - the need to protect the ozone, the effects of climate change, the impacts of air, water and soil pollution, and desertification. These were all identified as global environmental problems and the international community gathered to discuss and solve these issues.

Global problems also include transnational diseases such as HIV/AIDS, or the SARS outbreak that spread throughout East Asia. SARS quickly became a global problem as it could not be contained within national borders and soon threatened countries all over the world. It is evident that with globalization and increased communication occurring between countries, new threats to the global community have emerged on a worldwide level. The need to alleviate these issues has become a new purpose for providing aid in the globalized world.

Aid for Political Infusion

In addition to the major donor countries, such as the US, Japan and some European nations, the Soviet Union was also an aid-giver. Similar to how the US used aid as a political tool to propagate democratic values, the Soviet bloc provided aid to socialist countries to counterbalance US domination and to increase its influence within these countries. The socialist bloc of aid providers was mainly comprised of the Soviet Union, China and a few Eastern European countries. The Soviet Union and China each provided $1.1 billion in aid, whereas Eastern European countries totaled around $300 million. Of this aid, 75% was provided to developing communist countries,[23] which supports the claim that aid was utilized as a means for political infusion.

The competition and counterbalancing between socialist and democratic values was no longer necessary with the conclusion of the Cold War. With the expansion of democratic ideologies and the collapse of the Soviet bloc, Western interests in providing aid to promote democracy focused primarily on sub-Saharan African countries. In these countries aid was used to finance elections, creating capabilities for campaigning, voting and counting votes. It was also used to fund drafts of new constitutions, political party

23 *Ibid.*

training, or judicial reforms.[24]

It is estimated that bilateral aid used specifically for these new purposes was less than $13 billion of a total of $51 billion of bilateral aid in 2000. Nevertheless, this new motivation for aid-giving grew in importance during the 1990s and influenced how governments decided to allocate and provide their aid budgets.

As the world entered the new millennia, the international community continued to concentrate its efforts on creating a mechanism to effectively assist developing countries that were struggling with poverty. In an attempt to more effectively allocate aid, the United Nations created the Millennium Development Goals. The MDGs, which are discussed separately in Chapter 6, were a set of targets developed during the Millennium Summit aimed at alleviating poverty by 2015. They consisted of eight different quantifiable targets that concentrated on poverty alleviation in the Sub-Saharan African region. A key goal of foreign aid in the new century was poverty eradication and the international community continues to encourage aid that focused on poverty alleviation, especially in the poorest African countries.

A second key concept of the 21st century was sustainable development. It was increasingly obvious that aid provided on a one-time basis, such as food aid that disappears once it is consumed by recipient populations, was less effective than aid that can contribute to promote sustainable development in a developing country. In light of these ideas, donor countries have been motivated to provide kinds of aid that can contribute to sustainable development.

It is important to understand that diverse considerations are made before a donor country provides foreign aid. There is no country that provides foreign aid for a single reason. Donor motivations for giving aid are complex and intertwined amongst each other. Sometimes these reasons can be explicitly identifiable through government statements and action plans, but most times the motivations of different donor countries must be uncovered through a detailed analysis of aid allocation behaviors. Moreover, the general trends, values and beliefs of the international community have continued to influence individual state behaviors. This has added complexities and makes it even more difficult for scholars to understand the underlying reasons behind aid-giving.

24 *Ibid.*

2.4 Millennium Development Goals (MDGs)

The UN Millennium Summit (2000) saw the largest gathering of world leaders in history. United Nations Secretary General Kofi Annan presented his vision for future in a report entitled '*We the Peoples: The Role of the United Nations in the 21st Century*'. The three main pillars of the report were development, security and the environment. First, it addresses freedom from want, the development agenda, followed by freedom from fear, identifying the security agenda, along with the path towards a sustainable future, referring in content to the environmental agenda.

At the conclusion of the summit, the United Nations Millennium Declaration was adopted. This nine-page declaration saw world leaders reaffirmed their commitment to the purposes and principles of the Charter of the United Nations, especially all efforts to uphold the sovereign equality of all states, as well as respect for territorial integrity, political independence and resolution of disputes by peaceful means in conformance to the principles of justice and international law.

The effects of globalization have sparked debates across the world between pro-globalization and anti-globalization factions. At the Millennium Summit, world leaders agreed that the central challenge facing the international community is ensuring that globalization becomes a positive force. In light of these beliefs, leaders presented their commitment in promoting development and eliminating poverty. The urgency to address the needs of Africa was also highlighted during the Summit. The Millennium Declaration defined 8 specific goals, which came to be known as the Millennium

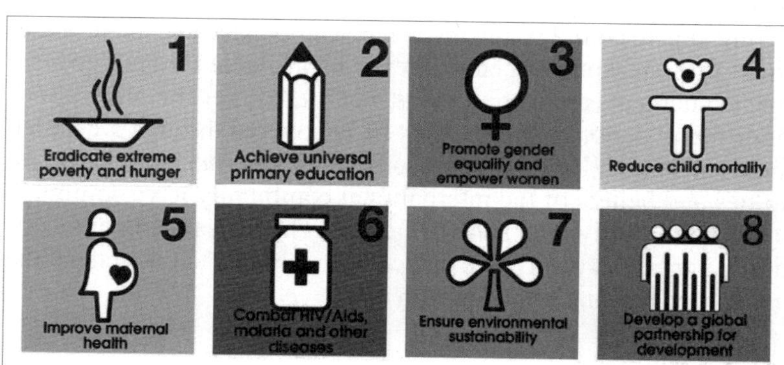

Millennium Development Goals(MDGs)

Development Goals (MDGs). All of these goals are founded on six fundamental values: freedom, equality, solidarity, tolerance, respect for nature and shared responsibility. These concepts are vital for governance in the 21st century.

The MDGs represent a culmination of global partnerships that have grown from commitments and targets established in the international community to promote poverty reduction, education, maternal health, gender equality, and combat child mortality, AIDS and other diseases. The MDGs consisted of eight goals set for the year 2015, which can be further broken down into twenty quantifiable targets measured by sixty indicators.

Box 2.2 Millennium Development Goals

There are eight goals in the framework of the Millennium Development Goals (MDGs) that have been endorsed by the UN member states to assist and improve all facets of the economic, social, and political conditions of impoverished countries by 2015.

Goal 1. Eradicate extreme poverty and hunger
Goal 2. Achieve universal primary education
Goal 3. Promote gender equality and empower women
Goal 4. Reduce child mortality
Goal 5. Improve maternal health
Goal 6. Combat HIV/AIDS, malaria and other diseases
Goal 7. Ensure environmental sustainability
Goal 8. Develop a Global Partnership for Development

Box 2.3 MDG 2015 Report

The Millennium Development Goals is a framework for development adopted by the international community, composed of twenty targets and over sixty indicators with which over 190 countries in ten regions are evaluated. MDG reports show the progress that has been made towards achieving the MDG targets by 2015. Each report considers the progress made by the international community for each of the eight MDGs. The most recent MDG progress report was published in 2015.

I. Eradicate extreme poverty and hunger

The report is generally optimistic that the progress to halve the number of people living on less than $1.25 a day in developing countries given the overall economic improvements worldwide. Extreme poverty rate has dropped to 14% in 2015 with the significant progress occurred since 2000. The Proportion of people living on less than $1.25 a day in sub-Saharan Africa has decreased by 28%, Southern Asia by 66%, South-Eastern Asia by 84%, Latin America and Caribbean by 66%, Western Asia by 46% and Northern Africa by 81% in 2015. However, it is apprehensive of the fact that this trend is mainly due to the rapid development of countries in East Asia whereas Western Asia, Sub-Saharan Africa, CIS, and South Eastern Europe are still economically depressed. The report also points to necessary improvements that must be made in stabilizing food prices, lest an additional 100 million people become indigents.

II. Achieve universal primary education

Statistical figures augur well for the bright future of the agenda. With respect to developing countries, the total enrollment ratio in primary education has reached up to 91% as of 2015 Not only that, but the number of students outside of primary school has decreased in number from 102 million in 2000 to 56 million worldwide and to 53 million in developing countries in 2015, despite an increase in the population of this group.

III. Promote gender equality and empower women

Most of the governments in all regions have done well in increasing girls' school enrollment rates in relation to boys'. As of 2015, Gender Parity Index for gross enrollment ratios in primary schools has increased in all regions almost all passing the 2015 target between 0.97 and 1.03 while Oceanic, sub-Saharan Africa, Western Asia and Northern African falling short. Also, over 96% for secondary school, except Sub-Saharan (83%), Western Asia (90%), Southern Asia and Oceania (92%). The number of women employed in non-agricultural sectors has increased worldwide, but problems still persist in developing countries where most occupy part-time and low-status jobs as well as unpaid caregiving and domestic work.

IV. Reduce child mortality

The MDG set forth its target to reduce the under-five year old child mortality rate by two thirds between 1990 and 2015, and the global under-five mortality rate has declined by more than half, dropping from 90 to 43 deaths per 1000 live births. While Sub-Saharan Africa has the world's highest child mortality rate, the absolute decline in child mortality has been the largest over the past two decades. However, Every day in 2015, 16,000 children under five continue to die, mostly from preventable causes.

V. Improve maternal health

Even though the maternal mortality ratio in the regions has fallen 46% between the time period of 1990 to 2013, it still has a long way to go in order to reach 2015 target of just above 100 maternal deaths per 100,000 live births. However it is worth noting that more than 70% of births were assisted by skilled health personnel in the developing regions by 2014.

VI. Combat HIV/AIDS, malaria, and other diseases

Preventive programs have been successful in reducing the number of people newly infected with HIV by 40 between 2000 and 2013. However, problems still exist in supplying enough drugs to those in need. Evidence suggests that the large-scale expansion of preventive programs and improved access to more effective antimalarial drugs can substantially reduce malaria cases and deaths.[25] However, most developing countries experience difficulty in affording the necessary drugs. The number of tuberculosis cases per 100,000 people has been consistently falling. Between 1990 and 2013, the tuberculosis mortality rate fell by 45% and the prevalence rate 41%.[26]

VII. Ensure environmental sustainability

Carbon emissions have increased by 38% worldwide from 2000 to 2012 and the IPCC asserted that anthropogenic emissions account for more than half of emissions. In order to mitigate and adapt to climate change, the Paris 2015 Agreement was adopted within the framework of UNFCCC, which is the first universal climate agreement with all countries participating in the process.

The report calls for enlarging the scope of forest protection. An increase in afforestation, a slight decrease in deforestation and the natural expansion of forests have reduced the net loss of forest from an average of 8.3 million hectares annually in the 1990s to an average of 5.2 million hectares annually between 2000 and 2010.[27] The population using an improved sanitation facility has reached 62% as of 2015.

---

25 United Nations, "The Millennium Development Goals Report" (New York: United Nations, 2008), 31.

26 United Nations, "The Millennium Development Goals Report" (New York: United Nations, 2015), 8.

27 *Ibid.*

However the 2015 target was set above 70%.

VIII. Develop a global partnership for development

In 2014, net ODA flows from DAC members totaled $135.2 billion which is 66% increase between 2000 and 2014. It is important to continue to increase bilateral and multilateral aid from developed countries, but to improve trade conditions between developed and developing countries is also critical issue.

Progress in increasing preferential trade mechanisms for developing countries to export their goods to developed countries is still stalled. Moreover, less developed countries need more trade-related assistances to achieve sound economic development. These goals can be traced back to the 1995 World Summit on Social Development (WSSD), which enjoys legitimacy among NGOs and activists from various parts of the world due to the broad involvement of governmental and NGO participants in the WSSD preparations and negotiations. But unlike the 1995 WSSD, the 1996 "Shaping the 21st Century" document, which became a foundation for the MDGs, emerged from the OECD's DAC and involved very little of this kind of input. Former DAC Director James Michel argues that the MDGs were "based largely on the formulation recommended in *Shaping the 21st Century*". In the World Bank/IMF 2000 paper "A Better World for All," a fact took the MDGs "from being disparate findings in various United Nations conferences to becoming a unified set of DAC recommendations to the international community…" For this reason, many NGO activists see the MDGs as a product of the OECD governments and the international financial institutions, a perception that compromises the MDGs' ability to mobilize social and political actors.[28]

Monterrey Consensus

The Monterrey Consensus was the product of the International Conference of Financing for Development, held in Monterrey, Mexico (2002), with the stated goal to address the challenges of financing development around the world, eradicating poverty, sustaining economic growth, and promoting sustainable development. During this conference more than 100 participating countries committed themselves to a basic compact of mutual accountability and partnership between developed and developing countries. Commitments involved mobilizing domestic resources, attracting inter-

28 Paul Nelson, "Human Rights, the Millennium Development Goals, and the Future of Development Cooperation," *World Development*, vol. 35, no. 12 (2007): 2041-2055.

national financial flows, promoting international trade, increasing international financial and technical co-operation, sustainable debt financing and external debt relief, and enhancing coherence and consistency of the international monetary, financial and trading systems.[29]

The Monterrey Consensus also placed ODA within a wider framework by urging an increase in all financial flows to developing countries and calling for countries to work coherently towards removing trade restrictions and reducing unmanageable debt. The role of donor-recipient partnerships as the basis for all aid-giving and the role of aid recipients in contributing to aid effectiveness were also emphasized at Monterrey. Donor efforts were linked to achieving the MDGs and it was suggested that the UN should monitor its performance to achieve these goals.

To this end the United Nations set up the Millennium Development Project, an institution tasked with assessing the UN's performance and progress towards the MDGs. In 2005, the Millennium Development Project released a report, *Investing in Development: A Practical Plan to Achieve the Millennium Development Goals* (UN Millennium Development Goals 2005). The report focused on the central notion of recipient-country ownership and recommended that each poor country should build on the MDGs to create separate development strategies that are uniquely designed to accommodate their specific conditions. It was also recommended that development finance be implemented to meet any necessary financial needs.

The global community has faced many obstacles in achieving the MDGs by 2015. Economic recession, food security crises and the effects of climate changes were issues that needed to be addressed but these challenges should not have prevented progress on achieving the MDGs. As identified by Secretary General Ban Ki-Moon, the strategies used to face these challenges must remain focused on the MDGs. He also called attention to the fact that some of these challenges would not have emerged had they been given sufficient attention in the past.[30]

The MDGs were first set in the year 2000, marking the beginning of a new millennium. The significance of the MDGs can be

29 See DAC, OECD paper DAC in Dates.

30 United Nations, "The Millennium Development Goals Report" (New York: United Nations, 2008).

understood in various ways. The MDGs are the first comprehensive framework set out for the global community with quantifiable goals for action. More importantly, the MDGs have been a truly global effort, adopted as a framework for international development by over 190 countries and going beyond governmental efforts to include the private sector and civil society.

The international community has achieved progress in some areas of MDGs, and some of the goals are expected to be reached by their target date. The ultimate goal for the MDGs is to alleviate poverty. According to the UN Millennium Development Goals Report (2008), the overarching goal of reducing absolute poverty by half is within reach globally.

The efforts of major actors played a critical role in achieving the MDGs by 2015. The Global Monitoring Report 2004, issued by the World Bank, suggested several areas of attention for developing countries, developed countries and international financial institutions. In the case of developing countries, it stressed the need to improve the environment and attract private investment, to strengthen capacity in the public sector and to improve the quality of governance, to scale up investments in infrastructure and to ensure its effectiveness, and to enhance the effectiveness of service delivery in human development. It is evidently important for recipient countries to strengthen ownership and commit themselves to cooperate fully with donor countries in development assistance projects.

The efforts of developed countries are also important in increasing effectiveness of aid to meet the MDG targets. In 2004, it was recommended that developed countries sustain stable and strong growth in the global economy. The economic downturn in 2008 evidenced the importance of a sustainable global economy to effectively improve conditions in developing countries. Other suggestions included ensuring a successful pro-development and timely outcome of the Doha Round, providing more and better aid, and improving policy coherence for development.

Multilateral institutions also play a pivotal role in development assistance. According to the World Bank, IFIs needed to refine and strengthen institutional roles in low-income countries and improve selectivity and coordination of agency programs. Thus, there needs to be a collaborative effort made by diverse actors, with different roles maintained by the actors based on their inherent strengths, so that each is able to fully contribute towards eradicating poverty and promoting development in impoverished countries.

Trade and MDGs

The World Bank and other international developmental organizations have adopted the MDGs as part of a structure to motivate and measure progress on sustainable development and as a means to accelerate the implementation of Agenda 2.[31] Most developmental institutions focus on economic growth. The articles set forth by the WB focus on economic health, with goals to facilitate the flow of capital to achieve productive purposes in countries seeking reconstruction.

The MDGs provide a basis for members of the UN family and the Bretton Woods institutions to work together.[32] The United Nations Development Program referred to the MDGs as an accountability system against which international organizations can be measured. Now development banks work with each other and other institutions to achieve these goals. For example, the Africa Stockpiles Program is a partnership between non-governmental organizations, such as the World Wildlife Fund for Nature International and the Pesticides Action Network, and UN specialized agencies, including the WB, along with other international agencies. The objective of the ASP is to support the Stockholm Convention on Persistent Organic Pollutants.

Millennium Human Rights Goals

The UN Millennium Declaration set forth the commitments of 189 countries to work in partnership for development and poverty eradication. Not only that, but the Millennium Declaration also set forth commitments for human rights, democracy and good governance. There were two reports for the implementation of the Millennium Declaration, the Millennium Development Goals and the Millennium Human Rights Goals. There are six Millennium Human Rights goals:

- Goal 1. To respect and fully uphold the Universal Declaration of Human Rights and strive for the full protection and promotion in all countries of civil, political, economic, social and cultural rights for all
- Goal 2. To strengthen the capacity of all countries in implementing the principles and practices of democracy and human rights, including minority rights

31 The World Bank and Agenda 21, July 2002.

32 Charles E. Di Leva, *Achieving the Millennium Development Goals: World Bank Projects, Partnerships and Policies for Sustainable Development*, American Law Institute (2005).

- Goal 3. To combat all forms of violence against women and to implement the Convention on the Elimination of All Forms of Discrimination against Women
- Goal 4. To take measures to ensure respect and protection of the human rights of migrants, migrant workers and their families, to eliminate the increasing acts of racism and xenophobia in many societies, and to promote greater harmony and tolerance in all societies
- Goal 5. To work collectively for more inclusive political processes, allowing for genuine participation by all citizens in all countries
- Goal 6. To ensure the freedom of the media to perform their essential role, and the right of the public to have access to information

Unlike the MDGs, the Millennium Human Rights Goals were not translated into time-bound targets and indicators. Moreover, human rights principles and goals presented in the Millennium Declaration are not integrated in the MDGs.[33] The MDGs and human rights have a common objective to protect human dignity. The relationship between human rights and development is one that deserves more analysis and will be further covered in Chapter 9.

2.5 Post-2015 and Promoting Global Cooperation

In 2010, the international community reviewed progress on the MDGs and issued a report. The report pointed out the necessity of common ground and a mechanism to discuss sustainable and inclusive development goals to replace the MDGs after their expiration in 2015.[34] According to these recommendations, the UN Secretary General launched the UN System Task Team on the Post-2015 UN Development Agenda in January 2012 and assigned it the task of assessing ongoing efforts within the UN system, consulting external stakeholders such as civil society, academia and the private sector, and defining a system-wide vision and roadmap.[35]

There are various reasons why the international community has

33 Gillian MacNaughton, "Decent Work, Human Rights and the Millennium Development Goals," *Hastings Race and Poverty Journal*, vol. 7, no. 2 (2010): 349-351.

34 United Nations, "Accelerating progress towards the Millennium Development Goals: options for sustained and inclusive growth and issues for advancing the United Nations development agenda beyond 2015," *Annual report of the Secretary-General*, A/66/126.

35 UN System Task Team on the Post-2015 UN Development Agenda, "Realizing the Future We Want for All: Report to the Secretary-General,"http://www.un.org/millenniumgoals/pdf/Post_2015_UNTTreport.pdf, Last visited June 2014.

had difficulty achieving the MDGs goals. UNDP indicated achievement was unequally distributed across and within regions and countries in *The Millennium Development Goals Report 2012*.[36] In target setting of MDGs, one argues that there was not proper consideration of individual state's and regional differing baselines and different capacities. Instead, the thing that MDGs set a common goals applied to all countries was one of limitation of MDGs. In addition, a global financial crisis in 2008 and 2009 resulted in the decrease of financing for development, and natural disaster affected negative influence by reducing global food production. Scholars also argue there was lack of consideration of war and fragile states.[37]

Ban Ki-Moon, the UN Secretary General, launched the UN High-Level Panel of Eminent Persons on the Post-2015 Development Agenda (HLP) consisting of twenty-seven persons. This panel took into account aspects such as region, gender, the level of development, as well as state and non-state actors. After a series of meetings and outreach, HLP released its report in May 2013: *A New Global Partnership: Eradicate Poverty and Transform Economies through Sustainable Development*. This report emphasized five transformative shifts that were necessary for sustainable development:

- Leave no one behind;
- Put sustainable development at the core;
- Transform economies for jobs and inclusive growth;
- Build peace and effective, open and accountable public institutions;
- Forge a new global partnership.

The HLP came up with 'Specific, Measurable, Attainable, Relevant, Time-bound (SMART),' a series of twelve universal goals and fifty-four national targets in order to achieve these five transformative shifts. New development agendas were added to the pervious agendas of MDGs, which are poverty, hunger, water, sanitation, education, and healthcare, and it further incorporated the concept of sustainable development.[38] The HLP report included, on the basis

36 UNDP, "The Millennium Development Goals 2012" (New York: United Nations, 2014).

37 Sojin Lim, "Post-2015 Development Framework and UN HLP Report," [In Korean] [*Development Cooperation Policy and Issue*] KOICA, vol. 2, no. 10 (2013): 7-8.

38 United Nations, "A New Global Partnership: Eradicate Poverty and Transform Economies through Sustainable Development," The Report of the High-Level Panel of Eminent Persons on the Post-2015 Development Agenda (New York: United Nations, 2013), 1-6.

of discussions by the UN system task team, issues such as inequality, peace and conflict, governance, and the efficient use of natural resource, all aspects that were not tackled by MDGs.[39] On the other hand, the HLP report also built on the MDGs success by creating a relatively limited number of targets, which are easily understandable, measurable and reachable.[40]

Box 2.4 UNIVERSAL GOALS, NATIONAL TARGETS

1. End Poverty:

1a. Bring the number of people living on less than $1.25 a day to zero and reduce by x% the share of people living below their country's 2015 national poverty line[1,2]

1b. Increase by x% the share of women and men, communities, and businesses with secure rights to land, property, and other assets[2,3]

1c. Cover x% of people who are poor and vulnerable with social protection systems2,3

1d. Build resilience and reduce deaths from natural disasters by x%[2]

2. Empower Girls and Women and Achieve Gender Equality:

2a. Prevent and eliminate all forms of violence against girls and women[1,2,3]

2b. End child marriage[1,2]

2c. Ensure equal right of women to own and inherit property, sign a contract register a business and open a bank account[1,2]

2d. Eliminate discrimination against women in political, economic, and public life[1,2,3]

3. Provide Quality Education and Lifelong Learning:

3a. Increase by x% the proportion of children able to access and complete pre-primary education[2]

3b. Ensure every child, regardless of circumstance, completes primary education able to read, write and count well enough to meet minimum learning standards[1,2]

3c. Ensure every child, regardless of circumstance, has access to lower secondary education and increase the proportion of adolescents who achieve recognized and measurable learning outcomes to x%[1,2]

39 Sojin Lim, "A life of dignity for all," [*Development and Issue*], KOICA, no. 12 (2013): 9.

40 Sojin Lim, "Post-2015 Development Framework and UN HLP Report, [*Development Cooperation Policy and Issue*], KOICA, vol. 2, no. 10 (2013): 10.

3d. Increase the number of young and adult women and men with the skills, including technical and vocational ,needed for work by x%[2,3]

4. Ensure Healthy Lives:
4a. End preventable infant and under five deaths[1,2]
4b. Increase by x% the proportion of children, adolescents, at-risk adults and older people that are fully vaccinated[1,2]
4c. Decrease the maternal mortality ratio to no more than x per100,000[1,2]
4d. Ensure universal sexual and reproductive health and rights[1,2]
4e. Reduce the burden of disease from HIV/AIDS, tuberculosis, malaria, neglected tropical diseases and priority non-communicable diseases[2]

5. Ensure Food Security and Good Nutrition:
5a. End hunger and protect the right of everyone to have access to sufficient, safe, affordable, and nutritious food[1,2]
5b. Reduces stunting by x%, wasting by y%, and anemia by z% for all children under five[1,2]
5c. Increase agricultural productivity by x%, with a focus on sustainably increasing small holder yields and access to irrigation[3]
5d .Adopt sustainable agricultural, ocean and fresh water fishery practices and rebuild designated fish stocks to sustainable levels[1]
5e. Reduce post-harvest loss and food waste by x%[3]

6. Achieve Universal Access to Water and Sanitation:
6a. Provide universal access to safe drinking water at home, and in schools, health centers, and refugee camps[1,2]
6b. End open defecation and ensure universal access to sanitation at school and work, and increase access to sanitation at home by x%[1,2]
6c. Bring fresh water with drawls in line with supply and increase water efficiency in agriculture by x%, industry by y% and urban areas by z%
6d. Recycle or treat all municipal and industrial waste water prior to discharge[1,3]

7. Secure Sustainable Energy:
7a. Double the share of renewable energy in the global energy mix
7b. Ensure universal access to modern energy services[1,2]
7c. Double the global rate of improvement in energy efficiency in buildings, industry, agriculture and transport
7d. Phase out inefficient fossil fuel subsidies that encourage wasteful consumption[1,3]

8. Create Jobs, Sustainable Livelihoods and Equitable Growth:

8a. Increase the number of good and decent jobs and livelihoods by x[2]

8b. Decrease the number of young people not in education, employment or training by x%[2]

8c. Strengthen productive capacity by providing universal access to financial services and infrastructure such as transportation and ICT[1,2,3]

8d. Increase new start-ups by x and value added from new products by y through creating an enabling business environment and boosting entrepreneurship[2,3]

9. Manage Natural Resource Assets Sustainably:

9a. Publish and use economic, social and environmental accounts in all governments and major companies[1]

9b. Increase consideration of sustainability in x% of government procurements[3]

9c. Safe guard ecosystems, species and genetic diversity

9d. Reduce deforestation by x% and increase reforestation by y%

9e. Improves oil quality, reduces oil erosion by x tones and combat desertification

10. Ensure Good Governance and Effective Institutions:

10a. Provide free and universal legal identity, such as birth registrations[1,2]

10b. Ensure people enjoy freedom of speech, association, peaceful protest and access to independent media and information[1,3]

10c. Increase public participation in political processes and civic engagement at all levels[2,3]

10d. Guarantee the public's right to information and access to government data[1]

10e. Reduce bribery and corruption and ensure officials can be held accountable[3]

11. Ensure Stable and Peaceful Societies:

11a. Reduce violent deaths per100,000 by x and eliminate all forms of violence against children[1,2,3]

11b. Ensure justice institutions are accessible, independent, well-resourced and respect due-process rights[1,2]

11c. Stem the external stressors that lead to conflict, including those related to organized crime[3]

11d. Enhance the capacity, professionalism and accountability of the security forces, police and judiciary[3]

12. **Create a Global Enabling Environment and Catalyze Long-Term Finance:**

12a. Support an open, fair and development-friendly trading system, substantially reducing trade-distorting measures, including agricultural subsidies, while improving market access of developing country products[3]

12b. Implement reforms to ensure stability of the global financial system and encourage stable, long-term private foreign investment[3]

12c. Hold the increase in global average temperature below 2℃ above pre-industrial levels, in line with international agreements

12d. Developed countries that have not done so to make concrete efforts towards the target of 0.7% of gross national product (GNP) as official development assistance to developing countries and 0.15 to 0.20% of GNP of developed countries to least developed countries; other countries should move toward voluntary targets for complementary financial assistance

12e. Reduce illicit flows and tax evasion and increase stolen-asset recover y by $x[3]

12f. Promote collaboration on and access to science, technology, innovation, and development data[3]

[1] Candidates for global minimum standards, including 'zero' goals.
[2] Indicators to be disaggregated.
[3] Targets require further technical work to find appropriate indicators.

Source: United Nations (2013) "A NEW GLOBAL PARTNERSHIP: ERADICATE POVERTY AND TRANSFORM ECONOMIES THROUGH SUSTAINABLE DEVELOPMENT (available at: http://www.post2015hlp.org/the-report/).

Promoting Global Cooperation

The MDGs are a set of goals that were established by the United Nations during the UN Millennium Conference. Hence, the leading coordinator of the MDGs is the UN, which has continued to spur the efforts of individual countries to implement the goals. The MDGs have been perceived as a framework for the entire UN system to work coherently towards a common ground. To this end, the UNDP network spans over 177 countries and is uniquely positioned to help advocate change, connect countries to knowledge and resources, and coordinate broader efforts at the country level.

As an international organization, what the UN can contribute towards achieving the MDGs is not sufficient in and of itself to eradicate global poverty. The UN has concentrated on establishing an overall framework for action, networking the efforts of donor and recipient partners, as well as management, monitoring and evaluation mechanisms to promote future efforts. At the same time, the UN needs to recognize the significant role played by participating countries and newly emerging actors. Based on this understanding of the potential contributions that different actors can make to the global aid effort, the UN must continue to govern the complexities inherent within this network of interactions between diverse participants of development assistance.

The United Nation's Core Strategy on MDGs identifies the UNDP's work as focusing on four main pillars: ① campaigning and mobilization, to support advocacy for the MDGs and work with partners to mobilize commitments and capabilities to build awareness; ② analyzing, to research and share the best strategies in achieving the MDGs in terms of innovative practices, policy and institutional reforms, means of policy implementation and evaluation of financing options; ③ monitoring to help countries report advancement towards the MDGs and to track progress; and 4) operational activities which promote goal-driven assistance to support governments to tailor MDGs to local circumstances and challenges, as well as addressing the key constraints to progress.[41]

The cooperative and collaborative efforts of all participating actors are critical for achieving the MDGs. The value of the MDGs rests in the establishment of quantitative goals that function as a strong motivator of action from donor governments. The MDGs also provide a mechanism that allows for comparative assessment and evaluation of the progress of recipient partners. A further achievement of the MDGs is their contributions towards achieving a widespread awareness in the general public. The MDGs have become a key agenda within the international arena, one that has continued to gain recognition and interest from diverse spheres including the public sector, the private sector, and academia. Thus, the MDGs have provided a mechanism to promote the efforts of participating actors. An increasing awareness of the importance of governmental support to achieve the MDGs by 2015 has led to enhanced efforts by both donor and recipient countries, and the relationship between the MDGs and ODA has proven mutually rein-

41 UNDP, "About the MDGs: UNDP's Role," http://www.undp.org/mdg/undps_role.shtml, Accessed March 2009.

forcing.

Chapter 2. Review Discussion Questions

1. What aspects of the international community induced the United States to consider the Marshall Plan?
2. During the early stage of foreign aid, what was the underlying rationale for providing development aid?
3. Why did countries generally refrain from providing aid before the 1950s?
4. How have the purposes or motivations for providing aid changed during the last fifty years?
5. How have the UN Development Decades contributed to the field of development assistance?
6. Why were the MDGs different from past efforts made by the international community to alleviate poverty?

Chapter 3
Aid Planning and Monitoring

> *"The peer review process is a unique experience for learning about the characteristics of effective development co-operation systems, in the light of internationally agreed standards, commitments and principles (the Paris Declaration and Accra Agenda for Action).... In an effort to make donor action more coherent and effective, and to improve accountability, co-ordination, learning and evaluation, these reviews attempt a critical, helpful and respectful commentary on practices by DAC members. It is a process that seeks a common understanding of aid practice and provides regular feedback on innovative ways in which donors have made progress towards more effective aid management."*[1]

Development cooperation programs or projects generally consist of the three stages of planning, implementation and evaluation. When donor countries design aid operations, they are requested to consider the recipient country's development plan and priorities, transparency, effectiveness, predictability of aid and their own interests and resources for aid. The aid planning stage decides the types of aid, which can be tied or untied, grant or loan, program or project, sector, and bilateral or multilateral. The donor countries execute aid operations according to their plans and during or after this operation they should conduct monitoring and evaluation jointly with their counterpart in the recipient country. The results of monitoring and assessment are recommended to be reflected in the amendment of ongoing aid operations or become lessons for better aid in the future. In this sense, aid planning and monitoring is an important part of the aid operation cycle.

3.1 Aid Planning

Aid operations reflect differing approaches and types. Since the

1 OECD DAC website, "Lessons from Peer Reviews," http://www.oecd.org/dac/peer-reviews/lessons-peer-reviews.htm.

late 1960s, USAID, UNDP and UNICEF developed manuals and mechanisms to design, implement and evaluate aid programs and projects systematically and effectively. European aid institutions such as German GTZ, NORAD and FINNADA in the 1980s, also sought effective management of aid operations by developing aid management frameworks.

Concept of PCM

Project Cycle Management (PCM) is a framework covering the whole process of aid operations from project formation, design, implementation, monitoring, and assessment to feedback. PCM evolved from the basic principles of the 'logical framework' of US-AID in the late 1960s. The basic framework of PCM includes project identification and planning, the formation of a Project Design Matrix (PDM), and monitoring and evaluation.

Box 3.1 Project Cycle[2]

Project Cycle refers to a process of project planning, implementation, and evaluation. A standard procedure of a project cycle is as follow:

Stage 1: identification of state and sectoral development strategies
Stage 2: project identification
Stage 3: project formation and design
Stage 4: project feasibility study
Stage 5: agreement between the donor and the recipient
Stage 6: procurement and bidding
Stage 7: implementation
Stage 8: conclusion of project and transfer
Stage 9: evaluation
Stage 10: follow-up support and management

Logical Framework (Logframe) by the USAID: Late 1960s

The origin of PCM is from the Logical Framework (Logframe) that USAID developed to make a budgetary report to US Congress in the late 1960s. Logframe is a framework linking each component — goal, target, output, activity, and input of aid — in a coherent and logical manner. Logframe is a systematic tool for designing, planning, implementing, and monitoring and evaluating a project (or

2 KOICA, *Understanding International Development Cooperation* (Seoul: Hanul, 2008), 364.

program). It is also a tool for organizing thought related inputs to the implementation of activities, activities to the production of outputs, outputs to the achievement of a defined purpose, and purpose to a high-level goal or impact. It can also be a tool for identifying and assessing risks by listing critical assumptions inherent in project design and implementation, measuring project progress through objectively verifiable indicators and means of verification, and for developing consensus and communicating a project's intent and strategy.

The logic of Logframe is based on organized thinking. It focuses on an effective mobilization of resources, the input of such resources for planned activities, and building logical relationships between activities and objectives and overall goals. This logical frame was later developed into ZOPP by GTZ and PCM, which is today the dominant framework in international development cooperation. However, it also has received criticism. Logframe is not a substitute for other technical, economic, social and environmental analyses. It cannot replace the use of professionally qualified and experienced staff. Rigidity in project management may arise when objectives and external factors specified during design are over emphasized. It also requires a team process with good leadership and facilitation skills to be effective. Moreover, the whole culture of Logframe can be alien in some societies.

Objectives-Oriented Project Planning (ZOPP) by GTZ: Early 1980s

In 1983, the German Organization for Technical Cooperation (GTZ) developed "Objectives-Oriented Project Planning (ZOPP)" by adding the concept of participatory cooperation to Logframe. ZOPP is a systematic structure for identification, planning, and management of projects. It is applied through iterative workshops with project authorities, beneficiaries, and stakeholders. Also, it utilizes problem analysis and stakeholder analysis to create a project-planning matrix of logical project frameworks. Due to its practical availability, ZOPP is used in the planning, monitoring and evaluation of aid programs by many development institutions.

ZOPP consists of 5 stages:

- Pre-ZOPP: an in-house exercise by agencies in preparation for a project.
- Appraisal ZOPP: an in-house appraisal for preparing Terms of Reference of a project.

- Partner ZOPP: prepared in-country; coordination of conclusions and recommendations with staff of project country
- Take-off ZOPP: prepared in-country; preparation of the plan of operations with personnel responsible for project execution and counterpart authorities.
- Replanning ZOPP: prepared in-country; adjustments during project implementation.

Each planning phase of ZOPP has a specific goal and each goal is the subject of a workshop. Each workshop is comprised of different stakeholders. Participants analyze key issues throughout the project cycle. There is no set formula for a successful workshop and participants need to create a common language and understand one another's divergent views.

Box 3.2 Project Planning Matrix (PPM)

The Project Planning Matrix (PPM) is a Logframe Matrix of ZOPP. It is central to ZOPP-based project work because the process of building relies on repeated, collaborative stakeholder input. The PPM is a one-page summary of:

- why the project is carried out,
- what the project is expected to achieve,
- how the project is going to achieve these results,
- factors crucial for the success of the project,
- how success can be measured,
- where data is needed to assess project success,
- what the project will cost.

Project Cycle Management (PCM) by EC: Early 1990s

USAID's Logframe and GTZ's ZOPP provided an important encouragement for the establishment of Project Cycle Management (PCM) in the early 1990s. PCM is different from Logframe and ZOPP in that PCM includes ① flexibility in project preparation, ② new procedures for project planning.

PCM is not an 'activity-driven' but a 'result-oriented' approach. PCM that aims to manage comprehensively the whole process of a project cycle puts priority on securing consistency and transparency in aid planning and operations and setting objectives and actions logically. This approach is expected to achieve aid effectiveness by increasing project planning and management.[3] It also allows a participatory stakeholder involvement in the process of aid planning, implementation and assessment. It works as a framework that can be applied to the evaluation of relevance, feasibility and sustainability of aid programs and projects by providing indicators for monitoring and assessment of aid objectives. Lastly, it includes external factors that can form an operational environment affecting the success or failure of an aid project.[4]

There are eight steps for PCM.

- Stakeholders Analysis: A stakeholder is any individual, group or organization, or community with an interest in the outcome of a program or project.
- SWOT Analysis: SWOT analysis is a tool for institutional appraisal and a brainstorming exercise in which the representatives of the organization participate fully. This is to assess the performance and capacity of the units or divisions of an organization.
- Problems Analysis: Problems Analysis visually shows the causes and effects of existing problems in the project area in the form of a Problem Tree. It clarifies the relationships among the identified problems.
- Objectives Analysis: Objective Analysis clarifies the means-ends relationship between the desirable situation that would be attained and the solution for attaining it. This stage also requires an Objective Tree.
- Project Selection: Project Selection is a process in which specific project strategies are selected from among the objectives and means raised in Objectives Analysis, based upon selection criteria.
- Formation of the Project Design Matrix (PDM): The PDM is formed through elaborating the major project components and plans based on the approach selected. The format of PDM is similar to that of the Logical Framework, and therefore can be commonly used worldwide (see below).
- Workplan / Plan of Operations: The Plan of Operation is prepared by the project implementers, based on the PDM and other information. It is an effective tool for project implementation and management, and provides important data for monitoring and evaluation of the project.
- Monitoring and Evaluation (M&E)

3 *Ibid.*, 365.

4 *Ibid.*

Project Design Matrix (PDM)

Project Design Matrix (PDM) is a matrix that shows key variables that should be considered in the stage of aid planning and the logical relationships between the project and these variables. PDM includes inputs, activities, project purpose, objectively verifiable indicators, and external conditions. Table 9.1 shows a basic Project Design Matrix.

Table 3.1 Project Design Matrix (PDM)

Project Summary	Objectively Verifiable Indicators- Standards for measuring project achievement	Means of Verification- Data sources from which indicators are derived	Important Assumptions- Conditions important for success of the project, but cannot be controlled by the projects. Whether these conditions develop or not is uncertain
Overall Goal- Direction that the project should take next			
Project Purpose- Objectives that the project should achieve within the project duration			
Outputs-Strategies for achieving the Project Purpose			
Activities-Specific actions taken to produce Outputs	Inputs-Human resource, materials, equipment, facilities and funds required by the project		Pre-conditions-Conditions that must be fulfilled before a project gets underway

Figure 3.1 PDM Mapping

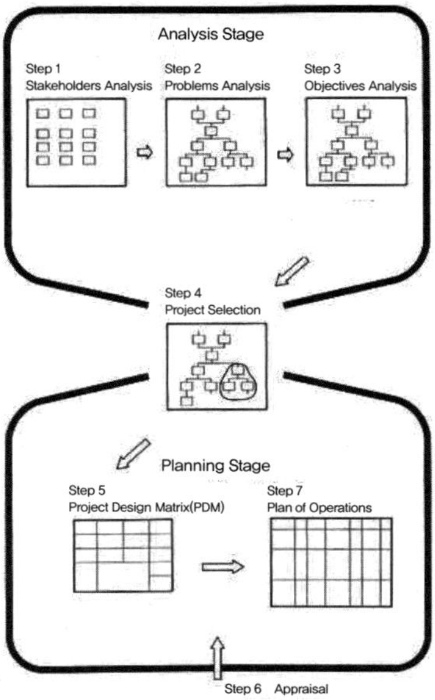

Source: KOICA International Development Education Academy, *Understanding of KOICA Project* (2012), 103.

Limitation of PCM and PDM

Although PDM is a document that is produced at the beginning stage of aid planning, it needs consistent amendment and updates throughout the duration of the aid operation. In case of sudden changes in the operational environment, for example, the entire project might need to be changed.[5] When PCM and PDM are adopted, however, they are not easy to amend due to the bureaucratic inertia, even if there is demand for alteration from the field. In addition, it is not easy to include detailed information on the project in the case of PDM because these are typically provided on a single sheet of paper.[6]

Poverty Reduction Strategy Papers (PRSP)

While the DAC Peer Reviews constitute donor-oriented efforts to promote effectiveness in providing aid, Poverty Reduction Strategy Papers are efforts by recipient-oriented developing countries to

5 KOICA International Development Education Academy, *Understanding KOICA Project (2012)*, 113.

6 *Ibid.*, 113-114.

increase effectiveness in implementation. PRSPs work as a means of encouraging governments of poor countries to develop unified strategies in collaboration with a diversity of stakeholders so that economic and political structures concentrate on the elimination of poverty. As such, they provide a comprehensive country-based strategy for poverty reduction.

PRSPs were first introduced and initiated by the International Monetary Fund and the World Bank in 1999. These institutions recognized the importance of ownership and the necessity to concentrate on poverty reduction, eventually leading to the development of PRSPs to work as a crucial link between national public actions, donor support and the development outcomes needed to achieve the Millennium Development Goals. They aimed to reinforce coordination among donors, enhance the design of financial support programs, and raise the domestic records of policy implementation in order to improve the time series properties of aid flows.

PRSPs are prepared by member countries through a participatory process involving domestic stakeholders as well as external development partners such as the World Bank or the International Monetary Fund. They contain information on the country's macroeconomic, structural and social policies as well as programs to promote broad-based growth and reduce poverty. A typical PRSP covers a span of three years and is further updated with annual progress reports. Interim PRSPs (I-PRSPs) summarize the current knowledge and analysis of a country's poverty situation, describe the existing poverty reduction strategy and lay out the process for devising a fully developed PRSP. Individual country PRSPs and I-PRSPs are available on the World Bank database.

Box 3.3 Core Principles of PRSP Approach

Poverty Reduction Strategies should be:

- country-driven, promoting national ownership of strategies through broad-based participation of civil society;
- result-oriented and focused on outcomes that will benefit the poor;
- comprehensive in recognizing the multidimensional nature of poverty;
- partnership-oriented, involving coordinated participation of development partners (government, domestic stakeholders, and external donors); and
- based on a long-term perspective for poverty reduction.

PRSPs are significant in the sense that they encourage greater national ownership and thereby more effectiveness in poverty reduction, but whether or not they can be successful in reducing poverty is yet to be seen. The IMF's low-interest lending facility, the Poverty Reduction and Growth Facility, utilizes the PRSPs of individual countries to identify appropriate strategies to accommodate each country's unique conditions. The PRSP is also used by the World Bank as a basis for developing Country Assistance Strategy (CAS).[7]

Poverty Reduction and Growth Facility (PRGF)

The Poverty Reduction and Growth Facility (PRGF) is the IMF's low-interest lending facility for low-income countries. It was established in 1999 to make poverty reduction and growth more central to the lending operations in its poorest member countries. PRGF-supported programs are framed around comprehensive, country-owned PRSPs, from which the targets and policy conditions are drawn. The principles of broad public participation and country ownership are central to PRGF, and supported programs adhere to each individual country's poverty reduction and growth priorities. As long as macroeconomic stability is maintained, it responds flexibly to changes in country circumstances and pro-poor priorities. PRGF-supported programs also concentrate on strengthening governance in order to assist countries' efforts in designing targeted and well prioritized spending. Measures to improve public resources management, transparency and accountability are of particular concerns, as are the poverty and social impacts of key macroeconomic policy measures.

3.2 Types of Aid

Development assistance generally can be distinguished into loan and grant aid, but according to the target beneficiary, delivery channel, and contents there are more diversified types of aid. It includes program and project aid, technical cooperation, budget support, di-

7 The World Bank prepares a Country Assistance Strategy (CAS) for active borrowers from the International Development Association (IDA) and the International Bank for Reconstruction and Development (IBRD). The purpose of the CAS is to set out a selective program of Bank Group support linked to the country's development strategy and based on the Bank Group's comparative advantage in the context of other donor activities. CASs are designed to promote collaboration and coordination among development partners in a country.

saster relief, debt relief, etc. This section reviews different types of aid.

Projects and Program Aid

Project aid refers to a situation in which the donor is fully in control of all the inputs required in the production of some part of the developmental good. Under the assumption that the donor is in full control of the project, a following implicit assumption is that it is possible to avoid the diversion of aid funds by the recipient. Most donors resort to project aid for developmental programs when recipient countries have weak monetary and fiscal systems, management skills, and accountability.

An inherent problem of project aid is "aid fungibility," which refers to reallocation of resources away from the developmental sector by recipient countries. In other words, the recipient country was ready and capable of investing its own money in the project but donors did it instead, allowing the government to allocate the funds elsewhere. Thus, donors have merely overlaid and substituted the government's work. For example, a government that initially intended to allocate resources to build a school may decide to use the resources elsewhere after donors provide project aid for building the school.[8]

The international community has recognized that aid effectiveness requires using different types of aid rather than just project aid. Since the mid-1960s, program-based support emerged. Contrary to project aid, program aid focuses on a comprehensive and inclusive program or cross-sectoral approach, i.e. poverty reduction programs, rather than project aid that tackles a single issue such as a school-feeding project. In other words, this approach is based on the principles of coordinated support for a locally owned program of development, such as a national development strategy, a sector program, a thematic program or a program of a specific organization.[9] Under program aid, each operation is linked closely and systematically and the agencies are able to collaborate more flexibly and in various aspects. To increase transparency and effectiveness in operations and to promote multilateral cooperation among donors and agencies, the program aid is prone to adopt a comprehen-

8 Tito Cordella and Dell Ariccia, "Budget Support versus Project Aid," *IMF Working Paper* (2003).

9 OECD, The Paris Declaration on Aid Effectiveness and the Accra Agenda for Action. http://www.oecd.org/dac/effectiveness/34428351.pdf.

sive management system and a result-based approach.

Program aid is composed of direct budget and sector support. It is important to distinguish the differences between program aid and budget support modality of aid. In the case of program aid, donors channel aid directly to the budget of the recipient countries, but the recipient governments have discretion in spending this money for development projects. After donor funds are disbursed into the host government's budget, the recipient government may use its own allocation, procurement, and accounting systems to implement its own development programs.[10] Another type of program aid is sector support. Donors grant aid to the recipient countries under the condition that funds will be used for specific sector, varying from health, education, to agriculture.

Policy makers in general accede that the level of financial and political development of a recipient country is the key success factor for program aids. Countries that have a strong budget system, macroeconomic policies, economic growth, and political will are more likely to attain their targets. As a result, countries that have stronger institutional infrastructures are more attractive to donor countries.

The OECD estimates that only around 5% of total foreign aid is in the form of budgetary support. Why is it so low? Much of the literature on this phenomenon seeks to explain it with reference to the relationship between donor and recipient countries; when preferences of both donors and recipients are aligned, budget support is preferable. However, recent writers have been analyzing the donor itself; that is, the agent (company or government) and principal (voters).[11] The main thrust of this argument is that because of information asymmetry, agents, for their own sake, are more prone to engage in projects with higher expected return even though program aid may be more efficient.

Donors and multilateral development agencies are improving their aid delivery mechanisms and planning in order to improve aid effectiveness. One example is that donors are expanding resources for aid and giving more priority to the PRSP of the recipient country. The IMF forecasts that donors will shift more from project aid to program aid. This shift will help reduce transaction costs and the

---

10 USAID, "General Budget Support and Sector Program Assistance," *PPC Evaluation Working Paper*, no. 19 (2004): 10.

11 Sanjay Jain, "Project Assistance versus Budget Support: An Incentive-Theoretic Analysis of Aid Conditionality," *Review of World Economics*, vol. 143, no. 4 (2007): 694-719.

drain on limited capacity caused by the need to implement a large number of projects. But program aid flows tend to be more volatile than project aid, which is usually committed up front and disbursed on a multiyear basis.[12] High volatility may characterize program assistance, given that it may depend on concessionality or on short-run macroeconomic performance, whereas project aid is relatively stable, given that it is designed to promote investment in physical and human capital.[13]

Tied and Untied Aid

At the DAC High Level Meeting in April 2001, a recommendation to untie aid to the least developed countries was adopted and came into force on January 1, 2002. There were several objectives underlying this decision. It aimed to foster coordinated, efficient and effective partnerships with developing countries and to strengthen the ownership and responsibility of partner countries in the development process. The recommendation also hoped to demonstrate responsiveness to requests from partner countries and to contribute to broader efforts at promoting integration into the global economy.[14]

The OECD DAC categorizations of aid type be divided into Untied Aid, Partially Tied Aid and Tied Aid. The official definition of tied aid indicates that "tied aid credits are official or officially supported Loans, credits or Associated Financing packages where procurement of the goods or services involved is limited to the donor country or to a group of countries which does not include substantially all developing countries (or Central and Eastern European Countries (CEECs)/ New Independent States (NIS) in transition)."[15] Because tied aid limits the procurement of goods and services to selected countries, tied aid practices can result in higher costs for developing countries. A further concern of tied aid is that flows of aid that were initially provided to recipient developing countries end up flowing back into the donor country economy. In this case, foreign aid is not really about poverty reduction in the recipient

12 Ben Eifert and Alan Gelb, "Coping with Aid Volatility," *IMF Finance & Development*, vol. 42, no. 3 (2005). http://www.imf.org/external/pubs/ft/fandd/2005/09/eifert.htm.

13 Pierre Richard Agénor and Joshua Aizenman, "Aid Volatility and Poverty Traps," *NBER Working Paper Series* (2007).

14 See DAC Recommendation on Untying Official Development Assistance to the Least Developed Countries.

15 "Tied Aid Credits", OECD Glossary of Statistical Terms.

country, but rather acts as a mechanism that provides incentives, like job creation, for the donor economy.

Table 3.2 DAC Definitions of Tying Status of ODA, Other Official Flows and Officially Supported Credits

Tying Status Category	Definition and Coverage
Untied Aid	Loans and grants whose proceeds are fully and freely available to finance procurement from all OECD countries and substantially all developing countries.
Partially Untied Aid	Loans and grants that are tied, contractually or in effect, to procurement of goods and services from a restricted number of countries which must include substantially all developing countries and can include the donor country.
Tied Aid	All other loans and grants not falling into the two above categories are classified as tied aid, whether they are tied formally or through informal arrangements.

Figure 3.2 OECD DAC: Tied and Untied Aid Trends (1995-2011)

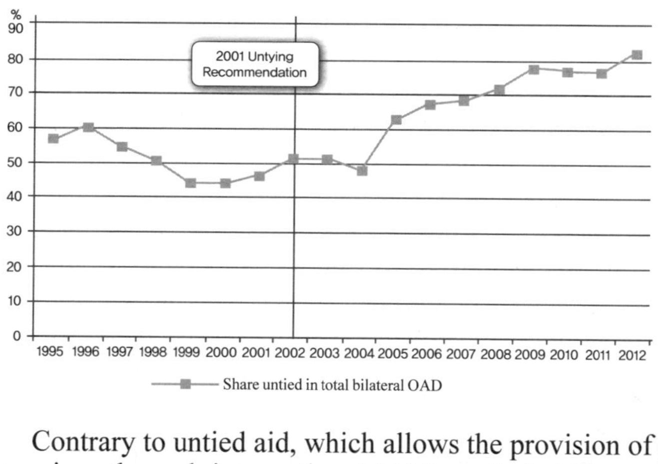

Contrary to untied aid, which allows the provision of goods and services through international bidding, tied aid is seen as a tool to achieve donor's political or economic interests as it limits the provider of goods and services to the donor country itself or a few countries. If the procurement of aid is limited to the donor country or a few countries, it is interpreted as tied aid regardless of the clear statement on tied condition in the agreement of procurement. The DAC Peer Review also recognizes this type of aid as tied aid.[16]

16 KOICA Annual Report (2008), 203.

Tied aid practices can result in higher costs for developing countries because it does not allow procurement to benefit from open competition in the market. Tied aid is known to increase costs by 15~30% compared to untied aid. From the perspective of donor countries, tied aid protects donor exports from international competition on contracts, but these acts lead to higher costs for the recipient country, many times incurring lower quality of goods and service. Estimates by the World Bank indicate that tying aid reduces effectiveness of aid by as much as 25%. Procurement of goods and services by the donor country reduces the possibility of increasing procurement from the markets of developing countries and imposes additional administrative costs on developing country governments. Donor countries may also distort aid allocations to sectors that are especially profitable for their domestic markets, seeking to increase commercial and political incentives rather than focusing on poverty reduction and economic growth in developing economies. Another serious problem following tied aid is that it can cause recipient countries to become dependent on large bilateral donors, which can stimulate a donor-driven approach to development assistance, further discouraging donor coordination and simplifying donor procedures. Due to these negative side effects, the OECD DAC, international organizations, and NGOs support untied aid.

Whereas tied aid restricts the procurement of goods and services from the donor country, untied aid allows recipient countries to buy goods and services from any country. The DAC defines untied aid as loans or grants that are freely and fully permitted to finance procurement from all aid recipient countries and from OECD countries. The categories of tied and untied aid are relatively unambiguous compared to that of partially untied aid. In the former two, the key issue is whether the sourcing of goods and services is either restricted or free from restriction. Partially tied aid refers to situations in which the donor wishes to allow local procurement in the recipient country or possibly even from a group of developing countries.

DAC Member countries agreed to untie ODA to the least developed countries by January 1, 2002 in the following areas: balance of payments and structural adjustment support; debt forgiveness; sector and multi-sector program assistance; investment project aid; import and commodity support; commercial services contracts; and ODA to non-governmental organizations for procurement related activities.[17]

For member countries of the DAC, an analysis of ODA statistics provides individual country ratios of tied aid and untied aid within their bilateral aid flows. The average proportion of untied aid within OECD DAC members has been increasing over time. While 58% of all bilateral aid commitments by OECD donors was tied in 1990, data for 2012 indicates that 82.2% of all aid provided by DAC member states was untied.

Table 3.3 DAC Members Tying Status of ODA, 2012[18]

	Bilateral ODA			
	Untied	Partially Tied	Tied	Not reported
Australia	99.9	-	-	0.1
Austria	37.3	-	62.6	0.2
Belgium	72.1	-	3.7	24.2
Canada	91.6	-	8.4	-
Czech Republic	45.1	-	54.9	0.0
Denmark	96.3	-	3.7	-
Finland	95.2	-	4.8	-
France	95.9	-	4.1	-
Germany	79.2	-	20.8	0.0
Greece	6.4	-	93.6	0.0
Iceland	100.0	-	-	-
Ireland	100.0	-	-	
Italy	82.0	1.1	15.7	1.2
Japan	71.0	-	11.6	17.4
Korea	49.4	0.3	50.3	0.0
Luxembourg	94.1	-	1.2	4.7
Netherlands	98.4	-	1.6	-
New Zealand	84.3	4.3	11.4	-
Norway	100.0	-	-	-
Poland	..	..	..	100.0
Portugal	24.6	-	75.4	-
Slovak Republic	..	..	..	100.0
Spain	83.4	0.1	16.5	0.0
Sweden	92.9	0.0	7.1	-

17 *Ibid.*

18 OECD, "Development Cooperation Report 2007 Statistical Annex" (2008).

Switzerland	93.1	-	6.1	0.8
United Kingdom	100.0	-	-	-
United States	74.7	-	25.3	-
Total DAC	**82.2**	**0.0**	**14.3**	**3.5**

Following the agreement to untie aid by its member countries, the DAC has encouraged all donors, including non-DAC member donors, to untie aid to the least developed countries. It expects untied aid to be more efficient than tied aid due to administrative burdens and technical incompatibilities among donor and recipient technologies that result from tied aid practices. Although some studies indicate that the effectiveness of tied and untied aid is not significantly different,[19] it is generally accepted that tied aid raises the costs of goods, services and works by 15-30% on average, with more than a 40% increase for food aid.[20]

On the other hand, the incentives for donor countries to provide tied aid are not limited to macroeconomic benefits but can also be understood from a political perspective. Some donor governments have explained that tying aid strengthens public and business support for a development aid agenda. In this case, some governments fear the possible negative impact that untying aid may have on already squeezed aid budgets. ODA is more complex than a simple economic exchange and contains the values and willingness of donor countries to cooperate with developing countries. In this light, tied aid provides a clear, visible connection/relationship/mutual incentive that the public can easily relate to.

Box 3.4 International Competitive Bidding

International competitive bidding refers to the procurement of goods and services from the international competitive bidding process.

There are two types of international biding markets. One is a multi-

19 Santanu Chatterjee and Stephen Turnovsky, "Tied versus Untied Foreign Aid: Consequences for a growing economy," *Computing in Economics and Finance*, vol. 2004, no. 8 (2004).

20 Edward J. Clay, Matthew Geddes, Luisa Natali and Dirk Willem te Velde, "Thematic Study, The Developmental Effectiveness of Untied Aid: Evaluation of the Implementation of the Paris Declaration and of the 2001 DAC Recommendation on Untying ODA To The LDCs, Phase I Report" (Copenhagen: Overseas Development Institute (ODI), 2008).

lateral ODA procurement market that is the World Bank, regional development banks, and UN multilateral development assistance organizations. The other one is a bilateral ODA procurement market where the donor government or its agencies procure goods and services for the specific recipient country's aid program or project.[21]

It is not easy to measure the volume of the international aid procurement market, but it is possible to estimate its volume by excluding tied aid and certain types of aid which are automatically excluded from the category of untied aid such as technical assistance, food assistance, debt relief, administrative cost.

The scale of international aid procurement market is increasing with a normative guideline in international development cooperation that supports untied aid.

Grant and Loans

Aid is divided into grants and loans, which can also be divided into bilateral aid, in which assistance is given directly to developing countries, and multilateral aid, which is provided through international organizations. A grant refers to a "free" form of assistance in cash, goods or services provided without stipulations of repayment or redemption. A loan refers to funding provided either in cash or goods with stipulations of liabilities for repayment. Concessional loans made as part of ODA are more favorable to the recipient country than other commercially available loans in terms of interest rates, maturity, and grace periods. In order to count as ODA, a concessional loan must have a grant element of 25% or greater.

OECD DAC countries' aid disbursement arrangement shows that grants count for 90% of total ODA. There is an international consensus that increasing grants and making loan aid more concessional is more desirable for poverty reduction and development from a humanitarian perspective. Because loan aid can cause an excessive external debt burden for developing countries, especially for the least developed countries, the international community recommends an increase of grant aid.[22]

21 Gye-Woo Lee, "South Korea's policy on international aid market," *Journal of International Development Cooperation*, vol. 2009, no. 4 (2009): 84-116.

22 Seung-Hoon Jeon et al., "Mid to Long-Term Bilateral Aid Policy of Korea" (Seoul: KOICA, 2006).

Figure 3.3 Grant and Loan Disbursements and Share (USD millions / per cent)

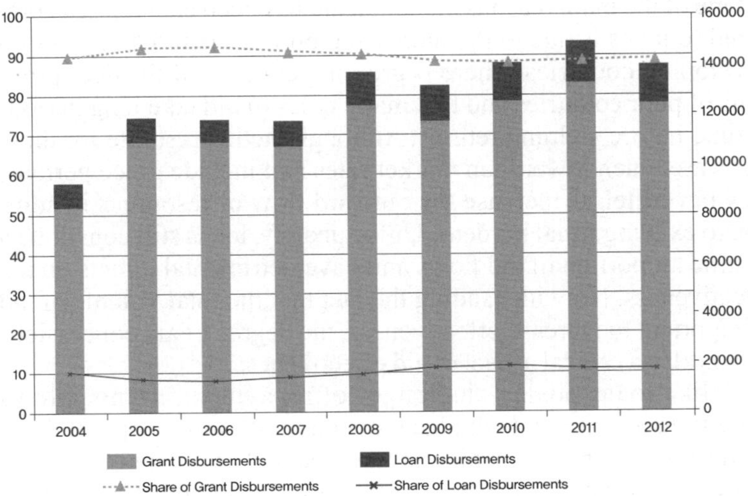

The international community recommends the increase of grant aid, but some insist that a loan type of aid is more effective in development. Supporters of loans find that development bank loans to middle-income countries are in fact highly profitable, and are essential for allowing institutions like the World Bank to subsidize aid to lower-income countries. Multilateral institutions have claimed that a superior debt enforcement capacity enables them to expand a country's debt capacity. A second argument is that the enforcement system of multilateral development banks helps international debt markets function more efficiently. In addition, by providing large-scale loans, development banks have obtained greater leverage over developing country policies than they would have with smaller volumes of grants.

In an argument made by Bulow and Rogoff, who support the transition of multilateral development banks from providing subsidized loans to grants, it is suggested that the incentives a recipient country may receive from utilizing loans is undermined by the risk of debt. While official lending expands a developing country government's borrowing capacity and can effectively enable the government to commit the country to repayment levels beyond that supported by domestic political consensus, this can lead to increased risk of debt crisis, which outweighs the gains that citizens might receive from their government's utilization of loans.[23]

One of the main reasons that grant aid has been encouraged compared to loans is due to the increasing burdens that debt leaves on developing countries. There is growing concern of the debt problems of poor countries and that many types of aid take long periods of time before yielding returns. Although the interest rate for these loans are much lower than market rates and include grace periods, they nevertheless increase the outward flow of resources in addition to existing fiscal burdens. Unfortunately, loans still constitute a significant portion of aid flows and have detrimental effects on aid effectiveness. Notwithstanding the fact that the total volume of aid is important to increase effectiveness, the degree of aid concessionality is also a critical aspect of aid effectiveness.

Unlike loans posing challenges of repayment, grants allows more transparency to take place together with more explicit demonstration of subsidies which in turn channel aid more effectively in theory. By increasing grants, it will also be possible to minimize "loan pushing". "Loan pushing" refers to cases wherein multilateral development banks induce politically fragile developing countries to take on unwanted debt because of their own internal pressures.[24]

Box 3.5 Korean Development Assistance

Korea's first experience as a development assistance donor country dates back to 1963, when Korea provided an education program under the sponsorship of USAID. This indicates that during the period between1960-90s, Korea was simultaneously a recipient and donor of ODA.[25] Since then, Korea has grown to become the 13th largest economy in the global community. In 2009, it submitted its application to become a member of the OECD DAC. Korea is now one of the few donor countries that continues to provide aid in the form of both grants and loans. It is also unique in that its aid management system is divided into agencies that specialize in either grants or loans.

The Korea International Cooperation Agency (KOICA) was established in 1991 to support the economic and social development of de-

23 Jeremy Bulow and Kenneth Rogoff, "Grants versus Loans for Development Banks," *American Economic Review*, vol. 95, no. 2 (2005): 393-397.

24 *Ibid.*

25 A list of ODA projects of the Korean Government during the period of 1960s to 1990s is given in Appendix 1.

veloping countries. It also aimed to promote friendly partnerships by sharing Korea's development experiences with developing countries. A unique characteristic of Korea's aid policy is that KOICA provides aid in the form of grants and technical assistance. There is a separate agency, the Export Import Bank of Korea (EXIM Bank), which organizes loan projects under the Economic Development Cooperation Fund (EDCF). The EDCF was enacted in 1987 and projects initiated by EDCF are repayable, whereas KOICA provides non-repayable concessional assistance.

Despite the recommendations of the international community to provide aid in the form of grants instead of loans, Korea continues to provide loans based on its past experience as a recipient country of ODA. Korea has had a successful experience with loans and they helped achieve its current economic growth. According to the EDCF, loans promote ownership in recipient country governments. They also empower recipient governments to act responsibly. In this respect, recipient governments are more involved in the implementation process when they receive aid in the form of loans.

Budget Support

Aid is categorized into budget support, program assistance and sector-specific project aid. The decisions of donor and recipient countries in how aid is allocated between budget support, program and project assistance are important because different types of aid require different considerations to be made in developing effective strategies. Budget support provides countries with flexibility to align their aid spending with national priorities by directly providing financial support to a recipient country government and has been found to be more effective in governments with sound policies. It differs from the project aid that we have discussed above since project aid is not directly implemented nor managed by the recipients but the donors on specific project. Other scholars have argued that budget support is favorable regardless of governance levels in recipient countries since it can save high transaction costs of implementing project aid.

During the 1980s, a debt relief plan established by then US Treasury Secretary Nicholas Brady contributed to alleviating debt overhang in countries that were suffering from excessive debt. The adverse economic conditions and poor policy choices substantially increased the risk of banks' loan portfolios during this period, and many countries suffered from severe debt.[26] The Brady Plan was effective in alleviating the debt crisis in Latin America at the end of the 1980s, allowing countries in the region to achieve rapid economic growth. These days, debt forgiveness has accounted for a large share of commitments made to Sub-Saharan Africa. There is also evidence that a large share of the aid flows to Sub-Saharan Africa since the late 1990s saw an increased emphasis on providing budget support to recipient governments, especially in the form of debt relief.[27] There has been an increase in commitments of budget aid since the year 2000, from 10% to 20% of total commitments by donors. During this period, the share of project aid has declined with debt forgiveness accounting for most of the increased commitments of budget aid. Since 1995, on average 70% of donor budget support commitments have been made in the form of debt forgiveness. Debt relief does not represent a write-off of the face value of concessional debt, so each dollar of debt forgiveness does not necessarily represent a one-to-one outward shift in the recipient country's budget constraint.[28]

Debt relief is also an important aspect for countries to consider when providing aid to developing countries. In many cases developing countries are struggling because they are unable to repay their high debts and most resources are allocated to debt repayment, which undermines the impact and effectiveness of aid. Thus, the debt problem is an important element in addressing the issue of aid effectiveness. The Enhanced Heavily Indebted Poor Country (HIPC) and the Multilateral Debt Relief Initiative have not resolved the problem of debt and debts continue to be accumulated by developing countries. The Enhanced HIPC initiative was set during the G7 meeting in Cologne during the fall of 1999. Under this initiative, countries began receiving debt relief as soon as they reached decision points by fulfilling a set of requirements posed by the Initiative including; be eligible to borrow from the World Bank's International Development Agency, and from the IMF's Poverty Reduction and Growth Trust, face an unsustainable debt burden that cannot be addressed through traditional debt relief mechanism, have es-

26 The 16 countries that are referred to as the Brady countries are: Argentina, Bolivia, Brazil, Bulgaria, Costa Rica, The Dominican Republic, Ecuador, Jordan, Mexico, Nigeria, Panama, Peru, Philippines, Poland, Uruguay, and Venezuela.

27 Sanjeev Gupta et al., "Are Donor Countries Giving More or Less Aid?" *Review of Development Economics*, vol. 10, no. 3 (2006): 535-552.

28 *Ibid.*

tablished a track record of reform and sound policies through IMF and World Bank supported programs and have developed a Poverty Reduction Strategy Paper through a participatory process in the country[29]. The enhanced framework of the Initiative provided more debt relief as it facilitated countries' efforts to reach decision points. Most HIPC countries began to receive debt relief after 2000. The initiative has also induced HIPC countries to institute economic reforms.

However, there are critics. Serken Arslanap and Peter Henry maintain that debt relief is an unlikely stimulator of investment and growth for the world's highly indebted poor since the biggest challenge to investment and growth in the world's poorest countries is not debt but a lack of basic economic institutions. Basic economic institutions are needed to provide a foundation for profitable economic activity.[30] They compare the different characteristics of the countries of the Brady Plan with those of the HIPCs. Debt relief is unlikely to work in the HIPCs since the HIPCs lack much of the basic infrastructure that serves as the basis for profitable economic activity. Thus, they conclude that without the requisite infrastructure, private foreign capital inflows will not be realizable from debt relief alone. Rather, debt relief will work best for countries that are relatively developed but have highly indebted economies suffering from debt overhang.

A complete debt cancellation of the IMF and International Financial Institutions (IFIs) has been called for.[31] Creditors have been accused that the burden of debt on low-income countries has forced them to cut back in other areas of government expenditure such as education and health, which has led to deleterious effects on poverty reduction and economic growth. The Paris Club Toronto terms of October 1998 culminated in the current enhanced HIPC initiative for the reduction of external debt.

29 IMF, "Debt Relief Under the Heavily Indebted Countries (HIPC) Initiative", https://www.imf.org/external/np/exr/facts/hipc.htm, last visited August 2015.

30 Serken Arslanap and Peter B. Henry, "Helping the poor to help themselves: debt relief or aid," *NBER Working Paper* (2004).

31 The International Financial Institution Advisory Commission sponsored by the US Congress has called for complete debt cancellation by the IMF and of the IFIs.

Box 3.6 General Budget Support (GBS)

General Budget Support is a new modality of budget support that has been developed to concentrate on the goal of reducing poverty in developing countries. GBS is intended to increase government ownership of aid-funded development policies and programs, reduce the transaction costs associated with fragmented aid delivery and strengthen domestic accountability. The GBS modality has been introduced to achieve these ends but has been criticized for overlooking political economic factors, which questions the role of donors in supporting institutional change. A number of expectations from GBS has been highlighted to include: improved co-ordination and harmonization among donors; alignment with partner country systems and policies; lower transaction costs; more efficient allocation of public expenditure; greater predictability of funding; increased effectiveness of the state and public administration or general budget support that is aligned with and uses government allocation and financial management systems; and improved domestic accountability through increased focus on the government's own accountability channels.[32]

GBS is found to have supported increases in pro-poor expenditure, allocation and operational efficiency and government discretion in spending of such financial support. It has also contributed to strengthening budget processes, in particular by 'requiring sector ministries to engage directly in the national budget process' and government capacity in public finance.[33] It has been found that GBS accounts for 20 to 40% of the government budget in a number of countries in Africa.[34] Several donors have expressed intentions to increase aid programs that rely on GBS, and recipient countries have also increasingly presented a preference to GBS aid.

Highly Indebted Poor Country (HIPC) Initiative

The HIPC Initiative was established in 1996 by the IMF and the World Bank under the goals to ensure that no poor country faces unmanageable debt burdens and to encourage the international community to reduce the external debt burdens of the most heavily

32 IDD and Associates, *Evaluation of General Budget Support: Synthesis Report* (Birmingham: International Development Department, University of Birmingham, 2006).

33 *Ibid.*

34 Andrew Lawson et al., "Does General Budget Support Work? Evidence from Tanzania," World Bank (London: Overseas Development Institute, 2005).

indebted poor countries. In 2005, the HIPC Initiative was supplemented by the Multilateral Debt Relief Initiative (MDRI), allowing for 100% relief on eligible debts by the IMF, the International Development Association (IDA) of the World Bank, and the African Development Fund (AfDF), the latter being a specific fund for countries that have completed the HIPC Initiative process.

A country must meet the following eligibility requirements for consideration under the HIPC Initiative: ① is eligible for IDA only and the Poverty Reduction and Growth Facility (PRGF); ② faces an unsustainable debt burden, beyond traditionally available debt-relief mechanisms; ③ establishes a track record of reform and sound policies through IMF and IDA-supported programs; and ④ has developed a Poverty Reduction Strategy Paper (PRSP) through a broad-based participatory process. A total of thirty five countries among the thirty nine eligible or potentially eligible countries for HIPC Initiative assistance are receiving full debt relief from the IMF and other creditors after reaching their completion points. Chad has reached its decision point stage and has benefited from interim debt relief. Three countries that have been identified as potentially eligible for HIPC Initiative assistance have not yet reached their decision points.[35]

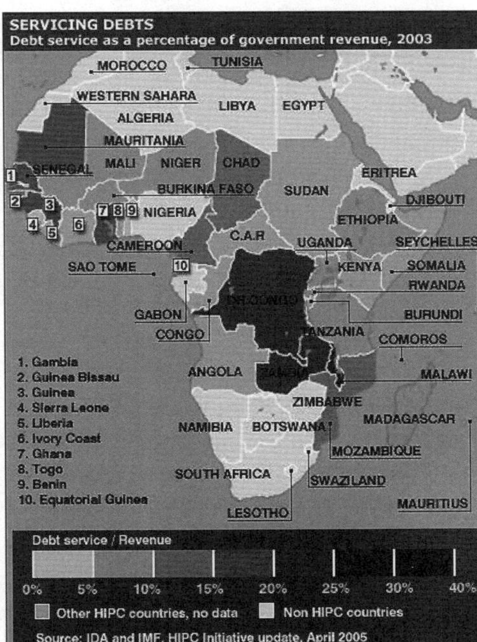

The total cost of the HIPC Initiative is estimated at $75 billion at net present value terms,[36] half of which will be funded by bilateral creditors, and the rest coming from mul-

35 IMF, "Debt Relief under the Heavily Indebted Poor Countries (HIPC) Initiative," http://www.imf.org/external/np/exr/facts/hipc.htm, last visited July 2014.

36 The estimated sum is at end 2007 net present value terms, based on data published in the annual report on the implementation of the HIPC initiative and the MDRI.

tilateral lenders. Nonetheless, for debt relief to have a positive impact on poverty reduction, additional resources need to be allocated to these countries.

Table 3.4 Eligible Countries for HIPC Initiative Assistance

List of Countries That Have Qualified for, are Eligible or Potentially Eligible and May Wish to Receive HIPC Initiative Assistance(as of end-March 2014)		
Post-Completion-Point Countries (35)		
Afghanistan	Ghana	Mozambique
Benin	Guinea	Nicaragua
Bolivia	Guinea-Bissau	Niger
Burkina Faso	Guyana	Rwanda
Burundi	Haiti	São Tomé & Príncipe
Cameroon	Honduras	Senegal
Central African Republic	Liberia	Sierra Leone
Comoros	Madagascar	Tanzania
Republic of Congo	Malawi	Togo
Democratic Republic of Congo	Mali	Uganda
Côte d'Ivoire	Mauritania	Zambia
Ethiopia		
Interim Countries (Between Decision and Completion Point) (1)		
Chad		
Pre-Decision-Point Countries (3)		
Eritrea	Somalia	Sudan

The Enhanced HIPC Initiative

The HIPC Initiative was enhanced in 1999 as a result of reviews by the IDA and IMF. The debt burden threshold was adjusted to embrace more countries as qualifying for debt relief. Qualifying countries must undergo two stages of policy and structural reforms to receive the relief: decision point, where a country needs to fulfill the conditions proposed in order to be considered for HIPC Initiative assistance, and completion point, where the country establish a further track record of good performance under programs, implement satisfactory key reforms agreed at the decision point and adopt the implement its Poverty Reduction Strategy Paper.

The Enhanced HIPC Initiative has three main components: the

modality used to calculate debt relief predicated on debt sustainability analysis; the Poverty Reduction Strategy Paper (PRSP) explaining the relation between debt relief and poverty reduction; and the poverty reduction and growth facility (PRGF) about macroeconomic policy reforms to follow during the processes of HIPC Initiative.

Multilateral Debt Relief Initiative

The Multilateral Debt Relief Initiative (MDRI) provides for 100% relief on eligible debt from three multilateral institutions to a group of low-income countries. The initiative intends to help them advance toward the United Nations' Millennium Development Goals (MDGs), which are focused on halving poverty by 2015.

All countries that reach the completion point under the enhanced Initiative for Heavily Indebted Poor Countries (HIPC Initiative), and those with annual per capita income below $380 and outstanding debt to the Fund at end-2004, are eligible for the MDRI.[37] MDRI has been criticized for its linkage with the HIPC Initiative because countries still have to meet the completion point of HIPC. In 2012, the IMF reported that 36 countries in total have received the MDRI relief.

Technical Assistance

More attention has been paid to the effectiveness and efficiency of expenditure on technical cooperation, which includes more coordinated support, greater use of country systems and increased use of local or other "southern skills."[38] Technical cooperation is a major component of development cooperation instruments, and should be given highest priority when supporting partners' efforts to formulate and implement poverty reduction strategies. Technical cooperation aims to strengthen institutional and human capacities of partner developing countries and plays a crucial role in strength-

37 IMF, "The Multilateral Debt Relief Initiative," http://www.imf.org/external/np/exr/facts/mdri.htm, last visited May 2009.

38 The Development Cooperation Report 2007 identifies six areas to measure progress for evaluating the success of development cooperation: aid volume, aid allocation, fragile situations, aid effectiveness, efforts of recipient countries and achieving results. The effectiveness and efficiency of technological cooperation is identified within these measures, however, according to the 2007 progress report the actual effectiveness is unclear due to difficulties of assessment, e.g. the types of assistance that fall within this category are diversified and numerous.

ening good governance, democratic processes, protection of human rights, and respect for the rule of law as well as market and private sector development. Although the significance of technical assistance is widely recognized within the international arena, there are no explicit measures that can identify the actual impact of technical cooperation on enhancing aid effectiveness.

Technical assistance comprises the most immaterial aspects of development cooperation: policy dialogue, capacity building with a minimum of financial support, technical advice, consultancy assistance and scholarship. Its rationale is that the greatest problem faced by developing countries today is not lack of capital but lack of knowledge about the correct, sound or good development model.[39]

Some of the challenges of technical assistance include the threat of weakening the institutional capacity of development due to the donor-driven nature of projects. In many cases of technical assistance, the project identification, design and implementation are all donor-oriented and can unintentionally threaten developing countries. Moreover, recipient countries do not have the resource capacity or financial stability to ensure continuing project implementation after the donor country leaves. In order for technical assistance aid to be successful, it is critical that donors and recipient governments have a lasting relationship. In particular, they should form a set of guidelines to follow, including statements about specific roles and responsibilities of each and the extent of project ownership.

IMF Technical Assistance Program

Technical assistance is one of the three main pillars of work by the IMF.[40] The IMF provides technical assistance to support the development of the productive resources of member countries by assisting them to effectively manage economic policy and financial

---

39 Degnbol-Martinussen et al., *Aid: Understanding International Development Cooperation* (London, Zed Books Ltd, 2003), 307.

40 The work of the IMF can be largely divided into three types. Surveillance involves the monitoring of economic and financial developments, and the provision of policy advice, especially in the case of crisis prevention. The IMF also lends money to countries with balance of payments difficulties, to provide temporary financing and to support policies and difficulties aimed at correcting the underlying problems. Loans to low-income countries are also aimed at poverty reduction. The third type of work at the IMF is providing countries with technical assistance and training in its areas of expertise.

affairs. It further helps these countries to strengthen their capacity in both human and institutional resources and to design appropriate macroeconomic, financial and structural policies. About 80% of technical assistance provided by the IMF is targeted to low and lower-middle income countries, or post-conflict countries, and seeks to contribute to building a more stable economy. Technical assistance provided by the IMF covers various areas of its expertise: macroeconomic policy, tax policy and revenue administration, expenditure management, monetary policy, the exchange rate system, financial sector sustainability, and macroeconomic and financial statistics.

Involvement and participation of the recipient country is especially important in technical assistance, and the recipient country needs to be aware of the whole process from identification of the need for technical assistance to implementation, monitoring and evaluation. The IMF has adopted a regional approach to delivering technical assistance. It operates eight regional technical assistance centers in the Pacific, the Caribbean, East, West and Central Africa, the Middle East, Central America, and Central Asia. Technical assistance accounts for about one-fifth of the IMF's operating budget and is financed through both internal and external resources, including funds from bilateral and multilateral donors. Bilateral donors to the IMF's technical assistance program include Australia, Austria, Belgium, Brazil, Canada, China, Denmark, Finland, France, Germany, India, Ireland, Italy, Japan, the Republic of Korea, Luxembourg, the Netherlands, New Zealand, Norway, Portugal, Russia, Singapore, Sweden, Switzerland, the United Kingdom, and the United States. Multilateral donors include the African Development Bank, the Arab Monetary Fund, the Asian Development Bank, the European Commission, the Inter-American Development Bank, the United Nations, the United Nations Development Program (UNDP), and the World Bank.

Table 3.5 Technical Cooperation Expenditure (USD million at current prices and exchange rates)[41]

Net disbursements							
	1996-1997 average	2001-2002 average	2008	2009	2010	2011	2012
Australia	404	412	899	1 131	1 650	1 946	2 048
Austria	132	89	210	201	212	216	198
Belgium	272	253	618	511	672	513	336
Canada	369	337	1 453	1 779	1 225	1 150	1 014
Czech Republic	..	1	31	26	0	0	16
Denmark	109	116	129	113	53	55	78
Finland	52	82	262	305	315	335	213
France	2 337	1 431	2 537	2 618	2 680	1 364	2 086
Germany	2 177	1 685	4 187	4 516	4 475	4 731	4 997
Greece	22	19	191	189	128	89	76
Iceland	..	..	..	..	..	..	2
Ireland	70	12	19	14	12	8	8
Italy	59	97	153	90	115	63	27
Japan	2 070	1 877	1 950	2 300	2 670	2 747	2 843
Korea	17	26	181	143	195	220	261
Luxembourg	2	4	7	7	6	11	12
Netherlands	935	573	372	331	396	453	385
New Zealand	54	39	58	52	62	64	79
Norway	170	164	555	454	276	279	272
Poland	..	..	..	..	..	..	..
Portugal	56	122	155	144	97	98	76
Slovak Republic	..	..	..	..	..	..	..
Spain	108	212	1 090	931	673	512	411
Sweden	153	62	188	136	697	653	610
Switzerland	330	133	157	176	161	163	211
United Kingdom	872	823	1 138	632	677	1 119	1 154
United States	2 764	5 986	722	767	595	1 034	921
TOTAL DAC	13 532	14 554	17 262	17 568	18 041	17 823	18 335
of which:							
DAC-EU countries	7 354	5 581	11 286	10 765	11 208	10 220	10 684

41 http://www.oecd.org/development/aidstatistics/statisticsonresourceflowstodevelopingcountries.htm.

Box 3.7 KOICA Training Program

The KOICA Training Program attempts to transfer knowledge and know-how in certain sectors to help developing countries build capacities for sustainable development and to bridge the gap between developed and developing countries. KOICA has been building partnerships with the least developed countries in Africa, the Middle East, and most parts of southern Asia. Today, the KOICA Training Program is offering fewer courses to some countries, such as China, that are now emerging as foreign aid donors in their own right.

The Training Program invites governmental officials and technicians to Korea and offers training courses; regular, special, country-specific, scholarship, and joint courses in cooperation with international organizations, NGOs, and other donors. It is reported that 2,007 courses have been provided since 1991, encompassing various sectors including agriculture, information technology, language, public sector management, human rights, energy and the environment.

Starting from 2008, KOICA has reformed the Training Program to offer more country-specific courses in response to developing countries' demands. In 2012, KOICA offered 245 courses and the top three courses were public governance and administrative capacity, industry and energy, and environment and gender.

3.3 Monitoring and Evaluation

Since the 1980s when the Logframe and PCM were adopted, the importance of aid monitoring and evaluation increased because these tools enabled systematic aid planning and assessment. The OECD DAC defines monitoring as a continuing function that uses systematic collection of data on specified indicators to provide the main stakeholders of an ongoing development intervention with indications of the extent of progress and achievement of objectives and progress in the use of allocated funds.[42] Therefore, monitoring is an ongoing activity to collect and analyze relevant data on aid operations. By doing so, monitoring can amend or adjust the aid operation in terms of input based on the recalculation of activity,

42 OECD DAC, *Glossary of Key Terms in Evaluation and Results Based Management* (2002), 27-28.

output and objectives of project.

According to the OECD DAC, an evaluation is an assessment of an ongoing or completed project, program or policy on its design, implementation and results. The main purposes of evaluation are: to determine the relevance and fulfillment of objectives, developmental efficiency, effectiveness, impact and sustainability; to improve future aid policy, programs and projects through feedback of lessons learned; to provide a basis for accountability, including the provision of information to the public.[43] An evaluation also should provide credible information, enabling the incorporation of lessons learned into the decision-making processes of both the recipients and donors.

Monitoring and Evaluation (M&E) is not an independent but a complementary relationship in which the data from monitoring is used in the evaluation of aid achievements.[44] In other words, monitoring and evaluation need to be understood as a complementary process because the data collected from monitoring becomes the baseline data for evaluation that also affects the establishment of evaluation criteria and direction.[45]

M&E is also important in the learning aspect and securing accountability. M&E provides information for effective management and helps determine what works well and what requires improvement. Such a process generates knowledge on development cooperation policy, programs and projects, and knowledge from the experience and practice can continually contribute to the development of international cooperation by being applied to other aid policies and operations. Securing accountability for the taxpayers is important for the sustainable financing for development in that resources for development mostly come from the pocket of taxpayers in the donor countries. Donor agencies have a duty of reporting the progress and result of aid operations to their taxpayers. In this sense, enhancing transparency in aid operation contributes to securing accountability.[46]

---

43 OECD DAC, *Principles for the Evaluation of Development Assistance* (1991), 5.

44 UNDP, *Human Development Report* (New York: United Nations Development Programme, 2009), 13.

45 Yool Kwon, *A Strategy for Advancing South Korea's ODA: Paradigm Shift in International Development Cooperation and South Korea's ODA Reform* (Seoul: KIEP, 2006), 29.

46 KOICA, *Development Cooperation Evaluation Guideline* (2008), 8-9; Jae-Hwan Hong et al., *A Study on the Evaluation System of the ODA Projects in Korea* (Korea Institute of Public Administration, 2012).

For M&E, international development organizations and state agencies have their own monitoring and evaluation mechanisms and tools. Some countries have an independent evaluation body. For instance, the Swedish Agency for Development Evaluation (SADEV) founded in 2006 is a representative evaluation institution at the state level. SADEV, which is governed by an expert board, independently establishes the objects and schedule of evaluation and conducts its monitoring process on the results, efficiency and effectiveness of Swedish aid operations. SADEV is also active in sharing its evaluation results with the Swedish development cooperation agency, SIDA, and the decision makers in other national and international development agencies.[47]

At the international level, the OECD DAC is operating the Creditor Reporting System (CRS) in order to monitor overall aid flows from its member states. Peer Review by the OECD DAC is another form of evaluation of donor state's aid policy, types, volume, sector and impact. In the early 1990s, an effective and inclusive evaluation mechanism was seen as a necessary step in increasing cooperation among donors. In 1991, the OECD DAC adopted the 'Principles for the Evaluation of Development Assistance' that clarified the five principle of relevance, efficiency, effectiveness, impact and sustainability and stipulated a list of eleven evaluation indicators. Based on this, the OECD DAC proposed the preparation of a manual to achieve the five principles by adopting the 'DAC Principles for Effective Aid.'[48] In addition, the OECD DAC introduced a joint evaluation and aggregate evaluation system.

The World Bank has been another pioneer in evaluation. The World Bank adopted the concept of participatory monitoring and evaluation (PM&E) in the late 1990s. PM&E is a process through which stakeholders at various levels engage in monitoring or evaluating a particular project, program or policy, share control over the content, the process and the results of the PM&E activity and engage in taking or identifying corrective actions. PM&E seeks to engage key project stakeholders more actively in reflecting and assessing the progress of their project and in particular the achievement of results.

---

47 *Ibid.*, 171-174.

48 *Ibid.*, 59.

Core principles of PM&E are:[49]

- primary stakeholders are active participants – not just sources of information
- building capacity of local people to analyze, reflect and take action
- joint learning of stakeholders at various levels
- catalyzes commitment to taking corrective actions

In 2009, the World Bank further published a book titled 'The Road to Results' which is considered an essential guideline for those involved in development evaluation. It presents concepts and procedures for evaluation in a development context. It provides procedures and examples of how to set up a monitoring and evaluation system, conduct participatory evaluations and do social mapping, and construct a "rigorous" quasi-experimental design to answer an impact question.

DAC Peer Reviews

The OECD DAC is the central organization that conducts evaluations of aid practices. Despite its efforts, the OECD DAC has been criticized for being a donor-oriented organization. The OECD DAC was initially developed as a forum for donor countries to share their experiences and challenges in providing aid. As such, DAC has contributed to building a framework for assessing and evaluating donor behaviors. In addition to its evaluation efforts, official statistics regarding development aid are gathered and distributed through the DAC. This database is used by numerous development agencies as a basis for analysis and study of donor aid evaluations. With a growing awareness of the importance of the participation of recipient countries in the international aid community, the OECD DAC continues to establish criteria for general assessment to include both donor and recipient aid implementation activities.

In 1991, the OECD DAC adopted a set of core principles for the evaluation of development assistance, focusing on the management and institutional arrangements of development agencies. Since then, these principles have been utilized as a guideline by most donors in development aid. In 1998, a review of the evaluation principles was conducted, and most DAC members reported hav-

49 World Bank, http://web.worldbank.org/WBSITE/EXTERNAL/TOPICS/EXTSOCIALDEVELOPMENT/EXTPCENG/0,,contentMDK:20509352~menuPK:1278203~pagePK:148956~piPK:216618~theSitePK:410306,00.html, accessed: 12/10/2014.

DAC and KOICA delegations at DAC Peer Review Session, held at KOICA Headquarters, Seoul

ing made progress in implementing the core principles set by the OECD DAC. Even today, the principles established in 1991 remain at the core of development evaluation and also serve as the basis for the DAC Peer Reviews.

According to the OECD, a "peer review is the systematic examination and assessment of the performance of a State by other States. Its ultimate goal is to help the reviewed State improve its policymaking, adopt best practices, and comply with established standards and principles. The examination is conducted on a non-adversarial basis, and it relies heavily on mutual trust among the States involved in the review, as well as their shared confidence in the process."[50] With the participation and involvement of member countries in the context of a peer review, a reciprocal evaluation system of mutual accountability is created.

OECD DAC members tend to evaluate each other every three to four years. Five different member countries are subject to peer review each year in order to assess the extent to which the development policies, strategies and activities of the reviewed country meet the standards set by the DAC. Through these reviews, member countries are provided with constructive critiques and recommendations regarding aid policies, volumes, institutions and field operations. However, it is important to note that peer reviews are non-binding in nature. They are meant as recommendations for the reviewed country, not demands.

Peer reviews are either a general examination of an individual

50 Fabrizio Pagani, "Peer Review: A Tool for Cooperation and Change," *The OECD Observer*, no. 235 (2002): 55-56.

country or a thematic examination that reviews a number of countries simultaneously. It is anticipated that these reviews will act like peer pressure, which can be utilized as a means of soft persuasion to stimulate change, achieve goals and meet standards. Peer pressure is particularly effective with quantitative assessments that rank countries according to performance, which highlights not only those countries that have performed well, but also those that are near the bottom of the list. These methods have gained importance in recent years as countries have become more aware of the importance of soft power. Most governments realize the potential benefits of having a "positive country image" in today's globalizing world.

Peer reviews are not only used by the OECD, but are also utilized by other intergovernmental organizations and international programs. These include the UN and the IMF Country Surveillance Mechanism, the World Trade Organization under the Trade Policy Review Mechanism and the DG Employment and Social Affairs of the European Commission, which uses a peer review process to identify good practices and assess the transferability for national labor market policies. Although there is no standardized mechanism for peer review, each contains common structural elements: a basis for proceeding, an agreed set of principles, standards and criteria against which the country performance is to be reviewed, designated actors to carry out the peer review, and a set of procedures leading to the final result.

The DAC Peer Reviews are the only internationally agreed mechanism that assesses the performance of OECD DAC members' development cooperation programs. DAC member countries conduct peer reviews in order to monitor the individual efforts and performance of other members. Each country is under review approximately every four years, which results in approximately five programs being examined annually. A team of representatives from the Secretariat prepares the Peer Reviews and officials from two DAC members are designated as examiners. Then the country under review is required to provide a memorandum that identifies the main developments in its policies and programs, which is scrutinized by the review team.

To further supplement the Peer Review and to facilitate assessment of how the country is implementing major DAC policies, principles and concerns, the review team interviews the country's government officials and civil society representatives to obtain first-hand insight. The team also reviews operations in recipient countries, highlighting areas of poverty reduction, sustainability, gender equality and local aid coordination.

It is important to note that there are no sanctions imposed for countries that receive poor peer reviews. Peer Reviews provide constructive criticisms and recommendations regarding aid policies, volumes, institutions and field operations, and although DAC members are not obliged to fulfill recommendations provided by the Peer Review, the recommendations are made to encourage positive change, support mutual learning and promote aid effectiveness.

Table 3.6 Twelve Lessons from DAC Peer Reviews[51]

Lesson 1	Have a clear, top-level statement of purpose, whether in legislation or another form, which has wide ownership and can remain relevant for a sufficient period.
Lesson 2	Avoid letting short-term pressures jeopardize long-term common interest in effective development.
Lesson 3	Set a clear mandate and establish mechanisms to ensure that policies are assessed for their impact on poor countries.
Lesson 4	Invest in delivering, measuring and communicating results of aid-financed activity.
Lesson 5	Task a sufficiently senior and publicly accountable figure with clear responsibility at the political level for delivery.
Lesson 6	Rationalize bilateral aid structures to facilitate coherent action at the country level.
Lesson 7	Promote coherence in diverse aspects of multilateral aid.
Lesson 8	Decentralization of responsibility on the field can be beneficial, but it needs high quality, lean-supporting systems.
Lesson 9	Radical reforms in delivery are vital, as donors must deliver more aid per head of agency staff while increasing effectiveness.
Lesson 10	Most donors should focus assistance on fewer countries, sectors and, in particular, activities.
Lesson 11	Develop a stronger culture of managing for results and align incentives accordingly, but to promote, not weaken, local structures of accountability.
Lesson 12	Secure and develop well-qualified, motivated local and expatriate staff to enhance effectiveness. Quality agencies attract quality staff.

The analysis of DAC Peer Reviews has provided valuable insight towards strengthening policy coherence for development. In order to consolidate political commitment and policies on policy

51 OECD, "Effective Aid Management: Twelve Lessons from DAC Peer Reviews" (DAC, 2008).

coherence, DAC members must work with civil societies, research organizations and partner countries to educate and engage the public, raise public awareness and build support for policy coherence in aid implementation. However, weak systems for monitoring, analyzing, and reporting development impacts remain a challenge to member countries seeking to achieve policy coherence in aid implementation. Donor countries must overcome these obstacles in order to better report the impacts of development policies to the government as well as to the public.

An inspection of any peer review will provide in-depth information on aid practices and efforts of a donor country. Peer Reviews are mostly used to promote understanding of a particular donor country's development assistance work and to encourage future effort by providing recommendations for better effectiveness. Peer Reviews have limitations and are often criticized because there is a perception that DAC Peer Reviews and donor countries are constantly complimenting one another. Nevertheless, it cannot be denied that peer reviews provide valuable information on aid practices. Not only that, but peer reviews are also open to the public and many countries can refer to Peer Reviews to identify the best practices of other donors. The next section will provide case studies of several peer reviews.

DAC Network on Development Evaluation[52]

What began as the Working Party on Aid Evaluation later developed into what is known today as the Network on Development Evaluation. This is an international forum of evaluation managers and specialists from development cooperation agencies in OECD member countries and multilateral development institutions. Its objective is to increase development effectiveness of aid policies and programs by promoting high quality, independent evaluation. It has developed into a platform for learning and coordination, enabling members to work together in improving the quality of development evaluations. Direct objectives of the Network on Development

52 Network members include Australia, Austria, Belgium, Canada, Denmark, European Commission, Finland, France, Germany, Greece, Ireland, Italy, Japan, Luxembourg, Netherlands, New Zealand, Norway, Portugal, Spain, Sweden, Switzerland, United Kingdom, United States, World Bank, Asian Development Bank, African Development Bank, European Bank for Reconstruction and Development (EBRD), Inter-American Development Bank, United Nations Development Programme (UNDP), and the International Monetary Fund (IMF).

Evaluation stated by the OECD are:

- to help the evaluation community make a vital contribution to development outcomes by strengthening member evaluation systems and improving the quality of development evaluations.
- to share good practices and develop useful guidance documents, standards and norms to inform development evaluation policy and practice.
- to improve harmonization, alignment and coordination of evaluation work, especially through facilitating joint evaluations.
- to support evaluation capacity development in partner countries.

Admittedly, it is difficult to create an effective mechanism that can provide the necessary evaluations of development aid projects. Obtaining information that can fully represent the scope and capacity of aid project performances remains a serious challenge. The current efforts are comprised mostly of guidelines for evaluation. Although there have been many discussions and lots of research done to better understand how to increase the effectiveness of aid implementation projects, it is difficult to establish a single set of standards that can be used for evaluation in all of the diverse contexts of the world's developing countries.

Asian Development Bank (ADB)

Country Assistance Program Evaluation (CAPE)

The country assistance program evaluation (CAPE) is an important evaluation instrument operated by the Operations Evaluation Department (OED) of the Asian Development Bank (ADB). The first CAPE was initiated in 1998, and at the time there was no internationally accepted methodology for assessing the performance of a country assistance program. After numerous experiments with trial and error, however, it was able to create some guidelines for evaluation. Now it works as a comprehensive evaluation covering all aspects of public and private sector operations, including policies, procedures and processes as well as country, sector, impact and thematic evaluations. The ADB's evaluation has two major dimensions, which include self-evaluation by operations departments responsible for preparing and implementing projects, programs and technical assistance operations, and independent evaluation by the OED.

CAPE builds on all available independent and self-evaluation materials, in addition to government plans and strategies, secondary performance data, country files, project records, stakeholder interviews, sample surveys and other information sources. It identifies opportunities that could work to improve program performance at the country level and support the formulation of future country strategy programs.

CAPE is used for both accountability and lesson learning, with a number of objectives such as; to provide credible assessment of the performance of ADB assistance in a particular developing member country, to identify factors affecting such performance, and to draw lessons and recommendations for improving the future performance of ADB assistance.[53]

In addition to CAPE, the ADB concluded its first regional cooperation assistance program evaluation for the greater Mekong Sub-region in 2009. The evaluation assessed Greater Mekong Subregion (GMS) operations, which were co-financed with the ADB during 1992-2007. The GMS program is an activity-based subregional economic cooperation program that began in 1992 under the sponsorship of the ADB. It is comprised of Cambodia, Laos, Myanmar, Thailand, Vietnam, and the Guangxi Zhuang Autonomous Region and Yunnan Province in the People's Republic of China. The ADB assumed the role of the GMS Secretariat as well as roles of a facilitator, financier, honest broker, and technical adviser. ADB sponsored the project, providing 40% of the funds (about $3.5 billion including GMS loans and grant projects and technical assistance), while another 35% came from member countries, and 25% more from other development partners.

Center for Global Development (CGD)

The Center for Global Development (CGD) in the United States along with the Global Economy and Development program at Brookings Institute issue a qualitative assessment on ODA. The CGD conducts research and analysis on a wide range of topics related to how policies and actions of the rich and powerful affect poor people in the developing world. The mission statement of the CGD emphasizes the reduction of global poverty and inequality through rigorous research and active engagement with the policy community.

53 http://www.adb.org/sites/default/files/related/30755/revised-cape-guidelines-2010.pdf

The CGD undertakes independent research in economics and other disciplines. The CGD's research investigates pivotal issues of development policy:

- Aid Effectiveness and Innovation: Characteristics of effective development assistance, debt relief, and donor accountability practices; support to weak and fragile states; new ways for donor countries to support people's efforts to escape poverty.
- Climate Change: Interactions between global warming and development; climate-related aid (e.g., adaptation assistance, technology transfers, carbon offsets); development-friendly ways to minimize greenhouse gas emissions; the impacts of climate change in developing countries.
- Global Governance: The roles of multilateral institutions such as the World Bank and the IMF; ways to make them more responsive to the needs of developing countries and more effective agents for collective action to provide global public goods.
- Global Health and Education: The relationships among health, education, demographic change, and development; innovative solutions for health and education financing and delivery; enhancing girls' well-being through education and other investments.
- Migration: Opportunities and challenges that large-scale migration presents to global development and poverty reduction; the effects of increased mobility on sending countries' development prospects.
- Private Investment and Access to Finance: Policies that affect the quantity and quality of capital flows to low-income countries; the roles of multinational firms in development; protection against adverse financial shocks; access to financial services including microfinance.
- Trade: Links between trade policy and global poverty reduction; the politics and policy of food and agricultural subsidies; development-friendly pathways for bilateral and multilateral trade negotiations; preferential market access for developing countries; intellectual property rights.

In 2010, the CGD conducted comprehensive research on the quality of Official Development Assistance targeting 23 OECD DAC member countries, 8 multilateral aid agencies, and 150 aid institutions. The report sought to improve the quality of ODA by comparing the strengths and weaknesses of each donor and aid institution, not simply ranking donors and agencies and comparing them. The report qualified the indicators of aid effectiveness to compare the development policies and practices of actors. For this, the report prepared four evaluation criteria based on the Paris Declaration, which are maximizing efficiency, fostering institutions, reducing burden, and transparency/learning.[54]

Throughout this chapter we have talked about planning and monitoring of aid and specific cases of those fields. Various mechanisms and institutions that make plans and keep an eye on aid facilitation do play great part when it comes down to aid but what we cannot overlook is the public support from the people. Even though the influence of public opinion does both good and bad, governments and aid activists claim that high levels of public support prove that there is no such thing as 'aid fatigue' while Non-governmental organizations cite this public support to lobby for increased government expenditures on aid or to obtain government financial support for their own activities.

As the public increasingly wants to be informed of development assistance activities, there is a growing incentive for an efficient systematic evaluation system domestically and a promotion of transparency and efficiency in implementation processes.

More parties are beginning to get involved in aid planning and monitoring process therefore more diverse interests and ideas should be taken into account and be reflected on the procedures, decisions and mechanisms regarding aid.

Chapter 3. Review Discussion Questions

1. What are the DAC criteria for assessing development assistance?
2. Why is it difficult for recipient countries to evaluate aid projects?
3. What are some of the benefits for developing countries to develop Poverty Reduction Strategy Papers (PRSP)? What are some of the limitations of PRSP?
4. What is the potential role of NGOs in aid evaluation practices? What needs to be done for NGOs to partake in coordinating the involvement of donor and recipient countries in the foreign aid pro-

54 Jae-hwan Hong et al., *A Study on the Evaluation System of the ODA Projects in Korea* (Korea Institute of Public Administration, 2012).

cess?

5. Why has the international community encouraged the untying of aid? What are some of the challenges faced by countries in untying aid? What are potential benefits of untying aid?
6. Identify how public support can promote aid effectiveness. Why does a donor government need to gain public support in order to provide effective aid projects?
7. Identify the challenges that donor countries confront when providing technical assistance to developing countries. What are some of the potential threats that must be considered before countries implement technical assistance projects?

Chapter 4

Foreign Aid and Official Development Assistance (ODA)

> *"Poverty is hunger. Poverty is lack of shelter. Poverty is being sick and not being able to see a doctor. Poverty is not having access to school and not knowing how to read. Poverty is not having a job, is fear for the future, living one day at a time. Poverty is losing a child to illness brought about by unclean water. Poverty is powerlessness, lack of representation and freedom."*[1]

4.1 Poverty Alleviation and Aid

It is difficult to measure poverty because it encompasses so many different aspects of life. The most common method of measuring poverty is based on income and consumption levels. A person is considered poor when his or her consumption falls below the minimum level necessary to meet the basic human needs, referred to as the poverty line. The World Bank set the poverty line as 1.25 dollar a day, meaning that if a person did not have consumption power equal to an American spending 1.25 dollar a day, that person was considered to be in extreme poverty. As of October 2015, reflecting the updated price data, the new global poverty line has been updated to $1.90.

It must be noted that in individual countries, poverty lines change overtime and according to different contexts, such as the country's level of development, societal norms or values. The 1.25 dollar a day standard provided by the World Bank is used to estimate poverty levels on a worldwide scale. Just over 900 million people globally lived under this line in 2012, and it is projected that in 2015, just over 700 million are living in extreme poverty.[2]

In order to understand poverty, it is necessary to consider both

---

1 World Bank, "Overview: Understanding, measuring, and overcoming poverty," http://web.worldbank.org/WBSITE/EXTERNAL/TOPICS/EXTPOVERTY/0,,contentMDK:20153855~menuPK:373757~pagePK:148956~piPK:216618~theSitePK:336992,00.html, Last visited December 2014.

2 The World Bank, "FAQs: Global Poverty Line Update," http://www.worldbank.org/en/topic/poverty/brief/global-poverty-line-faq, last visited August 2016.

hard and soft factors. Hard factors refer to the geography, topography, size, climate, soil, natural resources, population growth and density of a country, all factors which influence the wealth that a country possesses. The soft factors are more implicit and are integrated amongst each other. For example, the history of a country plays an important role in determining its current level of wealth.

There is a clear difference between countries with a history of being in isolation or under foreign dominion and a country that has had numerous opportunities to freely trade with other nations in the past.

Other significant soft factors include the terms of trade of a given country, which includes internal aspects such as transportation infrastructure, the culture, language and identity of its people and their levels of health.[3] These conditions help answer the question of why certain countries grow while others continue to struggle from severe poverty. They indicate that poverty is not simply a lack of material wealth but is a rather more complex situation that encompasses several different interrelated factors.

The first linkage between aid and poverty alleviation was made by the DAC in the late 1960s but the potential contributions of foreign aid towards poverty reduction were not recognized until the early 1970s. At that time, the World Bank and the International Labor Office (ILO) started to argue that development approaches aimed at raising growth rates and stimulating structural and institutional changes to an economy were insufficient in combating poverty. This idea was also further supported by the UNDP. In light of these assessments by various international organizations, there was pressure to construct a new strategy for poverty alleviation. The need to address poverty more directly and new approaches regarding the poverty issues were necessary. In particular, new strategies addressing the problems of extreme poverty and absolute poverty were required.

The development doctrine of the 1950s and 1960s was primarily a state-led approach. Foreign aid was motivated by national policymakers and their state-centric ideas and values. However, in the 1970s, the new key word in assistance was Basic Human Needs. This new emphasis continued throughout the 1980-90s. Fulfilling Basic Human Needs was supposed to be achieved by liberalizing economies and concentrating on open markets. Since the mid-

3 Thomas W. Dichter, *Despite Good Intentions* (Boston: University of Massachusetts Press, 2003).

1990s, development assistance has shifted its focus to institutional developments. This is in part due to the effects of globalization, which causes a blurring of national barriers and the proliferation of non-state actors. Nonetheless, it should be recognized that for much of the history of development assistance, the nation state was the dominant actor.

The DAC was first developed as a forum to discuss measures of cooperation among donor countries in order to facilitate implementation of development aid programs. The recipients of the aid from the DAC were primarily governments of developing countries. This point illustrates that from the beginning of the institutionalized form of aid, that donor counterparts were the governments or political actors at the governmental level that would facilitate discussions and ease donor-recipient relations.

Country Programmable Aid (CPA)

A newly devised measure of assistance called country programmable aid (CPA) has been developed by the DAC and is used in the first full Survey on Aid Allocation Policies and Indicative Forward Spending Plans to pinpoint just how fragmented aid is. CPA refers to the amount of aid that the providers can plan the use of the aid provided depending on the status of individual countries or the regions which in turn maximizes the say of the aid providers while it reduces the control of the recipients regarding the planning and spending of the aid. Such aid includes emergency relief, debt relief and other aid.

Table 4.1 CPA Rankings by Country[4]

	CPA Actual	CPA Planned			CPA/GNI		CPA per capita	
Partner	2010	2011	2012	2013	2010(i)	2013(i)	2010(ii)	2013(ii)
		2010 $ million			%		2010 $ million	
Viet Nam^	3164	3631	3644	3666	4.6	4.4	35.8	40.1
Kenya^	1515	1783	1860	1911	5	5.2	41.5	49.8
Tanzania^	2579	2579	2657	2431	12	9.3	62.4	55.4
Ethiopia^	2341	2418	2491	2517	8.6	7.3	27.6	27.6
Indonesia	3303	3180	3163	3129	0.7	0.6	14.1	12.8

4 Ranking by absolute increase (countries with increasing aid dependency are highlighted) – Gross disbursements.

Sudan*^	1015	1117	1126	1084	2	1.8	25.3	25
Nigeria^	2125	2055	2190	2190	1.2	1	14.6	12.9
Turkey	1426	1467	1493	1549	0.2	0.2	20	20.9
Pakistan^	2582	2810	2748	3012	1.5	1.6	15.5	17.2
Cameroon	659	709	702	675	2.8	2.6	32.3	30.7
Colombia	789	755	766	771	0.3	0.3	17.3	16.4
Ghana^	1584	1614	1651	1561	5.6	4.2	66.8	61.1
Nepal^	837	935	935	975	6.4	6.6	29.7	34.6
Serbia	566	534	562	565	1.3	1.1	76.5	75.9
Congo, Dem. Rep.*^	1441	1486	1566	1594	14.6	12.3	21.6	21.9
Uganda^	1501	1549	1548	1457	9.9	7.9	44.6	38.1
Cote d'Ivoire*^	560	446	440	407	2.5	1.7	25.4	16.9
Armenia	318	358	387	366	4.3	4.4	96.3	107.7
Philippines	1116	1063	1087	1091	0.7	0.6	11.9	10.9
Mozambique^	1729	1766	1752	1744	17.3	14	80.1	76.1
Malawi^	891	848	910	868	20.1	16.6	62.7	58.1
Malaysia	181	178	178	178	0.1	0.1	6.4	6
Mali^	1079	1177	1175	1109	12.2	10.7	77.2	74.1
Somalia*	245	257	233	292	..	..	26.1	28.8
Namibia	280	330	338	334	3	4.2	134.6	155
Liberia*^	417	353	349	336	64	41.1	109	79.7
Rwanda^	986	841	890	799	20.1	14.4	98.6	75.1
Burundi*^	508	476	462	385	41.2	27.2	61.4	44.8
Lebanon	531	515	509	511	1.6	1.3	135.8	125.7
Afghanistan*	5376	5136	5176	5164	59.4	45.6	181.3	160.9
Palestinian Adm. Areas	2062	2139	2126	2168	..	..	467.6	450.3
Croatia	136	113	120	154	0.2	0.2	30.7	34.8
Zambia^	821	990	1022	997	6.6	6.5	67.3	77.2

* State in situation of conflict or fragility (i.e. Low-income countries scoring 4.2 and below on the World Bank's Country Policy and Institutional Assessment - CPIA).

^ GNI/capita in 2005 below $1,000.

(i) GNI source: DCR 2006. GNI forecast based on IMF projected growth rates (World Economic Outlook database).

(ii) Population source: DCR 2006. Population is assumed to grow at 2% per annum.

4.2 Definition of ODA and Other Relevant Terms

ODA

The issue of poverty reduction through aid reemerged in the late 1990s as the primary purpose of development aid. Major agreements were reached to consolidate commitments made for the expansion of ODA into a wider set of initiatives to 'attack poverty.'[5]

The definition of ODA was set by the DAC as the quantities of assistance that the net volumes can be identified which enable the cross-country comparison. Other than the DAC definition, the international community does not yet have a set conceptualization of development aid or foreign aid. To date, the terms of development aid, development assistance and foreign aid have been used interchangeably within the global arena and development agenda. In this regard, ODA contains value in that it specifically has a set definition and can be measured by providing comparisons or data on the relative amounts of aid provided to developing countries, making it possible to trace the transaction patterns of aid within the global arena. This definition is especially important because it permits the establishment of an evaluation system. In addition, the concreteness of the concept of ODA promotes government-level dialogues, facilitating interactions between donor and recipient countries.

In order to identify the significance of ODA compared to other aid flows, it is necessary to understand the historical background of the term. The concept of Official Development Assistance (ODA) was first adopted in 1969 to separate ODA from "Other Official Flows (OOF)." ODA consists of flows to developing countries and multilateral institutions provided by official agencies, including state and local governments, or by their executive agencies, which meets the following test: a) it is administered with the main objective of promoting economic development and welfare of developing countries, and b) it is concessional in character and contains a grant element of at least 25%(calculated at a rate of discount of 10%).[6]

The DAC refined its definition of ODA in 1972 to distinguish ODA from Official Aid (OA). The distinction between ODA and

5 Roger C. Riddell, *Does Foreign Aid Really Work?* (London: Oxford University Press, 2007).

6 OECD, "Official Development Assistance – Definition and Coverage," http://www.oecd.org/investment/stats/officialdevelopmentassistancedefinitionandcoverage.htm, last visited July 2014.

OA lies in the status of the recipient country. Recipient countries are divided into Part I and Part II countries according to their level of development. While the poorest developing countries and lower and upper middle income countries are termed Part I countries, those categorized as Part II countries include more advanced developing nations, as well as countries and territories that are in transition. Aid flows are recognized as ODA only when they meet the conditions stated within the DAC definition and are given to Part I countries. All other aid flows are termed OA.

Under such circumstances, the DAC have been trying to refine the ODA reporting guidelines to ensure fidelity to the definition and the consistency among donors. The traditional definition ODA is as follows: ① Military equipment or services and anti-terrorism activities are excluded, but the cost of using donors' armed forces to deliver humanitarian aid is eligible; ② Most peacekeeping expenditures are excluded, but some developmentally relevant activities within peacekeeping operations are included; ③ Reportable as ODA, provided it is for civilian purposes, such as nuclear energy; ④ Eligible as ODA if they build the cultural capacities of recipient countries, but one-off tours by donor country artists or sportsmen, and activities to promote the donors' image, are excluded.[7]

Although ODA has evident advantages, there are also challenges to providing aid on the governmental level. The decision-making process of aid allocation is complicated due to the conflict between national interests and a desire to promote the global good. It is important to find the appropriate balance between these two agendas. However, the most serious obstacle posed for donor governments is their inability to bridge the feedback loop. Donor governments use money from taxpayers for ODA, so the support of taxpayers is an important aspect of government planning. However, because the feedback loop is disaggregated across geographical and political boundaries, there is a wide gap between the beneficiaries (recipient countries) and taxpayers (donors).

The performance feedback loop identifies the relationship between the provider, which would be the taxpayer, and the recipient beneficiary. Within a domestic context, where information flows are easier, it is possible for direct evaluations among actors. Thus, taxpayers can be fully aware of how their money is used and recipient beneficiaries can evaluate the performance of these funds. This

7 *Ibid.*

provides a check and balance mechanism, with the link between the taxpayer (donor) and beneficiary (recipient) forming a loop.

In comparison international aid contains more complexities. Two important factors to be considered are the geographical and political distance between the donor and recipient countries. Although it may have been possible for the taxpayer to receive direct feedback within the domestic sphere, geographical distance can function as a strong deterrence against direct communications in the case of international aid. Differences in political ideology, culture and even language cause further complications as well. Therefore, it is difficult for the recipient to provide adequate feedback to the taxpayer.

This disconnection between the recipient and donor poses many difficulties for evaluating aid effectiveness. Both the donor and recipient need to be informed of how allocated funds were used in order to make evaluations necessary for future decisions.

Non-ODA

Non-ODA includes Other Official Flows (OOFs) and Private Flows. Private Flows are divided into Market Terms and Private Grant. Most of international development and cooperation falls into the basic category of ODA and Non-ODA.[8]

Box 4.1 Types of Non-ODA

Other Official Flows (OOFs)		Transactions by the official sector with countries on the List of Aid Recipients which do not meet the conditions for eligibility as Official Development Assistance (ODA) of Official Aid (OA), either because they are not primarily aimed at development, or because they have a grant element of less than 25%.
Private Flows	Market Terms	Financed out of private sector resources, i.e. changes in holding of private long term assets held by residents of the reporting country (FDI, bank loans, bonds, guarantee).
	Private Grant	Grants by non-government organizations, net of subsidies received from the official sector.

8 Kyungyon Moon, "International Development Cooperation and Development Finance: Discussion and Analysis of Major Actor's Policies on Development Finance," *Journal of East and West Studies*, vol. 26, no. 2 (2014): 94.

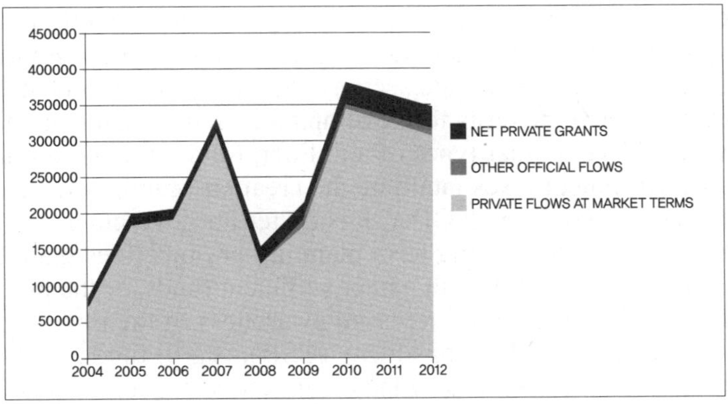

Figure 4.1 Total Non-ODA Flows by donor (unit: USD millions)

The discussion of financing for development, whether it is ODA or Non-ODA, started from the Monterrey Consensus in 2002. Those kinds of financing for Development emphasize three difference financial resources: ① mobilizing domestic financial resources for development (improving taxation, harnessing sustainable streams of natural resource revenue, improving expenditure efficiency, curbing illicit financial flows); ② private finance for development (FDI, trade as an engine for development, etc.); ③ innovative sources of finance (Unitaid, IFFIm, Product RED, etc.).

4.3 Success Cases of ODA

ODA flows are considered an important source of funds for capital expenditures for low-income and middle-income countries. ODA remains the most important component of aid, accounting for over 70% of all development and emergency aid. The impact of ODA on economic growth in developing countries is still under study, with many scholars attempting to identify the conditions that make ODA effective. Research has proven that ODA reduces poverty and spurs growth substantially when it goes to developing countries that have reasonably good policies and institutions.[9] This has led to a shift in aid allocation to developing countries with sound policies.

9 David Dollar and Lant Pritchett, "Assessing Aid — What Works, What Doesn't, and Why," *World Bank policy research report* (Washington D.C. : The World Bank, 1998).

Regardless of this continuing debate, contributions of ODA have also improved conditions in developing countries by promoting investments from the private sector. It has also been accepted that ODA has several benefits for developing countries that cannot be provided through other types of aid. First, funds attained through donor government taxes facilitate the creation of long-term goals for providing aid through ODA. It is easier for governments to allocate funds based on long term planning or objectives than it is for NGOs, which struggle to gather sufficient funds, or the private sector, which, in spite of increased awareness of the importance of Corporate Social Responsibility (CSR), is still fundamentally profit-oriented, and allocates funds or investments on a project-by-project basis.

To achieve sustainable development, it is especially important that aid is provided on a long-term basis. It has been found that short-term aid programs that concentrate on donor interests have detrimental effects on recipient countries. This is particularly true for countries that are struggling to escape the poverty trap. Foreign assistance and intervention is necessary on a long-term basis for these countries to develop infrastructure that will bring them out of the poverty trap and into the global economy. Without outside assistance, developing countries that are suffering from severe poverty are caught in a vicious cycle. Aid packages in the form of food or assistance that are consumed by the recipient without providing any framework for future incentives cannot lead to sustainable development but instead worsen the situation.

A second significant aspect of ODA lies in the role of the government in the donor country. With globalization there has been an emergence of new actors, multilateral international organizations, non-governmental organizations and even actors within the private sector that work to provide aid to developing countries. However it must be recognized that all types of aid are delivered to the governments of recipient countries. The benefits of government dialogues can contribute to increasing aid effectiveness by promoting partnerships. As such, donor governments that provide ODA have an advantage over other actors that provide aid since inter-governmental level discussions are possible.

Botswana

Botswana has successfully used development aid and achieved one of the highest economic growth rates in the world. Botswana is now independent from foreign aid and has been attracting a large amount of foreign direct investments. This success can be broken into three time periods.

First, in the period of 1960-75, the independent government of Botswana took the initiative in projecting development strategies and sought to maximize foreign aid for development. The government was successful not only with receiving enough aid but also with modernizing its political landscape.

Second, from 1975 to 1989, the government of Botswana was successful in integrating a market-based economy to a multi-party political system. It created several kinds of special funds and also integrated development planning with the budget system as to ensure that development projects were initiated locally.

Third, since 1990, the private sector started to direct many development projects and the government began to manage the transition from aid dependency to independence; foreign aid was no longer a dominant factor for its economy.

Botswana finally developed into an upper middle-income country. Botswana, as a diamond-rich country, achieved stable economic growth based on consistent high ranks in international anticorruption measures and political stability. However, the social development in Botswana still needs more attention. The country suffers from expensive food and fuel, high unemployment rate, and the world's highest HIV/AIDS infection rate. The Botswana government is also working to encourage economic diversification, but such efforts have yet to produce results.[10]

Indonesia

From 1975, the flow of aid to Indonesia has been quite volatile. Multilateral aid in particular increased significantly several times in the mid and late 1980s when the country suffered from falling oil prices and balance of payment difficulties, as well as during the severe financial crisis of 1997. Foreign aid helped Indonesia keep its budget in balance by financing deficits.

Up to date, Japan has been the biggest bilateral donor to Indonesia. As of 2005, it was estimated that Japan had contributed over $971.6 million. The government of Japan has focused on building democracy, promoting peace and stability, and sustainable devel-

---

10 Council on Foreign Relations, http://www.cfr.org/botswana/botswana-african-success-story-shows-strains/p15108 , last visited July 2014.

opment.

Mozambique

Mozambique is often quoted as the success story of stability, development, and peace in Africa. Since the end of a disastrous civil war in 1992, Mozambique has been receiving inflows of foreign aid and its economy has been growing at a steady rate of 8% since 1997. As of 2004, foreign aid comprised 23% of its national income. Scholars advised the government of Mozambique, considering its high dependency on aid, to be prepared with particularly sound macroeconomic policies and government spending strategies.

Recently, both the government of Mozambique and the19 donors that provide general budget support are focusing on attaining the goals of the Paris Declaration on Aid Effectiveness. As a result, Mozambique is currently the only country assessing donor performance via mutual accountability mechanisms and getting donors engaged in aligning their purposes with Mozambique's.

South Korea

South Korea overcame extreme poverty in just four decades through foreign aid and has emerged as a new donor. Korea started to receive ODA from 1945, when it became independent, until 1980s when it became one of the providers. Korea founded two aid agencies: the Economic Development Cooperation Fund in 1987 and the Korea International Cooperation Agency or KOICA in 1991 for supporting development and economic stability of developing countries and enhancing economic cooperation. In 2005, it joined the IDA of the World Bank and started to fund reconstruction in Iraq. Moreover, Korea became the newest member of the OECD's DAC in November 2009. South Korea hosted the 4th High Level Forum on Aid Effectiveness in Busan in 2011, and increased its ODA by 18.8% every year from 2008 to 2012, which was the highest increase rate among the DAC countries. This is happening in the middle of an economic crisis, and while many countries are holding back, Korea is signaling the way forward.[11] Since the pledge of 0.25% by 2015 in the Roh Moo-hyun Administration in 2005, South Korea is consistently increasing its ODA volume even in the

11 OECD, "OECD Development Assistance Committee (DAC) welcomes Korean membership," http://www.oecd.org/dac/oecddevelopmentassistancecommitteedacwelcomeskoreanmembership.htm, last visited July 2014.

negative global financial condition[12] which was met with its ODA contribution reached $2.01 billion in 2015.

Tanzania

The government of Tanzania started to receive foreign aid to finance development policies in accordance with the 1967 Arusha Declaration and the goals of socialist development. Since 1990, the aid flow to Tanzania has been around $1 billion on average. Tanzania used aid mainly for agriculture and transportation infrastructure in the 1960s and for the energy and industrial sectors during the 1970s. However, in the 1980s and 1990s, many projects and programs failed to meet their targets, which prompted the government of Tanzania and donors to cooperate to make aid more efficient and effective.

In 1997, both the Tanzanian government and donors followed the recommendations of the Helleiner Report and focused on aid and donor coordination and harmonization processes. These attempts were successful and Tanzania is now in the forefront of implementing strategies that make aid policies work. It has also promulgated the National Vision 2025, which set its national objectives for socio-economic development and development frameworks.

4.4 OECD DAC Member Countries[13]

The OCED DAC member countries continue to provide the majority of ODA. Despite concerns of aid fatigue, the overall volumes of ODA disbursements have continued to increase. An inspection of the trends of aid distribution by major OECD DAC member countries over the years will provide insight on how individual donor countries have contributed towards the global effort to eradicate poverty in developing countries.

Before diving into individual donor states case by case, the commonalities that the donor states share is ought to be presented as the following;

1) Donors are becoming more strategic and focused on allocating bilat-

12 *Ibid.*

13 Tables in this chapter were made based on data from the OECD database for each respective country.

eral and multilateral aid. For example, in recent years national security interests have changed allocations to some partner countries.

2) The focus on results and effectiveness has become an important factor that affects how allocations are made by donor countries. The performance of multilateral agencies is also taken into account. Consequently, donor countries have reduced or discontinued ODA to some multilateral agencies. In other cases, government-to-government programs in countries that present a poor record of respecting human rights and democracy have also been reduced or phased out.

3) Donors have also tried to maximize the use of ODA for development by reducing the administrative costs of projects and programs, but this remains a great challenge.[14]

4) Donors tend to concentrate on bilateral assistance and grants. Over two thirds of the total ODA from DAC member countries is made on bilateral terms.

United States

A major driving force for US aid to Western European countries after World War II was identified as a diplomatic tool to promote democratic values and beliefs as well as countering Soviet expansion. However, in the post-Cold War period this instrumental use of aid is increasingly criticized. The power imbalance inherent in ODA is particularly salient in cases of bilateral assistance. In bilateral arrangements, donor countries are able to specify the terms of aid provision to a particular recipient, and in many cases the aid program becomes donor oriented as a result. Regardless of the inefficiencies within the particular aid programs proposed by donor countries, recipient countries must accept the terms or risk losing the assistance to another country. Thus, if power relations exist among these partner countries, it is clearly the donor that wields more influence. Furthermore, in cases where the recipient country becomes dependent on foreign assistance, especially bilateral assistance, the donor countries will enjoy even more power. This is the foundation for the argument that aid has become a modern form of imperialism.

From another perspective, ODA can be seen as a tool to bolster soft power initiatives. Soft power, a term conceptualized by Joseph Nye, highlights cooption and attraction rather than force and coercion. Limitations on the effectiveness of traditional hard power capabilities, such as military power, are increasingly evident in inter-

14 OECD, *Better Aid Managing Aid: Practices of DAC Member Countries* (Paris: OECD, 2009), 49.

national relations. As a result, Nye argues, soft power is becoming an important form of power within international society:

> The basic concept of power is the ability to affect others to get the outcomes you want. There are three major ways to do that: one is to threaten coercion (sticks); the second is to pay (carrots); the third is to attract them or co-opt them, so that they want what you want. If you can get others to be attracted to want what you want, (to help set their preferences), it costs you much less in carrots and sticks.[15]

There are many different forms of soft power, but the term can encompass popular culture, political values, and foreign policies, such as ODA. Many countries are using foreign aid policies to enhance their national image, believing that this gives them more influence in the international sphere.

Overall the United States provides the largest amounts of ODA in net volume. However, it has continued to be criticized by the international development community because of its low ODA/GNI level. Its peak was a little over 0.2%, much lower than the recommended 0.7% target of ODA/GNI for DAC member countries.

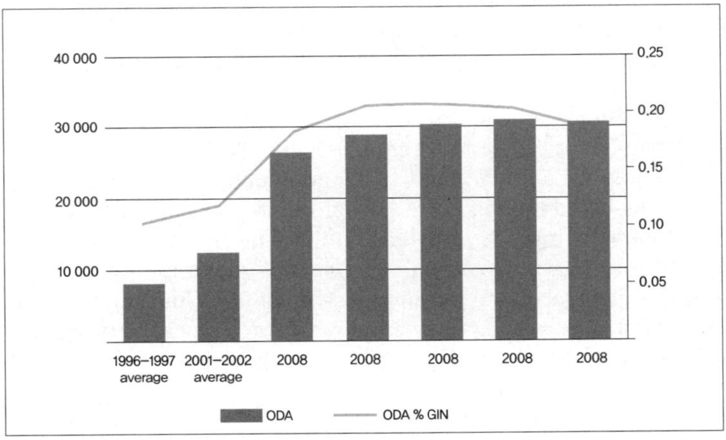

Figure 4.2 United States: Net ODA Volume and ODA/GNI from 1996 to 2012 (unit: USD million/per cent)

15 Carnegie Council, "Soft Power: The Means to Success in World Politics," http://www.cceia.org/resources/transcripts/4466.html, last visited Mar 2009.

In 2005, the US committed to double its aid to Sub-Saharan Africa between 2004 and 2010. It has launched the Millennium Challenge Account, with the aim of providing $5 billion a year to reduce global poverty by means of sustainable economic growth. Most of the $15 billion for Emergency Plan for AIDS Relief program was spent on 15 focus countries including Botswana, Ethiopia, Haiti and Uganda while $4 billion was reserved for the programs on the other parts of the world for HIV/AIDS research. Another $1 billion was contributed to the Global Fund that aims to attract resources to prevent and treat not only HIV but also tuberculosis and malaria.

Box 4.2 Millennium Challenge Account[16]

The Millennium Challenge Account is a new approach to foreign development aid that aims to encourage good governance. The Millennium Challenge Act of 2003 represents a major policy shift by donors, placing governance issues center stage and relying on highly transparent and objective empirical allocation criteria. The Act was passed on January 23, 2004. It appropriates foreign aid to specific infrastructure economic development grants in developing countries that show a commitment to ① just governance, ② investment in their people and ③ encouragement of freedom. It allows eligible countries to design their own programs based on internally identified priorities and increases host country ownership, accountability and control.

The Millennium Challenge Account established an independent government entity, the Millennium Challenge Corporation (MCC) and created the Millennium Challenge Account as a clearinghouse for results-based foreign aid. A Harvard study found that MCA candidate countries improve an average of 25% more than non-candidate countries on development indicator scores.[17] Countries continued to progress after receiving aid and the Millennium Challenge Account has become a powerful policy initiative that influences the regulatory environment and rule of law in developing countries.

16 Rebecca Stubbs, "The Millennium Challenge Account: Influencing Governance in Developing Countries through Performance-Based Foreign Aid," *Vanderbilt Journal of Transnational Law*, vol. 42, no. 621 (2009): 624-629.

17 Doug Johnson and Tristan Zajonc, "Can Foreign Aid Create an Incentive for Good Governance? Evidence from the Millennium Challenge Corporation 1," Kennedy School of

In recent years, about a quarter of US bilateral foreign assistance has been allocated to Sub-Saharan African countries, which is the poorest region in the world. US ODA to Sub-Saharan Africa rose by 26% in 2008. The commitments and policies made in the early days of the Obama administration further reinforce the prospects that US development assistance to Sub-Saharan Africa will continue to rise at least for several years beyond 2010. President Obama has pledged to double foreign assistance by 2015.[18] The President's budget for 2010 proposed an 8% increase for foreign assistance, and at least 10% more for Sub-Saharan Africa. The Obama administration's FY2012 bilateral Africa aid budget request, at $7.8 billion, represents an increase of roughly 10% compared to FY2010, albeit at a more restrained growth rate than in previous years.

In 2009, the US increased its assistance to Sub-Saharan Africa by 14% ($1.12 billion). The US exceeded its Gleneagles commitment one year in advance of its target, and is expected to show slight increase in aid spending up to 2018 as the impacts of financial crisis starts to wear off.

The US has made the largest ODA increases in volume to Sub-Saharan Africa among the G8 and has committed to double foreign assistance by 2015. In addition, it has concentrated its efforts on

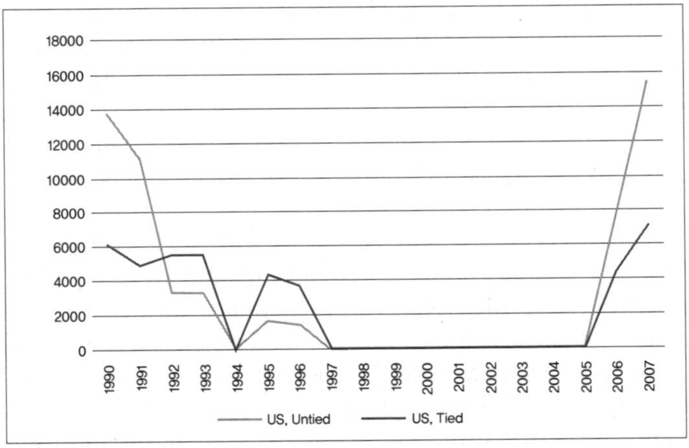

Figure 4.3 United States: Tied and Untied Aid Distributions[19]

Government, Working paper series (2006).

18 United States. H. Cong. Res.6. 114th Cong. 1st sess. (Washington: GPO, 1998). Proquest Congressional Publications, Web (1 September 2015).

global health programs and made large investments in agriculture.

Despite these efforts to concentrate US aid in Africa, the top recipients of ODA remain Middle Eastern countries. The largest proportion of ODA is allocated to Iraq and Afghanistan, followed by Sudan, Colombia and Egypt. The US continues to provide a proportion of its aid as tied aid, but the overall levels of untied aid have been rising consistently over the years.

United Kingdom

UK achieved its goal ratio of ODA to GNI of 0.7% in 2013 for the first time. British ODA radically developed since the foundation of the DFID (Department for International Development) in 1997, which is an independent ODA policymaking and implementation body. The DFID covers bilateral and multilateral aid and delivers 85% of British ODA. Other organizations in the British government also deliver ODA, but the DFID plays a strong and collaborative coordination role among the other agencies.

Before the establishment of the DFID, a humanitarian mandate was not the mission of British ODA. In other words, the UK government used ODA to further economic and foreign policy. With the establishment of the DFID in 1996, however, British government and civil society made clear that a humanitarian mandate is the fundamental goal of British ODA. In 2002, the UK adopted the International Development Act, which provides guidelines for British ODA. It stipulates that the purpose of ODA is as follows: to help the least developing countries by poverty relief and economic development assistance based on the priority of the recipient countries.[19]

The UK government also tries to coordinate its ODA with the 'EU Code of Conduct on Complementarity and Division of Labor.' Based on this code, the UK government puts priorities on the issues of capacity building, climate change, and humanitarian assistance. The top recipient countries of British ODA are the countries in Sub-Saharan Africa followed by South and Central Asia. The top 10 recipients are India, Ethiopia, Afghanistan, Democratic Republic Congo, Pakistan, Nigeria, Bangladesh, Tanzania, Uganda, and Ghana. Most of these countries were British colonies in the past

19 International Development Act 2002, http://www.legislation.gov.uk/ukpga/2002/1/contents, last visited July 2014.

and are currently members of the Commonwealth of Nations. Such a tendency testifies to the fact that British ODA has evolved from colonial experience and governance.

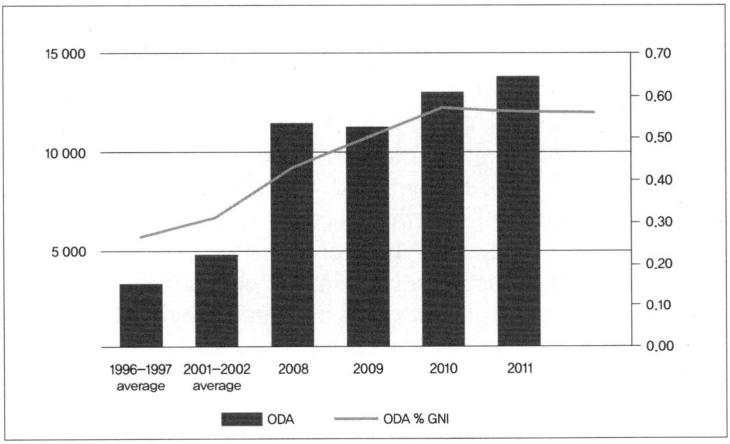

Figure 4.4 United Kingdom: Net ODA Volume and ODA/GNI from 1996 to 2012 (unit: USD million/ per cent)

France

France has provided aid contributions to make up for colonial ties. Due to France's history and links with African countries, Prime Minister Lionel Jospin voiced for reforms to French cooperation machinery and the creation of a Priority Solidarity Area (ZSP - Zone de solidarité prioritaire). The ZSP included some 60 of the world's least developed countries, mostly former colonies and other African countries, including Lebanon and the Palestinian territories, the Indochinese peninsula and the Caribbean, to allocate bilateral ODA. Over 40% of French ODA goes to the world's least developed and low income countries, and the African continent receives half of its bilateral aid. France also aims to increase ODA and fulfill its "duty of solidarity."[20]

France's ODA agenda included efforts to support regional integration within the Franc Zone and the Indian Ocean area. The eco-

20 French Embassy, "French ODA - Interview given by M. Charles Josselin to the La Croix daily newspaper, Paris 29.04.2001," http://www.ambafrance-uk.org/French-ODA-Interview-given-by-M.html, last visited March 2009.

nomic effects on neighboring countries from giving ODA to major economic players in the region, such as Côte d'Ivoire and Cameroon, two Francophone countries in West and Central Africa, were also taken into account before making decisions.[21]

Critics have pointed that French aid has been concentrated on supporting Francophone countries and French overseas territories. French Polynesia and New Caledonia, for example, account for about 7% of the French total bilateral aid. With the exception of Egypt, the rest of the top ten recipients are all ex-African colonies, receiving about 50% of bilateral aid. The rest of France's bilateral aid is dispersed among 130 different countries.

In 1999, the Cooperation Minister identified France's development priorities as focused on building up capacities for influence abroad, to identify and anchor elites in its partner countries, to confirm its position in development cooperation, and to associate civil society with its policy objectives.

At the International Conference on Financing for Development held in Monterrey in 2002, French President Jacques Chirac pledged to increase France's ODA to 0.5% of gross national income (GNI) by 2007, which was achieved in 2010, and ultimately to 0.7% by 2015. It was also identified that at least half of this aid would be directed towards Africa to help achieve the Millennium Development Goals (MDGs) and to support the areas specified in the New Partnership for Africa's Development (NEPAD).

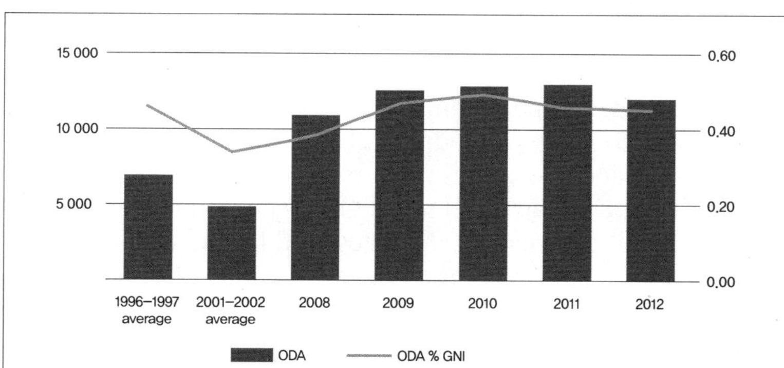

Figure 4.5 France: Net ODA Volume and ODA/GNI from 1996 to 2012 (unit: USD million/ per cent)

21 *Ibid.*

In recent years, more than half of France's ODA has been allocated to Sub-Saharan African countries, but in terms of income groups, French ODA has been provided mainly to lower-middle income countries. The top recipients of ODA include Nigeria, Iraq, Cameroon, Morocco, and Mayotte. France's aid is motivated by its historical relations with different countries and is concentrated on its past colonies. France's tied aid has continued to decrease since 1990 with small fluctuations and has been at minimal levels since 2002.

France's development assistance to Sub-Saharan Africa grew substantially in 2009, with an increase of $1.19 billion. This was actually a greater increase than was projected in the French budget. In 2013, bilateral ODA of France totaled $2.6 billion to the sub-Saharan Africa, the biggest allocation of ODAs compared to any other regions. The commitment France made at Gleneagles was the largest of the G7 as a proportion of GNI and the second largest in volume, focusing a higher proportion of resources on Sub-Saharan Africa than the rest of the EU. It has committed to reach 0.7% ODA/GNI by 2015. Also, it has committed to spend 66% of all bilateral ODA and 50% of all multilateral ODA in Sub-Saharan Africa. In absolute figures this would mean an increase in ODA to Sub-Saharan Africa from around $3 billion in 2004 to $4.5 billion in 2010.[22]

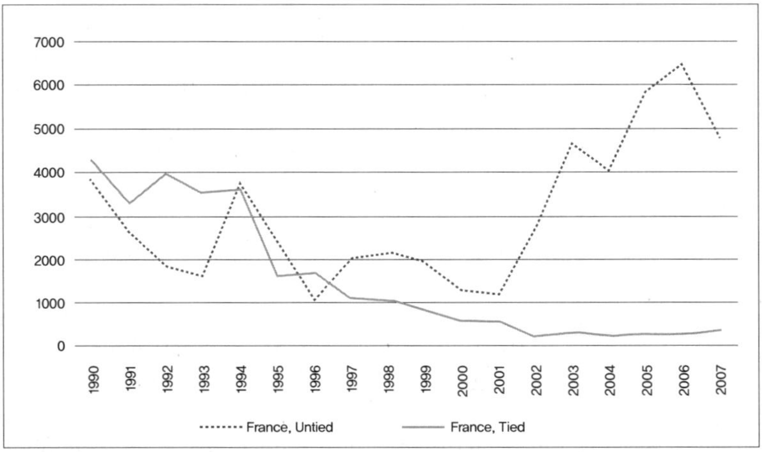

Figure 4.6 France: Tied and Untied Aid Distributions

22 The Data Report 2010, Monitoring the G8 promise to Africa, France – Development Assistance, http://www.one.org/report/2010/en/country/france/oda.html, last visited Jan 2011.

French aid is guided by a number of key principles: priority to Africa, global public goods, the regulation of globalization, sustainable development and democratic governance, cultural diversity and La Francophonie. France has also made a commitment to secure better integration of African countries into the world economy. France has been a major force behind the European Union's plan to create fairer trading conditions for African cotton producing countries.

Germany

Germany is the second largest donor of ODA, following the US. From the late 1980s to 1998, Germany's ODA volume fell due to its concentration on reunification and support to strategically important former Eastern bloc countries, such as Poland. Germany has committed to expand its ODA gradually to meet the 0.7% target by 2015, set interim targets of 0.33% by 2006, which was achieved in 2005, and 0.51% by 2010. In response to the 2005 EU commitment on development assistance, Germany has promised to reach 0.51% ODA/GNI in 2010 and 0.7% ODA/GNI in 2015. In 2008, bilateral development projects and programs in Germany overall rose by 12.5% compared to 2007 and aid to Africa also increased by 10%. However, financial difficulty in Europe and Germany in the 2010s became an obstacle for Germany in achieving its pledged goal of 0.7% by 2015. Due to such obstacles, Germany has reached ODA rate of 0.38% in 2015, which is expected to rise to 4.0% in 2016 and 0.46% by 2019.

In 2009, German ODA to Sub-Saharan Africa increased by only $79 million and it is projected to increase by $88 million in 2010. Despite drops in global development assistance, spending in Sub-Saharan Africa continued to increase in 2011.Within the G8, Germany has been a supporter of safe water supplies and sanitation in Sub-Saharan Africa, and has also emerged as a leader in generating funding from innovative financing mechanisms. It was the first country to direct financing from the sales of CO_2 emission certificates to development.[23] In 2010, ODA increases were mainly used to intensify assistance to Afghanistan and mitigate climate change.

23 The Data Report 2010, Monitoring the G8 promise to Africa, Germany – Development Assistance, http://www.one.org/report/2010/en/country/germany/oda.html, last visited Jan 2011.

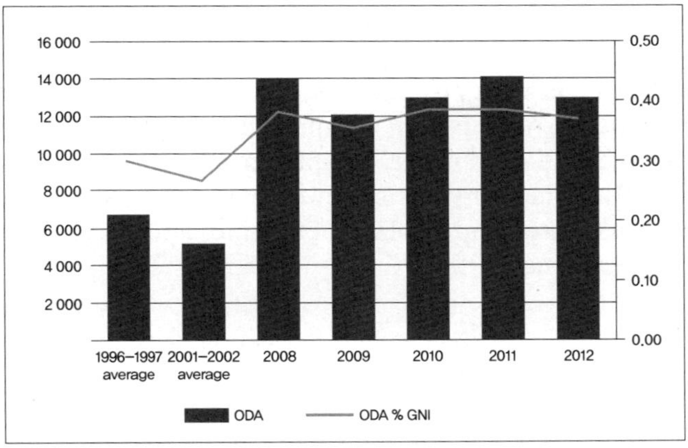

Figure 4.7 Germany: Net ODA Volume and ODA/GNI from 1996 to 2012 (unit: USD million/ per cent)

Germany was among the first DAC members to adopt a comprehensive government-wide policy statement, entitled "The Program of Action 2015 on Poverty Reduction." The underlying philosophy of the program is that in order to achieve the MDGs, economic growth together with governance is needed in addition to social development. Germany has spent more on water and sanitation in Sub-Saharan Africa than any other G8 country and is a clear leader in this sector.

Germany's ODA trends are similar to that of France. In recent

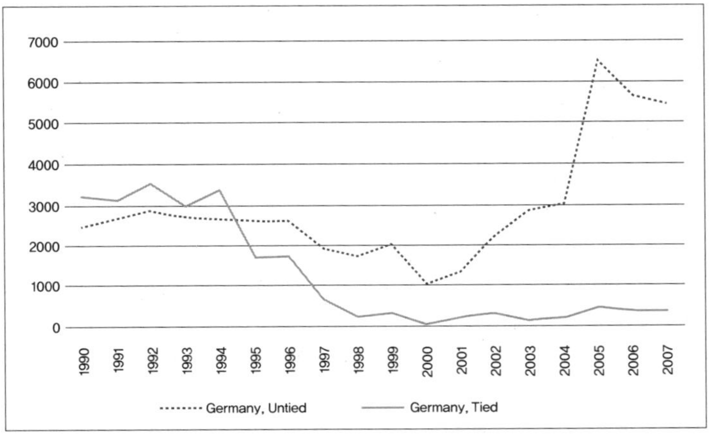

Figure 4.8 Germany: Tied and Untied Aid Distributions

years, the largest proportion of Germany's ODA has been allocated to Sub-Saharan African countries, but in terms of income groups, German ODA has been provided mainly to lower-middle income countries. The top recipients of German ODA include India, China, Afghanistan, Brazil, Indonesia, Egypt, Peru, Pakistan, Turkey, and Kenya in 2014. Germany has complied with the DAC guidelines that encourage untied aid in place of tied aid, and its levels of tied aid have fallen since 1995.

Japan

In many cases, the historical ties of countries play a strong role in decisions to provide aid. Following the global financial crisis in 2008, Prime Minister Taro Aso announced plans to hand out $17 billion to other Asian countries. He stated that Asian countries could lead the world out of recession through closer economic co-operation, and emphasized Japanese support for Asian countries by mobilizing funds.[24] Since its first contributions of aid, Japan has consistently shown a preference to provide ODA to Asian countries.

Japan's history of development assistance goes back to 1954, when Japan joined the Colombo Plan, launched in 1950 with the aim of facilitating economic and technical cooperation among the member countries of the British Commonwealth of Nations. Japan soon extended technical assistance to other Asian countries. Until 1976, Japan's economic foreign policy toward Asian countries was closely linked with reparations and aimed to promote friendly relations. This approach was redefined in the 1970s so that Japan's economic cooperation was recast as having two major objectives: ① to ensure its security and prosperity by creating a peaceful and stable world through assistance to developing countries; and ② to maintain friendly relations with developing countries for the sake of Japan's economic growth. The second point was important because Japan is dependent on developing countries, particularly in Asia, for supplies of natural resources.

Japan's ODA has contributed to the economic development of developing countries, particularly within Asia. Approximately 60% of Japan's ODA has been directed to Asian countries, the majority

24 CNN, "Japan unveils $17B Asian aid package," http://edition.cnn.com/2009/BUSINESS/01/31/davos.wef.japan/index.html, last visited March 2009.

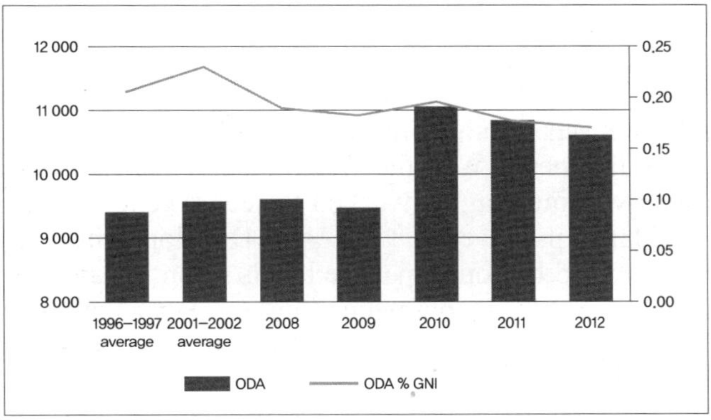

Figure 4.9 Japan: Net ODA Volume and ODA/GNI from 1996 to 2012 (unit: USD million/ per cent)

of which was allocated to developing economic infrastructure. This kind of assistance has helped create an environment conducive for foreign capital and private sector investment. Most ODA projects succeeded in attracting FDI to Asian countries and promoting the development of export industries.[25]

Japan has consistently contributed a large volume of development aid to the international community. The institutional framework of Japan's aid program encompasses some unique characteristics. In 1999, the Overseas Economic Cooperation Fund (OECF), which had been in charge of the loan part of ODA in industrial countries since 1991, and the Japan Export and Import Bank merged to create the Japan Bank of International Cooperation (JBIC). JBIC has an annual budget of $30 billion, which is as large as the budget of the World Bank.[26]

In 2005, Japan stated that it intended to increase its ODA volume by $10 billion (¥1.1 trillion) in aggregate over the next five years, and it committed to double its ODA to Africa over the next three years. Japan met this target in May 2008 and made a new commitment to double its bilateral ODA to Africa, net amounts without debt relief, by 2012. In addition, it also made several new sectorial commitments to Africa. It proposed to double rice production in the continent within a decade and to train 100,000 health workers. Ja-

25 Ministry of Foreign Affairs of Japan, "History of Official Development Assistance," http://www.mofa.go.jp/policy/oda/summary/1994/1.html, last visited March 2009.

26 Japan Bank for International Cooperation, http://www.jbic.go.jp, last visited March 2009.

pan has been a leader in providing technical assistance and support for water and sanitation improvements.

The largest proportion of Japanese ODA has been concentrated on Asian countries. A large amount of ODA is allocated to China, Nigeria and Indonesia. With the global financial crisis in 2008, the Japanese government again worked to secure funds for its Asian neighbors. Japan proposed that the Asian Development Bank triple its capital to $165 billion. Japanese levels of untied aid have consistently met the DAC recommendations and Japan continues to be one of the forerunners in providing ODA to developing countries.

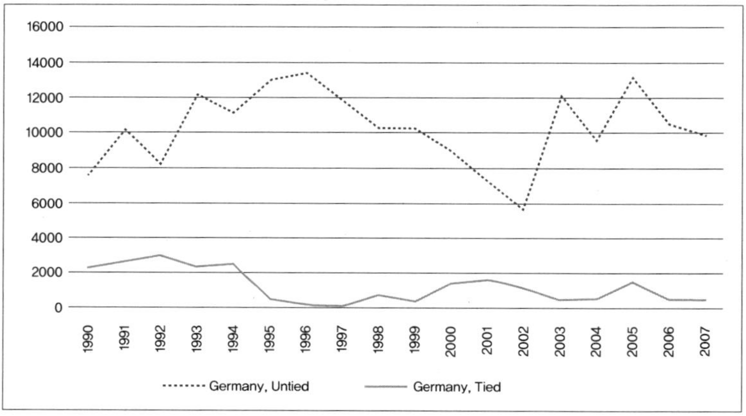

Figure 4.10 Japan: Tied and Untied Aid Distributions

Scandinavia and Netherlands

The Scandinavian countries, including Norway and Sweden, have continued to provide the highest levels of ODA/GNI ratios and met the OECD DAC target recommendation of 0.7% of total GNI.

In the case of Netherlands, about half of the aid was not allocated to any specific region or income group. Of the remaining aid that was allocated, the majority was provided to the Least Developed Countries and the Sub-Saharan African regions. The top recipients of aid from the Netherlands include Nigeria, Sudan, Indonesia, Tanzania and Ghana.

The aid practices of Sweden showed some similarities to that of the Netherlands. The largest proportion of aid in 2006 was not allocated to any specific income group or region. Among aid that was

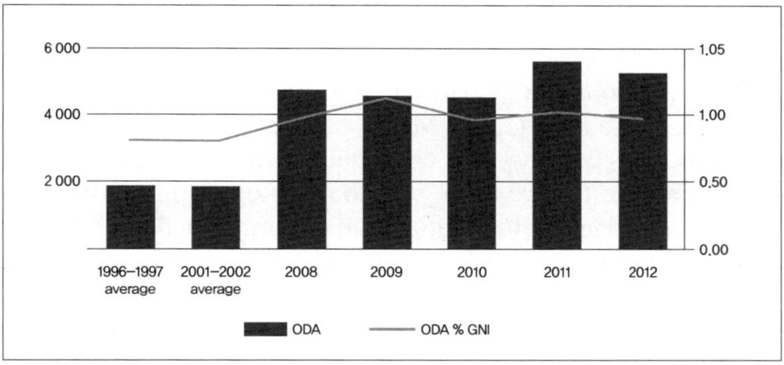

Figure 4.11 Sweden: Net ODA Volume and ODA/GNI from 1996 to 2012 (unit: USD million/ per cent)

allocated, the Least Developed Countries and Sub-Saharan Africa were the largest group recipients. As an individual country, Iraq received the largest amount of ODA. Other top recipients of Swedish ODA include Tanzania, Mozambique, Uganda and Sudan.

Swedish aid that was not allocated to a specific sub-region was smaller in quantity compared to the Netherlands, but the majority of aid was not specified and of the aid that was specified, the largest proportion was directed to promote pro-poor growth.

EU

The volume of aid that the European Union has provided to the Mediterranean region has increased substantially over the past years. A comprehensive EU Mediterranean policy that deals with Europe's political and economic interests in the region has emerged to promote aid to the region. In the past, the objectives of EU assistance were aimed at traditional development-related agendas, but in recent years these motives have shifted to focus on promoting transition and economic integration with Europe. Mediterranean Partner Countries (MPC) of interest includes the Arab states and the Palestinian Authority.

It was the ongoing conflicts of the 1970s that initiated EU interests in the Mediterranean region. The Global Mediterranean Policy (GMP) was constructed in an effort to formalize and harmonize relationships between the EU and the Mediterranean countries by signing trade and cooperation agreements. Most of these agreements were bilateral and included focus on direct security interests.

The GMP agreement waived tariffs for most of the industrial products and offered a degree of financial assistance. It also encouraged economic relations among participating countries.

Despite these efforts, the MPCs have experienced economic stagnation. This was in part a consequence of their small domestic markets and the failure of any regional integration among Arab countries. This lack of integration and governance along with protectionist policies all contributed to economic failure. Arab governments pursued protectionist trade policies, government intervention in the economy was rife and the regulatory system lacked free competition, efficiency or entrepreneurship. Globalization increased pressure on the MPCs to reduce the state's role and attract foreign investments through increasing competition and general systemic pressures.

Under these circumstances, reform was perceived as a prerequisite for development in the region. With the EU strategy, reforms were to be combined with regional integration to allow a larger market and economies of scale. It was anticipated that access to the European market would attract a growing level of FDI to promote economic growth. Unfortunately, FDI flows to the region remain weak. The MPCs' total annual FDI inflow is comparable to that of Poland. Although the Mediterranean aid works well in terms of its principles and objectives, it will not be enough to transform the political economies of recipient states. The limited integration that is offered to the Mediterranean is not sufficient to enable the MPCs to overcome the immense social and economic challenges that they face.

The EU's aid policy towards Africa began with the 1957 Treaty of Rome. It was initially influenced by France, and was limited to Francophone Africa. Following the first enlargement of the EU in the early 1970s, African members of the British Commonwealth and other former colonies in the Caribbean and the Pacific were covered by EU aid. The Lomé Convention from 1975 to 2000 has often been considered the most comprehensive, innovative and ambitious agreement for North-South cooperation. The EU jointly undertook decisions with the African, Caribbean and Pacific Group of States, or ACP countries, and attempted to be politically and economically neutral. It reversed the previous trade regime from reciprocal to non-reciprocal and now almost all ACP goods enter the EU free of any tariff or quota restrictions. The EU also agreed on separate trading protocols.

The Cotonou Partnership Agreement (CPA) was signed in 2000, introducing a number of radical changes to the EU-ACP relationship. Following a 7-year transition period, new free trade agreements known as Economic Partnership Agreements (EPA) would enter into force. The process proved controversial and few countries had concluded agreements with the EU by 2007. Within the CPA, issues that were considered outside of the realm of development assistance, such as arms trade, migration, drugs and corruption were included. The participation of non-state actors increased in the process of development cooperation and greater access to funds and capacity building support were achieved.

The adoption of the Cotonou Agreement occurred during a period in which the EU external assistance program was undergoing an extensive reform process. The EU was being criticized for being fragmented in its instruments, procedures and institutional mechanisms. At the management level, Europe Aid was launched as a structure in charge of implementation, monitoring and evaluation of all external aid instruments.

The EU-Africa Strategy was the first opportunity to implement the provisions of the European consensus. The Strategy was a platform for both EU and Member States aid, with overall goals to support African efforts in achieving the MDGs. The EU focused its activities on a limited number of areas: good governance and peace and security as prerequisites for developments; trade, regional integration and interconnectivity as actions promoting economic growth and ultimately poverty reduction; and actions to directly tackle the MDGs such as health, education, and safe environment.

4.5 Emerging Donors: China, Brazil, Russia and India

The role and contribution of non-DAC countries is increasing. The HLF 4 held in Busan in 2011 helped ignite the emerging role of non-DAC countries in the framework of South-South partnership. In fact, the volume of ODA from these countries is consistently increasing. Some non-DAC countries, such as Saudi Arabia, China, Turkey, and the United Arab Emirates, are providing more ODA than some DAC countries.

Figure 4.12 Estimate of gross concessional flows for development co-operation ("ODA-like" flows) from OECD Key Partners (unit: USD millions)[27]

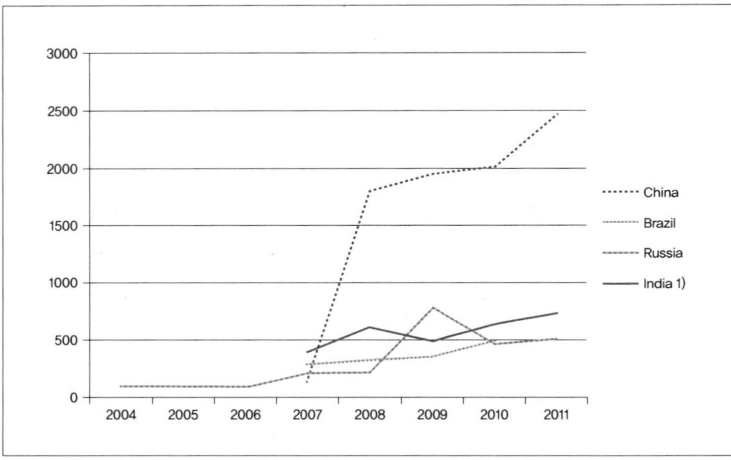

* Estimates on ODA-like flows as published in national publications
1) Figures for India are based on their fiscal years. 2011 data correspond to fiscal year 2011-12.

Figure 4.13 Concessional financing for development ("ODA-like" flows), 2011[28]

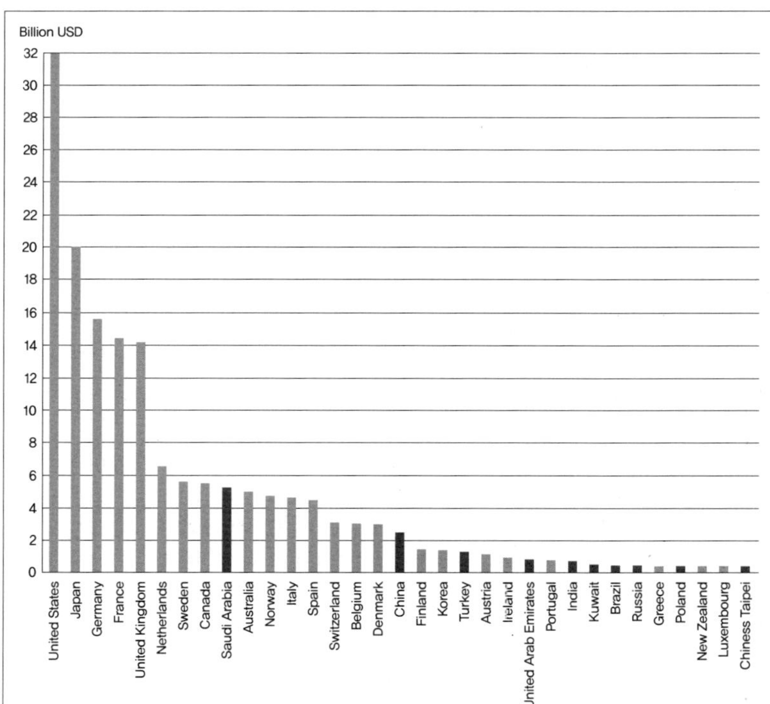

* 1) Blue: DAC countries; Grey: non-DAC countries. It includes all countries with a development co-operation program of at least $300 million in 2011. 2) The figures in this graph are presented on a gross disbursement basis to make them more comparable with the estimates of the development co-operation efforts of Brazil, China, India, Indonesia and South Africa, for which data on loan repayments are not available.

China

Emerging donors are expanding relationships with African countries based on trade, investment, development assistance and loans. While it is difficult to collect and evaluate data from emerging donors, there are some clear trends on the size and scope of these relationships. Many relationships between emerging economies and Sub-Saharan countries are motivated by trade and investment interests. South-South FDI has tripled from $14 billion in 1995 to $47 billion in 2000 and accounted for more than 26% of global trade by 2008.

China is a developing country that is providing aid to other developing countries, especially those in Africa. Although the scope of China's involvement in Africa has magnified in current years, its cooperation with Africa traces back to the late 1950s and early 1960s. China was able to position itself as part of South-South cooperation, emphasizing cooperation at similar levels, and refrained from identifying itself as a donor country. In January of 2006, China published its African Policy related to foreign aid, which is closely associated with a variety of projects in the field of education and other sectors. China has intense bilateral engagements with 48 out of the 53 African countries; the remaining 5 maintain diplomatic relations with Taiwan.[29]

In the 1970s and 1980s, Chinese engagement with African countries was concentrated on infrastructure and public works projects, technical assistance and scholarships. In line with China's rapid economic growth, it has started to focus on the oil and mineral resources available in Africa. The relationship between China and Sub-Saharan Africa has been strengthened through development assistance, loans, trade and investment. Today, China is Africa's most important trading partner and according to the Chinese Ministry for Commerce, its trade with Africa is estimated to be worth over $100 billion a year.[30] Major increases in Chinese development assistance to Africa increased with the launch of the Forum for China-Africa Cooperation (FOCAC) in 2000. The FOCAC is a platform designed to promote economic and political cooperation. China continues to increase its commitments to Africa. In the fourth ministerial meet-

---

27 OECD, *Development Co-operation Report 2013*, 251.

28 *Ibid.*, 250.

29 Kenneth King, *China's Aid to Africa: A View from China and Japan, lead paper to the JICA seminar on China's Aid to Africa the Beijing Summit and its Follow-up* (Tokyo: Japan International Cooperation Agence (JICA), 2007).

30 The Data Report 2010: Monitoring the G8 Promise to Africa, *Emerging Donors.*

ing held in November 2009 (FOCAC IV), China pledged to give more support for the social sector and additional debt relief incorporating government loans owed by Heavily Indebted Poor Countries (HIPCs) and most African Least Developed Countries (LDCs). In the latest meeting held in July 2012, China and Africa agreed on the outline of the next three years of mutual cooperation, especially in the area of people to people exchanges and African integration.

Mutual benefits are core values of Chinese assistance in Africa. The assistance provided should not be burdensome to the recipient, or make them dependent, but rather contributes to making rapid results, build income and accumulate capital. China has promoted what it calls the "Beijing consensus" in Africa by providing unconditional aid to African countries. China emphasizes that its activities in Africa are two-way exchanges and mutual cooperation. The declarations that have emerged from China's African Policy also emphasize the importance of parallelism and equal cooperation. Economic cooperation is also a key idea to Chinese-African relations, and there is little reference to poverty reduction as an objective of the relationship.

China does not use ODA or FDI as a means of infusing its values. Africa has welcomed China's unconditional approach to providing aid that does not link its aid to policies that are oriented from its national beliefs or value systems. China has sponsored a wide range of development activities in Africa. The integration of Chinese development initiatives are set within holistic bilateral frameworks. For example, grant assistance, the medical, health and educational support to Africa, or the increasing numbers of short and longer-term trainees going to China are some of the bilateral projects being undertaken.

Around 79% of the total amount of African operations by the Export-Import Bank of China is concentrated on infrastructure development, accounting for 259 projects in 36 countries. Infrastructure projects include road and rail transport, energy and power plants, transmission lines, oil and gas pipelines, water supply and sanitation. The Ex-Im Bank referred to these concessionary lending projects as a form of South-South cooperation on an equal and mutual beneficial basis, claiming that it promoted social and economic development and improved the living standards in developing countries.[31]

31 China, Export-Import Bank of 2006, "Infrastructure development in Africa supported by the

India

The Special Commonwealth African Assistance Program is India's African aid program. It currently provides funding for 19 African countries. In 2008, India committed more than $500 million to its aid to Africa program over a span of five years. From 1991 to 2008, India's trade with Africa increased from $967 million to $35 billion and the government has forecasted that it expects trade with Africa to triple, reaching a total of $100 billion over the next years to come. However, most cooperation is concentrated in South Africa, accounting for 68% of African exports to India, mostly minerals, precious stones, metals alloys and chemicals.

Brazil

Brazil is the biggest economy in Latin America and acts as a bilateral partner with more than seventy countries. The official Brazilian figure for expenditure on development cooperation between 2005 and 2009 is $1.4 billion, of which almost $1.1 billion was in the form of contributions to international organizations. Brazil used $126 million for technical cooperation (TC), $139 million for scholarships and $79 million for humanitarian relief. The technical assistance budget rose from $11 million in 2005 to $49 million in 2009, almost doubling its total share of the development cooperation budget from 7.2% to 14.5%. According to the Brazilian Cooperation Agency (ABC – Agência Brasileira de Cooperação), TC is the country's greatest strength.

Brazil has not yet published data on its development cooperation flows for 2011. The figures published by Brazil up to 2010 show that Brazil's development cooperation has been steadily increasing in recent years, with its 2010 flows representing a 33% increase compared to 2009. A large part of Brazil's development cooperation is channeled through multilateral organizations. Brazil's technical co-operation program, coordinated by the Agência Brasileira de Cooperação, is mainly focused on agriculture, food security and social policies. Geographically, the priority regions for Brazilian South-South cooperation are (in order of priority): South America, Central America, the Caribbean and Africa.

Among OECD key partners, Brazil is the largest supporter of

Export-Import Bank of China," Paper presented at the 3rd annual Meeting of the Infrastructure Consortium for Africa, January 17th, 2007, Berlin.

the multilateral system, with regional funds and organizations like FOCEM (Fund for Structural Convergence of Mercosur) as main channels of delivery. Organizations outside of Latin America, however, also receive contributions from Brazil. Already a contributor to the African Development Bank (AfDB) in 2010, an organization in Brazil's third priority region (behind South and Central America), Brazil signed an agreement with AfDB to create a South-South Cooperation Trust Fund in 2011.

Russia

The Russian Federation' ODA is consistently increasing to US $480 million in 2011. Two-thirds of the Russian Federation's ODA is delivered bilaterally, with the remainder as core contributions to various UN agencies, the Global Fund and the World Bank.[32] Russian bilateral and multilateral ODA is based on the regulations and conditions of the concept note "Russia's Participation in International Development Assistance" approved by the President of the Russian Federation in June 2007. Health is a priority sector for the Russian Federation – especially infectious disease control – however, the Russian Federation also invests in food security, education and humanitarian assistance. The Russian Federation's main partner countries are the members of the Commonwealth of Independent States (CIS) in Eastern Europe and Central Asia, followed by countries in the Asia-Pacific region and Sub-Saharan Africa.[33]

The Russian Federation's core contributions to multilateral organizations increased from 36% of Russian ODA in 2010 to 50% in 2011. The International Development Association (IDA) and the International Bank for Reconstruction and Development (IBRD), both part of the World Bank Group, were the main multilateral recipients, followed by the Global Fund to Fight AIDS, Tuberculosis and Malaria. Nicaragua was the principal recipient of the Russian Federation's bilateral cooperation – receiving 37% of its geographically specified development finance – followed by Korea, Serbia and the Kyrgyz Republic.

There are a number of main goals of Russia's ODA: To eliminate poverty and ensure sustainable economic development in develop-

32 Ministry of Finance of the Russian Federation, *The Russian Federation ODA National Report* (2011), 2.

33 OECD, "The Russian Federation's Official Development Assistance (ODA)," http://www.oecd.org/russia/russiasofficialdevelopmentassistance.htm, last visited July 2014.

Figure 4.14 Regional ODA Distribution in 2011

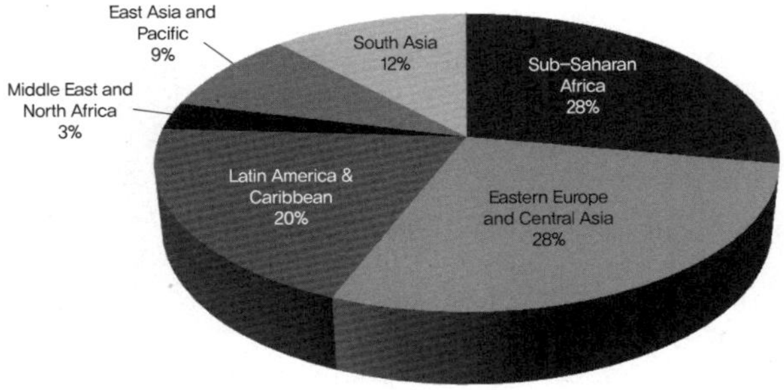

Source: Ministry of Finance of the Russian Federation, "The Russian Federation ODA National Report," (2011). 2.

ing and post-conflict countries; to liquidate the consequences of humanitarian, natural, environmental, and industrial disasters and other emergencies; to foster democratic processes, development of market-oriented economies, and observance of human rights in partner countries; to develop political, economic, educational ,social, cultural, and academic relations with other countries and international associations.

The general predictions for the overall ODA worldwide were optimistic; everyone foresaw that the world economy would recover soon and the assistance flow would again be back on its track for the better. Unfortunately, the data from 2015 is starting to illustrate grimmer picture. The ODA flows worldwide are not recuperating fast enough from the backdrop they have experienced from the consecutive economic downturns. However, the importance of ODA is continuing to be crucial in our day and age. The increasing importance of mutual accountability of the donor and receiver, basic and shared monitoring and accountability frameworks as well as global discussion and support seen at the latest United Nations Development Cooperation Forum are leaving us with hopes that the ODAs are moving toward the right direction where every stakeholder take part and get involved all the way.

Chapter 4. Review Discussion Questions

1. The current target for bilateral donors is set at 0.7% of total GNI. Does this mean that those countries that are providing large net amounts of aid should be criticized because they have not met the targets? How should aid commitments be evaluated, especially in terms of quantity?
2. Compare the aid allocations of different bilateral donors.
3. How is Official Development Assistance distinguished from other forms of development assistance? Wherein lies the significance of ODA? How is this comparable to other official flows?
4. What are some of the unique challenges faced in providing foreign aid?
5. Identify the factors that lead to economic growth and development for those countries that have successfully implemented development aid. Are there any commonalities among these countries?
6. Why is the international community concerned with the increasing amounts of Chinese aid in Africa? Why is China allocating so much of its aid to Africa?
7. In many cases aid is allocated to countries that have some relationship to the donor country. In light of the different cases of development aid that have been presented, are there any perceivable advantages of such aid allocations? Are there any distinct disadvantages?

Chapter 5
Bilateral, Multilateral and Multi-bi Aid

> *"Aid donors face growing demands to explain and justify the allocation choice between multilateral and bilateral aid channels. Among other reasons, this is because the aid disbursements of multilateral agencies looks, in many cases, quite similar to the disbursements of bilateral donors, offering aid on similar terms, within the same countries and to the same sectors. The possibility of substitution across these two channels creates a strategic opportunity for donors to direct funding through either bilateral or multilateral institutions."*[1]

Official aid can be largely categorized into bilateral and multilateral aid. Bilateral aid is provided directly by donor governments through their official aid agencies to the recipient country government. It is bilateral in the sense that there are two government agencies involved in the aid program, the agency of the donor country and that of the recipient country. Bilateral transactions also include transactions between national or international nongovernmental organizations active in development, and other internal development-related transactions, such as interest subsidies, disbursement for promotion of development awareness, debt reorganization and administrative costs.

Multilateral aid refers to aid that is provided through an international organization. In the case of multilateral aid, the implementation process is done by various international organizations, which minimizes the amount of direct contact that is often conducted in the case of bilateral transactions between donor and recipient countries. It must be noted that the funding for multilateral agencies still largely come from the contributions of large bilateral donors.

5.1 Bilateral Aid

Many factors can influence the allocation of budgets to bilateral

1 Nilima Gulrajani, "Bilateral versus multilateral aid channels: Strategic choices for donors" (London: ODI Report, 2016), 5.

aid. The opinions of political elites and the public in donor countries are significant since the source of funds for ODA comes from tax revenues, which is why government dialogues with domestic constituents are a critical agenda in setting goals for development assistance. Other influential aspects include concern for humanitarian relief and alleviation of poverty in countries that have strategic significance to the donor country, or the need for international economic and social stability. The historical relationship between donor and recipient countries or the potential of recipient countries as economic partners should also be considered for humanitarian relief. As economic partners, recipient countries can become a source of natural resources or markets for donor countries' trade.

Political agendas are an important aspect of donor governments' reason for giving development assistance. At the domestic level, within the political decision-making process of budget allocation, a government must consider the impact of aid before it can allocate its funds to foreign development assistance. Since national budgets are limited, it is crucial that government decisions strike a balance between domestic welfare and foreign aid. At the international level, providing development assistance has been recognized as a political tool that can be utilized towards security interests, strategic concerns, or fulfillment of regional responsibilities.

The inherent complexities in the decision-making processes of donor governments have resulted in an array of motivations. Each donor has different objectives for providing aid, which can be identified through analysis of political statements or relevant documents of these countries. Nonetheless, it is important to note that political, economic and humanitarian purposes are always present in a donor's decision to give aid. The difference between donors, however, is the weight given to each agenda in their overall motivations for providing aid.

In the 1950s the US accounted for half of all ODA, and one of the key factors for the success of the Marshall Plan was that the US was the predominant aid provider. Since there was only one aid donor, it facilitated implementation because the United States could oversee its complex policy with minimal transaction costs, unlike the case of multilateral aid.

About 75% of total ODA is bilateral aid, and considering that multilateral aid is also funded by governments of large donor countries, the behaviors and trends of donors is important in understanding both bilateral and multilateral aid. According to DAC statistics for 2007, the United States, the United Kingdom, Germany, France and Japan were the five largest bilateral donors of aid. The total ODA volume within the DAC in 2012 was $126.88 billion, and the sum of the five countries accounted for $80.15 billion, almost over 60% of all aid by DAC donors.

The United States

In the history of aid, the US has consistently been the largest official aid donor. In the 1950s, it provided half of all ODA, but the amount decreased to less than 20% in the 1990s when Japan emerged as the prominent donor. The US increased its volume in 2000, and further emphasized the importance of ODA ever since the 9/11 terrorist attacks. However, in relative terms to GNI, the aid provided by the US is far below the DAC average (0.46%), and has been criticized by many different aid agencies. During the 1990s, the ODA/GNI was as low as 0.1%, but has improved to 0.19% levels in recent years. Today, the US continues to be the largest donor country by net total ODA volume, contributing approximately 23% of the total ODA volume within the DAC.

The core purpose of the US aid program is to 'protect America,' through its emphasis of democracy and freedom. The key goal is to stimulate economic growth and development in countries that adhere to basic human rights. According to the USAID, foreign aid has been an essential tool of foreign policy, playing a vital role in supporting US geo-strategic interests.[2] Another goal of US aid is poverty alleviation for poor countries while creating job opportunities for Americans by reducing barriers to free trade. Other goals concentrate on supporting programs on HIV/AIDS, providing vulnerable people with food and humanitarian assistance, and promoting refugee programs.[3]

It is indicated in US law that bilateral aid, implemented through the USAID, must be tied to the procurement of goods and services from the US and aid goods and services have to be transported in US-owned planes and ships, which results in nearly 70% of US aid being tied. Tied aid refers to aid in which procurement with donor country affiliation is mandatory. This has been criticized because it results in high procurement costs for recipient countries and a large

2 USAID, *US Foreign Aid: Meeting the Challenge of the Twenty-first Century* (2004).

3 Roger C. Riddell, *Does Foreign Aid Really Work?* (Oxford University Press, 2007). drawn from the 2006 Federal Budget; www.house.gov/budget/prezbudget.html, last visited March 2009.

proportion of aid flowing back into the donor economy. A comparison of tied aid to untied aid is provided in Chapter 3.

The United Kingdom

The peak of ODA for the UK was in the early 1960s when it gave 0.59% of ODA per GNI. With the formation of the first Conservative government under Margaret Thatcher, however, ODA levels in the UK started to decrease. It was not until Tony Blair came to office that the first Labor government reversed the contraction and stagnation of development assistance. From 1997 to 2005, ODA doubled in real terms, and the government has further expressed its commitment to increase ODA in the future. The UK government increased ODA volume to 0.56% in 2012 and finally reached the goal of 0.71% in 2015 (unadjusted).

As well, a succession of initiatives to enhance the quality of aid and its effectiveness were introduced by the UK. Its approach to poverty eradication is multi-faceted, adopting methods for direct assistance to poor people, making efforts to stimulate economic growth and development and paying increased attention to capacity building and governance. The International Development Act was passed in 2002, which required ODA to be used solely for the purpose of poverty reduction and development in developing countries. The law limits commercial benefits for the UK, particularly that ODA cannot be tied to the purchase of UK goods and services and economic benefits must be secondary to poverty reduction purposes.

The UK has concentrated on providing ODA for the primary purpose of poverty alleviation, and in order to achieve this, it has continued to emphasize monitoring the impacts and results of its aid programs, especially in light of the MDGs. It has also pledged to allocate up to 90% of its bilateral aid to low-income countries. By 2004, nearly 75% of UK ODA was allocated to low-income countries. By 2014, 67.9% of ODAs were directed to the low income countries through official government channels and the total of 96% of ODAs were being spent on aiding the low income states. It was also decided in 2004 that the share of bilateral aid to middle-income countries should be limited to 10%. However, despite such pledge, the ODAs to low and upper middle states totaled 32.1% through official government channel and 71.9% through non-governmental channels.[4]

4 Department for International Development, "Statistics on International Development," 2015,

France

Until recently, France has been the largest ODA donor in Europe. More than 50 years ago, in 1961, the ratio of ODA to GNI was 1.36%, the highest record for all major donors, and for most of the 1960s, France exceeded the target ODA of 0.7% per GNI. Facing dramatic drops in ODA volume, France committed to raise its ODA progressively from 0.32% of GNI in 2000 to 0.42% in 2004 and 0.5% in 2005 to meet the target 0.7% by 2012. In 2012, the French government did not achieve 0.7% ODA/GNI. French ODA remained at 0.45% and then decreased to 0.37% of GNI in 2015.

Despite its large volume of ODA, France was without any comprehensive aid plan or framework, and it was only recently (2005) that it began to shape an overall aid budget, the Institutional Act on Financial Legislation (LOLF), which entails developing-country-specific budgets linked to the introduction of new financial legislation. France also committed itself to a reorientation of its development aid policy, including working with other donors to raise aggregate levels of aid.

Traditionally, French donor practices were largely influenced by its colonial past. Recently, global agendas have become of increasing interest for France, but its approach to poverty reduction is centered on trying to integrate the poor into globalization.

Japan

Japan began as a small aid donor but increased its volume to surpass the US and became the largest aid donor in 1993, providing almost 20% of all ODA. It continued to be the predominant aid donor for 8 years but afterwards its volume of aid decreased by an average of 12% each year, to the current level of $7.68 billion, which is less than 10% of total DAC ODA.

To date, Japan has not committed to any timeframe to increase its ODA to meet the 0.7% of GNI which is the target adopted by the resolution of the UN General Assembly in 1970. During its history of aid, Japan recorded 0.3% ODA/GNI in the 1980s and 0.25% in the 1990s, but dropped to 0.19% in 2004.

The Japanese government's core objective of providing aid is to contribute to peace and development of the international community as a means of ensuring its own security and prosperity. It is pos-

https://www.gov.uk/government/uploads/system/uploads/attachment_data/file/482322/SID2015c.pdf).

sible to categorize Japan's ODA as occurring within the context of five basic priorities: supporting the self-help efforts of developing countries; taking a human security perspective; applying principles of fairness while noting particular problems of vulnerable groups and differences between the rich and poor as well as regional differences; making full use of Japanese experience and skills; and working cooperatively with the international community. To this end, Japan has agreed to four basic policies for ODA allocation, which are poverty alleviation, sustainable growth, commitment to global issues, and peace-building.

Japan's contributions of ODA are based on the belief that it will benefit from improving security and prosperity, goals which were widely supported by its public as well. It has been identified by the Ministry of Foreign Affairs that 48.8% of the respondents to a national opinion poll conducted by the Association for the Promotion of International Cooperation (APIC) in December 1997 were of the opinion that Japanese ODA "does benefit developing countries." By contrast, 14.4% felt that ODA was of "no benefit" (36.8% of the respondents stated that they were not sure).[5]

In the late 1990s, however, Japan faced fiscal strain, and in 1997, structural reforms were made to the fiscal budget, calling for a shift in the emphasis of ODA from quantity to quality. Consequently, ODA budget allocations were reduced when the government enacted a fiscal reform law mandating cuts to ODA budgets. However, the Japanese government continued its efforts to implement ODA projects more efficiently and effectively, and an emphasis was set on building an effective evaluation system.[6]

Inefficiencies of Bilateral Aid

As early as 1969, the Pearson Commission warned that there were too many aid donors. Since then the number of aid donors has continued to increase. Today there are about 100 major official aid donors, including bilateral agencies, international and regional financial institutions, different UN organizations and agencies and 100 additional smaller agencies. The 23 OECD DAC member states have been providing over 95% of total bilateral ODA, while the rest is made of contributions from 14 non-DAC member countries.

---

5 Ministry of Foreign Affairs of Japan, "ODA Evaluations and Recent Trends in Japanese ODA," http://www.mofa.go.jp/policy/oda/evaluation/1998/japanese.html, last visited December 2008.

6 *Ibid.*

With this proliferation of aid donors, there is growing concern about possible inefficiencies in the development aid system. Since the international community currently lacks an overall governing system in supervising the flow of aid, the increase in aid donors may result in fragmentation of aid donors or increased inefficiency due to overlapping aid programs of diverse donors. Promoting the effectiveness of aid is an important agenda for donors, but with an overflow of donors with different political objectives central to their aid policies, it is highly possible that aid will not be disbursed evenly among recipients, but concentrated on specific countries. Within these recipient countries, aid agencies will propose different aid programs, but since the recipient country lacks a substantial governing structure to organize these aid programs, or the power to reallocate aid according to domestic needs, this can result in overlapping of aid for certain programs, thereby diminishing effectiveness. The complexities of implementation and lack of organizational structure within developing countries is the foremost concern for donor countries which has been intensified through the increasing numbers of bilateral donor relations.

A further concern of bilateral aid is excessive donor orientation of aid programs. In many cases of bilateral aid, aid programs are designed by donor countries and presented to recipient countries without consultations regarding recipient's country-specific needs. This type of aid will increase the threat of aid dependency for recipient countries. They will become increasingly dependent on countries that provide them with aid, and the donors will gain influential power, which can threaten the political and social independence of the recipient state. A central interest within the international community is promoting ownership and strengthening partnership among recipients and donors. It is evident that 'take it or leave it' program proposals by donor countries increase inefficiencies, and are thus discouraged by the international community, but nevertheless a large proportion of bilateral aid remains donor-oriented. These circumstances will lead to a waste of resources, further leading to a gap in the total volume of aid provided in terms of donor budget allocation and actual aid impact in the recipient country.

The influence of a donor country on a recipient is strongest in the case of bilateral aid, which is not always a bad thing. Some attribute the effective implementation of the Marshall Plan to the fact that the US was the predominant aid provider at the time. However, when any country is exposed to large amounts of bilateral aid, it is threatened by the possibility of aid dependency. Aid dependency refers to the power that a dominant donor country has on any single recipient country. The threat of the donor withdrawing its aid program from the recipient country becomes large enough for the donor to gain power over the government of the recipient country.

In light of the political motivations that underlie donor decisions in providing aid, development assistance in the form of bilateral aid has been recognized as a policy form that can contain imperialistic objectives. Donor countries can use aid as leverage to influence recipient countries with their cultural values and ideals, which in essence can be perceived as a means of imposing imperialism. Even without intending to do so, bilateral assistance exposes recipient countries to cultural infusions by donor countries.

5.2 Multilateral Aid

Multilateral assistance takes the form of contributions to funds managed by multilateral agencies, especially those of the United Nations. Contributions may come in the form of membership subscriptions or discretionary contributions. The biggest difference that distinguishes multilateral aid from bilateral aid is the fact that in the case of multilateral aid, the donor does not have any implementation power. It is with these contributions that the multilateral institution acts as an independent entity in designing and implementing aid programs in developing countries.

Box 5.1 When are multilateral contributions made?

Multilateral contributions are those made to a recipient institution that:

Conducts all or part of its activities in favor of development.

Is an international agency, institution or organization whose members are governments, or a fund managed autonomously by such an agency.

Pools contributions so that they lose their identity and become an integral part of its financial assets. If, however, the donor specifies the recipient or other aspects of disbursement (e.g. purpose, terms, total amount, reuse of any repayments), effectively controlling the disposal of the funds they contributed, the contribution is considered to be bilateral.

Multilateral aid is ODA provided through multilateral organizations. It has been encouraged by the international community because it is widely accepted that multilateral aid is less politically driven, more likely to be channeled to recipients on the basis of need, and has fewer conditions attached.

The first type of multilateral aid provider is international financial institutions (IFIs), which includes multilateral and regional banks and lending institutions. Examples of these types of organizations include the World Bank and the International Monetary Fund (IMF), or regional development banks like the Asia Development Bank, the African Development Bank (AfDB), the Inter-American Development Bank (IDB), and the Caribbean Development Bank (CDB). The World Bank group includes a number of different institutions, four of which play major roles in the development of poor countries: the International Bank for Reconstruction and Development (IBRD), the International Development Association (IDA), the International Finance Corporation (IFC) and the Multilateral Investment Guarantee Agency (MIGA). Both multilateral and regional banks conduct similar projects, but projects carried out by regional banks are smaller in size because they distribute funds into different types of projects.

The second type of multilateral aid provider includes large international organizations such as the United Nations, or the OECD. The United Nations continues to play an important role in multilateral aid. There are thirty separate UN bodies or groupings involved in humanitarian development work, all of which utilize aid funds. The Economic and Social Council (ECOSOC) has a primary role in coordinating development and humanitarian aid assistance programs. The UN's Office for the Coordination of Humanitarian Affairs (OCHA) has a world-wide presence and is responsible for coordinating the humanitarian aid of the UN and other agencies. The UN Development Group (UNDG) was formed to coordinate activities at the recipient country level.

There are also other multilateral aid funds and agencies. Some examples are global environmental funds, the Global Environment Facility and the Montreal Protocol Fund or different multilateral

Arab/OPEC funds. Global health funds have emerged, with an emphasis on assisting developing countries to protect their environment throughout the development process, or to fight diseases, such as AIDS, tuberculosis, or malaria. Some funds that have concentrated on promoting global health include the Global Fund to Fight AIDS, Tuberculosis and Malaria (GFTAM), and the Global Alliance for Vaccines and Immunization (GAVI), funded largely by the Bill and Melinda Gates Foundation.

The International Monetary Fund

The Articles of Agreement for the IMF were drafted and signed at the meeting in Bretton Woods in 1944. It was designed as an international monetary system that would foster full employment and price stability while allowing individual countries to attain external balance without imposing restrictions on international trade.[7]

From 1944 to 1971, it was required for member countries to fix their exchange rates to the US dollar, which was tied to gold at $35 per ounce. However, this system collapsed in 1971 as the dollar was seen as overvalued. Since the end of the Bretton Woods system, IMF members have been free to choose any form of exchange arrangement they wish: allowing the currency to float freely, pegging it to another currency or a basket of currencies, adopting the currency of another country, participating in a currency bloc, or forming a monetary union.[8]

President M. Buhari and the International Monetary Fund (IMF)

7 Paul Krugman, *International Economics: Theory and Policy* (Boston: Addison Wesley, 2003), 546.
8 IMF, "History," http://www.imf.org/external/about/history.htm, last visited December 2008.

IMF has responded to the balance of payments difficulties of many countries through various loan and debt relief programs including the Trust Fund, Enhanced Structural Adjustment Facility, and Multilateral Debt Relief Initiative (MDRI). The IMF's fundamental mission is to help ensure stability in the international financial system. It does so in three ways: keeping track of the global economy and the economies of member countries (surveillance); lending to countries with balance of payments difficulties (lending); and providing practical help to members (technical assistance).[9]

Since 2008, the IMF has been focusing on helping both less developed and developed countries to tackle the turmoil of global financial crisis. It has already provided loans and access to credit worth more than $100 billion to emerging markets including Belarus, Hungary, Iceland, Latvia, Pakistan, Serbia, Ukraine, Mexico, and others. Moreover, the IMF is planning to double its concessional loans to $11 billion in five years. For advanced economies, it proffers advice with respect to structuring fiscal stimulus packages. The IMF has been tracking financial environments and developments to provide up-to-date forecasts and recommendations to policymakers in order to restructure the international financial system.

World Bank Group

The World Bank, which is comprised of two development institutions, the International Bank for Reconstruction and Development (IBRD) and the International Development Association (IDA), was established in 1944 as a result of the Bretton Woods Conference.

9 IMF, "Our Work," http://www.imf.org/external/about/ourwork.htm, last visited December 2008.

It has expanded into the World Bank Group with the association of five other institutions — IBRD, IDA, the International Finance Corporation (IFC), the Multilateral Guarantee Agency (MIGA), and the International Centre for the Settlement of Investment Disputes (ICSID).

The main objective of the World Bank is to reduce poverty in less developed countries by providing financial, technical assistance and development programs.[10] In order to meet this objective, it has been focusing on ① building socio-political capacity; ② creating infrastructure; ③ developing financial systems; and ④ developing ways to combat corruption in those countries in order to address its global challenge to poverty. The World Bank has particularly been focusing on following six agendas:[11]

- poverty reduction and sustainable growth in the poorest countries, especially in Africa;
- solutions to the special challenges of post-conflict countries and fragile states;
- development solutions with customized services, as well as financing for middle-income countries;
- regional and global issues that cross national borders--climate change, infectious diseases, and trade;
- greater development and opportunity in the Arab world;
- and collaboration of the best global knowledge to support development.

International Bank for Reconstruction and Development (IBRD)

The International Bank for Reconstruction and Development (IBRD) aims to reduce poverty in middle-income and creditworthy poorer countries by promoting sustainable development through loans, guarantees, risk management products, and analytical and advisory services. The IBRD was established in 1944 as the original institution of the World Bank Group and is structured like a cooperative that is operated for the benefit of its 188 member countries.

The IBRD raises most of its funds in the world's financial markets and has become one of the most established lenders since issuing its first bond in 1947. The income that the IBRD has generated

10 In 2008, according to the World Bank website, the World Bank provided $23.6 billion for 279 projects in developing countries worldwide. The Bank is currently involved in more than 1,800 projects in virtually every sector and developing country.

11 The World Bank, http://web.worldbank.org, last visited December 2008.

over the years has allowed it to fund development activities and to ensure its financial strength, enabling it to lend at low cost and offer clients good borrowing terms.

At its Annual Meeting in September 2006, the World Bank committed to making further improvements to the services it provides to its members. In an effort to meet the increasingly sophisticated demands of middle-income countries, the IBRD is overhauling its financial and risk management products, broadening the provision of free-standing knowledge services and making it easier for clients to deal with the Bank.[12]

International Finance Corporation (IFC)

The International Finance Corporation is another member of the World Bank Group. Its purpose is to create opportunities for people to escape poverty and improve their lives by ① promoting open and competitive markets in developing countries; ② supporting companies and other private sector partners when there is a gap; and ③ helping to generate productive jobs and deliver essential services to the underserved. To meet these purposes, the IFC provides direct investments, advisory services, and other technical assistance.

The IFC emphasizes five strategic priorities for maximizing its impact on sustainable development: ① concentrating its focus on frontier markets, particularly the Small and Medium Enterprises (SME) sector; ② building long-term partnerships with emerging global players in developing countries; ③ promoting efforts to combat climate change, and environmental and social sustainability activities; ④ addressing constraints to private sector investment in infrastructure, health, and education; and ⑤ developing domestic financial markets through institution-building and the use of innovative financial products.[13]

Multilateral Investment Guarantee Agency (MIGA)

The MIGA's mission is to promote foreign direct investment (FDI) in developing countries to help support economic growth, reduce poverty, and improve people's lives. Since its inception in 1988, the MIGA has issued nearly 1143 guarantees, worth more than $28 bil-

12 The World Bank, "International Bank for Reconstruction and Development," http://web.worldbank.org/WBSITE/EXTERNAL/EXTABOUTUS/EXTIBRD/0,,menuPK:3046081~pagePK:64168427~piPK:64168435~theSitePK:3046012,00.html, last visited December 2008.

13 International Financial Group, "What We Do," http://www.ifc.org/ifcext/about.nsf/Content/WhatWeDo, last visited December 2008.

lion for projects in 155 developing countries.

The MIGA specializes in facilitating investments in high-risk, low-income countries, such as those in Africa and conflict-affected areas. The MIGA's technical assistance services also play an integral role in catalyzing FDI by helping developing countries define and implement strategies to promote investment. Moreover, the agency uses its legal services to further reduce possible impediments to investment. The MIGA helps governments and investors resolve their differences and ultimately improve the country's investment climate.[14]

Asian Development Bank (ADB)

The ADB is an international development finance institution. Its core mission is to help reduce poverty in its developing member countries and improve the quality of the lives of the people. It was established in 1996 and is currently headquartered in Manila. The ADB is financed by its sixty seven members, of which forty eight are from the region and 19 are from other parts of the globe. The ADB's main partners include member governments, the private sector, nongovernmental organizations, development agencies, community-based organizations, and foundations.

A long-term strategic framework, Strategy 2020, was adopted in 2008, through which the ADB has presented three complementary strategic agendas: inclusive growth, environmentally sustainable growth, and regional integration. The ADB utilizes loans, technical assistance, grants, advice, and knowledge in pursuit of its goals.

Although most lending is in the public sector and concentrated on governments, the ADB also provides direct assistance to private enterprises of developing countries through equity investments, guarantees, and loans. In addition, its triple-A credit rating helps mobilize funds for development.[15]

African Development Bank Group (AfDB)

The African Development Bank Group is comprised of the African Development Bank, the African Development Fund, and the Nigeria Trust Fund. Its mission is to help reduce poverty, improve living

14 Multilateral Investment Guarantee Agency, "About MIGA," http://www.miga.org/about/index_sv.cfm?stid=1588, last visited December 2008.

15 Asian Development Bank, "Our Vision- an Asia and Pacific Free of Poverty," http://www.adb.org/About/default.asp, last visited December 2008.

conditions for Africans and mobilize resources for the continent's economic and social development. Its shareholders include 53 African countries, known as regional member countries and 25 non-regional member countries, including countries from the Americas, Asia, and Europe.

The African Development Bank Group's primary objective is to promote sustainable economic growth to reduce poverty on the continent. It achieves this objective by financing a broad range of development projects and programs through ① public sector loans, including policy-based loans, private sector loans, and equity investments; ② technical assistance for institutional support projects and programs; ③ public and private capital investment; ④ assistance in coordinating development policies and plans of the regional member countries; and ⑤ grants of up to $500,000 in emergency support.[16]

The Economic and Social Council (ECOSOC)

The ECOSOC was established under the United Nations Charter as the principal organ to coordinate economic, social, and related work of the 14 UN specialized agencies, nine functional commissions and five regional commissions. The Council also receives reports from 11 UN funds and programs. The ECOSOC serves as the central forum for discussing international economic and social issues, and for formulating policy recommendations addressed to Member States and the United Nations system. It is responsible for ① promoting higher standards of living, full employment, and economic and social progress; ② identifying solutions to international economic, social and health problems; ③ facilitating international cultural and educational cooperation; and ④ encouraging universal respect for human rights and fundamental freedoms.

It has the power to make or initiate studies and reports on these issues. It also has the power to assist the preparations and organization of major international conferences in the economic and social and related fields and to facilitate a coordinated follow-up to these conferences. With its broad mandate, the Council's purview extends to over 70% of the human and financial resources of the entire UN system.[17]

16 African Development Bank, "About Us," http://www.afdb.org/en/about-us/profile/who-weare/, last visited December 2008.

17 United Nations Economic and Social Council, "Background Information," http://www.un.org/ecosoc/about/, last visited December 2008.

Office of Coordination of Humanitarian Affairs (OCHA)

In 1998, as part of the Secretary-General's program of reform, the Department of Humanitarian Affairs (DHA) was reorganized into the Office for the Coordination of Humanitarian Affairs (OCHA). Its mandate was expanded to include the coordination of humanitarian response, policy development and humanitarian advocacy.

OCHA's mission is to mobilize and coordinate effective and principled humanitarian action in partnership with national and international actors in order to: ① alleviate human suffering in disasters and emergencies; ② advocate for the rights of people in need; ③ promote preparedness and prevention; and ④ facilitate sustainable solutions.[18]

United Nations Development Group (UNDG)

The UN Development Group (UNDG) coordinates all the UN funds, programs, agencies, departments, and offices that play a role in development. The group's common objective is to deliver more coherent, effective and efficient support to countries seeking to attain internationally agreed development goals, including the Millennium Development Goals.

It was established by the Secretary-General in 1997 to design system-wide guidance that coordinates, harmonizes and aligns UN development activities. The group strengthens the UN development system at the country level, prepares it to meet future challenges and ensures that operations are conducted in accordance with mandates from UN governing bodies such as the General Assembly.

By strengthening the UN Resident Coordinator System and helping UN organizations work together in new and better ways, the UNDG generates synergies and efficiencies that increase the impact of UN programs and policy advice. Coordination of development operations promotes more strategic support for national plans and priorities, makes operations more efficient, and reduces transaction costs for governments. This helps the UN to be a more relevant and reliable partner for governments.[19]

Global Environment Facility (GEF)

The Global Environment Facility (GEF) is a global partnership of

18 OCHA, "OCHA Mission Statement," http://ochaonline.un.org/AboutOCHA/tabid/1076/Default.aspx, last visited May 2009.

19 UDG, "About the UNDG," http://www.undg.org/index.cfm?P=2, last visited May 2009.

183 countries, international institutions, civil society organizations and the private sector to address global environmental issues while supporting nation-wide sustainable development initiatives. It provides grants for projects related to six focal areas: biodiversity, climate change, international waters, land degradation, the ozone layer, and persistent organic pollutants.

The GEF is also the designated financial mechanism for a number of multilateral environmental agreements (MEAs) or conventions, including the Convention on Biological Diversity, United Nations Framework Convention on Climate Change, Stockholm Convention on Persistent Organic Pollutants, and UN Convention to Combat Desertification.

The Global Environment Facility was established in October 1991 as a $1 billion pilot program in the World Bank to assist in the protection of the global environment and to promote environmentally sustainable development. In 1994 at the Rio Earth Summit, the GEF was restructured and moved out of the World Bank system to become a permanent, separate institution.[20]

Global Fund to Fight AIDS, Tuberculosis and Malaria (GFTAM)

The Global Fund to Fight AIDS, Tuberculosis and Malaria (GFTAM) was officially formed in 2002. In January of 2009, it became an independent International Financial Institution (IFI). The Global Fund is a unique global public/private partnership dedicated to attracting and disbursing additional resources to prevent and treat HIV/AIDS, tuberculosis and malaria. This partnership between governments, civil society, the private sector and affected communities represents a new approach to international health financing.

Since its creation, the GFTAM has approved funding of $11.4 billion for more than 550 programs in 151 countries. It is responsible for nearly a quarter of all international funding to fight AIDS around the world. It also provides 82% of the funding for tuberculosis and 50% of the funding for malaria.[21]

Global Alliances for Vaccines and Immunization (GAVI)

Launched in 2000, the GAVI Alliance is a global health partnership

20 Global Environment Facility, "What Is the GEF?" http://www.gefweb.org/interior_right.aspx?id=50, last visited May 2009.

21 Health GAP, "History of the Global Fund," http://www.healthgap.org/gfatm.htm, last visited May 2009.

representing stakeholders in immunization from both private and public sectors: developing world and donor governments, private sector philanthropists such as the Bill & Melinda Gates Foundation, the financial community, developed and developing country vaccine manufacturers, research and technical institutes, civil society organizations and multilateral organizations like the World Health Organization (WHO), the United Nations Children's Fund (UNICEF) and the World Bank.

The Alliance members' objectives are to: ① accelerate access to existing underused vaccines; ② strengthen health and immunization systems in countries, and ③ introduce innovative new immunization technology, including vaccines. To meet its missions to save children's lives and protect people's health, the GAVI has announced the GAVI Alliance Strategy for 2007-2010 and has also been making contributions to meet goals outlined in the WHO/UNICEF Global Immunization Vision and Strategy. The target on pentavalent vaccines introduction were met in 2012 while vaccines for pneumococcal disease and rotavirus were met in 2014. However, the actual vaccine coverage is still behind the target except for the case of pneumococcal disease which the target of 40% were met in 2015. The rest two coverages fell short; pentavalent vaccines by 8% and rotavirus by 7%.

As a result of the GAVI Alliance support, the WHO projects that 3.4 million future cumulative deaths caused by Hepatitis B, Haemophilus influenza type b (Hib) and pertussis have been averted. This is an increase of 600,000 on the estimate of future deaths averted at the end of 2007. Moreover, the WHO projects a cumulative 213 million additional children have been reached with GAVI-supported underused vaccines from 2000 to 2008.[22]

22 GAVI Alliance, http://www.gavialliance.org/, last visited May 2009.

Benefits of Multilateral Aid

There has been a proliferation of multilateral aid agencies, but over 90% of multilateral aid is still provided by 15 agencies, while the latter 10% is dispersed among 150 different multilateral institutions. The international community has supported the increase in multilateral aid agencies and aid funds for several reasons.

First, in order to achieve political objectives through aids, it is more efficient using multilateral aid than bilateral aid. Instead of direct participation in providing aid to specific countries, donor governments provide ODA to multilateral institutions, which manage accumulated donor funds to use in various projects for developing countries. Since the donor government does not have control over the actual aid implementation process, multilateral aid reduces potential inefficiencies caused by aid selectivity and aid conditionality. Aid selectivity is the process of selecting recipients of aid. One problem of aid selectivity is the unequal distribution of aid to developing countries. Multilateral institutions must also go through the toilsome process of selecting where to provide aid, but compared to individual donor countries, political interests are not as influential in determining these decisions.

The biggest problem of aid conditionality is that it distorts aid implementation by increasing inefficiency. Many bilateral aid donors continue to provide aid to selected countries. Moreover, specific conditions for procurement are outlined before aid is provided to these countries. Donor countries can profit by providing tied aid, which results in economic gains through procurement or employment opportunities for domestic personnel. In extreme cases of tied aid, a majority of aid actually flows back into the domestic economy of the donor country by setting restrictions on aid flows through enforcement of various conditions.

Aid Harmonization

The importance of aid harmonization is presented within the Paris Declaration of Aid effectiveness. The Paris Agenda refers to a commitment to reform the delivery of development assistance entailing ① systematic support for recipient country plans to achieve development; ② the increased use of national administration systems; and ③ a more coordinated and predictable action among multiple aid actors. It has achieved an agreement in principle, which is set on observable targets for changes in donor, recipient and joint behaviors. The significance of harmonizing aid has emerged with the increasing participation of various actors in development assistance and which are also in accord with current trends that encourage multilateral aid in place of traditional bilateral aid projects.

Multilateral aid has the potential to bring the global community closer together. It will be difficult to construct a proper network that includes diverse types of actors within a framework so as to promote aid effectiveness, but increasing and developing strong multilateral institutions is a step in the right direction. The transformation from bilateral to multilateral aid will minimize the pursuit of individual interests and donor funds will be allocated to increase effectiveness in the most needed areas, limiting the temptation to use aid as a policy tool. Multilateral aid also adheres to global trends of cooperation and collaboration. A fundamental change within the global economy is that countries understand that each nation is now set within the context of a regional and global atmosphere, and the increasing linkages among countries have made it important for countries to cooperate to facilitate development. The failure or devastation of any single country can impact its neighboring countries and these effects will continue to spill over to affect other countries. With globalization, it has become impossible to contain policies within domestic boundaries. In fact, closed policies have posed problems for countries because the international community is encouraging liberalization of policies.

Challenges of Multilateral Aid Efforts

The increasing number of aid donors has complicated the sphere of development aid by building a complex web with diverse international actors. Within these complexities, an overlap between different actors exists, including both bilateral and multilateral institutions and agencies. The Brandt Commission recognized the increasing rise in the number of multilateral agencies with concern, arguing that this growth had already led to fragmented and diffused activity, overlapping responsibilities and organizational rivalries.[23]

This is evidenced in many cases. The United Nations system has received criticisms for the extensive overlap between and across organizations. Different organizations within the UN implement similar aid projects or programs. For example, UNESCO, the WB, UNICEF and UNFPA are all directly involved in education; the FAO, IFAD, WB and WFP are involved in agriculture; the WHO,

23 Taken from the Brandt Commission Papers (1980).

WB, UNICEF, and UNFPA all deal with health; and UNCTAD, the WB, and the World Trade Organization (WTO) are all involved in trade issues.

In addition to inefficiencies posed by unnecessary overlap of institutions and agencies, a second aspect of concern is that multilateral institutions remain predominantly donor-orientated. Most membership of international organizations is composed of developed countries and the international community still lacks an effective institution that revolves around developing countries. With increasing interest in promoting partnerships, there has been considerable effort to include participation of developing countries. Partnerships aim to emphasize the importance of ownership and empowerment of recipient countries. Regardless of these efforts, there still exists an imbalance within international agencies, which give more weight to initiatives of the developed countries.

Before multilateral assistance can increase its effectiveness, it is necessary to construct a broader cooperation mechanism between developed and developing countries. One way to give developing countries a stronger voice in these issues would be strengthening South-South cooperation. Increased exchange of resources, technology, and knowledge between developing countries can counter the predominance of donor-oriented policies by allowing recipient-based perspectives to flourish. For recipient countries to strengthen their voice within the international arena, it will be necessary for developing partners to form a consensus of common ideas regarding these issues. In order to achieve this, developing countries should not limit their efforts to governmental contacts but need to encourage the involvement of non-governmental organizations and civil societies.

5.3 Multi-bi Aid

One of the emerging aid types in international development and co-operation is multi-bi aid. Earmarked by sector, theme, and country or region, it is defined as bilateral aid, even if it is routed through multilateral agencies.[24] Earmarked aid is called "non-core" or "multi-bi aid" and DAC statistics count this type of aid as bilateral aid.[25] According to the DAC categorization, multilateral aid is ①

24 OECD, *2008 DAC Report on Multilateral Aid* (Paris: OECD, 2009), 26.

25 *Ibid.*, 21.

made to an international institution whose members are governments and which conducts all or a significant part of its activities in favor of development; and ② those contributions are pooled with other amounts received so that they lose their identity and become an integral part of the institution's financial assets.[26] Multi-bi aid is delivered by a multilateral system to which the donor country belongs, but multilateral agencies do not have the authority to decide where and how pledged aid is used. As donors make aid conditional by earmarking for specific objectives, it is instead considered as "bilateral aid."

International Trends on Multi-bi Aid

The reasons why donor countries prefer multi-bi aid are that donors believe multi-bi assistance is an effective tool to achieve aid goals, increase the synergy effect with bilateral aid, and expand political influence over multilateral agencies.[27] Through multi-bi aid using multilateral institutions, donor countries are able to deliver their aid to the countries where donors do not have their own field offices. By doing so, donor countries can complement their bilateral aid flows and reduce administrative costs. In addition, multi-bi aid is a tool that decision makers in the donor government use to appeal to tax payers because it is easier to incorporate national policy interests rather than funneling aid purely through a multilateral channel. It is also believed that multi-bi is an option which can mitigate the issue of aid fragmentation which is commonly identified in bilateral aid flows. Multi-bi aid also allows donor countries to maintain their focal sector and area in ODA and political influence over multilateral institutions.[28] Multilateral agencies do not avoid this type of multi-bi aid because it allows them additional financial resource flows and project opportunity.[29]

The portion of multi-bi aid gradually increased from 28% in 2007 to 33.3% in 2012. In regional allocation, Sub-Saharan Africa counts for 40% while 20% of the allocation counts for South and

26 *Ibid.*

27 Yul Kwon et al., "*Dajawonjoeui hyogwajeok silhangeul wuihan tonghapchujinjeonryak [Korea's Multilateral Aid: Recent Developments and Future Challenges]*" (Seoul: KIEP, 2013), 20.

28 OECD, *2012 DAC Report on Multilateral Aid* (Paris: OECD, 2009): 6, 28; Jione Jung, et al, "Woorinara dajawonjo chujin jeonryakgwa jungchakgwaje *[Enhancing the Effectiveness of South Korea's Multilateral Aid]*" (Seoul: KIEP, 2010), 115-116.

29 Jione Jung et al., "Woorinara dajawonjo chujin jeonryakgwa jungchakgwaje *[Enhancing the Effectiveness of South Korea's Multilateral Aid]*" (Seoul: KIEP, 2010), 115-116.

Central Asia. In the sector aspect of multi-bi aid, humanitarian aid slightly decreased, but it increased in the sectors of economic infrastructure and service, government and civil society.[30] Among UN agencies and funds in 2011, the top five recipients of multi-bi aid, who received over 80% of all multi-bi funding, were the World Food Programme (WFP), United Nations Development Programme (UNDP), United Nations' Children's Fund (UNICEF), United Nations High Commissioner for Refugees (UNHCR), and World Health Organization (WHO).[31]

Figure 5.1 DAC Donors' Core Multilateral and Non-Core(multi-bi) Multilateral ODA (in constant 2011 USD million)

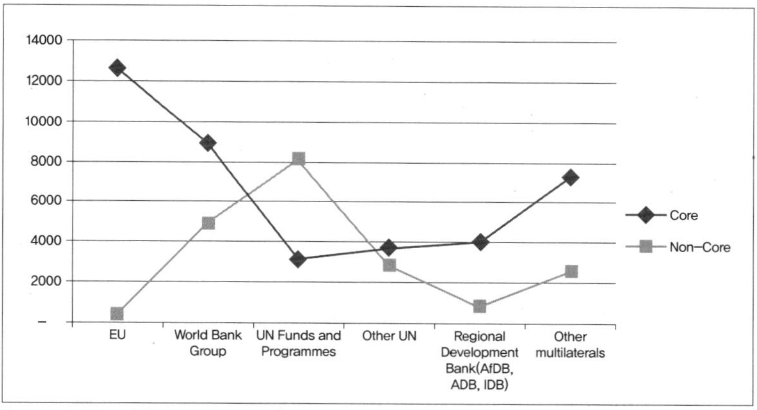

Source: OECD DAC (http://www.oecd.org/dac/aid-architecture/multilateralaid.htm), last visited June 2014.

In 2011, DAC donors' multi-bi ODA was $19,800 million dollars, which is a half of $40,900 million dollars of multilateral (core) ODA. The countries that show high levels of multi-bi aid compared to multilateral aid were Australia, Iceland, Canada, United States, and Norway in that order. The United States, United Kingdom, Canada, Japan, Australia were the highest multi-bi aid countries in volume. The UN recognizes core resources, which is un-earmarked aid funneled through the multilateral institutions, as a desirable financial flow than can promote coherence and harmonization in aid and its effectiveness so the funds do not need to be put aside for

30 OECD DAC, "Data on total use of multilateral system: All DAC members," http://www.oecd.org/dac/aid-architecture/multilateralaid.htm, last visited June 2014.

31 OECD DAC, *The DAC Multilateral Aid Report in 2013-14* (Paris: OECD, 2013), 7.

the purposes of the donors. The non-core resources, which are the opposite as the name may suggest, are contributions from various sources earmarked for certain purposes. The United States and Japan are two countries giving the same amount of the core and non-core ODA through the World Bank and UN Funds but countries like the United Kingdom, Canada and Australia prefer core ODA through the World Bank and allocate more than a half of non-core ODA to UN Funds and Programs.

With regard to the top five multi-bi donors' aid allocation by region, the United States, United Kingdom, and Canada provided Sub-Saharan Africa region with most of their multi-bi aid, and Japan and Australia's multi-bi aid for South and Central Asia was 58% and 32% for Far East Asia. By sector, 64% of the United States' contributions through multilateral institutions in 2011 were concentrated on 'humanitarian aid.' However, the other four countries spread their multi-bi aid between economic infrastructure and service, government and civil society, education, and health as well as humanitarian aid.[32]

Limits of Multi-bi Aid

Despite the increasing ratio of multi-bi aid in international development and cooperation, there are limits to this practice. First of all, there is a fundamental limit of multi-bi aid in that donor countries decide which sector and which region or country will be the beneficiary. Although this is not entirely an intrinsic limitation of multi-bi aid, like other types of ODA and aid, it is prone to increase 'aid orphans' as a result of insufficiently coordinated aid. Second, multi-bi aid can mitigate the limitation of aid fragmentation which is a common problem identified in bilateral aid, but it also can weaken accountability of aid by disaggregating responsibility between the donor country and multilateral agencies in charge of implementation. Third, it can weaken the autonomy of multilateral institutions' policymaking on aid.[33] Donor countries utilizing the form of multi-bi aid in aid delivery seek to enhance their influence on aid policymaking and the decisions of multilateral agencies, and that can

32 OECD DAC, http://www.oecd.org/dac/aid-architecture/multilateralaid.htm, last visited June 2014.

33 OECD DAC, *2011 DAC Report on Multilateral Aid* (Paris: OECD, 2012), 16; Hyuk-Sang Sohn et al., *A Study on Multilateral Aid Strategies of OECD/DAC Members and Policy Implications for South Korea* (Seoul: KIEP, 2013), 41.

cause confrontations with multilateral agencies.[34] Last, this kind of funding weighs heavily on the total budget of some UN funds/agencies and it may increase these organizations' reliance on non-core funding. In 2011, for example, the WFP's non-core funding was almost eight times larger than core funding, accounting for 88% of its total financial inflows. The non-core share of total funding was between 78% and 68%.[35]

Table 5.1 Advantages and Disadvantages of Non-Core Multilateral Aid (multi-bi ODA)

From the perspective of:	Advantages	Disadvantages
Partner country	- Trust fund steering committee may offer more representative governance arrangements for partner countries than organization's Board - Enhanced harmonization among donors, especially where it replaces parallel bilateral initiatives	- Trust fund steering committee may offer less representative governance arrangement for partner countries than organization's Board - Blurred lines of accountability in disbursement
Multilateral organization	- Increases overall resource envelope of the organization - If multi-donor, preferable to multiple parallel bilateral initiatives - For specific, critical and time-bound purposes, preferable to the creation of a new organization	- Hollows out governance, bypasses Board decisions - Increases transactions costs (including reporting) - May conflict with the organization's core policies of strategy
Bilateral donor	- Ability to focus specific sectors, regions, countries (including fragile states) where multilaterals have more expertise or a stronger presence to complement bilateral programming - Can make contributions more visible - Can circumvent onerous Board decisions - "Pilot" for setting up stand-alone funds or organization	- Core contributions from donors may subsidize non-core funds' administrative costs - "Multilateralization" of bilateral aid

OECD, *2011 DAC Report on Multilateral Aid* (Paris: OECD, 2012), 16.

The UN General Assembly expressed its concern over the increase of non-core funding which is earmarked aid, while emphasizing the importance of untied aid in international development

34 OECD DAC, *2011 DAC Report on Multilateral Aid* (Paris: OECD, 2012), 16; Hyuk-Sang Sohn et al., *A Study on Multilateral Aid Strategies of OECD/DAC Members and Policy Implications for South Korea* (Seoul: KIEP, 2013), 41.

35 OECD DAC, *The DAC Multilateral Aid Report in 2013-14* (Paris: OECD, 2013), 7.

and cooperation.

Box 5.2 UN General Assembly's Stance on Non-core (Multi-bi) Aid[36]

In 2008, the General Assembly issued a policy review on operational activities for development of the UN system at the 62nd session in March. Based on this policy review, the General Assembly adopted A/RES/62/208 and this resolution included the discussion on funding for operational activities for development of the UN system and reform of UN development system.

According to the resolution, the General Assembly emphasizes the importance of core contribution (multilateral aid), which is untied aid, in order to maintain the UN development system (para. 18, 20). Simultaneously, it recognizes that the increase of non-core resources contributes to the diversification of financing for development (para. 20). While the General Assembly raises the issue of increase of imbalance between core and non-core aid with the increase of non-core aid and the issue of aid effectiveness caused by fragmentation in aid operation (para. 21), it recommends donor countries increase funds and programs for the United Nations development system and specialized agencies (para. 19).

Dilemma and International Initiative

The United Nations launched the Multi-Partner Trust Fund (MPTFs) office to enhance coherence and efficiency at the country and global levels and to increase joint UN activities in 2006. The MPTF's office tackles major concepts, approaches and principles embodied in the Aid Effectiveness Agenda and the United Nations Reform initiative of 'Delivering as One.' Particularly, 'Delivering as One' tackles the issue of fragmentation of development financing and overlapping administration among various UN agencies.

Under the charge of the United Nations Development Group (UNDG), the UNDP manages the MPTF's office. The MPTF's office is operating $7.1 billion through 100 finance mechanisms. There are around 100 recipient countries participating in this scheme and 114 projects are operating under the coordination of the UN Resident Coordinator. MPTFs make public all information on

36 UN General Assembly, *Triennial Comprehensive Policy Review of Operational Activities for Development of the United Nations System*, A/RES/62/208 (19 December 2007), 5.

funds for UN agencies under the cooperation of developing country governments and donor governments, from the initial fund contribution, management, and annual reporting to audits.

Throughout this chapter we have taken a look at multilateral and bilateral aid programs and various actors that play parts in them. The imbalance among the donor organizations and lack of cooperation between them are pointed out as the hindrance to realizing the full potential of multilateral aids while multi-bi aids, which was brought about as a possible alternative to overcome such shortcomings, are being criticized for giving too much power to the donors instead of empowering the recipients through increasing non-core funds. However, we cannot say that the future for aid is dark and glim; through proper means that encourages more united forms of aid and that monitors the contribution and management the international community will get closer to achieve more unity and prosperity.

Chapter 5. Review Discussion Questions

1. Compare the implementation processes of bilateral and multilateral aid programs. How are they different? How are they similar?
2. Why has the international community encouraged multilateral aid? What are some of the potential benefits of multilateral aid programs?
3. There have been a number of large bilateral donors since the beginning of development aid. Why have these large donors preferred to provide bilateral aid?
4. Identify some concerns the international community has regarding bilateral aid practices.
5. How will increasing multilateral aid contribute to minimizing aid selectivity and aid conditionality?
6. What are some challenges that must be overcome before it is possible to increase effective implementation of multilateral aid programs?
7. Identify some of the main actors in international development assistance. How do the roles of these actors differ?

Chapter 6

NGOs in International Development Cooperation

"The phenomenal growth of nongovernmental organizations (NGOs) at both international and national levels is due to the changing attitude of donor agencies about development assistance and the increased demand for NGO services in Third World countries. NGOs are non-membership support organizations involved in relief, rehabilitation, or community development work in developed and, especially, developing or Third World countries. Considered part of the civil arena in society which also includes trade unions, people's associations and membership organizations, cooperatives and religious-based charities, NGOs provide a third approach to development between market-led and state-led strategies."[1]

There are a wide variety of non-government organizations (NGOs), ranging from multilateral development organizations to charity relief organizations. A core element of non-governmental organizations, and perhaps their greatest advantage, is that they are non-profit organizations involved in grassroots development projects.

Compared to the top-down implementation process of government donors, NGOs are able to provide a bottom-up approach to development assistance. A bottom-up approach is valuable for several reasons. First, it is able to provide a system of checks and balances. Since donor governments are balancing foreign aid on one hand and domestic interests on the other, it is difficult to behave solely in the best interests of recipient partner countries. As non-profit organizations, on the other hand, NGOs are not compromised by home country agendas. In these cases, NGOs are able to encourage donor governments to maintain a more balanced perspective. Second, NGOs are better able to understand recipient needs and desires. The involvement of NGOs can provide donor countries with a practical perspective during the aid implementation process because these organizations are able to conduct field research in recipient countries and provide valuable information and insights. Moreover,

1 J. Wagona Makoba, "Nongovernmental Organizations (NGOS) and Third World Development: An Alternative Approach to Development," *Journal of Third World Studies*, vol. 19, no. 1 (2002): 53-63.

NGOs can perform basic human-needs operations at a grassroots level in a more effective way than larger aid organizations because they are more flexible and adaptable.

Transnational NGO networks have constructed large networks of relationships to share information. For example, the capacity to collect and publicize credible information on human rights violations in parallel with state-level reporting is an important function of NGOs. The role of NGOs to provide an effective monitoring and evaluation mechanism has also been emphasized in development assistance activities.

Since the countries have grown closer together due to globalization that has increased economic, political and social ties among countries, compared to when nation states were the predominant actors within the international community, numerous non-state actors have now emerged. The diverse new actors have attempted to combine their work in an effort to collaborate and increase the effectiveness of many global issues. However, multilateral institutions need to organize and manage the different actors to establish a mechanism that effectively promotes global cooperation. These multilateral institutions contain the potential to become a tool for increasing effectiveness by promoting cooperation among these diverse actors. It is imperative to develop the role of multilateral institutions to partake a governing role so that it will be possible to organize the complexities and inefficient overlaps among actors that currently exist.

6.1 Non-Governmental Organizations (NGOs)

The term non-governmental organizations can refer to many different types of agencies, encompassing both local and global levels. NGOs that are based in developed countries are mostly considered northern NGOs, while those based in the developing countries are categorized as southern NGOs. Despite these differences, NGOs that work in the development sector, or Non-governmental Development Organizations (NGDOs), share certain commonalities. For one, they are all directly or indirectly involved in humanitarian and development work. However, they are distinct and separate from governments and private for-profit organizations because most NGOs are working on a non-profit basis.

International NGOs (INGOs) refer to organizations that work

across borders of different countries. Compared to the work of NGOs that concentrate on activities within domestic boundaries, INGOs engage in advocacy, lobbying and campaigning at the international level. INGOs can implement projects and programs with poor communities, and these activities can cover a variety of agendas and issues that are not related to humanitarian or government work, such as the environment or human rights.

The funds for NGO activities come from private donations, governments, and private foundations. The amount of ODA allocated by DAC member countries to NGOs increased by 62% between 2007 and 2009. In 2009, DAC members, excluding EU institutions, disbursed $15.5 billion to and through NGOs, accounting for 13% of total aid disbursements. Despite this increasing volume of money and the expanded role that NGOs have been playing in effectively implementing aid in recipient countries, one should not lose sight of the most important role played by NGOs—monitoring and evaluating aid implementation practices in donor and recipient countries.

Traditionally, the roles played by NGOs involved the support or implementation of specific projects and programs for poor communities, encompassing service delivery activities such as health, housing, education, water and sanitation, as well as activities to promote economic growth and well-being of peoples in impoverished countries. However, the purpose of the majority of NGO projects and programs today are to give poor people and poor communities a voice and the power to take control of their lives. In an attempt to empower poor populations, many NGOs have worked to strengthen and build the capacity of poor communities.[2]

Because the current international aid community has an extremely fragmented feedback loop, it is anticipated that NGOs will be able to play an important role by functioning as a mechanism that coordinates the involvement of donor and recipient countries within the whole aid process. The current process involves internal assessments by recipient countries in identifying country strategies for poverty reduction, which is then utilized by donor countries in aid implementation activities. The final stage of aid evaluation is left to donor countries for self-assessment, resulting in a donor-oriented evaluation that lacks the actual impact of aid as assessed by recipient countries at the point of destination. In order to increase

2 Roger C. Riddell, *Does Foreign Aid Really Work?* (London: Oxford University Press, 2007).

interactions among recipients and donors throughout the process, the involvement of an objective third party, such as NGOs, may prove to be effective.

Non-governmental organizations often have a high profile both within their domestic arena and abroad. At times, the general public is more aware of NGO activities than it is of the government's development work. NGOs can make a strong contribution to increasing public awareness of development issues, and partnerships with local NGOs help donors deliver humanitarian assistance because NGOs are able to work effectively with highly vulnerable groups.

NGOs also monitor and assess the activities of their government, other aid agencies or the private sector. The principal role of NGOs is to examine the impact of the aid provided by other relief and development agencies. They also aim to ensure that the poorer and more marginalized communities are included in development aid practices. The final role of NGOs is to monitor the quality of services provided by the private sector in order to ensure that they are affordable but also meet minimum standards.

Box 6.1 NGOs in the Philippines

The Philippines has one of the largest Non-Governmental Development Organizations (NGDOs) communities in the world. Development NGOs refer to NGOs that work directly or indirectly with grassroots and whose primary interventions include community and sectoral services. Philippines NGDOs have gained influential power in political and socioeconomic spheres through implementation of various social programs. For example, NGDOs have been successful in areas of national policies related to agrarian reform, environment, housing and urban land reform, decentralization and local governance, co-operatives, health reform, generics laws, gender and women's rights, and indigenous people's concerns.

According to the Securities and Exchange Commission, there were some 60,000 registered non-stock, non-profit organizations in 1995. 50,000 of these have been identified as NGDOs, while the remaining 10,000 are people's organizations.[3] In 2000, the estimated numbers of NGDOs working specifically in the field of providing social programs

3 Robert Gonzales, *A Strategy to Increase Participation of Philippines NGOs in the Policy Formulation and Programming of Official Development Assistance* (Asian Institute of Management, 1998).

and services ranged from 3,000 to 5,000 organizations. A problem that has emerged with the increasing numbers of NGOs in the Philippines is dependency on foreign donor grants, such as Northern non-government and official aid agencies. Most NGDOs rely on program and project funds from donor NGOs, through direct funding from official development assistance or through public service contracts. Unofficial estimates of donor dependency of Philippines NGDOs are estimated to be between 50% and 95% of their annual budgets.[4]

6.2 NGOs in the Field of Development

The term NGO encompasses a diverse range of organizations with differing institutional capabilities and interests. There are a number of prominent organizations leaving footsteps in the field of international development.

British Overseas NGOs for Development (BOND), which is one of those organizations, was established in 1993 and now has over 350 member organizations. It is a United Kingdom-based entity for non-governmental organizations that was created in an effort to promote and support the work of NGOs in the field of international development. It provides a network for diverse NGOs to cooperate and encourages its members to strengthen the quality and effectiveness of the sector through the exchange of experiences, ideas and information. Through this network, members exchange views and experiences to share best practices. BOND also provides a platform for collective advocacy so that member organizations can work together on specific issues with increased efficiency and to leverage more lobbying power.

The vision of BOND encompasses the core value of development, seeking a world without poverty, inequality or injustice in which human rights are upheld and the environment is protected. Its mission statement is to strengthen the quality and effectiveness of UK-based international development organizations and harness the power of collective action to influence public, private and political bodies in the pursuit of BOND's vision.

The International Institute for Sustainable Development (IISD),

4 Fernando Aldaba et al., "NGO Strategies Beyond Aid: Perspectives from Central and South America and the Philippines," *Third World Quarterly*, vol. 21, no. 4 (2000): 669-683.

established in 1990, is a Canada-based not-for-profit organization with a diverse team of more than 150 people located in over 30 countries. The IISD works on projects related to sustainable development. It is a policy research institute that engages decision-makers in government, business, civil society and other sectors in the development and implementation of policies. It emphasizes the importance of open and effective international negotiation processes.

The IISD engages in a range of issues related to sustainable development. For example, it works in areas of climate change and energy, economic developmental issues and foreign investment and governance for sustainable development. Other major directions of this organization's work include information society, international trade, measurement and assessment, natural resources, security and the future.

Green Cross International was founded upon the idea proposed by Mikhail Gorbachev (the former President of the USSR) in 1989 for an organization that would apply the medical emergency response model of the International Committee of the Red Cross to ecological issues and expedite solutions to environmental problems that transcend national boundaries. The mission of Green Cross International is to help ensure a just, sustainable and secure future for all by fostering a value shift and cultivating a new sense of global interdependence and shared responsibility in humanity's relationship with nature.

Green Cross International is involved in activities to prevent and resolve conflicts that result from struggles over natural resources. It also addresses the environmental consequences of wars and conflicts. In 1993, a mandate was created to safely eliminate weapons of mass destruction (WMDs) and mitigate the social, health, and environmental impacts of conflicts and nuclear, chemical, and biological contamination. It continues to serve as a core activity of Green Cross International. Finally, it works to promote values and behaviour changes, promoting programs that highlight the nexus between security, poverty and the environment.

Oxfam International was established in 1995 by a group of independent non-governmental organizations. The aim of this institution is to have a significant impact on poverty reduction and injustice by working together. Oxfam International implements long-term development programs in vulnerable communities. Today, there are seventeen member organizations in the Oxfam International confederation. They are based in Australia, Belgium, Canada,

Oxfam Germany

France, Germany, Great Britain, Hong Kong, India, Ireland, Italy, Japan, Mexico, Netherlands, New Zealand, Quebec, Spain and the United States.

Oxfam works in approximately ninety countries to overcome poverty and injustice. In collaboration with thousands of local partner organizations, Oxfam works with impoverished populations to protect their human rights and take control of their lives. The work of Oxfam is founded on the belief that ① poverty and powerlessness are avoidable and can be eliminated by human action and political will; ② basic human needs and rights can be met; ③ inequalities can be significantly reduced both between rich and poor nations and within nations; and ④ peace and substantial arms reduction are essential conditions for development.

Box 6.2 Oxfam Australia in Zimbabwe

Oxfam Australia has been working in Zimbabwe since 2001 to support 11 HIV and AIDS service organizations. It attempts to reduce the rate of new infections and strengthen community capacity to care for and support people infected with HIV.

20.1% of Zimbabwe's population is infected with HIV. This is the fifth highest in the world. Zimbabwe also has the fourth-lowest life expectancy. 1.7 million people are infected with HIV, but only 8% receive anti-retroviral treatment. Very few hospitals are equipped to provide adequate care. Oxfam Australia supports partners to provide integrated prevention, care and support services for orphans and vulnerable children and people living with HIV and AIDS. Local partners encourage people to adopt behaviors that reduce their vulnerability to HIV. They use educational plays, or establish youth clubs, and support groups to promote awareness within Zimbabwe in efforts to prevent the spread of HIV.

6.3 Transnational Networks

For the last twenty years, transnational network and activities have radically increased. In the 1990s, in fact, transnational exchange and cooperation was limited and largely restricted to the US and European countries. While American and European NGOs evolved from national organizations into international NGOs with local branches and offices scattered around the world, NGOs in developing countries had difficulty evolving due to a lack of financial and human resources, weak civil society and domestic political restrictions. Thus, they remained as the targets of aid from NGOs based in the western rich countries.[5]

Asian NGOs Expand Global Influence(The Asian Foundation)

The end of the Cold War and the spread of democracy in the

5 Daeseok Choi and Seokhyang Kim, "The Characteristics and Dynamics of NGO Networks in Northeast Asia," *Discourse* 201, vol. 10, no. 1 (2007): 106.

1990s provided a favorable operational environment for the activation of transnational networks for NGOs. Further, World Conferences organized by the UN in the 1990s to discuss trans-border agendas facilitated the building of transnational networks. The increase of face-to-face meetings at international conferences and growing awareness and consensus on the specific issues and agendas promoted building of transnational networks, and such networks developed into significant political actors of modern world politics. NGOs began to exert influence on the agenda setting and policymaking of the international community by widening their alliances and strengthening their solidarity.[6] The development of transportation and IT technology in the 20th century facilitated information and human resource exchange among NGOs, and provided effective tools for transnational network operations. In addition, globalization is gradually blurring national borders by framing national agendas and issues as cross border concerns and may even be contributing to the birth of a nascent global citizenship.[7]

Working Mechanism of Transnational Networks?

Constructivist scholars who examine the role of civil society in state policymaking focus their analysis on the role of NGOs. Margaret E. Keck, Kathryn Sikkink and Ann Florini in particular argue that NGOs and their transnational advocacy networks shape and change the policy and practice of states and international organizations. Audie Klotz in the area of anti-apartheid, David P. Forsythe and Kathryn Sikkink in human rights, Richard Price in banning landmines and Karl Raustiala in environmental institutions trace how norms and ideas have changed state policies and practices. Through their tremendous empirical studies, these scholars argue that non-state actors, such as NGOs and their transnational advocacy networks, play a significant political role in the process of state norm adoption and internalization.[8]

One of reasons that NGOs prefer building transnational networks is the 'boomerang effect.' The NGO uses external channels to pressure the target government when the channels to deliver the

6 *Ibid.*, 107.

7 Jinsoon Bae and Sungho Kang, "Study of Transnational NGO Network and Activities: Territory Issues and Conflict Resolution," *OUGHTOPIA*, vol. 24, no. 1 (2009): 37.

8 Kyungyon Moon, "The role of humanitarian NGO's: impact on South Korean food aid policy towards North Korea from 1995 to 2007," PhD Dissertation, Cranfield University (2011): 15.

NGO's demand or ideas are blocked. By appealing to the international community and its members through transnational networks, NGOs seek to pressure its own government or target government to change its behavior. If this boomerang effect did not exist, then governments could simply ignore the demands of domestic civil society actors or NGOs.[9]

Figure 6.1 Boomerang Effect[10]

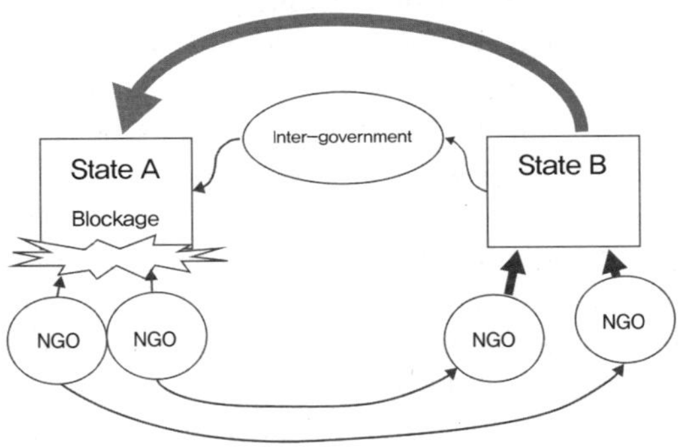

The "boomerang pattern," developed by Keck and Sikkink, to activate TANs, Interrupting Oppression in Repressive States Prone to Mass Violence: Are humanitarian technologies effective in local contexts where civil society encounters its predatory state-society counterparts?

NGOs that organize transnational networks increase opportunities in the international arena for countries to contact other national entities and strengthen their alliances and solidarity. Such transnational networks provide NGOs with access to targets, leverage, and information.[11] NGOs also share and exchange tactics, values and strategies for movements through transnational networks. In particular, transnational networks allow its members a common response strategy for advocacy and movement. Using these tools, strategies and solidarity, NGOs oversee and pressure local or central governments and target entities to induce changes in policy and practice. In addition, such networks enable NGOs to expand local issues and

9 Jinsoon Bae and Sungho Kang, "Study of Transnational NGO Network and Activities: Territory Issues and Conflict Resolution," *OUGHTOPIA*, vol. 24, no. 1 (2009): 37.

10 Margaret E. Keck, Kathryn Sikkink, *Activists Beyond Borders: Advocacy Networks in International Politics* (Ithaca: Cornell University Press, 1998): 13.

11 Jinsoon Bae and Sungho Kang, "Study of Transnational NGO Network and Activities: Territory Issues and Conflict Resolution," *OUGHTOPIA*, vol. 24, no. 1 (2009): 38.

agendas into national and transnational issues by framing them in particular ways. When NGOs are able to frame local issues as global issues, it allows them to combine a transnational social movement with a local movement, which creates powerful synergies. Such framing and combination can successfully incorporate global norms and ideas with those of local and national governments.[12]

Types of Transnational Networks

Transnational networks among NGOs can be categorized by networking style, issue and region. In practice, it is not easy to distinguish the differences between these networks, but theoretically there are five primary types of transnational networks.[13]

First, there is a 'transnational federation of NGOs', such as Oxfam and World Vision. A feature of this type of network is that the members share identical images and values that are already established by a central headquarters and use the same name for their organization. This network has national branches around the world and is considered to be one organization, but national branches have their own autonomy in operation and administration. As this network shares identical ideas and values and is linked together by a close network, it is considered to be the most systemic and incisive network.

The second type of network is a 'formal coalition' formed by differing NGOs. The meaningful function of a formal coalition for the various NGOs comprising it is that it provides an opportunity to discuss agendas and issues, develop common stances or policy, and cooperate. The member NGOs under this type of network do not share a common identity but maintain a loose confederation.

Third, there is an 'issue network' that is organized to jointly deal with specific issues. While the member NGOs of this type of network engage in their ordinary activities, the members also exchange information, organize joint campaigns and actions, and conduct cooperative projects and programs on issues of common interest.

Fourth, there is a 'transnational networking through aid'. De-

12 *Ibid.*, 38.

13 Youngrae Kim, Hasoo Lee and Kiho Lee, "A Comparative Study on the Transnational Network of Non-Governmental Organization (NGO) and the Strengthening Strategy of Civil Society: Korea, Japan and America," *Korean Association of International Relations*, vol. 41, no. 4 (2001): 11-13; Jinsoon Bae and Sungho Kang, "Study of Transnational NGO Network and Activities: Territory Issues and Conflict Resolution," *OUGHTOPIA*, vol. 24, no. 1 (2009): 5-31.

CONCORD: European NGO Confederation for Relief and Development

velopment sector is one of the fields that NGOs' participations are most active and these NGOs provide development programs and educations to the developing world through governmental ODAs and some aids from private channels. The NGOs in the development area were already covered by the chapter above.

Finally, there are networks called an 'issue caucus,' which are a similar type of issue-based grouping. This type of network focuses on lobbying as a major strategy. The unique feature of this network is that it is organized only when a conference on the specific issue is held, and therefore its activity is limited to certain periods. During inter-government or UN conferences, NGOs organize this type of network in order to pressure the target governments participating in the conference to incorporate the issues and agendas espoused by the NGOs. Due to these characteristics, these temporary alliances are also called a 'shadow network.'

Box 6.3 Better Aid

International NGOs organized the 'Civil Society International Steering Group' (ISG) in 2007 to participate in the governmental discussion of aid effectiveness at the 3rd High Level Forum on Aid Effectiveness held in Accra in 2008 and it developed into 'Better Aid.'[14]

Better Aid, as a transnational network, unites over 700 development organizations from civil society. It provides an open platform, and participating organizations can get involved in discussions and policy-influencing opportunities on a wide range of issues to deepen aid and development effectiveness. Better Aid drafts policy and positioning papers in participatory processes, and promotes its messages through advocacy activities on an international and national level.[15] The OECD DAC allowed Better Aid, representing global civil society, to participate in the Working Party on Aid Effectiveness.

6.4 Dynamics of NGOs Operation[16]

This section draws up a mechanism of how NGOs work. It draws particularly from the works of Richard Price, Keck and Sikkink.[17] This identifies four stages in the process of an NGO advocacy movement. These four stages are ① agenda setting, ② networking, ③ grafting and ④ institutionalization. At each stage of NGO advocacy, the different operational environments facilitate or circumscribe an NGO's influence on state policymaking. The capability to set the agenda, build networks, graft norms and institutionalize policy goals within state policy is different for each NGO and these different capacities are consequential. By tracing NGO activities through these four stages, therefore, it is possible to trace the evolution of NGO influence on state policymaking.

Agenda Setting

The NGO advocacy movement begins with 'agenda setting.' In this initial stage, an individual NGO generates attention towards issues that previously have not been a matter of public debate or that have

14 Hyuksang Sohn, "Busan HLF4 and Global Civil Society: Case Study of Better Aid and Open Forum," *Journal of International Development Cooperation*, vol. 2011, no. 3 (2003): 116-117.

15 Better Aid, "About Better Aid," http://www.betteraid.org/en/about-us/about-better-aid.html, last visited June 2014.

16 This part has been imported from, one of authors of this book, Kyungyon Moon's PhD Dissertation, 49-58. Kyungyon Moon, "The role of humanitarian NGOs: impact on South Korean fod aid policy towards North Korea from 1995 to 2007," Ph.D. Dissertation, Cranfield University, 2011.

17 Margaret E. Keck, *Activists Beyond Borders: Advocacy Networks in International Politics* (Ithaca, London: Cornell University Press, 1998), 1-38.

not been considered as problems. To set a problem as a policy agenda, Keck and Sikkink argue, NGOs first of all attempt to change the 'value context' in which policy debates take place.

To change the value context, NGOs exploit various tactics related to information politics and symbolic politics to make issues or ideas resonate with both the state and public or even the international community. First, NGOs try to disseminate facts related to the issues through the media, debates, hearings, testimonies, meetings on the issues and public campaigns. At this time, the facts must be reliable and well documented. Second, to maximize its effectiveness, information used by NGOs must be timely and dramatic. For this, as Deborah A. Stone argues, NGOs reframe the issues into sufficiently short and clear causal stories that identify the root of the problem, the responsible party or parties and credible solutions. This tactic allows NGOs to persuade the state and public more effectively. Thirdly, another tactic exploited by NGOs to make their issue appear more dramatic is the use of symbolic politics. NGOs try to reframe the issue by drawing on symbolic events. By developing convincing explanations for powerful symbolic events and linking them with the given issues, they catalyze domestic and transnational mobilization and thereby help set the new issues as policy agendas. In the same vein, whether a given issue is framed as a bodily harm issue or not is another factor that determines the success and failure of agenda setting. When a given issue is framed as potentially causing bodily harm to vulnerable and innocent people, the issue raises strong feelings that make it easier to resonate with the public. As Lisa McIntosh Sundstrom argues, whether the issue is framed by norms of the international regime or not can also make it relatively difficult or easy to set an agenda. When the given issues are framed by norms and ideas that are underpinned by international principles or regimes, NGOs find it easier to acquire support from the state or public.

In summary, agenda setting, as the first stage of NGO advocacy, is important in that it provides a basic groundwork for the next three stages: networking, grafting and institutionalization. An individual NGO's capability to generate reliable and well-documented information, to reframe the issue by symbolic events or norms and values, and to exploit various tactics to disseminate this information effectively are important factors required for agenda setting.

Networking

Networks are essential instruments for successful NGO advocacy movements. Since NGOs do not have powerful tools such as electoral punishment or financial power, their legitimacy in generating broad support from the public or leverage to proselytize government depend to a large extent on their ability to build different levels of networks. Networks enable NGOs to maximize their influence by facilitating exchange of information about ongoing issues and activities. Networks act as a coordinative body linking individuals and organizations, consolidating them and mediating relationships between individuals and between organizations at the individual level, inter-organizational level and transnational level.

Networking follows agenda setting. Networks, as Richard Price argues, are deemed to provide chances and forms of participation for the socialization of individuals and organizations to specific sets of values. For these reasons, NGOs endeavor to mobilize broad networks. These can be categorized into three levels: the individual level, inter-organizational level and transnational level. The individual level of networking refers to prior social ties operating as a basis for broader recruitment and networks. It becomes a locus of movement emergence. At the individual level of networking, relationships may be either direct or indirect, formal or informal, or private or public. Personal friends, relatives, colleagues and neighbors for instance may all affect individual decisions to become a member of a movement. In this stage, by exploiting various kinds of relationships NGOs endeavor to amplify their quantitative influence through the recruitment of volunteers, staff and activists and through public support. NGOs also seek to deepen their qualitative network by recruiting technicians and experts, bureaucrats, political elites and leaders, journalists and reporters.

Second, inter-organizational networking is another form of NGO networking. It has the same reasoning as individual networking, but there is more focus on building formal and public networks. This inter-organizational network provides the functions of information production and circulation, resource mobilization and the allocation of mobilized resources. Mario Diani and Doug McAdam argue that this inter-organizational network facilitates the negotiation of agreed goals, joint participation in specific actions and events, exposure to the media, personnel sharing and the protection of small individual organizations against oppositional groups.

Third, as Tomas Risse-Kappen has explored, transnational advocacy networks are one of the critical factors that ensure successful advocacy movements. By building transnational networks, particularly with norm and idea entrepreneurs, NGOs can acquire their legitimacy by relying on the international principles underpinning international society. Transnational networks also pressure the host or target states to comply with policies and practices that NGOs pursue. It furthermore provides expertise and material resources.

Grafting

What happens before the institutionalization of new norms or ideas introduced by NGOs and their networks? Richard Price uses the term 'grafting' to describe the process of norm adoption. This is a process in which new norms and ideas introduced by NGOs compete with existing norms within the public and the state's political system before finally being accepted as a norm governing state behavior or practices. If the previous two stages, agenda setting and networking, are the preparatory stages, the stage of grafting is a substantial stage. NGOs attempt to persuade the state and the public to embrace new norms and ideas through their advocacy activities and thereby seek to induce the state, their fundamental target, to change their policy and practice.

Before looking at how NGOs incorporate their voices into state policy and practice, it is necessary to examine what motives induce states to adhere to new norms and ideas. There are two motives: material motives and normative motives. Some states generally in need of material resources, such as the countries in the category of Least Developed Countries (LDC), tend to adopt international norms and ideas in order to acquire material compensation or aid rather than to promote their reputation in the international community. For NGOs targeting these countries, it is an effective strategy to make access to material resources conditional on the promotion of international norms and ideas. Conversely, more powerful states tend to have normative motives. For example, a state that desires to be perceived as an important global actor cares about its reputation or image as recognized by other states and international society. These states proclaim themselves to be and behave as protectors of liberal democratic values such as individual rights, equality of opportunity and the democratic decision-making process. Therefore, these states are sensitive to shaming, condemnation and blacklisting which are exploited by NGOs. To avoid reputational damage, these states adhere to norms and ideas introduced by NGOs. By incorporating the values and views of NGOs into state policy making, these countries attempt to show that they are a member of international society.

In this stage of grafting, then, how do NGOs incorporate their voices into state policy and practice? NGOs exert their influence through the mechanisms of persuasion and argument. NGOs disseminate important information, reframe a given issue by drawing on international principles, symbolize events more dramatically, build broader networks and link the issue explicitly with normative and material leverage. By doing so, they endeavor to persuade the public and states to adopt new norms and ideas.

NGOs deploy different strategies according to the type of target that they are seeking to persuade: public campaigns for the public and lobbying for the state. These advocacy strategies, though, are neither mutually exclusive nor competitive. NGOs in general exploit both public campaigns and lobbying policymakers simultaneously to achieve their fundamental goal. First, NGOs organize public campaigns to proselytize the public to change their norms and ideas embedded in their practice and attitude. NGOs exploit a broad range of 'promotion and recruitment' strategies using various communication skills. These include mass media such as TV, radio and newspapers, telecommunications such as the internet, telephone, email and paper-based letters, magazines and issue-specific reports and newsletters. NGOs also exploit face-to-face or door-to-door leafleting and petitioning, protests and parades, movement-sponsored events, conventions, festivals, conferences such as hearings and testimonies and seminars for the general public and experts. Second, as Thomas R. Dye argues, state policymaking flows not only upward from the masses but also downward from the governing elites. For the same reason, NGOs target political elites, leaders and bureaucrats who are deemed to be significant within state policymaking institutions. By lobbying these key policymakers, NGOs attempt to exert direct influence on the policymaking process. By recruiting lobbyists or establishing organizational units for lobbying within the organization, NGOs monitor and assess policymaking institutions and the roles and activities of individuals and groups of key policymakers in the state policymaking process. After identifying key players as lobbying targets, NGOs mobilize human or material resources which can be exploited in lobbying them successfully.

Another question raised is how one can explain or know which norms and ideas get selected and finally grafted? This question is related to methodological issue of how to identify norm and idea change. The difficulty in measuring normative change in the social sciences has often resulted in intentional exclusion of normative and ideational factors in foreign policy analysis. With the recent efforts of constructivist scholars, however, it has become possible to explore how norms and ideas are incorporated into state policy through the norm adoption process, which is referred to variously as 'socialization,' 'internalization,' or 'institutionalization.' It also became possible to assess which norms and ideas emerge, cascade and finally become internalized. By using empirical methods such as tracing changes in public opinion polls, the amount of media coverage, the number and scale of events such as parades and protests, and changes in human and material mobilization of norm advocacy organizations, it is possible to recognize norm grafting and adoption. A more convincing and comprehensive methodology to assess norm and idea grafting, however, is to examine the stage of norm institutionalization within the state policymaking structure.

Institutionalization

'Institutionalization' is the final stage of incorporating NGO influence into state policy. The notion of 'institutionalization' means to what extent the influence of NGOs is embedded in the state's constitutional, regulative and judicial system, and in the attitudes and beliefs of political actors such as political leaders, politicians and bureaucrats. The different level of institutionalization means, as Robert O. Keohane and Friedrich V. Kratochwil argue, the strength of norms and ideas that various entrepreneurs seek to resonate with the target states. Since NGOs' fundamental goal is to incorporate their advocacy movements into state policy and practice, it is important to assess to what extent NGOs have changed state policy and practice. To assess the influence of NGOs in state policymaking, this section distinguishes the institutionalization of NGO influence into four types: 'state agenda setting,' 'discursive position change,' 'institutional change' and 'policy change and rule-consistent behavior.'

The first type of institutionalization of NGO influence can be identified from changes in 'state agenda.' NGOs endeavor to pressure their government to adopt the issues that had never previously been a matter of public debate. When these discussions are held at official and public places such as conferences, meetings, or seminars convened or sponsored by the government or within the policymaking process in executive or legislative bodies, it signifies that the issue begins to germinate as a 'state agenda.' Although it is difficult to identify the existence of such debates when they are managed informally or in secret forums, as time goes on these kinds of debates rise to the surface, and then one can say that it is the beginning of state policy change.

The second type of institutionalization is changes in the state's discursive position. NGOs pressure the state to support their norms and ideas. When the states change their position in relation to norms and ideas espoused by NGOs by making public pronouncements and commitments or supporting international covenants, laws and conventions, this second type of institutionalization occurs. The public pronouncements or remarks themselves, however, do not carry an obligation to do anything. Since there is no enforcement mechanism in international politics to compel states to comply with their commitment to international conventions or declarations, this second type of change is sometimes exploited by the state to divert NGOs or to save face temporarily.

The third type of institutionalization generally comes after verbal or normative changes in domestic and international politics: changes in 'institutional procedures' of the state policymaking process. NGOs pressure the state to incorporate their ideas and norms into state policymaking processes. In this process, NGOs persuade the state to establish 'official consulting bodies' or 'councils' for the discussion of issues within the government institutions or to change state decision-making procedures and institutions. These procedural and institutional changes contribute to the increase of opportunities for NGOs to contact key policymakers within the state policymaking process. This change in institutional procedures becomes a precondition that leads to actual policy changes in the future.

The final type of institutionalization of NGO influence is state 'policy change' and 'rule-consistent behavior.' These two types are closely related but need to be differentiated. The main criterion for distinguishing between these two types is whether the states 'consistently' comply with their policy commitments or not. In the stage of 'policy change,' new policies initiated or consulted by NGOs are established. The states incorporate new norms and ideas into its policies by adopting domestic policies, legislation and international conventions. They try to establish relevant institutions and procedures to implement new policy. Despite state policy change, however, there can be still inconsistencies between the state policy and its actual behavior. In this sense, Kathryn Sikkink, Margaret E. Keck, and Thomas Risse-Kappen differentiate the stage of 'policy change' from the stage of 'rule-consistent behavior.' According to their differentiation between these two stages, the stage of 'policy change' can be defined as 'prescriptive status' that precedes 'rule-consistent behavior.' As the final stage of 'norm compliance' and 'self-reliance,' the stage of rule-consistent behavior comes when the states consistently commit themselves to their policy by exerting enforcement power as well as by making verbal or legislative commitments regardless of the existence of external monitoring or pressure. This stage of 'rule-consistent behavior' thus comes when norms and ideas introduced by NGOs are fully institutionalized internally and organizationally so that "national governments are continuously pushed to live up to their claims."

Chapter 6. Review Discussion Questions

1. What is the potential role of NGOs in aid evaluation practices? What needs to be done for NGOs to partake in coordinating the involvement of donor and recipient countries in the foreign aid process?
2. How can the impact or influence of NGOs in state policymaking be recognized or measured?
3. What are the factors for successful NGO movement or a key leverage for their movement?
4. What role are NGOs playing in the sector of international development and cooperation?
5. What are the most important factors in agenda framing for NGO movement and advocacy?
6. Why do NGOs organize transnational networks and how do they exploit such networks?

Chapter 7

Private Sector & Public-Private Partnership (PPP)

"Donors have increased their engagement with the for-profit private sector to catalyse contributions to development objectives. Likewise, partner countries are recognising the private sector in national poverty reduction and development plans. New collaborations are forged, most notably so called public-private partnerships (PPPs), to combine the strengths of different stakeholders."[1]

7.1 Private Sector

The Private Sector Development Strategy (PSD) was established by the Asian Development Bank (ADB) to create enabling conditions for private businesses to strive, to generate business opportunities for the private sector in ADB-financed public sector projects and to catalyze private investments through direct financing, credit enhancements and risk mitigation instruments. The ADB attempts to provide opportunities for private sector involvement, especially in the provision of essential goods and services. Private investment in infrastructure projects can assist public budgets, and also improve the delivery and efficiency of essential services and extend these to the poor.

An example of PSD is the gas transportation project in Indonesia in 2004. Indonesia is particularly well endowed with natural gas resources and 70% of produced gas is exported through pipelines as liquefied natural gas. Unfortunately, Indonesia lacks the gas infrastructure required to meet potential domestic demands. As a result, the government of the Republic of Indonesia requested the ADB to provide technical assistance for a gas transportation project through a public-private partnership.

Technical assistance provided by the ADB aimed to support Indonesia's strategy for promoting the domestic use of natural gas in the interest of sustainable economic growth. The costs of develop-

1 Penny Davies, "The Role of the Private Sector in the Context of Aid Effectiveness; Consultative Findings Document Final Report." (OECD, Doll) http://www.oecd.rog/doc/effectiveness/4708812/pdf.

ing gas pipelines were high, and the funding was provided by several donors including the World Bank and the Japan Special Fund. In the implementation process of a project such as building infrastructures for gas pipelines, donor governments need to closely collaborate with international organizations and the private sector to promote effectiveness.

Strategic Private Sector Partnerships for Urban Poverty Reduction (STEP-UP)

The Strategic Private Sector Partnerships for Urban Poverty Reduction in Metro Manila (STEP-UP) Program plans to help improve the lives of 5,823 poor urban households in twenty three poor communities in Metro Manila, Philippines through public-private sector partnerships. The distinct character of this three-year project is the strategic and focused participation of the private sector, whose contribution will match that of the Japan Fund for Poverty Reduction.

A total of twenty eight different corporations different corporations support the STEP-UP efforts, including well-known corporations like Nestle, Pfizer, IBM or Credit Suisse First Boston. According to their interests and expertise, corporations can choose which programs to support. For example, Business World simply supports STEP-UP by featuring stories on STEP-UP in its magazine while the University of Asia and the Pacific provides a venue for STEP-UP orientations. The Manila Electric Company provides technical assistance in fixing electrical grids, Pfizer has conducted a medical mission in Pasig, and students at De La Salle University volunteer to conduct computer literacy sessions.

Overall assessment of STEP-UP is that the program was successfully able to demonstrate that the business sector can participate in urban poverty alleviation. It also showed that Homeowners Associations have the capability to improve their current condition with support from other sectors. One of the most significant accomplishments of STEP-UP is in showing the credit worthiness of the urban poor. People from the informal sector managed to implement their own housing loan programs and registered high repayment rates of 95%. Thus, STEP-UP can be considered a successful case because it meets a real and urgent need.[2]

---

2 Asian Development Bank, "PHI: Strategic Private Sector Partnerships for Urban Poverty Reduction in Metro Manila (STEP UP)," (2007), http://www.adb.org/sites/default/files/projdocs/2007/36020-PHI-JFPRICM.pdf, last visited July 2014, 12.

United States Agency for International Development (USAID) and Privatization

During the Clinton administration in 1993, the National Performance Review was announced as a campaign to reinvent government to make it better, more efficient and more businesslike. USAID was encouraged to reform the procurement process and improve the agency's management of development assistance. A major strategy undertaken by USAID was to contract out public services to private providers, a method known as privatization. This means that the government draws on the expertise of private firms to provide services that had previously been performed by the public sector.

It was anticipated that contracting out development programs and projects for private for-profit firms as well as to non-profit organizations and NGOs would promote efficiency in USAID. The advantages of privatization were threefold. First, it increased efficiency to create a more businesslike environment in USAID. Second, since private corporations possessed the expertise for effective implementation, privatization cut costs. Finally, it benefited the US economy by creating jobs and income for domestic firms.

Contracting out is defined as public financing or private provision. Governments use competitive bidding to determine who should provide the service or goods. The benefit for the government is a reduction in costs by obtaining services from the private sector in place of using federal employees. On the other hand, governments must be cautious that businesses and private groups do not possess too much influential power over aid policies. It is necessary for the government to cooperate with the private sector; however, both entities must be careful when working together to find a balance that helps achieve effectiveness.

7.2 Foreign Direct Investment

Foreign direct investments (FDI) refer to the transfer of capital mechanisms or a transfer of technology and know-how. FDI can bring much needed extra capital as well as technology transfers, better formation of human capital, deeper international trade integration, and a more competitive business environment.[3] Liberal-

3 OECD, *Promoting Private Investment for Development: The role of ODA*, OECD DAC Guidelines

ization or free market mechanisms have led to increasing capital inflows. The most frequently cited factors of FDI inflow are current market size and potential market size. Other factors that have contributed to larger capital inflows in developing countries include labor costs, availability of infrastructure and political and macroeconomic stability.

According to the UNCTAD, there are several reasons for the increase in FDI.[4] Four main determinants include the following: market size and growth prospects; natural and human resource endowment; physical, financial and technological infrastructure; and openness to international trade and access to international markets.[5] These factors suggest that countries with stronger infrastructures are expected to achieve better results with allocated capital and are more attractive sites for FDI. A key factor appears to be government policies, especially tariffs or other barriers on imported products. The stronger the import restriction, the faster FDI replaces trade. Increased competition is another factor that encourages investment in a foreign market. Many companies resort to foreign production in an attempt to reduce transportation and production costs. Costs of transportation and customs duties increase the price of goods, making them lose competitiveness in a foreign local market. By internalizing operations in a local market, companies can gain price competitiveness.

Interestingly, it has been found that FDI flows are more sensitive to the corruption of governments than ODA.[6] At the same time, though, ODA has also been identified as a factor that leads to greater FDI inflows. Developing coun-

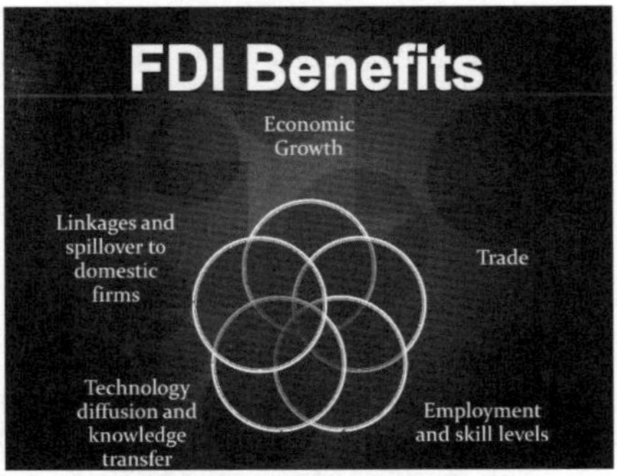

Slideshare, http://www.slideshare.net/Lordnikhil/fdi-economic-growth

and Reference Series (2003).

4 UNCTAD, *Word Investment Report 1996, Investment, Trade and International Policy Arrangements* (New York & Geneva, 1996), 76-78.

5 OECD, *Promoting Private Investment for Development: The role of ODA*, OECD DAC Guidelines and Reference Series (2003).

6 Alberto Alesina and Beatrice Weder, "Do Corrupt Governments Receive Less Foreign Aid?," *NBER Working Paper series* (Cambridge: National Bureau of Economic Research, 1999).

tries that receive ODA will use this ODA to develop basic infrastructure resulting in a better environment for private sector activities. It has been identified by the OECD that ODA can play a critical role in improving the environment for private sector activities and in helping enterprises respond to new and changing demands and pave the way for robust growth.

In countries that have shown high growth rates, the total domestic and foreign investment often exceeds 25% of gross domestic product. Countries with low growth rates, such as Sub-Saharan African countries, lack basic physical infrastructures that are necessary to attract investments. By building physical infrastructure in these countries it is expected that an improved investor climate will encourage capital inflows.

Thus, ODA should promote infrastructure development. This infrastructure development makes a significant contribution to economic growth in a developing country because it can further attract private investments. A positive causal relationship exists between budget and balance of payments support, infrastructure and aid for productive sectors and economic growth. In light of these assessments, it was proposed that support in the form of ODA should be appropriately distributed to improve the investment climate. To this end, the development agencies that implement aid projects should concentrate on achieving several important mutually reinforcing objectives.

ODA should aim to lower the costs of investments because the cost of doing business in a developing country is an important consideration made by any private entity before making a decision. The costs include the need to comply with the host country's policies and legal and regulatory frameworks. The threats of extra costs incurred because of inadequate infrastructure, crime and corruption must also be considered before it is possible to do the cost-benefit analysis. As well, the costs of any foreign investment must be balanced with the potential returns and possible risk factors.

Development agencies are also aware that it is important to reduce the risk of making an investment for private entities. In order to reduce risk for foreign investments, policy and institutional reforms need to be made so as to improve the stability of the investment climate and the predictability of returns on investments. Therefore, a stronger mechanism to enforce the rule of law can also contribute to reducing the risks for investors. As well, a stable financial market is a critical part of managing the possible risks of increasing firms and expanding production.

Competitiveness increases efficiency, innovation and productivity. Protectionist policies or policies and laws that allow anti-competitive behavior by public and private sectors need to be restricted. A culture that encourages competition will lead to a more attractive investment climate. ODA can also be utilized in developing the capacity of public and private sector stakeholders to reform the investment climate through implementing change. The innovative capacity of the private sector can be promoted by adopting new technologies and expanding entrepreneurial skills.

Global Trends in Foreign Direct Investments

The overall amounts of FDI continued to increase in 2007. Six of the top ten recipient countries in the FDI Confidence Index are emerging markets, and global investors have indicated optimism for opportunities in the developing world. Global FDI was at its low point in 2003 and has continued to increase until 2007. FDI flows remained at $1.3 trillion in 2013 after two years of decrease in 2008 and 2009.[7][8] In 2016, it is reported that the North American region enjoyed the highest growth in FDI inflows in 2015 of around 194%. The EU came in second in terms of inflow growth followed by the emerging Asian regions. In terms of the total amounts of FDI inflows, developing Asia was the most popular destination for FDI over $500 billion followed by North America around $400 billion and the EU of $420 billion.[9]

Figure 7.1 Foreign Direct Investment, Net Flows (BoP, Current US dollar)[10]

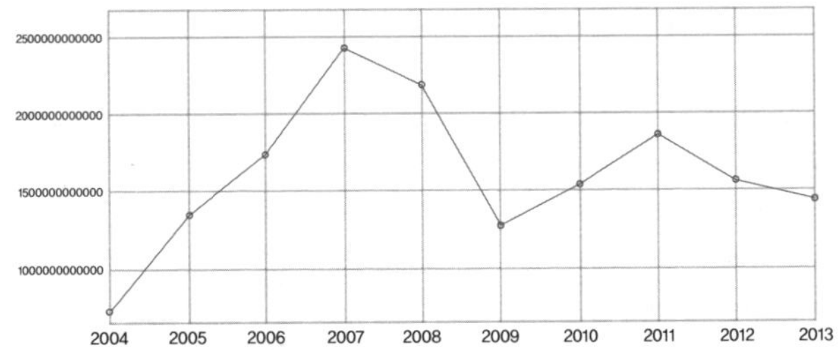

7 OECD, *FDI in Figures* (2014).

8 AT Kearney, *New concerns in an uncertain world: The 2007 AT Kearney FDI Confidence Index* (2008).

9 AT Kearney, "FDI on the Rebound?" 2016, https://www.atkearney.com/gbpc/foreign-direct-investment-confidence-index/publication/-/asset_publisher/lsBVD71WgZDd/content/2016-a-t-kearney-foreign-direct-investment-confidence-index/10192, last visited August 2016.

In 2003, AT Kearney projected possible global developments that were most likely to influence FDI decisions. The recovery of the US economy was the most important factor to influence FDI decisions. Other significant influential factors included increased government regulations and security or terrorism concerns. The global developments that would influence FDI developments can be found in Table 7.2.

Figure 7.2 Global Developments Most Likely to Influence FDI Decisions[11]

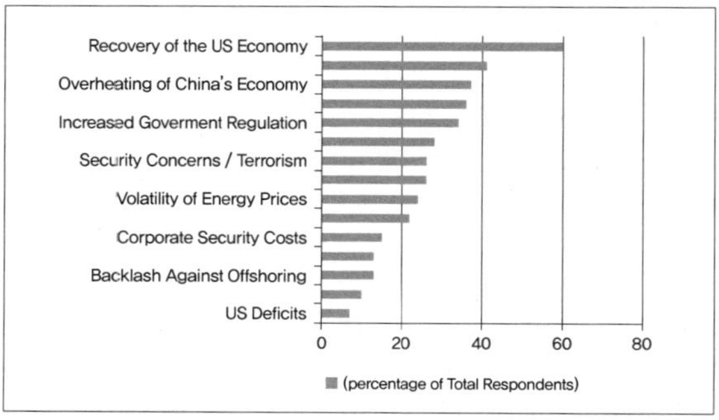

The factors that led the private sector away from offshoring or foreign investments were also identified in the 2003 FDI Confidence Index, as presented in Table 7.3. It was found that the strongest factor dissuading companies from adopting offshore strategies was the higher labor skills and education levels found in the domes-

Figure 7.3 Leading Reasons for Not Offshoring[12]

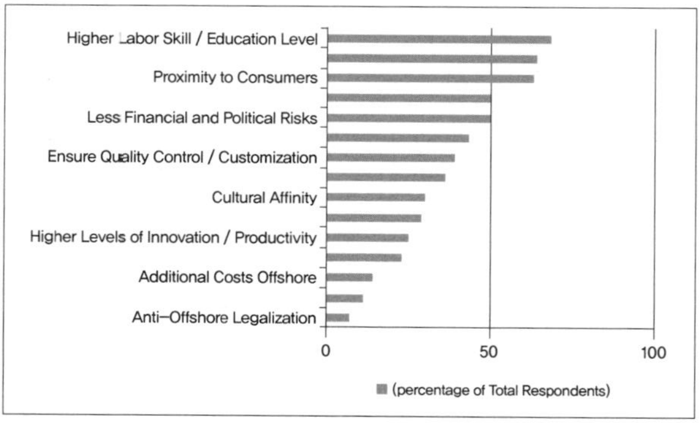

10 World Bank, http://data.worldbank.org/indicator/BX.KLT.DINV.CD.WD/countries?display=graph, last visited July 2014.

11 AT Kearney, *The 2003 AT Kearney FDI Confidence Index* (2004).

tic market. 64% of respondents also indicated that better domestic infrastructure was a reason for refraining from offshore investments.

It is difficult to find a causal link between geographical size and the potential returns on investments. A comparison of per-capita FDI inflows from large to small countries and rich to poor countries found that while the size of a country was not proportionate to its FDI inflows, richer developing countries received larger amounts of FDI. The tendency for richer countries to attract more FDI is due to stronger expectations for higher returns of investments. This is because a developing country with more capital wealth will have a stronger domestic market economy and less risk. Compared to the relationship between wealth and market stability, the geographical size of a country is not directly related to any of these factors.

Figure 7.4 Per-capita FDI Inflows, 1997–2000: Large versus Small and Rich versus Poor Developing Countries[13]

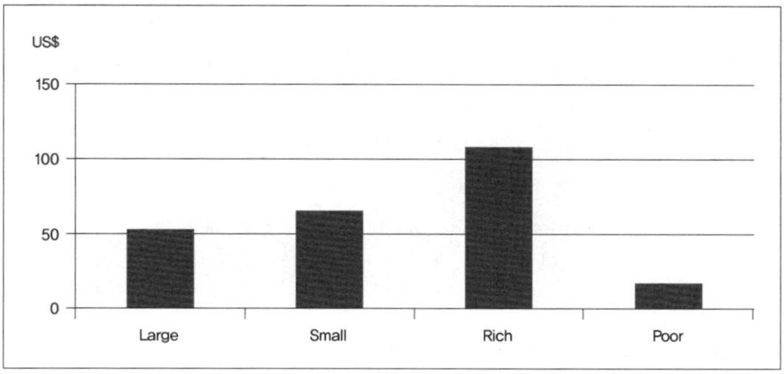

East Asian Economic Miracle

East Asian economies have achieved dynamic economic growth in the past few decades. In this period, the influence of inbound capital flows to the region in the form of FDI and ODA was significant.

12 *Ibid.*

13 The figures refer to the annual average. Countries are considered large (small), if their population in 1999 was above (below) the median of 8.0 million for the overall sample; countries are considered rich (poor), if their per-capita income (PPP) in 1999 was above (below) the median of 3,390$. The figures for Small countries exclude Hong Kong and Singapore; if included, average per-capita FDI inflows would increase to 155$. The figures for Rich countries exclude Hong Kong and Singapore; if included, average per-capita inflows would increase to 209$. Taken from UNCTAD, online database and World Bank (2002b).

The forerunner country in East Asian economic development was Japan, followed by the Four East Asian Tigers: Singapore, Hong Kong, Taiwan and South Korea. Although Singapore and Hong Kong have developed at a faster pace than Taiwan and Korea, the dynamic rate of economic development of all four countries was recognized under the title of the East Asian Tigers. The ASEAN-4 countries followed the trends of East Asian economic growth and began to gain momentum in the mid-1980s. These trends of development in East Asia are presented in Table 7.1 and Table 7.2.

Table 7.1 GNP per Capita in Current U.S. Dollars in East Asia

	1967	1970	1975	1980	1985	1990	1995
Japan	1,190	1,940	4,920	10,390	10,900	26,410	39,640
Singapore	660	1,050	3,080	5,130	7,570	12,740	26,730
Hong Kong	940	940	2,500	5,790	6,080	12,680	22,990
Taiwan	267	389	964	2,344	3,297	8,111	12,439
Korea	140	270	640	2,330	2,260	5,770	9,700
Malaysia	350	390	890	1,800	1,900	2,370	3,890
Thailand	170	210	390	720	810	1,520	2,740
Philippines	210	220	370	690	520	740	1,050
Indonesia	50	80	230	500	530	620	980

Sources: World Bank, World Development Indicators. Taiwan Statistical Data Bank.

Table 7.2 Average Annual Growth Rates of GDP

	1965-80	1980-90	1990-95
Japan	6.3	4.0	1.3
Singapore	10.1	7.1	8.5
Hong Kong	8.6	6.9	5.6
Taiwan	9.8	7.9	6.6
Korea	9.5	9.1	7.5
Malaysia	7.4	5.9	8.7
Thailand	7.2	7.9	8.4
Philippines	5.9	1.6	2.3
Indonesia	8.0	6.3	7.8

Sources: World Bank, World Development Indicators. Taiwan Statistical Data Bank.

7.3 Promoting Private Investments

The significance of private investments was well recognized in the Monterrey Consensus, which explicitly identified that private investment was a catalyst for innovation, economic growth and poverty reduction. According to the United Nations:

> Private international capital flows, particularly foreign direct investment, are vital complements to national and international development efforts. Foreign direct investment contributes toward financing sustained economic growth over the long term. It is especially important for its potential to transfer knowledge and technology, create jobs, boost overall productivity, enhance competitiveness and entrepreneurship, and ultimately eradicate poverty through economic growth and development.[14]

The relationship between ODA and private investments can be understood at multiple levels. In 2003, the OECD launched a policy guide for donors to use ODA more effectively and to promote private investment for development.[15] It was found that donors spent around 20% of their aid on a variety of investment-enhancing activities, emphasizing the need for strategic actions by donors and stronger coordination through a more systematic analysis of what actually works in developing country economies.

The OECD has encouraged donors to focus on helping to lower the costs of investments, reduce risks, improve competition and develop human and institutional capacities in the promotion of pro-poor growth. It further stressed economic infrastructure, financial market development and capacity building of enterprises as priority areas for mobilizing investments.

It is important for developing countries to improve their socio-economic and political settings in order to foster an attractive investment climate. Developing countries are prone to market failures, lack basic infrastructure, suffer from corrupt governments and have many other structural impediments. Before these countries benefit from foreign investments, they must provide stable socio-economic and political environments for investment. Improving

---

14 UN, "Final Outcome of the International Conference on Financing for Development," http://www.un.org/esa/ffd/0302finalMonterreyConsensus.pdf, last visited April 2009.

15 The document launched by the OECD was entitled the "Initiative on Investment for Development."

the coherence of different policy areas, including trade, tax, competition and investment promotion, or pursuing macroeconomic stability will attract more private investments. Other measures that can be taken by developing country governments include improving market-regulating institutions and strengthening procedures for contract enforcement and dispute settlement.[16]

Recommendations brought forth by the OECD DAC to help developing countries mobilize more productive investments and improve the effectiveness of interventions encourage development agencies to:[17]

- Be more strategic, and their interventions need to be harmonized and guided by more systematic learning of lessons.
- Focus on helping to lower the costs of investment, reduce risks, improve competition and develop human and institutional capacities in developing countries.
- Give high priority to economic infrastructure, investment and financial market development as key areas for promoting investment in the near term.
- Pay greater attention to the determinants of domestic investment, both formal and informal, and to strengthening the capacities of local firms to respond to new investment opportunities and to expand business relationships with foreign investors.
- Enhance the contribution of investment to pro-poor growth (i.e. increase the impact of growth on poverty reduction) by making labor, land and other markets work better for the poor, tackling constraints to women's entrepreneurship, reducing barriers to formalization, promoting environmental sustainability, expanding access to knowledge and technology and unleashing the economic potential in rural areas.
- Encourage entrepreneurship and innovation by supporting education and vocational training, research and development activities and technology transfers.
- Promote responsible business practices in areas such as labor relations, the environment and anti-corruption. Build on analyses of country and sector-specific constraints, at national and local levels, to private sector development and encourage publication and public debate about the results. Help build up the capacities of developing countries to carry out such assessments.
- Seek out reliable, representative and accountable domestic partners

16 OECD, *Promoting Private Investment for Development: The role of ODA*, (Paris: OECD DAC Guidelines and Reference Series, 2003).

17 *Ibid.*

who can drive reform programs and help catalyze change.

- Use market-based approaches in supporting firms. Targeted assistance should avoid distortions and firms receiving direct support should be selected based on their expected capacity to innovate, create jobs and provide services at local market conditions.
- Promote structured and inclusive public-private dialogue, at national and local levels, so as to bring micro and small entrepreneurs and informal firms and workers into consultation and decision-making processes. This will help to build demand for reform and investments that will improve the investment climate.
- Evaluate the cumulative impact of their interventions on promoting investment and share examples of successful and unsuccessful practices.

Box. 7.1 Development Business[18]

If development agencies are also considered to be a part of the aid industry and function as a business under the objective to promote investments, the OECD DAC has made several recommendations encouraging development agencies to change their way of approaching the business.

1) Development agencies should ensure that their internal incentive and evaluation systems do not work against staffs that pursue longer-term, programmatic and possibly higher risk interventions. Institutional and policy reforms are not one-off events and efforts may not come to fruition within an agency's typical three or four-year program cycle, or the period of one staff member's posting to a developing country.
2) Staff working on private sector development, agriculture, infrastructure, public governance, capacity development, environment and gender are often located in different organizational units and sometimes in different organizations only loosely associated with the core ODA program. To effectively promote investment, these staff need to work in close association and, ideally, under a common strategic framework.
3) The capacity of staff in development agencies may need to be further developed, to help them adopt appropriate approaches, determine which aid instruments to use and decide the sequence of

18 *Ibid.*

reforms, based on differences in a country's investment climate and stage of development.

4) Some development agencies may need to encourage their public sector partners to engage more with the private sector in developing countries. Development agencies can facilitate public-private partnerships by strengthening public authorities' capacities to negotiate contracts and exploring how the mitigation of non-commercial risks can be improved, including through coordinated responses by donors.

5) Development agencies can help develop the local private sector by procuring as many goods and services as possible in developing countries, subject to value-for-money considerations. This may require capacity building in the local private sector to enable firms to participate in competitive and transparent processes and so, take advantage of these opportunities. Development agencies can also encourage their suppliers and contractors to adopt responsible business practices.

6) Development agencies potentially have a wide selection of ODA instruments at their disposal including the direct supply of goods or services, free-standing technical cooperation, grants, concessional loans, partnerships, alliances, equity acquisitions and guarantees. However, few DAC members use all of these instruments and the use of some, such as concessional loans or equity acquisitions, may be limited to a development bank, development finance institution or other specialized agencies. Given the variety of domains that need to be addressed to promote investment, there is a risk that relying on a few aid instruments may inhibit the effectiveness of development agencies' efforts. DAC members should consider whether the selection of aid instruments at their disposal is right for reaching their objectives, especially in addressing, albeit indirectly, the private sector.

7) To help ensure that the range of DAC members' policies have positive impacts on investment mobilization, development agencies may need to expand their capacity to analyze the impact of non-ODA policies on developing countries and engage with representatives of other policy communities to influence policy formulation processes.

7.4 Public Private Partnerships

Public private partnerships (PPP) refer to a sustained collaborative effort between the public sector and the private sector in achieving a common objective while both players pursue their own individual interests. The motivation behind a public-private partnership (PPP) is to deliver public services, such as water, electricity or telecommunications, more efficiently and to more people, and to improve the quality and the affordability of access to services provided.[19]

World Bank Blogs

Within a PPP, both partners are involved throughout the entire process. They both share in creating the design. Each partner also contributes a fraction of the financial, managerial and technical resources needed to execute and operate the project. The decisions to divide labor are made after considering the comparative advantage that each partner has. Both partners are responsible for the risks associated with the project and they also share the benefits that are created.[20] A further advantage of PPP is that governments can be motivated to identify and prioritize their needs. Since governments are fully involved from the initial stage to the final outcome, it is important that they are aware of their individual needs in order to express these desires in the process of implementing a PPP.

Several assumptions can be identified in this conceptualization of PPP. First, the concept requires a shift in the roles and attitudes of both public and private entities. The new role of public authorities is concentrated around the core functions of supervision and regulation. In the past, the public sector was the client and the private sector assumed the role of contractor. This public sector's new role encourages the private sector to take on greater responsibilities and risks in execution, operation and the mobilization of resources.

19 OECD, Promoting Private Investment for Development: The Role of ODA (Paris: OECD DAC Guidelines and Reference Series, 2003).

20 Argentino Pessoa, "Public Private Partnerships in Developing Countries: Are infrastructures responding to the new ODA strategy," *Journal of International Development*, vol. 20, no. 3 (2008): 331-325.

Although the roles of government and private sector entities are changing, they are nevertheless pursuing a sustained collaborative effort in order to attain a common objective. Thus, a PPP represents a stronger partnership compared to the contractual relationships that existed in the past. It is important to recognize that both the public and private sectors have responsibilities in the areas of their comparative advantage.

A critical part of success in a PPP is an awareness of the individual interests of each partner. In the case of the private sector, net returns on investments are a strong motivation for participation. On the other hand, the interests underlying the public sector's involvement in PPPs differ from those of the private sector because it is pursuing a net benefit to society and the economy as a whole.[21]

The ineffectiveness of aid project implementation in the past has led donor governments to find new methods that will promote effectiveness. It has been found that private providers can play an important role in infrastructure and public utilities provision. However, the reason why PPPs are sustainable is that although the private sector has proved to be more effective in building infrastructure or completing projects, the financial engagement of the public sector is necessary for achieving long-term sustainability.

The use of PPPs continues to encounter difficulties that must be addressed to develop effective partnerships. Developing countries have become more dependent on a limited number of large companies, which gives these corporations extremely strong bargaining power and enforcement capabilities. The capacities of developing countries to design a regulatory framework are limited, but non-competitive industry structures and lack of capital market discipline make these regulations a necessity.

Box.7.2 Tobin Tax

A new form of development finance was proposed by James Tobin in the 1970s. It was proposed that the currency transactions tax (CTT), more widely recognized as the Tobin Tax, should be applied to foreign-exchange markets, such as spot, forward, future, swaps and other derivatives. The objective of the Tobin Tax was to reduce destabilizing fluctuations in currencies following the breakdown of the

21 *Ibid.*

Bretton Woods System, and was later taken up as a potential source of development finance. The biggest challenge to implementing global taxes like the Tobin Tax is that they require strong international political agreements, which are difficult to achieve.

Private Sector Contribution to Implementation

Cooperative efforts between the public and private sectors have gained more attention due to mounting concerns that governments do not possess the necessary capacity to implement aid projects in an effective and efficient way. Some of the problems with government implementation include the inability to secure sufficient funds, a lack of quality or efficiency of services, ineffective resource allocation and poor management. It is anticipated that greater competition leads to higher quality, but the public sector does not have incentive for competition. Franceys and Weitz found that conventional support to public sector providers through loans and capital investment have not achieved the desired results in reducing poverty.[22] In this light, public private partnerships have been identified as possible policy instruments in attaining multiple purposes such as adequate infrastructure, improving welfare and enhancing efficiency.[23]

Despite increasing efforts by developed countries, domestic public finances and ODA are not sufficient by themselves to finance the infrastructure needed by the developing world. According to the OECD, the cost of maintaining existing infrastructure is estimated to be about 7% of a developing country's GDP, which is equivalent to approximately $600 billion per year. The actual public spending on infrastructure in developing countries is around 3%. In most developing countries, the public sector does not have adequate funds to fulfill the requirements, which could be supplied by greater private sector participation. On the other hand, due to weak incentives or excessive risks, most infrastructure building projects in developing countries are not financially viable options for private sector entities.

The private sector possesses several strengths such as the capa-

22 Richard Franceys and Almud Weitz, "Public-Private Community Partnerships in Infrastructure for the Poor," *Journal of International Development*, vol. 15, no. 8 (2003): 1083-1098.

23 United Nations, *Report on the International Conference on Financing for Development* (New York: United Nations, 2002).

bility to improve quality, customer services and management standards. The private sector also has the funding to make investments in research and development. It would also be more effective than the public sector in developing new services and market-based systems of rationing. It is possible for donor governments to save costs by outsourcing certain activities to the private sector. On the other hand, the costs of outsourcing must also be taken into consideration when identifying whether outsourcing increases cost efficiency. In particular, the additional contracting and monitoring costs that will be incurred through outsourcing must also be accounted for in the cost-balance calculations.

The involvement of the private sector in public activities can be categorized into six basic forms including short-term service contracts, management contracts, leases, Greenfield projects, concessions and divestiture:[24]

1) Short-term Service Contract: The typical duration of a short-term service contract is from six months to two years. Specific jobs such as everyday maintenance jobs are contracted to the private sector while overall services management remains the role of the public sector. Short-term service contracts can be understood as a stepping-stone to PPPs.
2) Management Contracts: These contracts entrust the private company with various types of tasks relating to the organization and the maintenance operations usually performed by the public authority. A management contract involves fees to the private company, which is entrusted with the responsibility to respond to day-to-day routine maintenance jobs by contracting private companies on behalf of the public entity. The typical duration of a management contract is from three to five years to provide gains in managerial efficiency.
3) Lease: A lease has a typical duration from ten to fifteen years during which a private company leases the assets of a utility, and maintains and operates them in return for the right to revenues. In this case, commercial risks are born by the private sector, which provides strong incentives for better performance.
4) Greenfield Projects: These are usually built and operated by the private sector. The private sector is responsible for the commercial risk, but can share the political and exchange rate risk with the public sector. The most common form of a Greenfield project is the Build-

24 Argentino Pessoa, "Public Private Partnerships in Developing Countries: Are Infrastructures Responding to the New ODA Strategy," *Journal of International Development*, vol. 20, no. 3 (2008): 311-325.

Operate-Transfer (BOT). In this option the private sector develops, finances and operates bulk facilities. BOT arrangements stress the responsibility of the private entity during construction and operation of the infrastructure and the transfer of the assets to the public entity at the end of the operation period.

5) Concession: The public entity owns the assets in a concession, but contracts with the private sector for operations, maintenance and investment. A road concession is an arrangement under which the owner of the road delegates to a private entity the responsibility for providing and maintaining a specified level of service to road users in exchange for the right to collect revenues from users. A concession has high efficiency in operations and investments, but requires considerable commitment and regulatory capacity.

6) Divestiture: When the assets of a public utility are sold to the private sector, it is called a divestiture. This type contains the potential for high efficiency gains, but requires a credible regulatory framework and careful preparation.

It has been proposed to expand the use of public-private agreements in infrastructure projects by relying on ODA to enhance the quality of projects that reduce risks and raise profitability. If ODA can be effectively utilized in improving the environment of developing countries to attract investments, additional projects in developing countries will become financially viable.

7.5 Private Sector Contributions to Governance

Governance is the activities, institutions and processes involved in effectively managing and running a country's affairs in all of its different spheres, including the relationships between the state and society.[25] Governance is important in aid effectiveness. A relationship between ineffectiveness of aid and the quality of governance exists, but it is difficult to identify the actual impact of aid on the overall quality of governance.

Good governance requires domestic political commitment. Without effective governance, financing for development and trade-related concessions to assist developing countries will have a limited impact. Good governance is an essential requirement for the implementation of sound economic and social policies. It has been

25 Roger C. Riddell, *Does Foreign Aid Really Work?* (London: Oxford University Press, 2007).

identified as a key priority for eradicating poverty and promoting development. Four of the seven commitments in the Brussels Action for the Least Developed Countries are related to governance: fostering people-centered action; promoting good governance at national and international levels; building human and institutional capacities; and mobilizing financial resources, including official development assistance.

Governance is a comprehensive concept that encompasses all aspects of development assistance. As such, in order to achieve a good governance structure, it is important to create a mechanism that can incorporate diverse actors that participate in development assistance activities. The network of actors has become more complex with the emergence of new actors. Private sector involvement in development assistance has especially contributed to complicating the traditional web of development actors.

The benefits of private public cooperation and private sector participation in development activities necessitate an organizational structure that can encourage their efforts and contribute to achieving good governance. Good governance within development requires the facilitation of all the diverse actors that can contribute to the development of a country that is struggling from poverty.

Chapter 7. Review Discussion Questions

1. Explain the relationship between ODA and FDI. Does ODA encourage FDI? If so, why? On the other hand, does FDI encourage ODA? Why or why not?
2. What are some of the unique roles of ODA in promoting FDI?
3. Identify the benefits and disadvantages of private sector involvement. Should it be encouraged to achieve success in development assistance activities?
4. What is 'development business?' Elaborate on your view regarding the recommendations by the OECD to change the approach to 'development business.'
5. Explain the difference between PPC and PPP.
6. Is the Tobin Tax a plausible option for development financing? Why or why not?

Chapter 8
Aid Effectiveness

> *"Aid flows have significantly increased over the last decade, but at the same time aid has become increasingly fragmented. There has been an explosion in the number of donors, and while the number of projects has multiplied, their average size has dropped. Small projects being often limited in size, scope and duration, they result in little lasting benefit beyond the immediate impact. With more players, aid has become less predictable, less transparent and more volatile."*[1]

8.1 Increasing Aid Effectiveness

An assumption that countries make in providing aid to developing countries is that aid has positive effects on economic growth and poverty reduction. The central question of this chapter is simple - does aid work? It is generally believed that aid promotes poverty reduction, and there is considerable evidence supporting the existence of a positive link between foreign aid and economic growth. Widely circulated empirical data suggests that economic growth would be lower in the absence of aid.[2] Nevertheless, scholars have continued to question the effectiveness of aid, and some have even argued that its detrimental effects are counterproductive in reducing poverty.

The conditions and environmental factors that enhance aid effectiveness are a key focus of academic study. These preconditions influence donor decisions to provide aid to specific countries. Donors favor countries with strong commitments to development and good governance. In light of these trends, most research on aid effectiveness has concentrated on empirical studies of the impact of aid on growth, infant mortality, and the composition of government spending and the influence of aid quality on governance.[3] Numer-

1 M.G. Fengler and H. Kharas, *Delivering Aid Differently: Lesson from the Field* (Washington D.C.: Bookings Institutions, 2010).

2 Mark McGillivray, *Is aid Effective?* (OECD, 2004).

3 See Peter Boone, "Politics and the Effectiveness of Foreign Aid," *European Economic Review*, vol. 40, Issue 2 (1996): 289-329; Tarhan Feyzioglu, Vinaya Swaroop and Min Zhu, "A Panel Data Analysis of the Fungibility of Foreign Aid," *The World Bank Economic Review*, vol. 12, no.

ous scholars have assessed the effectiveness of ODA in promoting growth and reducing poverty in recipient countries. A related topic for study is the capacity of aid to influence main macroeconomic variables such as investment, savings, consumption, tax burden, and the role of inflation. Research in these areas seeks to measure the effectiveness of aid on economic growth. Despite studies that are skeptical of the impact of aid on economic development, these arguments do not sufficiently support the claim that aid has failed. Rather, they should be understood as explanations of the reasons why aid has not worked better and as indicators of how future improvements can be made.

A broad consensus is that sound institutions and policies are important determinants of long-term growth and poverty reduction. As well, the rules, norms and behaviors, social infrastructure, property rights and the legal rules and behaviors that enforce growth-enhancing institutions are important as well. A well-functioning civil service based on merit and transparency is also a factor that determines economic growth and poverty alleviation.

Burnside and Dollar have argued that aid has a positive impact on growth in countries that have a good political environment with sound policies.[4] This is not to imply that aid has a negative impact on countries with bad governmental policies, but rather to emphasize that a good political environment will facilitate a more desirable outcome of aid on economic growth. Burnside and Dollar advocate a redistribution of aid so that more aid is allocated to those countries with stronger policy environments, which will thus increase the effectiveness of aid, Burnside and Dollar's results rely on the existence of poor countries with sound policies, i.e. it is necessary to identify how many countries can be favored with financial aid to maximize poverty reduction because of the existence of sound governmental policies. Due to the worldwide trend toward economic reform in the 1990s, it was found that 32 countries with poverty rates over 50% had above average policies, accounting for nearly 75% of the world's poor.[5] The gain from allocating aid to

1 (1998): 29-58; Craig Burnside and David Dollar, "Aid, the Incentive Regime, and Poverty Reduction," *The World Bank Development Research Group, Macroeconomics and Growth* (June 1998) ALL; Stephen Knack, "Aid Dependence and the Quality of Governance: Cross-Country Empirical Tests," *Southern Economic Journal*, vol. 68, no. 2 (2001): 310-329.

4 Burnside and Dollar, "Aid, Policies, and Growth," *NBER Working Paper 9846* (July 2003).

5 This data was taken from a World Bank presentation (1998), which identified that the measure of policy used here was a broad one, covering macroeconomic and financial policies, structural

poor countries with good policies is anticipated to be very beneficial. For example, it is expected that if $10 billion in new assistance is allocated to poor countries that have sound policies, an additional 18 million people per year could be lifted out of poverty compared to the 7 million people that would be lifted out of poverty with the current allocation. Aid allocated to countries with sound policy environments has a higher return for investments, raises incomes and reduces poverty levels.[6]

The literature regarding the impact of aid on various categories of public expenditure and revenue clearly points to a general conclusion that aid contributes to higher public expenditures than would have been the case in the absence of aid.[7] However, it has also found that an overdose of aid can lead to diminishing returns. A number of studies have tested the linearity of aid with growth and found that aid is positively related to growth only to a certain point, but with excess amounts of aid the relationship between aid and growth becomes negative, with more aid leading to a diminishing growth rate for the recipient country. Studies have found that the negative returns are prevalent when aid inflows reach between 15% and 45% of GDP.[8]

---

issues, property rights and the rule of law, government quality and absence of corruption, social policies, governance, and safety nets.

6 World Bank, Development Research Group, "Assessing Aid, What Works, What Doesn't and Why?" Policy Research Report (1998).

7 See arguments by Tarhan Feyzioglu, Vinaya Swaroop and Min Zhu, "A Panel Data Analysis of the Fungibility of Foreign Aid," *The World Bank Economic Review*, vol. 12, no. 1 (1998): 29-58; Franco-Rodriguez Susana and Morrissey Oliver, "Aid and the Public Sector in Pakistan: Evidence with Endogenous Aid," *World Development* vol. 26, no. 7 (1998): 1241-1250; Mark Mcgillivray and Akhter Ahmed, "Aid, Adjustment and Public Sector Fiscal Behaviour in the Philippines," *Journal of the Asia Pacific Economy* vol. 4, no. 2 (1999): 381-391; Vinaya Swaroop, Shikha Jha and Andrew Sunil Rajkumar, "Fiscal Effects of Foreign Aid in a Federal System of Governance: The Case of India," *Journal of Public Economics* vol. 77, no. 3 (2000): 307-330; Mark McGillivray and Oliver Morrissey, "Aid Fungibility in Assessing Aid: red herring or true concern?" *Journal of International Concern* vol. 12, no. 3 (2000): 413-428; and Mark McGillivray and Bazoumana Ouattara. "Aid, debt burden and government fiscal behaviour in Côte d'Ivoire," *Journal of African Economies* vol. 14, no. 2 (2005): 247-269.

8 See arguments by Durbarry et al.: New Evidence on the Impact of Foreign Aid on Economic Growth, Credit Research Paper/ Collier and Dollar (2002): "Aid Allocation and Poverty," *European Economic Review*, vol. 46, Issue 8 (Sept. 2002)/ Hansen and Tarp, "Aid effectiveness disputed, Foreign Aid and Development: Lessons Learnt and Directions For The Future" (2000), "Aid and Growth regression," *Journal of Development Economics*, vol. 64, Issue 2, April 2001 (2001)/ Dalgaard and Hansen, "On Aid, Growth and Good Policies," *The Journal of Development Studies*, vol. 37, Issue 6 (2001); Hudson and Mosley, "Aid politics and growth: in search of the holy grail," *Journal of International Development*, vol. 13, Issue 7, Oct. (2001)/

Other challenges faced by countries in aid implementation include increasing transparency and minimizing corruption. The international community has shown growing interest in aid effectiveness and recognizes that money alone is not enough to achieve the goals of poverty alleviation and economic development in struggling countries. The importance of aid effectiveness was emphasized in 2002 at the International Conference on Financing for Development, during which the Monterrey Consensus was established. The following year, participants of the High Level Forum on Harmonization committed to work together to cooperate and coordinate activities with developing countries.

8.2 DAC Principles for Effective Aid

The international community organized four High Level Forums, Rome in 2003, Paris in 2005, Accra in 2008, and Busan in 2011 in order to seek ways to enhance aid effectiveness. After preliminary talks in Rome, the Paris Declaration on Aid Effectiveness established the basic principles of aid effectiveness, emphasizing the importance of ownership, alignment, harmonization, managing for

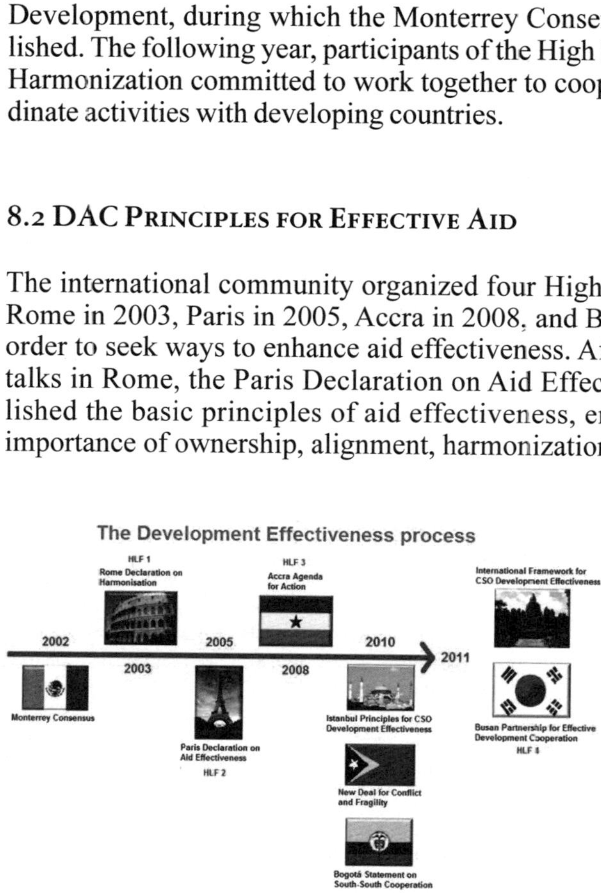

http://cso-effectiveness.org/-histoire-du-processus,017-.html

Lensink and White, "Are there negative returns to aid?" *The Journal of Development Studies*, vol. 37, Issue 6 (2001)/ Dalgaard et al., "On the empirics of foreign aid and growth," *The Economic Journal*, vol. 114, Issue 496 (2004)/ McGillivray, "Aid and Public Sector Behavior in Developing Countries," *Review of Development Economics*, vol. 4, Issue 2 (2000).

results and mutual responsibility. The Paris Declaration specified twelve performance targets to be reached by 2010. Mid-point progress report studies found that progress in attaining the 2010 targets was uneven, both across targets and among countries. In order to meet these goals, stronger commitment and better implementation will be necessary, not only involving donor and developing country governments but also the civil society, the private sector and other emerging actors. An emphasis was put on refining monitoring and evaluations methods in order to incorporate the new challenges that are being faced by the core principles of the Paris Declaration.

Box 8.1 Principles of the Paris Declaration on Aid Effectiveness

The Paris Declaration, endorsed on March 2, 2005, is an international agreement to which over one hundred Ministers, Heads of Agencies and other Senior Officials adhered and committed their countries and organizations to continue to increase efforts in harmonization, alignment and managing aid for results with a set of monitorable actions and indicators.[9]

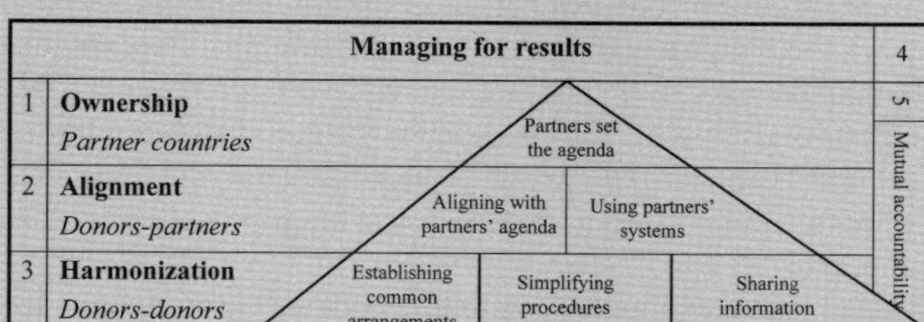

The Declaration is focused on five mutually reinforcing principles:

- Ownership: Developing countries must lead their own development policies and strategies, and manage their own development work on the ground. This is essential if aid is to contribute to truly sustainable development. Donors must support developing countries in building up their capacity to exercise this kind of leadership by strengthening local expertise, institutions and management systems.
- Alignment: Donors must line up their aid firmly behind the priorities outlined in developing countries' national development strategies.

9 OECD, http://www.oecd.org, Accessed March 2009.

Wherever possible, they must use local institutions and procedures for managing aid in order to build sustainable structures. In Paris, donors committed to make more use of developing countries' procedures for public financial management, accounting, auditing, procurement and monitoring. Where these systems are not strong enough to manage aid effectively, donors promised to help strengthen them. They also promised to improve the predictability of aid, to halve the amount of aid that is not disbursed in the year for which it is scheduled, and to continue to "untie" their aid from any obligation that it be spent on donor-country goods and services.

- Harmonization: Donors must coordinate their development work better amongst themselves to avoid duplication and high transaction costs for poor countries. In the Paris Declaration, they committed to coordinate better at the country level to ease the strain on recipient governments, for example by reducing the large numbers of duplicative field missions. They agreed on a target of providing two-thirds of all their aid via so-called "program-based approaches" by 2010. This means aid is pooled in support of a particular strategy led by a recipient country—a national health plan for example—rather than fragmented into multiple individual projects.
- Managing for results: All parties in the aid relationship must place more focus on the end result of aid, the tangible difference it makes in poor people's lives. They must develop better tools and systems to measure this impact. The target set by the Paris Declaration was for a one-third reduction by 2010 in the proportion of developing countries without solid performance assessment frameworks to measure the impact of aid.
- Mutual accountability: Donors and developing countries must account more transparently to each other for their use of aid funds, and to their citizens and parliaments for the impact of their aid. The Paris Declaration said that all countries must have procedures in place by 2010 to report back openly on their development results.

The first of these elements, ownership, commits the development community to "respect the right and responsibility of the partner country" to establish a development agenda setting out its own strategies for poverty reduction and growth. Alignment commits donors to align their development assistance with the "development priorities and results-oriented strategies set out by the partner country" and to "progressively depend on partner countries' own systems" simultaneously stressing that partner countries should strive to improve their own systems. The third element, harmonization, commits donors to implement food practices in aid delivery, including to "streamline and harmonize their policies, procedures and practices... and development staff and management incentives... to foster recognition of the benefits of harmonization."[10]

However, the indicators identified within the Paris Declaration are not sufficient measures of aid effectiveness. The most important aspect of aid effectiveness is the actual impact that aid has on recipient countries, especially a positive impact on local people's lives. Eradicating poverty and providing basic necessities such as water and education, sustainable jobs and livelihoods, food security, and environmental security are among some of the pertinent issues at hand. To increase effectiveness, aid should not be viewed as a gift or an act of charity. It is important to instill in developing countries the values of responsibility and ownership.

While country ownership usually refers to the responsible commitment and active participation of recipient governments, there are concerns that a broader conceptualization of ownership should include the role of the citizens as well. People's ownership or democratic ownership refers to the centrality of citizen's concerns within development plans and processes with the meaningful engagement of key stakeholders, including the poor or other marginalized populations that had been left out of past aid implementation activities.

In a similar light, to increase the participation of recipient countries, the concept of accountability must be applied to both donor and recipient countries. Within the current system, donor countries are evaluated and monitored through peer reviews and recipient countries are largely left to the responsibility of the World Bank. This has resulted in a one-way flow of accountability, which limits the possibility of openness and transparency from all partner countries.

In 2008, the Third High Level Forum, which took place in Accra, Ghana, saw more than 1700 participants including 100 ministers and heads of agencies from developing and donor countries, emerging economies, multilateral institutions and eighty civil societies gather to review the progress of the Paris Declaration implementation. The Accra Agenda for Action (AAA) was adopted, reflecting an international commitment to support necessary reforms in an attempt to accelerate the effective use of development assistance

10 Andrew Rogerson, "Aid Harmonization and Alignment: Bridging the Gaps between Reality and the Paris Reform Agenda," *Development Policy Review*, vol. 23, no. 5 (2005): 531-552.

and to reinforce efforts to achieve the MDGs by 2015. The AAA focused on the main institutional and political challenges to full implementation of the principles identified in the Paris Declaration. It found that progress in increasing country ownership, building more effective and inclusive partnerships, and achieving development results was limited, so it laid out an additional list of commitments for participating countries to fulfill.

Table 8.1 Center for Global Development's Estimates of Aid Effectiveness by Country

Donor Country	2003	Donor Country	2004	Donor Country	2005
United States	1.7	Italy	1.6	Japan	1.4
Italy	2.2	New Zealand	2.0	Italy	1.6
Greece	2.3	United States	2.1	United States	1.9
Canada	2.4	Greece	2.5	New Zealand	2.1
New Zealand	2.8	Austria	2.7	Australia	2.5
Portugal	2.8	Canada	2.9	Spain	2.6
Australia	2.9	Japan	2.9	Greece	2.8
Japan	3.0	Germany	3.0	Portugal	2.8
Spain	3.2	Spain	3.1	Canada	2.9
Germany	3.6	Australia	3.1	Austria	3.0
Austria	3.8	Portugal	3.5	Germany	3.4
France	4.3	United Kingdom	4.3	France	4.1
Finland	4.6	France	4.4	Finland	4.9
United Kingdom	5.0	Finland	5.1	Belgium	5.4
Ireland	5.5	Switzerland	5.3	United Kingdom	5.6
Switzerland	5.8	Ireland	5.4	Ireland	5.6
Belgium	5.9	Belgium	5.5	Switzerland	6.0
Norway	8.8	Netherlands	8.9	Netherlands	8.7
Sweden	9.5	Norway	10.3	Sweden	9.8
Netherlands	10.0	Sweden	12.0	Norway	10.8
Denmark	14.8	Denmark	14.3	Denmark	12.3

Source: Centre for Global Development (http://www.cgdv.org)

The Center for Global Development has made estimates of donor countries' aid effectiveness from the years 2003 to 2005. This index penalized tied aid and subtracted debt repayments by poor countries to the rich. It also favored aid to countries in which poverty is high but governance is relatively good, and it penalized donors for overloading recipient governments. Finally, it rewarded governments that allowed taxpayers to write off charitable contributions.

In 2011, a report on the achievements of the Paris Declaration was published before the Busan Conference. The results of the 2011 Survey on Monitoring the Paris Declaration showed that at

Table 8.2 Paris Declaration Indicators and Target Achievement in 2010[11]

	Paris Declaration Indicator	2010 Actual	2010 Target[1]	status
1	Operational Development Strategies % of countries having a national development strategy rated "A" or "B" on a five–point sosle*	37% (of 76)	75%	Not met
2a	Relliable public financial management (PFM) systems % of countries moving up at least one measure on the PFM/CPIA sosle since 2005*	38% (of 52)	50%	Not met
2b	Relliable procurement systems % of countries moving up at least one measure on the four–point sosle since 2005	–	No Target[C]	–
3	Aid flows are alligned on national priorities % of aid for the government sector reported on the government's budget*	41%	85%	Not met
4	Strengthen capacity by co–ordinated support % of technical co–operation implemented through co–ordinated programmes consistent with national development strategies*	57%	50%	Met
5a	Use of country PFM systems % of aid for the government sector using partner countries' PFM systems*	48%	55%	Not met
5b	Use of country procurement systems % of aid for the government sector using partner countries' procurement systems	44%	No Target[C]	–
6	Strengthen capacity by avoiding parallel PIUs Total number of parallel project implementation unite(PIUs)*	1 158	585	Not met
7	Aid is more predictable % of aid for the government sector disbursed within the fiscal year for which it was scheduled and recorded in government accounting systems*	43%	71%	Not met
8	Aid is united % of aid that is fully united*	88%	More than 89%	Not met
9	Use of common arrangements or procedures % of aid provided in the context of programme–based approaches*	45%	66%	Not met
10a	Joint missions % of donor missions to the field undertaken jointly*	19%	40%	Not met
10b	Joint country analytic work % of country analytic work undertaken jointly*	43%	66%	Not met
11	Results–oriented frameworks % of countries with transparent and monitorable performance assessment frameworks*	20% (of 44)	66%	Not met
12	Mutual accountability % of countries with mutual assessment reviews in place*	38%	100%	Not met

Notes:

a. Assessment against 2010 target uses data for all 78 countries participating in 2011 for which data were available. Where data are available for only a subset of these countries, the sample size is indicated in brackets.

b. Assessment against 2010 target uses data for the 32 countries participating in both the 2006 and 2011 Surveys, as the indicator target is formulated in relation to the 2005 baseline. Targets may differ from those published in previous years as baselines have been recalculated, omitting data from two countries (Nicaragua and Yemen) which formed part of the original panel of 34 countries participating in 2006, but which did not participate in 2011.

c. No targets are presented for indicators 2b (reliable procurement systems) and 5b (use of country procurement systems) as the sample of countries for whom data on the quality of systems are available is too small to allow for meaningful analysis.

d. The targets shown may differ from indicative targets published in previous years as a result of adjustments to historical data (e.g. indicator 8, where final data on tying led to adjustments to the underlying datasets after publication of reports on the previous surveys). The target for indicator 5a (use of country PFM systems) has been computed to consider the 2010 scores on the quality of PFM systems (indicator 2a), consistent with the approach agreed in the Paris Declaration and described in Chapter 3.

the global level, only one out of the thirteen targets established for 2010 were met. There was considerable variation in the direction and pace of progress across donors and partner countries since 2005. For the indicators where responsibility for change lies primarily with developing country governments, progress has been significant. However, this report showed that many of these changes require deep reforms that go beyond aid management to broader aspects of government processes. In this sense, the report emphasizes global attention on achieving many of the remaining twelve

11 OECD DAC, *Aid Effectiveness 2005-10: Progress in Implementing The Paris Declaration* (2011), 19.

targets.

One of the most significant gains from these evaluations is a chance to improve future activities. In this sense, the main objectives outlined within the DAC Principles for Effective Aid aim to promote future effectiveness through feedback and accountability. The ultimate goal of the DAC recommendation is to contribute to improving future aid policies and that the feedback from these programs and projects will provide valuable lessons and a basis for improved accountability in the future.

The DAC principles provide general guidelines for aid evaluation in the aid management process while adhering to the following:

- Aid agencies should have an evaluation policy with clearly established guidelines and methods along with a clear definition of its role and responsibilities and its place in institutional aid structure.
- The evaluation process should be impartial and independent from the process concerned with policy-making and the delivery and management of development assistance.
- The evaluation process must be as open as possible with the results made widely available.
- For evaluations to be useful, they must be utilized. Feedback to both policy-makers and operational staff is essential.
- Partnership with recipients and the cooperation of donors in aid evaluation are both essential; they are an important aspect of recipient institution-building and of aid coordination, which may reduce administrative burdens on recipients.
- Aid evaluation and its requirements must be an integral part of aid planning from the start. Clear identification of the objectives that an aid activity is to achieve is an essential prerequisite for objective evaluation.

Table 8.3 DAC Principles for Evaluation of Development Assistance

Criteria	Definition
Relevance	The extent to which the aid activity is suited to the priorities and policies of the target group, recipient and donor.
Effectiveness	A measure of the extent to which an aid activity attains its objectives.
Efficiency	Efficiency measures the outputs – qualitative and quantitative – in relation to the inputs. It is an economic term that is used to assess the extent to which aid uses the least costly resources possible in order to achieve the desired results. This generally requires comparing alternative approaches to achieving the same outputs, to see whether the most efficient process has been adopted.

Impact	The positive and negative changes produced by a development intervention, directly or indirectly, intended or unintended. This involves the main impacts and effects resulting from the activity on the local social, economic, environmental and other development indicators. The examination should be concerned with both intended and unintended results and must also include the positive and negative impact of external factors, such as changes in terms of trade and financial conditions.
Sustainability	Sustainability is concerned with measuring whether the benefits of an activity are likely to continue after donor funding has been withdrawn. Projects need to be environmentally as well as financially sustainable.

8.3 The 4th High Level Forum on Aid Effectiveness in Busan

The 4th High Level Forum on Aid Effectiveness in Busan (HLF4) was the fourth and final conference on aid effectiveness. It was organized to review and evaluate progress towards aid effectiveness based on the Paris Declaration. The South Korean government, which hosted HLF4, raised the issue of development effectiveness, a new concept focusing on the actual developmental changes in the recipient countries rather than simply measuring the result of the aid. The HLF4 also tried to build a new global partnership including all development actors. This inclusive approach was a reason why HLF4 became the largest conference on aid effectiveness yet, with 3,000 participants from all over the world, including donor countries, multilateral agencies, recipient countries, civil society and the private sector.[12]

Busan Outcome Document (BOD)

At HLF4, the international community adopted the Busan Outcome Document (BOD). The BOD emphasized a new partnership among all development actors for effective development cooperation, including governments of all levels, international and regional organizations, civil society as well as the private sector.

12 So-jin Lim, "Busan HLF4 Conference Outcome and Challenge of Korean ODA," *Development Cooperation Policy and Issue*, vol. 3, no. 3 (2011): 11-12.

Table 8.4 Principles and Actions adopted in HLF4[13]

Common Principles	Actions
Ownership of development priorities by developing countries	Deepen, extend and operationalize the democratic ownership of development policies and processes
A focus on results	Strengthen our efforts to achieve concrete and sustainable results
Partnerships for development	Broaden support for South-South and triangular cooperation, helping to tailor these horizontal partnerships to a greater diversity of country contexts and needs
Transparency and shared responsibility	Support developing countries in their efforts to facilitate, leverage and strengthen the impact of diverse forms of development finance and activities, ensuring that these diverse forms of cooperation have catalytic effects on development

BOD also included complementary efforts and actions for effective development to achieve MDGs by 2015. Considering a new type of development partnership such as the South-South development cooperation, the BOD envisioned an inclusive development whereby new actors in development and cooperation participate on the basis of common goals, shared principles and differential commitments. The BOD welcomed the inclusion of new actors, such as civil society and the private sector. Also, the BOD pointed out the

The Climate Change Fourth High Level Forum On Aid Effectiveness

13 OECD DAC, *Busan Partnership for Effective Development Co-operation* (Busan: OECD, 2011), 3.

importance of complementary action to improve the quality and quantity of development cooperation. For this, the BOD emphasized the importance of sustaining a high-level political leadership to ensure that the commitments made in Busan are implemented. Drawing on the evidence generated through periodic monitoring and the independent evaluation of the Paris Declaration, the participants of HLF4 confirmed the importance of sustainable results that meet the priority needs of developing countries and recognized a list of urgently needed changes to improve the effectiveness of partnerships for development. These changes are ① ownership, results and accountability, ② transparent and responsible cooperation, ③ promoting sustainable development in situations of conflict and fragility, and ④ partnering to strengthen resilience and reduce vulnerability in the face of adversity.[14]

The BOD also reflected a new awareness of development effectiveness, not just aid effectiveness. HLF4 suggested the following framework to improve development effectiveness:[15]

- Development is driven by strong, sustainable and inclusive growth.
- Governments' own revenues play a greater role in financing their development needs. In turn, governments are more accountable to their citizens for the development results they achieve.
- Effective state and non-state institutions design and implement their own reforms and hold each other to account.
- Developing countries increasingly integrate both regional and globally, creating economies of scale that will help them better compete in the global economy.

To this effect, the BOD confirmed the reconsideration of what aid should be spent on and how, in ways that are consistent with agreed international rights, norms and standards, so that aid catalyzes development. Such new framework includes following agendas.

- South-South and triangular cooperation for sustainable development
- Private sector and development
- Combating corruption and illicit flows
- Climate change finance

---

14 *Ibid.*
15 *Ibid.*

Development Effectiveness Discourse in the HLF4

Development Cooperation Discourse, introduced by civil society for the first time and adopted by the South Korean government for HLF4, emerged as an alternative to the aid effectiveness paradigm which has been a dominant framework in international development cooperation since the first HLF in 2003.

The principles of the Paris Declaration in 2005 constituted a dominant framework for understanding aid effectiveness, although there was an undercurrent of criticism highlighting how the principles focused too much on procedural and technical aspects from the donors' perspective. As the 2011 report on the Paris Declaration indicators and targets has shown, however, all of the indicators were unmet, with the sole exception of the technical cooperation indicator.[16] As a result, the international community came into HLF4 facing criticism that aid effectiveness mechanism is not effective and recognized the necessity of a new approach to achieve MDGs.[17]

Civil society saw the development effectiveness framework as an alternative approach to aid effectiveness discourse. Global civil society networks such as Better Aid and Open Forum emphasized an inclusive development cooperation encompassing all actors such as civil society and the private sector as well as governments, as well as crosscutting agendas like human rights, gender and environment. Civil society argued that aid is just one of the tools to achieve the goal of development and therefore the discourse of development cooperation should focus on actual development itself.[18]

The demand for a new framework comes from the government level as well. Right after the Accra Conference in 2008, the Canadian and Moroccan governments issued a report that recommended the development effectiveness as the theme of HLF4. The South Korean government and the United States supported this recommendation. Especially the South Korean government, as the host of HLF4, was under pressure to initiate a specific principle or norm related to international development cooperation. As a result, the South Korean government sought to establish a development effec-

16 Hyuk-Sang Sohn, "Framing Theory and Discourse Contestation of 'Aid Effectiveness' and 'Development Effectiveness' in International Development Cooperation," *The Korean Journal of International Relationship*, vol. 53, no. 1 (2013): 9.

17 *Ibid.*, 10.

18 *Ibid.* 24; BetterAid, "CSOs on the Road to Busan: Key Messages and Proposals," (2011); BetterAid, "BetterAid Response to the Busan Outcome Document," (2011); BetterAid, "Key Demands from Women's Right Organizations and Gender Equality Advocates," (2011).

tiveness framework which included effective institutions, gender equality, the expansion of the private sector in development cooperation, the establishment of a monitoring framework in the collaboration with the UN, and sustainable development.

However, it is difficult to say that this paradigm shift from aid effectiveness to development effectiveness was successful. Opposition to this paradigm shift came from several countries in the European Commission who traditionally steered aid effectiveness frameworks and UN agencies that were reluctant to see the OECD expand its influence through such a paradigm shift. Consequently, HLF4 concluded with the adoption of the BOD, which only indirectly includes development effectiveness discourse under the expression of 'Global Partnership for Effectiveness Development Cooperation.'

Outcome of HLF4

HLF4 was an inclusive framework that overall actors in development cooperation participated in and discussed aid effectiveness to achieve MDGs. There were four key accomplishments.

First, HLF4 tried to reach a realistic consensus by allowing the participation of emerging donors and by recognizing new actors' differing interests and positions on development cooperation. This conference was a place where differing actors, such as civil society, the private sector and governments were able to participate and raise their development agendas and build a comprehensive development partnership. Non-DAC countries, such as China, India and Brazil, also participated and raised their concerns.[19]

Second, HLF4 was a moment when the OECD and UN agencies could work together for more effective development cooperation. This meeting provided an opportunity for the OECD and UN to reach a consensus on the joint collaboration for the implementation of the BOD and MDGs evaluation.[20] One result of this collaboration between the OECD and UN agencies is South-South cooperation, a process where developing countries pursue their shared capacity development goals through exchanges of required knowledge, skills and resources across the regions in the Southern hemisphere,

19 Soo-Kyung Park et al., "Busan segyegaebalwonjo chongheo(HLF-4)eui juyo noneuiwa sunggwa [Busan HLF4 Key Issues and Outcome]," *KIEP jiyukgyungje Focus [KIEP Regional Economic Focus]*, vol. 5, no. 48 (2011): 11-13.

20 So-jin Lim, "Busan HLF4 Conference Outcome and Challenge of Korean ODA," *Development Cooperation Policy and Issue*, vol. 2011 no. 3 (2011).

and the triangular cooperation, a Southern-drive partnerships between two or more developing countries that are heavily supported by the UNDP.

Third, HLF4 sought to overcome key challenges facing the international community, such as a lack of financing for development, a need for the harmonization of multiple actors' development cooperation policies and the difficulty of accommodating the differing interests, perspectives and roles of these actors. Triangular cooperation and innovative financing for development are examples of how this conference attempted to improve international development cooperation.[21]

8.4 Global Aid Harmonization Mechanism

Need of Aid Harmonization

There are several reasons why aid harmonization is important. First, the global aid architecture can be characterized as the combination of various development actors. This global aid architecture consists of states, inter-governmental organizations, non-governmental organizations, expert groups, policy networks, ad hoc groups, international conferences and forums, the private sector, and transnational movements.[22]

Second, the current aid architecture is divided between the UN mechanism and the Bretton Woods system. This bilateral mechanism reflects a division of labor: the UN mechanism consists of specialized UN agencies such as the UNDP, UNICEF, and WFP. The Bretton Woods system consisting of the International Bank for Reconstruction and Development (IBRD), International Development Association (IDA) and International Monetary Fund (IMF) tackle the issue of financial assistance. In the UN system, the member states have equal voting rights, but the Bretton Woods system is controlled by major developed countries through a weighted voting system. In other words, the policies and norms related to international development cooperation are the specialty of the UN and its agencies, but the resources for their implementation are provided

21 Soo-Kyung Park et al., "Busan HLF4 Key Issues and Outcome," *KIEP Regional Economic Focus*, vol. 5, no. 48 (2011): 11-13.

22 Dae-Won Koh, "Accountability and Coherence in Global Governance for Development and Poverty Reduction," *Local Development Studies*, vol. 19, no. 2 (2010): 135-138.

by the Bretton Woods system. Therefore, there is always a gap between policymaking and implementation in the international development cooperation.[23]

Third, there is a highly asymmetric relationship in global aid governance between the donor countries and the recipient countries, a reflection of the fact that most of the resources for development cooperation traditionally came from donor countries. However, the recipient countries have been able to gradually increase their resources for development due to the increase of emerging donors and their own economic development. This has diversified the power relationship in the international development cooperation.[24] This increasingly diversified power relationship among development actors means that coordination in aid planning, implementation and evaluation at the global level is more important than ever.

International Effort for Aid Harmonization

The issue of aid harmonization was first raised at the 1st High Level Forum (HLF1) in Rome (2003). This arose from the recognition that differing donor requirements for delivering and monitoring development assistance were generating unproductive transaction costs for partner countries. The international community was also aware of partner country concerns that donors' practices do not always fit well with recipients' national development priorities and systems, including their budget, programs, and project planning cycles and public expenditure and financial management systems.[25]

In March 2005, the OECD organized the High Level Forum on Harmonization and Alignment of Aid Effectiveness. This forum further clarified the concept of aid harmonization and adopted 'harmonization' as one of the principles of aid effectiveness. The principle of aid harmonization means that donors must coordinate their development work better amongst themselves to avoid duplication and high transaction costs for poor countries. In the Paris Declaration, the international community promised to coordinate better at the country level to ease the strain on recipient governments, for example by reducing large numbers of duplicative field missions. Thus, aid should be pooled in support of a particular strategy led by a recipient country—a national health plan for example—rather

23 *Ibid.*

24 *Ibid.*

25 OECD, "Rome Declaration on Harmonisation," in *DAC Guidelines and Reference Series: Harmonising Donor Practices for Effective Aid Delivery* (Paris: OECD, 2003), 10-12.

than fragmented into multiple individual projects.

However, harmonization at the global level is just as necessary as it is at the country level. Yet, attempts to ensure global aid harmonization are themselves split between the two components of global aid architecture: the UN system and OECD DAC. The OECD DAC has focused on aid harmonization among donors through improvement in aid effectiveness mechanisms. On the other hand, the UN is prone to tackle the issue of inclusive development cooperation between donors, recipients and other development actors, putting priority on social and human development.

The OECD established the Development Assistance Group, which is the predecessor of the DAC, in 1960 in order to shape the discourse of international development cooperation. The OECD DAC in fact played a key role developing the aid harmonization concept by adopting the Paris Declaration in 2005 and the Accra Agenda for Action in 2008. The donor countries participating in the OECD DAC mechanism were able to have a forum to discuss the challenges of development cooperation. Although the OECD DAC has worked for inclusive governance including emerging donors, civil society, developing countries and the private sector by building comprehensive partnerships, the intrinsic limitation of the OECD DAC — its membership consists of few rich member states — limits its ability to be the coordinator of global aid architecture.[26]

The UN General Assembly steers the discourse of aid harmonization at the UN level. The UN mechanisms reflecting this effort include the establishment of the United Nations Development Group (UNDG) in 1997 and United Nations Development Cooperation Forum (UN DCF) in 2005.

In 1997, responding to the consensus that it was necessary to coordinate the activities of different UN development agencies, Kofi Annan established the UNDG to avoid duplication and lower transaction costs. The steering authority of the UNDG goes to the General Assembly and United Nations Economic and Social Council (ECOSOC). The UNDG unites the 32 UN funds, programs, agencies, departments, and offices that play a role in development. The group's common objective is to deliver more coherent, effective and efficient support to countries seeking to attain internationally agreed development goals, including the Millennium Development Goals. The UNDG designs system-wide guidance to coordinate,

26 *Ibid.*, 143-145.

harmonize and align UN development activities.

UNDG also sought to increase aid effectiveness by reinforcing the UN Residence Coordinator system.[27] However, this attempt to increase coordination among UN agencies by restructuring UN aid architecture appears to have failed. ECOSOC in particular since the restructuring has shown lack of coordination with the agencies outside of UN mechanisms, especially the organizations those were based on the Bretton-Woods system. Also, the UNDG's coordination was impossible for UN agencies because the UNDG had difficulty exerting influence over the individual sovereign states.

The resolution adopted at the UN World Summit in 2005 recognized the necessity of a global forum for developing countries to express themselves. This momentum led to the establishment of the UN DCF. The creation of the UN DCF was one of the most proactive actions taken by the UN to increase accountability and coordination among the UN agencies in international development and cooperation.[28] It sought to provide an inclusive framework to reflect differing demands and voices from developing countries, donors, civil society, local and central governments, and the private sector.[29] The UN DCF convened three conferences in 2008, 2010 and 2012 where it covered the issues of coherence, mutual accountability, aid effectiveness and South-South cooperation in international development and cooperation.

Developing countries, especially the Group of 77 (G77), played an important role in establishing the UN DCF. The G77, with the support of NGOs, preferred discussing development cooperation issues in the UN, where they have more influence, rather than the OECD DAC, which is steered by the developed countries. However, in spite of the wishes of developing countries to work through UN DCF is unlikely to develop enough capabilities to respond fully to their wishes. Developed countries still prefer the OECD DAC system for the discussion of development cooperation. Moreover, the UN DCF does not have enforcement mechanisms.[30]

The establishment of the UNDG and UN DCF signifies that the

27 United Nations Development Group, "About the UNDG," http://www.undg.org/content/about_the_undg, last visited June 2014.

28 Dae-Won Koh, "Accountability and Coherence in Global Governance for Development and Poverty Reduction," *Local Development Studies*, vol. 19, no. 2 (2010): 123-152.

29 Ji-young Yoon, "UN DCF and International Development Cooperation," *Journal of International Development Cooperation*, vol. 2012, no. 4 (2012): 144.

30 Dae-Won Koh (2010).

UN system recognizes the importance of governance in global aid architecture. However, the operation of these mechanisms still have limitations in coordinating between various UN agencies because of a lack of enforcement mechanisms. The UN's key strength is in tackling social development and human development but it does not have strong enough governance systems to implement these agendas and compel its umbrella agencies. As a result, the OECD DAC is maintaining the initiative in the discussion of aid effectiveness.[31]

In 2005, the UN launched another initiative to harmonize differing UN development and humanitarian agencies, which is "Delivering as One." Based on the principle of 'One UN', the UN opened the 'United Nations Country Team,' which is a field office to coordinate UN aid operations in recipient countries. In February 2006, the UN conducted six pilot projects in eight countries under the initiative of 'Delivering as One': Albania, Cape Verde, Mozambique, Pakistan, Rwanda, Tanzania, Uruguay, and Vietnam. In these cases, the UN unified its structure in the recipient countries and sought to increase effectiveness in program and project management, budgeting, resource mobilization and distribution, communication, and other administrative issues. The resident coordinator of the single field office plays a critical role in this initiative.[32]

In sum, the establishment of efficient global aid architecture is a critical agenda in aid effectiveness. The priority of development cooperation is building a cooperative relationship between the OECD DAC and the UN system for increasing aid and its effectiveness. The first step in the harmonization between development actors will be avoiding meaningless competition for hegemony in development cooperation between the OECD DAC and the UN system. Overcoming a dichotomous division between the developing countries and the developed countries and building mutual accountability is also important. The desirable global aid architecture of the future would be authoritative and inclusive, combining enforcement mechanisms with deep coordination between the OECD DAC, the UN system and the Bretton Woods system.[33]

---

31 ODA Watch, "UN DCF: the Possibility of Collaboration for Future Development Cooperation?" *Newsletter OWL* 67 (2012).

32 Jione Jung et al., *Enhancing the Effectiveness of South Korea's Multilateral Aid* (Seoul: KIEP, 2010): 121-122.

33 Dae-Won Koh, "Accountability and Coherence in Global Governance for Development and Poverty Reduction," *Local Development Studies*, vol. 19, no. 2 (2010).

Chapter 8. Review Discussion Questions

1. How did the aid effectiveness regime develop?
2. What are the principles of aid effectiveness?
3. What limitation does the aid effectiveness regime have?
4. What were the differences between HLF4 and previous HLF conferences?
5. Why are there still limitations in the global aid architecture?
6. Who are the major actors in today's global aid architecture?

Chapter 9
Poverty, Security and Human Rights

"The challenge now is to demonstrate how the assets represented by human rights principles, a form of international public goods, can be of value in pursuing the overarching development objective: the eradication of poverty."[1]

"Democracy, development and respect for human rights and fundamental freedoms are interdependent and mutually reinforcing."[2]

9.1 Pro-poor Development for Poverty Eradication

The interest in pro-poor growth has developed from two concerns that emerged in the 1990s. First, the rate of growth in developing countries had to increase if they were to narrow the gap with the industrialized countries. Second, poverty had to be reduced. Poverty reduction was also a goal that had been emphasized through the Millennium Development Goals. Pro-poor growth implies distributional effects that favor the poor. However, there is still no set definition of what constitutes pro-poor growth. The current discussions of pro-poor growth are significant since it has been identified that growth will reduce poverty more effectively when the distribution of income is more equitable.

As identified by the DAC, pro-poor growth is the pace and pattern of growth that enhances the ability of poor women and men to participate in, contribute to and benefit from growth.[3] Growth is clearly pro-poor when it raises the incomes of the poor. However, the standard or extent of increase in income that is necessary for the growth to be defined as pro-poor is still under debate. From a policy perspective, pro-poor growth has also been defined as growth that maximizes the income gains of the poor and thus accelerates progress toward meeting MDG1.

---

1 "Bridging the Gap between Human Rights and Development" (Presidential Lecture, World Bank, December 2001).

2 Vienna Declaration and Program of Action.

3 OECD, *Promoting Pro-Poor Growth: Policy Guidance to Donors* (Paris: OECD, 2006).

Some policy implications are credited with promoting pro-poor growth. Incentives to invest and raise productivity are pre-conditions for economic growth. To achieve this, a stable macro-economy, institutions that allocate property rights, lower transaction costs and predictable policies need to be implemented. While economic growth has positive effects on poverty alleviation, to reduce poverty countries need to provide physical access to markets so that people can obtain the resources needed to make investments, especially in education and health. These types of policies will be able to direct the pattern and location of the poor in promoting pro-poor growth.

For pro-poor growth strategies to increase aid effectiveness, it is important to find strategies that reflect country conditions. Successful strategies need to be built on a thorough analysis of what limits participation of poor households in the growth process, and binding constraints need to be addressed before it is possible for these poor households to fully participate in promoting growth. In a study conducted by the World Bank, six characteristics have been identified as being particularly relevant:

- Population density and degree of urbanization determine the extent to which transaction costs and remoteness preclude rural households from participating in growth and the relative importance of a targeted infrastructure strategy.
- Asset and income inequality influences poverty reducing impact of future growth and can reveal gender or ethnic discrimination or other inequality traps that prevent equal footing in factor or input markets of different groups.
- Importance of agriculture in the economy and the workforce determines the need to raise agricultural earnings and encourage mobility.
- Climate instability affects agricultural earning and the need for risk management initiatives to protect poor farmers.
- Fertility rate indicates how women can participate in the workforce.
- Institutions with better quality and capacity to increase accountability and transparency for service delivery affect how public investments can link the poor to growth.

Aid Selectivity

A fundamental question in development assistance is how countries allocate the aid that they provide to foreign countries. Berthélemy finds that most donors behave in an egoistic way, targeting assistance to their most significant trading partners. However, the results also indicate that most donors do assist the neediest recipient countries and on average target recipients with better governance indicators, such as democracy or absence of violent conflicts. This suggests that in spite of egoistic values behind aid policies, bilateral donors also implement rules of selectivity based on recipient needs and merits.[4]

Aid selectivity refers to the quality of aid allocation decisions. The most selective aid is aid which maximizes its effectiveness in respect to the objectives set forth by the donor and recipient countries. It is a general concept that envisions a geographical pattern of aid allocation that maximizes poverty reduction. Poverty reduction is the primary legitimate goal of aid allocation. The concept is also defined under more narrow terms by which it designates an allocation of aid that gives preference to countries with good policies and institutions.[5]

Considerable evidence points to institutions and policies as key determinants in promoting effectiveness of financial assistance, i.e. a government with a sound framework for growth and poverty reduction is also more likely to use financial resources to complement policies with necessary public investments in roads or schools. This has given rise to an institutional selectivity approach, which is the term for when donor countries channel more aid resources to countries that possess the institutional and policy framework to utilize the aid properly.[6] There is also a broad agreement that concessional assistance should concentrate on the poorest countries. Compared to the lowest income countries, middle-income countries with sound institutions and policies generally have access to food in the international markets. In the case of middle-income countries, therefore, allocated aid concentrates on poverty selectivity and institutional selectivity.[7]

An interesting point to note is that studies show that selectivity has been changing over the years. The patterns of selectivity that

4 Jean-Claude Berthélemy, "Bilateral Donors' Interest vs. Recipients' Development Motives in Aid Allocation: Do All Donors Behave the Same,"*Review of Development Economics*, vol. 10, no. 2 (2006): 179-194.

5 Jacky Amprou et al., "Aid Selectivity According to Augmented Criteria," *The World Economy*, vol. 30, no. 5 (2007): 733-763.

6 David Dollar and V. Levin, "The Increasing Selectivity of Foreign Aid, 1984-2003," *World Development*, vol. 34, no. 12 (2006): 2034-2046.

7 *Ibid.*

were observed in the period from overall relationship between the institutional goal of aid and both bilateral and multilateral aid have achieved alignment in the 21st century. Also it has been found that the donors have consistently taken democracy into account when providing aid, especially when it comes to bilateral aid.[8] Moreover it is worth noting that as the time progresses, more and more donors are becoming aware and monitoring the will and power of economic governance of the recipient administration to make sure that the aid are used effectively rather than completing the quota that international institutions such as OECD dictates. In addition, another interesting point has been raised by scholars like Gourinchas and Jeanne who coined the term, "allocation puzzle". Gourinchas and Jeanne criticized that the aid model that was widely accepted as an established theory, which argued that the international capital including aids flows to the countries with relatively higher capital, is no longer valid and observable since the capital flows from developed and developing countries.

9.2 International Security

It was during the 17th century that a new state-centric international order was created to sustain peace and order in the world. Governments of different countries imposed different values on their people, and the state was given primary responsibility for action within the international arena. Since the development of the sovereign state and the establishment of the Westphalian order, the nation-state has been the central actor of international relations. By definition, 'international' means between and among nations. Traditional international relations analysis of security focused on external military threats to states, which meant that international security has been defined almost exclusively in terms of national survival needs. Security has meant the protection of the state-its boundaries, people, institutions and values from external shock.[9]

8 These results can be accounted for in part by the assistance of the European Commission which is largely considered multilateral. Other major multilateral agencies such as the African Development Fund, the IDA and the IMF have no relationship with democracy and are consistent with provisions in their charters indicating that political factors should not influence lending decisions. D. Dollar, V. Levin, "The Increasing Selectivity of Foreign Aid, 1984-2003," *World Development*, vol. 34, no. 12 (2006): 2034-2046.

9 Commission on Global Governance, *Our Global Neighborhood*, (Oxford: Oxford University Press, 1995).

During the Cold War, military power was perceived as an important foundation of development. The United States was especially concerned with its national interest and used development assistance as a tool to counter communism by making non-communist governments more powerful. Development assistance and military aid were perceived as complementary elements of successful development programs by the United States and other Western countries, as well as the Soviet Union and its allies.

However, as globalization erodes the barriers or boundaries around individual states, traditional views of security, which were based on the concept of national security, have started to shift. Today we require a more comprehensive definition of security.

Just like the definitions for the term security vary, the agendas for achieving security are also diverse as illustrated in the box below.

Box 9.1 Security Development Agenda	
Conflict prevention	Governments and donor countries have worked to prevent conflicts in developing countries. However, the international community has not been able to form a consensus on whether conflict prevention should include military means or be limited to civilian instruments. The costs of conflict prevention are high, largely because of the peacekeeping element included in conflict-prevention packages. A rough estimate indicates that global spending on conflict prevention, excluding peacekeeping operations, is around $1 billion to $2 billion per year.[10]
Peacekeeping	There has been some controversy regarding the objectives of peacekeeping activities. Some believe that peacekeeping activities are an effort to promote economic and social development while others question the possibility of safeguarding national security interests of those donors that send troops. Peacekeeping missions are expensive. Those managed by the United Nations are comparatively cheaper, and for the 2013/14 budget year, total costs amounted to $7.83 billion, excluding the additional national expenditures of at least some countries providing troops.
Disarmament, Demobilization and Arms Reduction	There is a consensus that practical disarmament is highly beneficial for economic development. A rough estimate of average expenditure during the early 2000s is about $500 million.
Direct Subsidies to security forces	Military aid and other types of direct subsidies to promote security have received a bad reputation as instruments to promote economic development due to the history of using military aid as an instrument of influence and control over the armed forces of recipient countries.

10 Michael Brzoska, "Extending ODA or Creating a New Reporting Instrument for Security Related Expenditures for Development," *Development Policy Review*, vol. 26, no. 2 (2008): 131-150.

9.3 Human Security

New threats have emerged due to globalization. Threats to human security are no longer exclusively military threats posed by neighboring states but now include trans-boundary issues such as environmental pollution, trans-boundary terrorism or infectious diseases. Compared to traditional relations analysis of security, which concentrated on the state as the sole actor within the international field, an expansion of the traditional concept of security since the end of the Cold War has resulted in the alternative conceptualization of human security. Human security is an expansion from traditional state-centric views of security along both vertical and horizontal axes. Human security vertically changes the focus from the state actor to the individual human being. From a horizontal perspective, the previous focus on military threats and power struggles is expanded to include other issues, such as criminality, defense of human rights, economic threats, environmental threats or threats to human health and well-being. Today, human security promotes human development and good governance.

UNDP, Human Security Report 2012

Former UN Secretary General Kofi Annan stated at the UN General Assembly in 2000 that individual sovereignty precedes national sovereignty, and that national sovereignty should not violate individual rights. The concept of human security was formulated during the post-Cold War era as the international community became increasingly aware of individual security concerns in place of traditional state-centric interpretations of security. However, the international community has yet to provide a single conceptualization of human security; the definitions that exist today are still diverse. Notwithstanding the differences that exist, certain commonalities can be identified. First, human security has shifted from traditional security, which centered on the sovereign state, to the individual; second, it is intertwined with a wide array of socio-economic elements; and third, multilateral co-operation and networks are crucial for establishing a human rights regime.

Human security is evidently a concept that has been derived from the traditional concept of state security to incorporate the changes that are perceivable within the current international order. Nonetheless, it is important to recognize that human security is not a replacement for the previous approach that concentrated on the state; rather, the two concepts are becoming increasingly interdependent. That is, state security cannot be achieved without human security and human security is complementary to attaining state security. The mutually reinforcing nature of human security and state security can be understood in four respects:

- Its utmost concern is with the individual and the community rather than the state;
- Menaces to people's security include threats and conditions that have not always been identified as threats to state security;
- The range of actors is expanded beyond the state; and
- Achieving human security includes more than just assisting people to fend for themselves.[11]

In 1994 the UNDP introduced new dimensions of human security in its Human Development Report. Following the UNDP's definition, in 1999, the Human Security Network was established by fourteen countries from all regions. The Commission on Human Security (2003) defines human security as protecting the vital core of all human lives in ways that enhance the human freedoms and human fulfillment.[12] Human security attempts to protect individuals from direct threats to their well-being. In addition to protecting the individual, the idea of human security contains the power for people to act on their own behalf, which can be interpreted to mean that in order to promote human security, individuals must be encouraged to build and develop capabilities and awareness of human dignity, which will ultimately lead to avoiding future threats.

The Commission on Human Security calls for a strategy of protection and empowerment to secure the lives of people and their

11 Commission on Human Security, *Human Security Now: Protecting and Empowering People* (New York: United Nations, 2003), 4-6.

12 *Ibid.*

livelihoods and dignity. Core policy agendas include:[13]

- Protecting people in violent conflict
- Protecting people from the proliferation of arms
- Supporting the security of people on the move
- Establishing human security transition funds for post conflict situations
- Encouraging fair trade and markets to benefit the extreme poor
- Working to provide minimum living standards everywhere
- According higher priority to ensuring universal access to basic health care
- Developing an efficient and equitable global system for patent rights
- Empowering all people with universal basic education
- Clarifying the needs for a global human identity while respecting the freedom of individuals to have diverse identities and affiliations

Although some dispute the idea that human security can be a means of resolving the current impasse between security and human rights issues, it is necessary to understand human security within the context of both traditional security agendas and human rights issues. The concepts of human security, the right to security and the responsibility to protect both may be used to temper the authoritarian overtones of the language of security as well as provide a potentially new legitimating framework for human rights.

Box 9.2 Trust Fund for Human Security

In December 1998, late Prime Minister Obuchi Keizo in Japan announced that a Trust Fund for Human Security would be established in the United Nations. Since 1999, the UNTFHS has committed over $350 million to projects in over seventy countries around the world. Japan contributed ¥500 million in 1999 and by 2006 had made total contributions of ¥33.5 billion to make the Trust Fund the largest of its kind within the UN. The objective of the Fund was to translate the concept of human security into concrete activities implemented by UN agencies through supporting projects that address threats like poverty, environmental degradation, landmines, conflicts, refugees, illicit drugs or infectious diseases to secure people's livelihoods and dignity. The Fund has set its focus on each individual and supports projects that are designed to protect the people from threats and empower them to enhance their resilience. The projects that are supported by the Fund are largely categorized into eight areas: poverty, health, drug, refugees, conflict, disaster, environment and other.

13 Commission on Human Security, www.humansecurity-chs.org, Last visited March 2009.

9.4 Human Rights and Development

Seventeen million people in developing countries die each year from curable infections and parasitic diseases such as diarrhea, measles, malaria and tuberculosis.[14] Unfortunately the suffering imposed by conditions of poverty is rarely analyzed as a violation of human rights. Until recently, human rights work has ignored investigating the systemic relationship between poverty and violations of human rights.

The rights-based approach is critical to understanding the role of human rights within the realm of development. Article 1 of the Declaration on the Right to Development indicates that a rights-based definition of development is a comprehensive economic, social, cultural and political process. The core objective of the rights-based approach is to improve the well-being of the entire population and all individuals based on their active, free and meaningful participation in development and the fair distribution of the benefits that result from development efforts.[15]

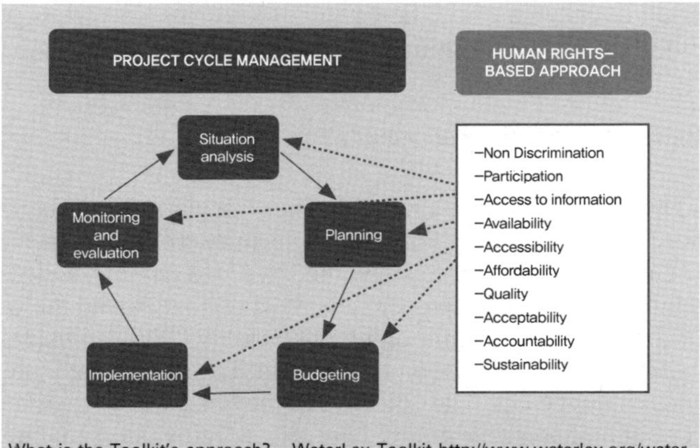

What is the Toolkit's approach? – WaterLex Toolkit http://www.waterlex.org/waterlex-toolkit/about-the-toolkit/what-is-the-toolkits-approach/

14 UNDP Human Development Report 1997.

15 The Declaration on the Right to Development was adopted by the General Assembly in December 1986. Article 1.1. The right to development is an inalienable human right by virtue of which every human person and all peoples are entitled to participate in, contribute to, and enjoy economic, social, cultural and political development, in which all human rights and fundamental freedoms can be fully realized. Article 1.2. The human right to development also implies the full realization of the right of peoples to self-determination, which includes, subject to the relevant provisions of both International Covenants on Human Rights, the exercise of their inalienable right to full sovereignty over all their natural wealth and resources.

The link between human rights and development was reaffirmed by the Copenhagen Declaration in 1995. The Copenhagen Declaration established a new consensus that placed people at the center of concerns for sustainable development. It explicitly points to human rights as a core element of development.

The ultimate goal of social development is to improve and enhance the quality of life of all people. It requires democratic institutions, respect for all human rights and fundamental freedoms, increased and equal economic opportunities, the rule of law, the promotion of respect for cultural diversity and the rights of persons belonging to minorities and an active involvement of civil society.[16]

The Office of High Commissioner for Human Rights (OHCHR) defines a rights-based approach to development as a conceptual framework for the process of human development that is normatively based on international standards and operationally directed to promoting and protecting human rights. It integrates principles of the human rights system, such as equality, equity, accountability, empowerment and participation, into the plans, policies and processes of development. Through this process the rights-based approach contains the potential to empower the poor. Empowerment has been recognized as an essential element of poverty reduction.

With a rights-based approach, the rationale of poverty reduction derives from the fact that the poor have rights which are being violated. In the case of the traditional needs-based approach, the obligations to poverty reduction were moral. However, with the recognition of fundamental rights, poverty reduction becomes a legal entitlement for the poor and a legal obligation for others towards the poor.[17] Thus, the rights-based approach provides a stronger mechanism to motivate the international community to provide aid to assist the poor in poverty reduction.

The international human rights framework states that all people have a human right to a standard of living that is adequate for their health and well-being, to food, clothing, housing, medical care, social services and civil and political freedoms. However, many people struggling from poverty are deprived of their human rights. Poverty is a direct violation of human rights. The human rights of those populations that are struggling from poverty need to be pro-

16 United Nations, *Report of the World Summit for Social Development* (Copenhagen: UN, 1995).

17 OHCHR, "Principles and Guidelines for a Human Rights Approach to Poverty Reduction Strategies" (New York, Geneva: United Nations, 2002).

tected. Thus, the relationship between human rights, poverty and development is complex and interconnected. It is evident that in order to achieve poverty reduction, efforts to protect the poor from human rights violations are necessary. However, the perception of threats to the national security of developed nations that emerged after the terrorist attacks on the World Trade Center has challenged this approach.

In the post-9/11 world there is an insuperable opposition between the ideals of security and human rights. There is a debate over whether states should pursue security or human rights, a debate aggravated by voices advocating a retreat from human rights. On the other hand, there also exists the notion of security as a human right.[18] Neil MacFarlane argues that the evolution of the discourses surrounding security may considerably enhance the capacity for international protection of the human rights of individuals and communities from the risk of violence.[19] Indeed, the United Nations Declaration of Human Rights identifies that individuals have the right to life, liberty and security of person.[20]

The Universal Declaration of Human Rights was adopted by the United Nations on December 10, 1948. It consists of thirty articles which recognize the inherent dignity and the equal and inalienable rights of all members of the human family to create a world in which human beings are provided four freedoms: freedom of speech, freedom of assembly, freedom from fear and freedom from want.

Box 9.3 Universal Declaration of Human Rights

The Universal Declaration of Human Rights was adopted by the United Nations General Assembly in 1948. Its thirty articles epitomize a fundamental set of rights that all human beings are entitled to. The world was shocked by the atrocities of World War II and cried for the need to promulgate basic human rights and this Declaration was adopted against such a background.

Articles 1 and 2 are the foundation blocks for the Declaration,

18 Benjamin Gould and Lira Lazarus, *Security and Human Rights* (Oxford: Hart Publishing, 2007), 19.

19 *Ibid.*

20 Universal Declaration of Human Rights (1948), Art. 3.

identifying principles of dignity, liberty, equality and brotherhood. The seven paragraphs of the preamble set out the reasons for the Declaration. The main body of the Declaration is comprised of four parts: Articles 3–11 constitute the rights of the individual, such as the right to life and the prohibition of slavery; Articles 12–17 constitute the rights of the individual in civil and political society; Articles 18–21 focus on spiritual, public and political freedoms such as freedom of religion and freedom of association; and finally the Articles 22–27 set out social, economic and cultural rights, which also articulate the duty of individuals to societies.

The Universal Declaration on Human Rights was the first declaration to articulate the rights inherent in human beings to protect individuals from external forces and pressures. It is not legally binding and thus not a treaty. Nonetheless, it has been utilized in many diplomatic settings to induce countries to make commitments for their peoples. The Declaration also serves as the foundation for many international covenants, conventions and institutions.

The fundamental question at the core of human rights is whether universal human rights exist. Or is it merely a concoction of Western countries to infuse Western ideologies and values throughout the world? Even if a universal set of human rights existed, the next challenge would be to define these rights. There have been many international efforts to draft a set of human rights, but all are drafted to accommodate diverse interpretations and development during adjudications. What should be absolute? Where should exceptions be permissible?

One of the basic assumptions made to deal with human rights is that there exists a universal norm to govern the way individual persons should deal with one another. This is the assumption that underlies the Universal Declaration of Human Rights. The right to inherent human dignity and the equal and inalienable rights of all people and the rights to freedom, justice and world peace are recognized within the Declaration. It also contains fundamental principles such as the right to life, the rights not to be subjected to torture or to cruel, inhumane or degrading treatment or punishment and the right not to be subjects to arbitrary arrest.

The Covenant on Civil and Political Rights, a separate international covenant concentrating on the rights of economic, social and cultural issues, was adopted in 1966. This covenant reflected the growing scope of human rights; that is, human rights refers to more than classic civil liberties and should consider fundamental economic, social and cultural developments. Nonetheless, the process of interpreting these "universal" human rights to specific contexts and situations has resulted in numerous dilemmas and conflicts.

Human rights policies may result in interfering with the domestic affairs of other nations. Conflicting objectives have emerged as a result of the process of formulating a development aid policy. The basic foundation for countries to provide economic aid to developing countries can be understood from two levels. First, reaching a basic standard of living is a fundamental human right for all mankind and as such rich countries should assist poor countries to reach a minimum standard of living by providing them with financial and technical support. Second, from a donor-country perspective, it is also in the interests of rich countries to provide aid.

A human rights approach must deal with both civil and political rights and economic and social rights in the development process. It must capture the essential active nature of human rights and apply human rights practices to the aid program instead of simply assessing the human rights implications of aid.[21] The international human rights framework provides a solid foundation for practical and effective official development assistance policies and programs.

Today, about ninety regional and subject-oriented international human rights regimes currently exist around the world. Most of these regimes are state-oriented or based on mutual agreements among nation states.[22] Human rights regimes are agreements accepted by individual governments and require the efforts of both donor and recipient countries for the realization of fundamental human rights.

Box 9.4 Four Freedoms

"The first is freedom of speech and expression—everywhere in the world. The second is freedom of every person to worship God in his own way—everywhere in the world. The third is freedom from want—which, translated into universal terms, means economic understandings which will secure to every nation a healthy peacetime life for its inhabitants—everywhere in the world. The fourth is freedom from fear—which, translated into world terms, means a world-wide reduction of armaments to such a point and in such a thorough fashion that no nation will be in a position to commit an act of physical aggression against any neighbor-anywhere in the world."

21 Andre Frankovits, "Rejoinder: the Rights Way to Development Elsevier Science Ltd," *Food Policy*, vol. 21, no. 1 (1996): 123-128.

22 UNESCO Korea, "Principal International Documents Regarding Human Rights" (Seoul: UNESCO, 1995).

The four freedoms refer to the freedom of speech and expression, the freedom of religion, the freedom from want and the freedom from fear. The four freedoms were identified within the State of the Union Address to Congress given by Franklin D. Roosevelt on January 6, 1941. These freedoms have become the basis for the human security paradigm.

9.5 Regional Human Rights Efforts

Europe

Efforts to prevent human rights violations became an international object after World War II. During the reconstruction of the continent following the world war, Europe renewed its peacekeeping efforts and encouraged cooperation. The Council of Europe, the European Union and the Organization for Security and Cooperation in Europe were all founded in this period to promote peace and stability in Europe. Although all three of these organizations deal with human rights, their purposes of development differed:

- The Council of Europe promotes the rule of law, human rights and democracy.
- The European Union was devised as an institution to promote trade and economic stability for its members.
- The Organization for Security and Cooperation in Europe (OSCE) was founded to maintain peace and military security within Europe.

The Council of Europe (COE) was established in 1949 by ten member states.[23] It was founded on the principles of pluralist democracy, human rights and the rule of law. To date, the Council has forty five member states with over 875 million people and is in dialogue with over 400 non-governmental organizations (NGOs), which hold consultative status.

European Convention on Human Rights (ECHR) was the COE's first legal treaty to protect human rights, as well as the first international human rights treaty with enforceable mechanisms. It was inspired by the United Nations Universal Declaration of Human

23 The ten members to join the Council of Europe at its inception in 1949 were Belgium, Denmark, France, Ireland, Italy, Luxembourg, the Netherlands, Norway, Sweden, and the United Kingdom.

Rights (1948), which was signed in Rome on November 4, 1950, and entered into force on September 3, 1953. Only member states of the COE can become a party to the ECHR. The European Court of Human Rights was established in 1953. It is located in Strasbourg and has jurisdiction over Council of Europe member countries that have accepted the Court's optional jurisdiction, after which court decisions are binding.

The Organization for Security and Cooperation in Europe (OSCE) is the largest regional security institution in the world. The OSCE began in the early 1950s when the Soviet Union proposed the creation of an all-European security conference for the first time. On August 1, 1975, the leaders from thirty five states gathered in the Finnish capital of Helsinki to sign the Final Act of Conference on Security and Cooperation in the European region, hence the name Helsinki Accords. The Accords is not a treaty but rather an aggrement that is politically binding. These countries pledged to make human rights their top policy regarding the Soviet Union and other Eastern European countries. This agreement aimed to improve relations between the Communist bloc and the West.

Today the OSCE deals with conflict warning, prevention, crisis management and post-conflict rehabilitation. Its tasks include arms control, preventive diplomacy, confidence and security building measures, human rights promotion, and democratization, election monitoring and guaranteeing economic and environmental security. OSCE members now include all European nations, as well as Canada and the United States (who were both original members) and members from Central Asia.[24]

The Act contains a broad range of measures to enhance security and cooperation in the region with an emphasis on human rights and fundamental freedoms. Since 1975, the number of countries who have signed the Helsinki Accords has expanded to fifty five. In the early 1990s the Helsinki Accords were officially transformed into the Organization for Security and Cooperation (OSCE) in Europe.

24 The 55 member states are: Albania, Andorra, Armenia, Austria, Azerbaijan, Belarus, Belgium, Bosnia and Herzegovina, Bulgaria, Canada, Croatia, Cyprus, Czech Republic, Denmark, Estonia, Finland, France, Georgia, Germany, Greece, the Holy See, Hungary, Iceland, Ireland, Italy, Kazakhstan, Kyrgyzstan, Latvia, Liechtenstein, Lithuania, Luxembourg, Malta, Moldova, Monaco, the Netherlands, Norway, Poland, Portugal, Romania, the Russian Federation, San Marino, Serbia and Montenegro, the Slovak Republic, Slovenia, Spain, Sweden, Switzerland, Tajikistan, the Former Yugoslav Republic of Macedonia, Turkey, Turkmenistan, Ukraine, the United Kingdom, the United States and Uzbekistan.

The European Union was established in July 1952 with only six members: Belgium, France, Germany, Italy, Luxembourg and the Netherlands.[25] At the time, it was named the European Coal and Steel Community (ECSC). Originally designed to address economic issues, the organization later became the European Economic Community (EEC) following the Treaty of Rome (1957). The institution was finally renamed the European Union with the Treaty on European Union (signed in Maastricht on February 7, 1992 and entering into force on November 1, 1993).

Asia

Despite the region's phenomenal economic growth, there are still many violations of human rights in East Asia. The region has received a fair share of funds from the international community in an effort to protect it populations from these violations. For example, according to the UN OCHA (Office for the Coordination of Humanitarian Affairs), between 2014 and 2015, more than $18 million, or roughly 6% of the total field operation budget, was allocated to Asia to provide humanitarian aid and prepare for emergencies and response.[26/]

Over 7 million people in Asia are infected with HIV/AIDS, with more than one million new infections annually. Within East Asia, China is threatened most by HIV/AIDS infections. The infection rates are still relatively low, but current estimates suggest that by 2010, up to 10 million people in China alone will be infected with HIV/AIDS. An epidemic of this size, according to UNAIDS estimates, indicates that the magnitude of resources needed to respond to epidemics in Asia will soon be equivalent to that needed in Africa.[27] HIV/AIDS issues and human rights issues are not separable in that the people suffering from such disease become vulnerable within the society and may not be able to realize their civil, politi-

25 The European Union has also expanded from its six original members to include: Denmark, Ireland, and the UK, which joined in 1973; Greece, which joined in 1981; Spain and Portugal, both joining in 1986; and Austria, Finland, and Sweden, which all joined in 1995. In 2004, the EU expanded from 15 to 25 states, with the accession of the Cyprus, Czech Republic, Estonia, Hungary, Latvia, Lithuania, Malta, Poland, Slovakia and Slovenia.

26 OCHA, *OCHA in 2006: Activities and Extra-Budgetary Funding Requirement* (New York: UNOCHA, 2006), 126-127.

27 Helene Gayle, Nafis Sadik and Naruo Uehara, "The Human Security Impact of AIDS and Other Communicable Disease in Asia," presented in the Human Security Challenge of HIV/AIDS and Other Communicable Disease: Exploring Effective Regional and Global Response hosted by Asia Society and JCIE, on March 22, 2004.

cal, economic, social and cultural rights to the fullest and also be subjected to discrimination and stigmatization due to their medical condition. Moreover, all of these effects on the patients of HIV/ AIDS drive the people and related communities underground, making it hard to seek treatment and education on their conditions. Such impacts are laid harder on those without adequate social, legal and economic conditions provided especially if it is the case of women and children in poverty.[28]

Sri Lanka was torn apart by the tsunami in the Indian Ocean along with the long-term internal strife and armed conflict between the government and LTTE (Liberation Tigers of Tamil Elam). These events were identified as resulting in a complex humanitarian emergency. The Democratic People's Republic of Korea (DPRK) has continued to pose threats to the international community both on international and regional levels. It attempted to take a strategic position against the US through nuclear programs. It was also open to more serious direct violations of human rights of its people who were arrested and repatriated from Northern China. The DPRK government has used imprisonment, torture, forced labor and public execution on its own population.

Despite the human rights violations that continue to threaten East Asian human security, the region has yet to create a regional mechanism to counter these challenges. It is the only region in the world that has not established a regional framework to promote human security. Moreover, the efforts to establish a regional human security regime in East Asia have been limited. While there has been a gradual recognition of the importance of a regional approach, attempts in this direction continue to face many obstacles such as argument on universality of human rights and respect for cultures among the states of the region.

African Union

There exist specific mechanisms to protect and promote human rights within the African regional context. The African regional human rights system is a part of the African Union. The African Union was established in 2001, replacing the Organization of African Unity. It is a regional organization that aims to protect African sovereignty and its territorial integrity and is committed to decoloniza-

28 United Nations Human Rights Office of the High Commssioner, HIV/AIDS and Human Rights, http://www.ohchr.org/EN/Issues/HIV/Pages/HIVIndex.aspx.

tion through the incorporation of human rights principles as well as democratic principles and good governance. The objectives of the African Union include the promotion of peace, security and stability on the continent, democratic principles and institutions, popular participation and good governance and promoting and protecting human rights in reference to the African Charter on Human and People's Rights.

The New Partnership for Africa's Development (NEPAD) is a specific program of the African Union representing the commitment by African leaders to eradicate poverty and place the African continent on a path to sustained growth and development. Within this program, African leaders have recognized peace, security, democracy, good governance and human rights as key conditions for sustainable development and to work together to promote these principles on national and regional levels. Member states have also adhered to the African Peer Review mechanism in an effort to hold each partner morally accountable. In addition to these efforts, the African Court of Human and People's Rights was established in 2004 with a mandate to complement the protective mandate of the African Commission on Human and People's Rights.

9.6 Rights to Security

Poverty is a part of national and international security. In this regard, efforts to achieve poverty reduction are direct contributions to building sustainable, long-term peace, which is a fundamental necessity of a stable economy. In the past, internal and international conflicts caused anguish and devastation to civilian populations.

In addition, it is also possible to gain insight into human rights issues within the realm of social development as an indication of the interrelated nature between poverty alleviation and promotion of human rights.

The idea of a larger freedom, identified by the former UN Secretary General Kofi Anan in 2005, encapsulated the idea that development, security and human rights must go together. It is also identified in this report that the UN, as an organization, strives to ensure respect for human rights, establish conditions under which justice and the rule of law can be maintained and promote social progress.

OECD defines Official Development Assistance (ODA) as those

flows to countries and territories on the DAC List of ODA Recipients and to multilateral institutions which are provided by official agencies, administered with the promotion of the economic development and welfare of developing countries as its main goal and is concessional in its traits and carries a grant element of at least 25%.[29] This definition includes some important aspects of the term but also excludes some as states on the following table.

Table 9.1 Security related elements included/excluded in the OECD DAC definition of ODA[30]

Category	Included	Excluded
Conflict prevention		
Civilian peace-building, conflict prevention and conflict resolution	Support for civilian activities related to peace-building, conflict prevention & resolution, including capacity-building, monitoring, dialogue and information exchange	Activities supporting defense ministries or armed forces; direct use of military forces for such activities
Peace missions		All costs except the following:
Post-conflict peace-building operations	Cost of a donor's bilateral participation in the following activities, when they are part of the post-conflict peace-building phase of a UN peace operation, net of any compensation received from the UN: human rights; election monitoring; rehabilitation assistance to demobilized soldiers; rehabilitation of basic national infrastructure; monitoring or re-training of civil administrators & police forces; training in customs & border control procedures; advice or training in fiscal or macroeconomic stabilization policy; repatriation and demobilization of armed factions, and disposal of their weapons; explosive mine removal	net cost of bilateral activities authorized by and in support of action by the UN, calculated as the excess over what the personnel & equipment would have cost to maintain had they not been assigned to take part in a peace operation; net costs of non-UN-supported peace-building operations

29 OECD, Official development assistance -definition and coverage, http://www.oecd.org/dac/stats/officialdevelopmentassistancedefinitionandcoverage.htm

30 Michael Brzoska, "Extending ODA or Creating a New Reporting Instrument for Security Related Expenditures for Development," *Development Policy Review*, vol. 26, no. 2 (2008): 131-150.

Security-sector reform		
Security system reform	Technical cooperation provided to parliament, government ministries, law enforcement agencies & the judiciary to assist review & reform of the security system to improve democratic governance and civilian control; Any such support to defense ministries must be part of a national security-system reform strategy & be approved by the partner country ministry with overall responsibility for coordination of external assistance	Military competence/capacity-building and strategic planning activities
Management of security expenditure	Technical cooperation to improve civilian oversight & democratic control of budgeting, management, accountability and auditing of security expenditure, including military budgets, as part of a public expenditure management program	Technical support to armed forces and defense ministries, not aimed at improving democratic control of aspects of security expenditure
Enhancing civil society's role in security system	Assistance to civil society to enhance its competence & capacity to scrutinize the security system so that it is managed in accordance with democratic norms & principles of accountability, transparency and good governance	Training in military skills assistance to defense ministry or armed forces
Child soldiers	Technical assistance to government and civil society organizations to support & apply legislation designed to prevent recruitment of child soldiers; Assistance to improve educational or employment opportunities for children so as to discourage their recruitment as soldiers & build capacity (including advocacy) within civilian government & civil society to prevent children from becoming soldiers; Efforts to demobilize, disarm, reintegrate, repatriate & resettle child soldiers	Costs of military operations against groups that may have recruited child soldiers; Support to armed forces themselves; Assistance that contributes to strengthening of military or fighting capacity of armed forces
Training, material	Training of police & other non-military security forces if the objective is the promotion of economic development & welfare	Training of military personnel, even in non-military matters such as civil engineering, surveying, or human rights law; Training of all other security forces unless see left

Practical disarmament		
Assistance for Demobilization	Support for repatriation & integration of demobilized military personnel into the economy & conversion of production facilities from military to civilian outputs	Support of disarmament; Support of demobilization & subsidies to combatants prior to official discharge
Mine clearance, small-arms control	In UN peacekeeping operations; If main objective is economic development & welfare; Education of general public; Institutional reform (as element of good governance);Weapons collection and destruction, except by the military	General mine clearance; Seizures of small arms by force; Involvement of militaries in small arms collection & destruction
Direct subsidies, military aid		
Military equipment or services	Additional costs of military personnel delivering humanitarian aid	Grants, official loans, or credits (guaranteed or not) for supply or financing of military equipment or services, including direct participation in military expenditures and other contributions linked to a specific defense effort; Use of military personnel to control civil disobedience, even in emergency situations
Police forces, customs, other public security forces	Support to police forces if main objectives are promotion of economic development and welfare	Support to police training, police equipment where main objective is not economic development & welfare
Anti-terrorism activities		Training of police and other security forces in anti-terrorism, including intelligence-gathering

Three important concepts are introduced in this chapter: poverty, security and human rights. Each of these concepts are interlinked with each other. Poverty is central to both security and human rights. Human security cannot be achieved separately from poverty alleviation and the protection of human rights. Likewise, human rights cannot be separated from either poverty or security issues. The interconnectedness and the complexities inherent within these relationships are evident.

Within the context of an understanding of these concepts, the final part of this chapter proposes to identify the linkages existing within this network. First of all, poverty is at the very core of the three concepts. Poverty eradication is a precondition for achieving human security or protecting individuals from human rights violations. Thus, current international efforts to provide development assistance and eradicate poverty can be perceived as a fundamental stepping stone.

The relationship between human security and human rights is more complex. At the surface, the two concepts seem to merge together and the boundaries between them are not clear. Nonetheless, it is important to recognize that the two concepts are interrelated and one cannot be achieved while the other is being violated. Poverty reduction and development will provide the poor with basic security to their livelihoods. Once these people are able to escape from the trap of poverty and achieve human security, this will contribute to protecting them from certain human rights violations.

It is difficult to argue which comes first—human rights or human security. It is more important to understand both human security and human rights as distinctive concepts and recognize the significant influence they have on one another. Furthermore, the potential contributions that poverty eradication and development can have on enhancing human rights and human security need to be acknowledged by all of the actors participating in development assistance.

Chapter 9. Review Discussion Questions

1. How does pro-poor growth contribute to poverty alleviation?
2. How have traditional views of security transformed with the new international order?
3. Compare traditional views of international security and human security. How can the relationship between these two concepts be defined?
4. Do universal human rights exist? Identify the debate that underlies the efforts to protect human rights at a global level.
5. Explain the relationship between poverty alleviation and the human rights-based approach.

Chapter 10

Sustainable Development and Green Growth

> *"Far from being a burden, sustainable development is an exceptional opportunity - economically, to build markets and create jobs; socially, to bring people in from the margins; and politically, to give every man and woman a voice, and a choice, in deciding their own future."*[1]

10.1 Growth, Environment and Sustainable Development

It was at the 1972 UN Conference on the Human Environment held in Stockholm, Sweden that the UN Environment Program was created and world leaders produced a declaration comprising of twenty-six principles that provide the guidelines for environmental preservation. The principles included using natural resources wisely to prevent depletion for future generations, protecting the capacity of the Earth to create resources for use, and adopting rational planning to reconcile the conflict between the utility of nonrenewable natural resources and their preservation.[2] In 1983, the Bruntland Commission first introduced the term 'sustainable development.' It was defined as development that "meets the needs of the present without compromising the ability of future generations to meet their own needs."[3] However, it is challenging to clearly conceptualize the goals of sustainable development. A broad, more complex definition explains sustainable development not as "a fixed state of harmony, but rather a process of change in which the exploitation of nonrenewable resources, the direction of investments, the orientation of technological development and institutional change are made consistent with the future as well as present needs."[4]

1 Former UN Secretary-General Kofi Annan, From a lecture at the London School of Economics (4 October, 2012).

2 Ellie Carroll, "Twenty-five Years in the Making: Why Sustainable Development has Eluded the UN and How Community Driven Development Offers the Solution," *Houston Journal of International Law*, vol. 32, no. 2 (2010): 2.

3 United Nations, "Report of the World Commission on Environment and Development," *General Assembly Resolution* 42/187 (1987).

4 Ellie Carroll (2010), 4.

http://www.tankonyvtar.hu/hu/tartalom/tamop425/0032_kornyezetiranyitas_es_minosegbiztositas/ch04.html

Sustainable development can be categorized into environmental sustainability, economic sustainability and sociopolitical sustainability. Hughes and Johnston address sustainability through three major components: continued economic growth and human development, protection and extension of social capital with a special emphasis on social equity and the protection of the natural environment. In light of this understanding, they propose a strategy for a globally networked knowledge economy with greater innovation, efficient environmental technologies and business practices and measures to reduce environmental impacts.[5]

The focus of this chapter is to understand the concept of environmental sustainability. Environmental sustainability has emerged in response to concerns that economic growth and development will

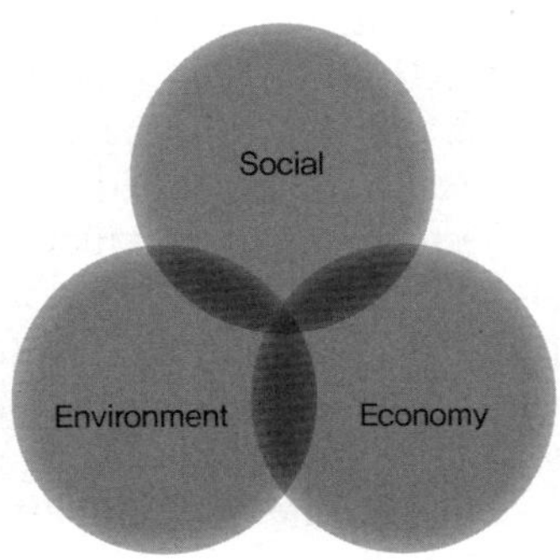

Figure 10.1 Conceptual Framework of Sustainable Development

5 Barry Hughes and Peter Johnson, "Sustainable Futures: policies for global development," *Futures*, vol. 37, no. 8 (2005): 813-831.

lead to environmental degradation and that the two concepts face a contradictory relationship. However, today it is recognized that the relationship between the environment and development can be complementary or mutually reinforcing. Moreover, the international community has increased its efforts to establish development projects that are in relative harmony with the environment.

North-South Relations and the Environment

The concept of sustainable development has evolved based on how countries perceive the emerging threats to the global environment. Today, environmental issues have become more important, since they are perceived to be directly related to the economic and social development of countries, leading to global negotiations that encompass environmental and economic policies. As the relationship between the environment and the economic welfare of countries has been widely recognized, North-South inequalities have become a pressing issue in global environmental politics.

The North-South divide is founded on a basic understanding that there exists a wide gap between economies in the Northern and Southern countries. It has been accepted that developing countries lack the global economic relations that would fundamentally enable them to shape adequate policy responses regarding global environmental issues, including necessary strategies for negotiations. This results in a weak bargaining position for Southern countries compared to their Northern counterparts.

In the 1970s, developing countries called for a redistribution of wealth. The first of these calls was proposed in the New International Economic Order (NIEO) in 1974. The NIEO included a list of demands to lessen the gap between the North and South in an attempt to redistribute wealth. It demanded ① a new system of international commodity agreements, ② a unilateral reduction of barriers to imports from developing countries in industrialized countries, ③ a strategy to enhance developing countries' capabilities in science and technology, ④ calls to increase Northern financing of technology transfers, and ⑤ demands to change the patent laws to lower the cost of transfers. Despite Southern efforts, the NIEO was unsuccessful and North-South inequalities continued to deepen.

The disturbing gap of North-South economic relations has also resulted in degradation and depletion of natural resources. The increasing demand for resources in the North has led to exploitation of resources in Southern countries. In addition, developing countries have increased exports of domestic resources to respond to Northern protectionism and in attempts to reduce debt burdens. Protectionism in the form of subsidies to agricultural exporters in developed countries deprives developing countries of markets and depresses world market prices.

Regarding the current threats to the global economy, most developing countries believe a relationship exists between global environmental issues and the North-South economic divide. The consensus is that developed countries' historical industrialization process, their production and consumption of CFCs and combustion of fossil fuels are responsible for the thinning of the ozone layer and global warming. The excessive consumption of resources has caused global environmental degradation.

Since the North was responsible for creating the threat to the global environment, developing countries have asserted that the North should bear the financial burdens of reversing this ecological damage. This call from the South for Northern action has been identified as the principle of "common but differentiated responsibilities."[6] It acknowledges that different countries have caused different levels of damage to the environment, and hence, they should recognize their responsibility to address these impacts accordingly. This idea has been reflected by the different emissions reductions standards that have been set for countries according to their respective levels of development. A further concern of the South is its lack of environmental technology such as solar-light power generation. The South has demanded that it receive transfers of environmental technologies on concessional or preferential terms.

History of Environmental Aid

The United Nations Conference for Environment and Development was held during the summer of 1992 in Rio de Janeiro. 172 governments participated with 108 heads of state or government present and 2,400 representatives of non-governmental organizations. During this conference, which later came to be referred to as the Earth Summit, participants discussed the world's ecological challenges and debated the relationship between the environment and economic growth, whether the two could be mutually achieved, or whether they were contradictory concepts, in which case one would

6 Pamela Chasek et al., *Global Environmental Politics* (Boulder: Westveiw Press, 2006), 234-243.

inhibit the success of the other. The central question at issue was if environmental conservation was possible while countries pursued economic growth and development.

At the Earth Summit, environmentalists pressured their governments to act on issues such as deforestation in the Amazon, ozone depletion or global climate change. However, many countries with abundant natural resources were still in the developing stage, and if developed countries persuaded these countries to preserve the environment it would be more difficult for them to industrialize. For developing countries, the continued struggle with issues like alleviating poverty, or providing health care and education systems to their people meant that preserving the environment was not a prioritized issue.[7]

As discussed above, the North-South divide refers to how the world has developed at uneven rates, with the majority of developed countries concentrated in the Northern hemisphere, while most of the population in the Southern hemisphere continued to struggle with poverty and under-development. With this recognition emerged a debate on inequality and responsibility, especially regarding environmental issues. Most of the environmental issues that pose threats to the global economy in the 21st century are by-products of the industrialization process of developed countries in the North.

Having achieved industrialization, developed countries were able to look around and broaden their perspectives, and gradually became aware of the importance of the environment and natural resources. To some extent, environmental issues became a global agenda due to inequalities between the North and South. Ironically, since the Southern hemisphere was underdeveloped, it contained more potential for future damage to the environment. If the South, which has rich natural resources, starts to industrialize, it may lead to threats of deforestation of the Amazon in South America, desertification in the Saharan region of Africa, and climate change on a global scale.

The central issue in the environmental agenda was simple: who should pay? It was obviously unfair for the developed countries to expect the developing South to pay for the degradation of the global environment that the North had caused during their efforts

7 Robert Hicks et al., *Greening Aid? Understanding the Environmental Impact of Development Assistance* (New York: Oxford University Press, 2008), 1.

to industrialize. Furthermore, the North was ready to understand the importance of the environment in sustaining their economic developments and well-being. On the other hand, for most Southern countries, a more pressing issue was to promote economic growth to uplift their poverty-stricken populations and start them on the path to growth and development. The South was neither ready nor willing to pay for the protection of the environment. Even though the North recognized the need for investments to protect the environment, it also was not a willing giver of capital investments. It was in this context that negotiations between the North and South continued over who should pay the costs of the global environmental crisis.

The South, which depended on assistance from developed countries, was also concerned that this new interest in environmental protection would lead to a redistribution of Northern aid away from the much needed areas of poverty alleviation, health care and providing basic human needs in impoverished developing countries. The Beijing Ministerial Declaration on Environment and Development in 1991 argued for a special 'Green Fund' to provide adequate and additional financial assistance to developing countries, targeting problems such as water pollution, coastal pollution affecting mangrove forests, shortages and degradation of fresh water resources, deforestation, soil loss, land degradation and desertification.[8] The following year, in 1992, the Kula Lumpur Declaration on Environment and Development emphasized the importance of distinguishing environmental aid from ODA and called for a specific and separate fund for the implementation of Agenda 21.

Agenda 21, a 300-page plan to persuade poor countries to participate in environmental agreements while assisting them in economic development, developed and refined the definition introduced by the Brundtland Commission. Agenda 21 is the fundamental program of action for achieving sustainable development. The importance of allocating new funds for these programs was explicitly recognized within Agenda 21, and the total estimate to achieve its goals was $561.5 billion a year, of which $15 billion was to go to global environmental issues while the rest would fund localized sustainable development programs in developing countries. Environmental issues were discussed in detail within Agenda 21, with

8 Helen Sjöberg, "Restructuring the Global Environmental Facility. Working Paper," http://thegef.org/Outreach/outreach-PUblications/WP13-Restructuring_the _GEF.pdf (1999).

14 chapters allocated to environmental issues and only eight dedicated to social and economic issues.

Table 10.1 Agenda 21 Chapters of Environmental Issues

Agenda 21: Environmental Issues
Protection of the Environment
Planning and management of land resources
Combating deforestation
Combating desertification and drought
Sustainable mountain development
Sustainable agriculture and rural development
Conservation of biological diversity
Environmentally sound management of sound technology
Protection of oceans and seas
Protection of the quality and supply of freshwater resources
Environmentally sound management of toxic chemicals
Environmentally sound management of hazardous wastes
Environmentally sound management of solid wastes and sewage
Safe and environmentally sound management of radioactive wastes

Sustainable development strategies are important mechanisms for enhancing and linking national capacities to bring together priorities in social, economic and environmental policies. In order to achieve sustainable development, it is necessary to integrate diverse policy making levels at operational levels to understand the impact of economic sectors, such as industry, agriculture, energy, transportation and tourism, on human well-being and the physical environment. Priority actions for the full implementation of the Program of Action of the World Summit for Social Development that acts upon the follows up on the principles of Agenda 21 include[9]:

1) Improving access to sustainable livelihoods, entrepreneurial opportunities and productive resources, including land, water, credit, technical and administrative training and appropriate technology, with particular efforts to broaden the human and social capital basis of societies so as to reach the rural poor and the urban informal sector;
2) Providing universal access to basic social services, including basic education, health care, nutrition, clean water and sanitation;

9 Taken from the "Program for Further Implementation of Agenda 21," Resolution Adopted by the General Assembly (s/19-2).

3) Progressively developing, in accordance with the financial and administrative capacities of each society, social protection systems to support those who cannot support themselves, either temporarily or permanently; the aim of social integration is to create a "society for all";
4) Empowering people living in poverty and their organizations by involving them fully in the formulation, implementation and evaluation of strategies and programs for poverty eradication and community development and by ensuring that these programs reflect their priorities;
5) Addressing the disproportionate impact of poverty on women, in particular by removing legislative, policy, administrative and customary barriers to women's equal access to productive resources and services, including access to and control over land and other forms of property, credit, including micro-credit, inheritance, education, information, health care and technology.
6) Working together of interested donors and recipients to allocate increased shares of official development assistance to poverty eradication. The 20/20 initiative is an important principle in this respect, as it is based on a mutual commitment among donors and recipients to increasing resources allocated to basic social services.[10]
7) Intensifying international cooperation to support measures being taken in developing countries to eradicate poverty, to provide basic social protection and services and to approach poverty eradication efforts in an integral and multidimensional manner.

At the 2000 Millennium Summit in New York, eight new millennium goals incorporated sustainable development in less explicit terms. The new set goals were; ① eradicate extreme poverty and hunger, ② achieve universal primary education, ③ promote gender equality and empower women, ④ reduce child mortality, ⑤ improve maternal health, ⑥ combat HIV/AIDS, malaria, and other diseases, ⑦ ensure environmental sustainability and ⑧ develop a global partnership for development.[11]

---

10 A compact between developing and industrialized countries, the 20/20 Initiative calls for the allocation of, on average, 20% of the budget in developing countries and 20% of official development assistance to basic social services, and has become a critical aspect of sustainable development, particularly in light of inadequate social outcomes in many areas, such as the deepening of poverty, continued high debt burdens, declining official development assistance, and also from a brighter perspective, the increasing prominence of human rights in development.

11 United Nations, Conferences, Meetings and Events http://www.un.org/en/events/pastevents/millennium_summit.shtml.

Goal 7 aimed to ensure environmental sustainability by 2015. The second Earth Summit, the World Summit on Sustainable Development, was held in 2002, in Johannesburg, South Africa to further discuss the issues pertaining to sustainable development. The Summit produced the Johannesburg Declaration, the Johannesburg Plan for Implementation and three hundred voluntary partnerships and other initiatives to support sustainable development. The Johannesburg Declaration was a pledge by world leaders to commit their countries to the goal of sustainable development, whereas the Johannesburg Plan for Implementation set out a comprehensive plan for action, including quantifiable goals and targets with fixed deadlines.

The following significant international meeting was at Gleneagles in 2005 when the leaders of the G8, the United States, Germany, France, Britain, Italy, Japan, Russia and Canada, gathered to reiterate their commitments to global environmental issues. They made promises to help poor countries identified within the Gleneagles Plan of Action and to explore opportunities within existing and new lending portfolios to increase the volume of investments made on renewable energy and energy efficient technologies.

The United Nations Commission on Sustainable Development (CSD)

The United Nations Commission on Sustainable Development was established by the UN General Assembly in December 1992 following the United Nations Conference on Environment. Its core responsibilities are to review progress in the implementation of Agenda 21 and the Rio Declaration on Environment and Development. The CSD is an inter-governmental body with members including thirteen members elected from Africa, eleven from Asia, ten from Latin America and the Caribbean, six from European and thirteen from other regions including Western Europe.

The Division for Sustainable Development (DSD)

Founded to implement Agenda 21, the Johannesburg Plan of Implementation and the Barbados Program of Action for Sustainable Development, the UN Department of Economic and Social Affairs, Division for Sustainable Development (DSD) is the authoritative source of expertise on sustainable development. The goals set forth by the DSD are to integrate the social, economic and environmental dimensions of sustainable development in policymaking at international, regional and national levels; to adopt an integrated, cross-sectoral and broadly participatory approach to sustainable development; and to measure the progress in the implementation of the goals and targets of the Johannesburg Plan of Implementation.

https://sustainabledevelopment.un.org/

In order to achieve these goals, DSD activities attempt to ① facilitate intergovernmental negotiations, consensus-building and decision-making; ② provide technical assistance, expert advice and capacity building to support developing countries and countries with economies in transition in their efforts to achieve sustainable development; ③ to facilitate inter-agency and inter-organizational cooperation, exchange and sharing of information and catalyze joint activities and partnerships within the United Nations system and with other international organizations, governments and civil society groups; ④ to promote and facilitate monitoring and evaluation of, and reporting on, the implementation of sustainable development at the national, regional and international levels; and ⑤ to undertake in-depth strategic analyses to provide policy advice on cross-cutting and emerging sustainable development issues.[12]

Box 10.1 Ecovillages[13]

An ecovillage is a cohousing community that generally has access

12 UN Department of Economic and Social Affairs, "*About the DSD*," http://www.un.org/esa/dsd/dsd/dsd_index.shtml, last visited April 2009.

to land surrounding the cohousing unit for agriculture, recreation and preservation purposes. They encourage the mixed use of land for commercial, residential and agricultural purposes. They also promote the use of energy-efficient methods and structures to conserve the daily use of resources. Many contain a cohousing unit and feature a "common house" for daily community activities including meals and recreation. They aim to create livable environments where human activities and development coexist with the natural world. According to the Global Ecovillage Network, there are 385 registered ecovillages. Ecovillages have been cited as an effective way to live sustainably by integrating and reinforcing sustainable education. Ecovillages also localize economic activity to build social capital and create awareness of the importance of sustainability.

It has been proposed that ecovillages can be a model implemented by developing countries to ensure long term sustainability by utilizing a community-driven development strategy. This strategy will empower communities to determine how financial aid should be spent and may be used to develop successful sustainable solutions to other concerns that developing countries have.

10.2 Climate Change and Poverty

Environmental challenges in the 21st century have moved across national boundaries and spread across regions and even impacted the globe as a whole. This section introduces seven different cases of concern to the global environment. For each environmental issue an explanation of the background is provided along with the efforts set forth by the international community to resolve these challenges. The cases studied include ① transboundary air pollution; ② ozone depletion; ③ climate change; ④ toxic waste; ⑤ loss of biodiversity; ⑥ desertification; and ⑦ deforestation.

Transboundary Air Pollution

Transboundary air pollution emerged as an environmental issue in the late 1960s. In 1968, Svante Oden presented scientific evidence citing the long-range transport of sulfur dioxide emissions as the

13 Ellie Carroll, "Twenty-five Years in the Making: Why Sustainable Development has Eluded the UN and How Community Driven Development Offers the Solution," *Houston Journal of International Law*, vol. 32, no. 2 (2010): 10-14.

source of Swedish aquatic acidification. Sweden advanced efforts to put the issue of long-range transboundary air pollution on the international agenda. Sweden and other Nordic states were able to persuade the OECD to monitor transboundary air pollution in 1972, and the OECD conducted a monitoring program from 1972 to 1977 to confirm that pollution was being exported across boundaries and that the problem required attention from the international community.

Countries that were victims of the export of acid rain, such as Sweden, Finland and Norway, took the initiative to negotiate binding regulations on sulfur dioxide and nitrogen oxide emissions. On the other hand, industrialized countries that were the main exporters of acid rain vetoed this motion. States that participated in the veto coalition include the United States, the United Kingdom, Germany, Belgium and Denmark. However, Finland, Norway and Sweden continued to pressure these countries to reduce transboundary air pollution and succeeded in concluding the Convention on Long-range Transboundary Air Pollution (CLRTAP) with 35 signatories, which established the principle that transboundary air pollution should be reduced. They also created a mechanism for collecting and disseminating information on air pollution flows, national reduction strategies and abatement technologies.

In 1984, countries pledged to reduce sulfur dioxide emissions and to substantially reduce other pollutants, especially nitrous oxide. An agreement on the Protocol on the Reduction of Sulfur Emissions or Their Transboundary Fluxes by at least 30%, more widely known as the Helsinki Protocol, was signed by 21 states in 1985. The second sulfur protocol was signed in 1994 by 28 parties to the convention, establishing different requirements for each country to attain the greatest possible effect for the environment. Protocol agreements by states continued to be adopted throughout the 1990s.

These international efforts persisted despite opposition from several states, including the United Kingdom, the US and Germany. The international agreements negotiated since 1972 have strengthened the international regime for transboundary air pollution through regular reviews and action.

Ozone Depletion

The ozone is a gas composed of three oxygen atoms. Ninety% of the ozone can be found in the stratosphere. The ozone helps to shield the earth from ultraviolet radiation produced by the sun and plays a critical role in absorbing UV-B radiation, without which living organisms on the earth would be seriously harmed.

The problem is that chlorofluorocarbons (CFCs) have been found to release chlorine atoms into the stratosphere, which acts as a catalyst that destroys ozone molecules. CFCs were created in the 1920s and were found to be very useful. They are inert, nonflammable, nontoxic, colorless, odorless and can be used in various applications. They became the main chemical for coolants in air conditioning, refrigerating systems and propellants in aerosol sprays, among other usages. Even once the hazards that CFCs posed to the ozone became known, it was difficult to form an international consensus to control their usage.

The United States was one of the primary producers of CFCs, producing around 40% of the world supply. Nonetheless, it banned the use of CFCs in aerosol sprays and advocated the participation of other countries in taking measures to protect the ozone. The European Community, also accounting for more than 40% of global CFC production and exports, vetoed the US move to control CFC usage. The EC was supported by other industrialized countries like France, Italy, Germany and the United Kingdom. In addition to the veto coalition of developed countries, a second veto coalition was formed by large developing countries with the potential to produce CFCs in the future. These countries included Brazil, China, India and Indonesia.

With strong opposition, the Vienna Convention for the Protection of the Ozone Layer (1985) affirmed the importance of protecting the ozone layer and included provisions on monitoring, research and data exchange, but lacked any specific obligations to reduce the production or use of CFCs. However, the threat that CFCs posed to the environment was further underscored by reports on the Antarctic ozone hole.

In 1987, the Montreal Protocol on Substances that Deplete the Ozone Layer mandated that industrialized countries reduce their production and use of popular CFCs by 50%. It was also agreed that a grace period of ten years would be given to developing countries, permitting them to increase their use of CFCs before the commitments took hold. Scientists also produced studies suggesting that CFCs were responsible for the hole in the ozone layer, which in 1989 was further confirmed by studies conducted by the Scientific Assessment Panel.

Today the ozone regime is one of the strongest and most effective global environmental regimes. The worldwide consumption of

CFCs has been reduced to 100,000 tons in 2003, compared to the 1.1 million ton level in 1996. The Ozone Secretariat has stated that in the absence of the Montreal Protocol, global CFC consumption would have reached 3 million tons in 2010 and 8 million tons by 2060. It is estimated that CFC consumption at these levels would have resulted in a 50% depletion of the ozone layer by 2035.

Climate Change

The threats of climate change have been well recognized by the international community. Climate change, also known as global warming, is caused by the emission of heat-trapping gases produced by cars, power plants, industrial processes and deforestation. The buildup of these gases overheats the planet, threatening our health, economy and the environment. Global warming is changing the distribution of plants and animals in the ecosystem by influencing animal population sizes, growth rates and the timing of plant flowering or animal migrations. It has also resulted in changes to the weather, such as intense storms and tsunamis, droughts and fire. With a warmer climate, the glaciers have been melting, leading to higher a sea level, which is expected to produce mass numbers of climate refugees. Other impacts of climate change include the threat of mass extinctions as well as coral bleaching and disintegration.

A study by scientists at the World Health Organization found that 154,000 people died yearly from the effects of global warming, but the more alarming fact is that these numbers could nearly double by 2020. Professor Andrew Haines of the London School of Hygiene and Tropical Medicine suggested that climate change could bring some health benefits like greater crop yields but these benefits would be outweighed by negative impacts. For example, small increases in temperatures could lead to the spread of malaria in developing countries with a more diverse range of mosquitoes.[14]

Greenhouse gas (GHG) emissions are a major cause of global warming. Emissions from burning fossil fuels account for roughly 80% of total world emissions, with deforestation and natural resources of methane accounting for the rest. Fossil fuel burning has increased the atmospheric concentration of carbon dioxide by 30% since pre-industrial times. The difficulty of stabilizing global concentrations of carbon dioxide is that it would require countries to reduce their current emission levels by half; however, GHG emis-

14 The World Health Report 2002: Reducing Risks and Promoting Healthy Life.

sions are directly related to energy, which is a critical part of every country's economy, development and welfare.

Formal negotiations for a climate convention were started by the Intergovernmental Negotiating Committee for a Framework Convention on Climate Change in 1991. In 1992, the United Nations Framework Convention on Climate Change (UNFCCC) was signed by 154 countries agreeing to take measures to reduce the GHG emissions. The Kyoto Protocol was adopted in 1995 to stabilize greenhouse gas concentrations in the atmosphere at a level that would prevent dangerous anthropogenic interference with the climate system. It established legally binding commitments for the reduction of four GHGs, carbon monoxide, methane, nitrous oxide and Sulphur hexafluoride, and two groups of gases, hydrofluorocarbons and perfluorocarbons, for Annex 1 countries[15] and general non-binding commitments for all other countries. The following table illustrates the targeted greenhouse gas emission reductions of the signatory states.

Table 10.2 Target Greenhouse Gas Emissions Reductions by 2012, Kyoto Protocol[16 17]

Country	Kyoto Target (per cent changefrom 1990 emissions)
Australia	+8
Bulgaria	-8
Canada	-6
Croatia	-5
Estonia	-8
European Union	-8
Hungary	-6
Iceland	+10
Japan	-6

15 Annex I countries, industrialized countries, include: Australia, Austria, Belarus, Belgium, Bulgaria, Canada, Croatia, Czech Republic, Denmark, Estonia, Finland, France, Germany, Greece, Hungary, Iceland, Ireland, Italy, Japan, Latvia, Liechtenstein, Lithuania, Luxembourg, Monaco, Netherlands, New Zealand, Norway, Poland, Portugal, Romania, Russian Federation, Slovakia, Slovenia, Spain, Sweden, Switzerland, Turkey, Ukraine, United Kingdom, United States of America. Annex II countries are classified as developed countries which pay for the costs of developing countries.

16 United Nations Kyoto Protocol to the United Nations Framework Convention on Climate Change, Article 3, Annex B.

17 Taken from UN references.

Latvia	-8
Liechtenstein	-8
Lithuania	-8
Monaco	-8
New Zealand	0
Norway	+1
Poland	-6
Romania	-8
Russian Federation	0
Slovakia	-8
Slovenia	-8
Switzerland	-8
Ukraine	0
United States	-7

Toxic Waste

The United Nations Environment Program estimates that between 300 and 500 million tons of hazardous wastes are generated each year.[18] Historically, around 10% of this amount was moved across international borders, primarily among OECD countries. But as OECD countries began to regulate hazardous waste disposal, there emerged a need for new sites to dispose of this waste. In the 1970s and 1980s waste shipments from the North to the South began to increase, particularly to the poorer developing countries of Africa, Central America and the Caribbean, which were tempted by offers of revenues for accepting waste, while lacking the technology or administrative capacity to dispose of it safely.

The UNEP working group of legal and technical experts established a set of guidelines in 1984 on the management and disposal of hazardous wastes, stated within the Cairo Guidelines. In 1988, a nonaligned movement demanded a ban on the international trade in wastes and called for industrialized countries to prohibit waste exports to developing countries. The Basel Convention (1992) on the control of Transboundary Movements of Hazardous Wastes and Their Disposal banned exports of hazardous wastes to countries with less advanced storage and disposal facilities.

18 Katherine Krumme, *International Management of Hazardous Wastes: The Basel Convention and Regulated Legal Rules* (Oxford: Clarendon Press, 1995).

Similar to hazardous wastes, toxic chemicals are released into the environment through the use of products, pesticides or fertilizers, industrial and manufacturing practices that involve or produce hazardous chemicals, leakage from wastes, mismanagement, accidents and intentional dumping. Once released into the environment, toxic chemicals are difficult to clean up and produce a diverse range of harmful effects for long periods of time.

The use of chemicals for commercial purposes began after World War II. In the 1960s, people started to become concerned about the potentially negative impacts pesticides and other chemicals were having on the environment and human health. In light of these threats, the 2001 Stockholm Convention on Persistent Organic Pollutants (POPs) attempted to eliminate or reduce the production, use, trade and emission into the environment of twelve POPs which are classified among the most toxic pollutants.[19]

Loss of Biodiversity

The Convention on International Trade in Endangered Species of Flora and Fauna (CITES) concentrates on a single cause of species loss — human predation. The worldwide market for animals plays an important role in species loss through overexploitation of certain natural resources. It is estimated that nearly 350 million individual plants and animals are bought and sold each year, with a large portion of this trade conducted illegally.[20] The illegal market of wildlife is the third largest international market of illicit goods, following drugs and weapons. CITES protects 33,000 species from illegal trade, but participating parties have many difficulties in deciding which species should be restricted from trade.

Biological diversity is not limited to the plants and animals of the earth, but encompasses diversity at all levels, including genes, species, ecosystems and landscapes. Ecosystems are an aspect of diversity through which interactions among living creatures exist, occurring within or between forests, wetlands, mountains, deserts and rivers as well as the air, water and soil around them, thereby

19 The POPs identifies within the Stockholm Convention on Persistent Organic Pollutants are aldrin, chlordane, dieldrin, dioxins, DDT, endrin, furans, heptachlor, mirex, toxaphene, PCBs and hexaclorobenzene. Of these, particular attention was given to aldrin, chlordane, dieldrin, endrin, heptachlor, mirex, toxaphene, PCBs and hexaclorobenzene, and parties were called on to eliminate the production and use of these chemicals.

20 Sarah Fitzgerald, *International Wildlife Trade: Whose Business is It?* (Vaud: World Wildlife Fund, 1989).

forming an interconnected community. Biodiversity also refers to the genetic differences within species, such as different breeds and varieties, chromosomes, genes and genetic sequences (DNA).

The loss of species has been perceived as a threat to future generations of humans. The rates of extinction of species have increased through human activity, and some 12% of birds, 23% of mammals, 25% of conifers and 32% of amphibians are threatened with extinction. The world's fish have been reduced by 90% since the start of industrial fishing. More effective fishing technologies and an increase of fishing vessels have given fleets more catching power than was sustainable. By the 1990s, the global fishing industry had more than two-and-a-half times more capacity than could be used sustainably. The United Nations Agreement for the Implementation of the Provisions of the United Nations Convention on the Law of the Sea was the first binding global agreement addressed to overfishing.

It was in the 1980s that scientists reached a consensus that the rate of species extinction was increasing at an alarming rate. The Convention on Biological Diversity (CBD), which was completed in 1992, aimed to achieve the sustainable use as well as the fair and equitable sharing of the world's genetic resources. It obligated parties to inventory and to monitor biodiversity in an attempt to incorporate the concepts of conservation and sustainable development into national economic development strategies and to preserve indigenous conservation practices. The CBD is more centered on economic incentives than on legal obligations for preserving biodiversity.

Desertification

Desertification is a serious environmental problem that affects the lives of 1 billion people in more than 110 different countries around the world. Desertification has been defined as sustained land degradation in arid, semiarid and dry sub-humid areas resulting from adverse human impact.[21] Desertification does not involve resources or life support systems of global level and the impact on countries that are not directly suffering from desertification are not severe. These countries are only indirectly influenced by the weakened economy and societies of the affected countries. Thus, it has been questioned whether desertification should be dealt with as a global environ-

21 United Nations Environment Program, "Desertification: The Problem that Won't Go Away" (1992).

mental issue.

For many African countries, however, desertification can be directly linked to poverty alleviation. The United Nations Conference on Environment and Development addressed desertification as an agenda in 1992, largely due to the persistence of African countries with US support. The Intergovernmental Negotiating Committee on the International Convention to Combat Desertification began in 1993 and was completed by 1994.

Deforestation

Forests cover over 3.8 million hectares, which is equivalent to around 30% of the world's landmass, excluding Greenland and Antarctica. However, only 40% of remaining forests are relatively undisturbed and are large enough to provide habitats for large species. Actual forestland has increased in recent years as a result of plantation forests. In spite of these efforts, which slowed the speed of deforestation in the 1990s, deforestation and forest degradation have continued to occur. Deforestation refers to forests that are permanently converted to non-forest areas, such as agriculture, highways or urban settlements, and is caused through overharvesting of industrial wood and fuelwood, overgrazing, fire, insect pests and diseases, storms and air pollution. Between 1990 and 2000 the world's forests decreased by an average of over nine hectares annually, with larger figures for African and South American regions.

It was during the 1992 UN Conference on Environment and Development that forests were discussed within the context of sustainable development. Chapter 11 of Agenda 21 on Combating Deforestation and the "Forest Principles" are two non-legally binding agreements about forests. Both reaffirm the rights of sovereign nations to use their forests in accordance with their national priorities and policy objectives. The Intergovernmental Panel on Forests (IPF) developed more than one hundred proposals for action on issues related to sustainable forest management, including national forest programs, forest assessment, criteria and indicators, and identifying the underlying causes of deforestation. In 1997, the Intergovernmental Forum on Forests was established to promote and facilitate implementation of the IPF's proposals for action and to review, monitor and report on the progress in the management, conservation and sustainable development of all types of forests. The United Nations Forum on Forests (UNFF) was established as a central intergovernmental forum to deliberate international policy in 2000.

10.3 Environmental Aid

The negative human impacts on the environment are striking. Approximately 1.6 million people die prematurely every year from indoor air pollution and 1.7 million people die prematurely every year due to unsafe water, sanitation and hygiene.[22] Environmental aid is aid that is concentrated to resolve these environmental challenges. In this section, several cases in which environmental aid has played a critical role are introduced to provide an understanding of how environmental aid is distinguished from development aid.

Water and Sanitation

At the 1992 Earth Summit, the international community estimated that approximately $6.1 billion a year of water and sanitation aid would be needed to satisfy global needs. This figure was also identified within Agenda 21. The United Nations Development Program estimates that it will cost about $10 billion annually for low-cost sustainable technology with an increase of $20-30 billion for universal access depending on the technology to achieve the Millennium Development Goal of halving the proportion of people without access to water and sanitation by 2015.[23]

Actual funds concentrating on improving the quality of water are estimated to have amounted to $78 billion between 1980 and 2000, or about $3.9 billion annually. In this time frame, foreign aid agencies financed 7,660 water and sanitation projects. Compared to the $78 billion allocated to improving water, all other environmental causes received just over $51 billion over the same period, a strong indication of how much emphasis was put on water sanitation. The patterns of aid from bilateral donors were comparable to the patterns of multilateral aid. The number of projects funded annually by bilateral donors increased steadily during this period and an exceptionally high increase was observed after the Earth Summit in 1992. The annual level of bilateral aid increased by 200% over this period, climbing from $600 million in 1980 to $1.8 billion in 1999 and hitting its peak in 1996 at just over $3 million.[24]

During the period from 1980 to 1999, bilateral donors spent

---

22 UNDP, *Human Development Report 2006* (New York: Palgrave McMillan, 2006).

23 *Ibid.*

24 Robert Hicks et al., *Greening Aid? Understanding the Environmental Impact of Development Assistance* (New York: Oxford University Press, 2008), 39-40.

$31.7 billion to finance 6,682 water projects, while multilateral donors funded 980 larger projects, totaling $46.2 billion. The number of projects funded by multilateral agencies increased at a more modest pace, but the amount of money allocated to each project was larger than that of bilateral aid projects. Multilateral aid increased from thirty two projects in 1980 to fifty four in 1999, and annual aid increased from $1.8 billion in 1980 to $2.3 billion in 1999.

The average amount of aid allocated to water sanitation during the period, approximately $3.9 billion, is significantly less than the $6.1 billion called for by Agenda 21 or the $10-30 billion suggested by the UNDP. Statistics point to a relative increase following Agenda 21, with the annual amount of water aid rising to $5.6 billion from 1993-9. This may be seen as a representation of the significance of Agenda 21 initiatives on the aid commitments of donors.

The average amount of aid for a single water project was around $4.7 million for bilateral donors, whereas it was a little more than ten times that amount, $47.1 million, for multilateral assistance projects. There was a difference in the types of projects that were undertaken by bilateral and multilateral aid donors. In the case of bilateral aid donors, the majority of water aid projects were smaller in scope, many of them in the form of grants to fund local projects. On the other hand, multilateral agencies would fund large infrastructure projects, which often utilized loans. Bilateral and multilateral agencies have also shown differences in which countries they allocate aid to. The top three recipients of bilateral water aid in 2011-2013 were India, Vietnam and China,[25] while the top three recipients of multilateral aid in 2014 were Afghanistan, Vietnam and Syria.[26]

Climate Change

A basic underlying principle of the 1992 UN Framework Convention on Climate Change reflects the irony of global warming for developing countries. Regardless of the causes of climate change, the effects of global warming will be spread all over the world and, unfortunately, the poor developing countries may suffer more than the developed North. The conditions in the Southern hemisphere indicate that developing countries are more exposed to the negative

25 WaterAid, "Essential Element: Why International Aid for Water, Sanitation and Hygiene Is Still a Critical Source of Finance for Many Countries" (2015).

26 The World Bank, "Net Official Development Assistance and Official Aid Received," http://data.worldbank.org/indicator/DT.ODA.ALLD.CD?year_high_desc=false, last visited August 2016.

consequences of climate change, such as rising sea levels, droughts, storms and a reduction in agricultural yields. Further considerations must be made to fully understand the seriousness of global warming and to face the complex challenges that will emerge with these changes to the environment.

For example, global warming will cause the sea levels to rise, but how will rising sea levels impact people? The very existence of the Maldives, a country that is comprised of nearly 1,200 islands in the Indian Ocean with its beautiful resorts and beaches, the economy has been sustained through tourism, which accounts for 28% of its GDP and more than 60% of its foreign exchange. The Maldives are of a combined land mass of a mere 115 square miles, is at question. Rising sea levels are an imminent threat to the Maldives, which at the highest point is only 8 feet above sea level

Twenty-two years ago, then president of the Maldives, Maumoon Abdul Gayoom, stood before the United Nations to warn the world that rising sea levels would eventually destroy his country, predicting that a one-meter rise in sea level could lead to a catastrophic storm surge.[27] Climate change and rising sea levels in the Maldives pose a threat to its people, and its government is discussing options to relocate the country, because as a country, they feel threatened to become a part of the 150 million environmental refugees that the Intergovernmental Panel on Climate Change (IPCC) has predicted to exist by 2050. The UN University's Institute for Environment and Human Security has predicted that there will be 50 million 'environmentally displaced people' by 2010. In the mid-1990s, the British environmentalist, Norman Myers, became the most prominent proponent of the 'maximalist' school, which argues the world has to act to support sustainable development in order to address the mass migration, noting that "environmental refugees will soon become the largest group of involuntary refugees."[28] Additionally, he stated that there were 25 million environmental refugees in the mid-1990s, further claiming that this figure could double by 2010, with an upper limit of 200 million by 2050. More recently, Myers has suggested that the figure by 2050 might be as high as 250 million.[29]

---

27 Nicholas Schmidle, "Wanted: A New Home for My Country," *The New York Times* (May 8, 2009).

28 Norman Myers, "Environmental Refugees: A Growing Phenomenon," *Philosophical Transactions: Biological Sciences,* vol. 357, no. 1420 (2002): 609.

29 http://en.wikipedia.org/wiki/Environmental_migrant.

These discussions have effectively conceptualized a new type of refugee, the environmental or climate refugee. Climate refugees are persons that are displaced from their countries due to environmental reasons an extreme case would be the disappearance of their country, as in the potential case of the Maldives. The problem with climate refugees is that they are a new category of persons who must be separately treated from political refugees who are currently protected under the 1951 Geneva Convention.

On the other hand, some, like Paul Kench, state that there is no scientific evidence to support this apocalyptic claim, as it is a gross exaggeration that the Maldives are going to disappear. Rather, the government of the Maldives is using this scenario as a political weapon.[30] The threat that the entire population of the Maldives will become climate refugees may be overblown, but this does not mean that the Maldives are free from the threats of global warming. Even if the Maldives are safe from rising sea levels, the increase in temperatures poses a problem for the islands. For example, in 1998, an influx of warm water killed large portions of its coral.

The international community has become more aware of the threats of global warming and climate change in recent years, and in accord with this recognition, climate aid has gained prominence starting in the early 1990s. It is expected that foreign assistance in the form of climate aid will continue to increase, especially with massive funding coming from the Clean Development Mechanism (CDM) projects under the Kyoto Protocol. The CDM allows developed countries to buy carbon from developing countries by paying for projects like reforestation, power plant energy efficiency and capturing of methane from landfills to meet their carbon emissions reductions level, as set by the Kyoto Protocol.

Energy

Energy is an essential requirement for development, but from a negative perspective, energy is also closely associated with negative side effects to the environment. Most energy comes from nonrenewable natural resources such as oil and fossil fuels. As countries struggle to secure stable sources of energy, foreign aid has become a tool to exploit abundant resources in developing countries, which has led to increasing criticism that foreign aid is a new form of imperialism. The recent inflows of aid from China into Africa are a

---

30 *Ibid.*

good example of recipient countries trading their natural resources for aid. Moreover, as the inflows of aid from China to Africa are becoming larger, some have voiced concern that aid dependency will develop.

Governments have recognized the importance of securing energy resources and realize that available sources of fossil fuels are scarce, so they are working to improve energy security by building technologies to improve efficiency, developing alternative energies like renewable energy sources, or promoting the use of environmentally friendly energy sources. Efforts in these areas are also a key to achieving sustainable development. Building capacity, strengthening institutions and promoting investments in the energy sector are all measures that can increase energy efficiency for sustainable development.

Natural Disasters

The World Bank lent funds to finance the construction of 487 schools over a 20-year period in Mozambique. In 2000, floods in Mozambique singlehandedly overturned the WB's 20-year project by destroying or damaging about 500 primary schools and 7 secondary schools. In Pakistan, the Kashmir earthquake of 2005 was responsible for $5 billion worth of damage, which is roughly equivalent to the total official development assistance for the three preceding years and the amount that the World Bank had lent to Pakistan over the preceding ten years. The tsunamis of 2004 devastated the shores of countries from Indonesia to Somalia, killing an estimated 220,000 people and leaving 1.5 million people homeless.[31]

It is becoming increasingly costly to recover from natural disasters. The costs of disastrous crises were fifteen times higher in the period from 1990 to 1999, estimated at $652 billion in material losses, compared to the $38 billion (at 1998 values) for the period 1950 to 1959. In addition to the material costs, human costs have also grown. Over the 1984 to 2003 period, more than 4.1 billion were affected by natural disasters. The numbers have continued to grow during this period, with 1.6 billion in the first half (1984-93) to 2.6 billion in the latter half (1994-2003).[32] With increasing

31 Independent Evaluation Group, *Hazards of Nature, Risks to Development: An IEG Evaluation of the World Bank Assistance for Natural Disasters* (Washington D.C.: World Bank, 2006).

32 *Ibid.*

numbers of natural disasters affecting developing countries, natural disasters have become a large obstacle to sustainable development.

One of the biggest problems with natural disasters is that when they occur, funds are needed instantaneously and end up diverting resources from other development projects. Another important consideration that must be made to understand the effects of natural disasters is that they have a disproportionate impact on developing countries. That is, natural disasters have caused more damage to developing counties than to developed countries. According to statistics by the International Federation of the Red Cross and Red Crescent Societies (IFRC), 98% of the 211 million people affected by natural disasters each year from 1991 to 2000 were from developing countries.[33]

There are several possible reasons for this disparity. The impact of natural disasters on different societies is directly related to their level of development, with poor countries being exposed to more damage. The quality of construction in developing countries is not equal to that of developed countries, and there are also differences in building codes, land registration processes and other regulatory mechanisms, which are essential conditions for a strong national infrastructure. It is also likely that developing countries are faced with pressing challenges that take priority away from preparing for natural disasters. Most of these developing countries are without any insurance systems which can cover the costs of natural disasters. In the US, private insurance covers approximately half of the costs of natural disasters, while in the developing countries, not even two per cent of the costs are covered by private insurance. Finally, the disproportionate effects of natural disasters can also be accounted for by the differences in climatic conditions of countries. Some areas have harsher climates than others, suffer from extreme weather conditions, or have unstable geology.

A critical part of natural disaster aid is the immediate response and support by donors. It is commonly the case that numerous donors respond to natural disasters, which increases the need for cooperation and coordination among these diverse actors. The report by the World Bank working group titled "Hazards of nature, risks to development: an IEG evaluation of World Bank assistance for natu-

33 International Federation of Red Cross and Red Crescent Societies (IFRC), "Relief, recovery and Root Causes," in *World disasters Report 2001* (Geneva: International Federation of Red Cross and Red Crescent Societies, 2001).

ral disasters" (2006) identified that 38% of all World Bank projects relating to natural disasters included the involvement of NGOs, and 170 of the 528 natural disaster projects mention coordination with other donors on diverse levels.[34]

The World Bank Response to Natural Disasters

As the participation of various multilateral and non-governmental groups related to recuperating from natural disasters rises, the international community needs to find ways to efficiently assist developing countries in recovering from natural disasters. The World Bank is the largest funder for disaster recovery and reconstruction. Its approach to natural disaster assistance concentrates on maintaining flexibility in the application of its aid projects. Flexibility in implementation of aid for natural disasters is especially important since the circumstances are more dynamic compared to other development projects. Projects need to be specifically designed to provide solutions to unique situations, taking into account geographical, cultural and sociopolitical factors.

The World Bank has learned how to manage its responses to various events and has demonstrated its ability to work together with donors to adopt policies and procedures that ensure the expeditious delivery of aid. The World Bank has worked to ensure that country assistance following disasters can contribute to long-term development and that future impacts of disasters can be reduced or prevented.

A total of 528 projects, representing 9.4% of all World Bank loan commitments since 1984, contained activities involving natural disasters and the total amount in dollar amounts which focused on natural disasters amount to $26,281 million. The general trends of lending have increased during the years and the most frequent type of disaster for which countries requested financing was flooding. Of the 528 projects, 234 had a flood-related activity, drought activities accounted for 107 projects, followed by fire with 95 projects. The Sub-Saharan region had the largest number of disaster projects followed by Latin America and the Caribbean regions. The Middle East and the North African regions accounted for the smallest portion of projects.

34 Independent Evaluation Group, *Hazards of Nature, Risks to Development: An IEG Evaluation of the World Bank Assistance for Natural Disasters* (Washington D.C.: World Bank, 2006).

10.4 Sustainable Development Goals (SDGs)

One of the main outcomes of the Rio+20 Conference was the agreement by member states to launch a process to develop a set of Sustainable Development Goals (SDGs), which will build upon the Millennium Development Goals (MDGs) and converge with the post 2015 development agenda. This new paradigm comes from the recognition that the UN used to heavily focus on environmental issues, neglecting economic, sociopolitical and environmental aspects. To overcome the limitation of this narrow focus and to implement sustainable development more effectively, the UN launched the SDG effort. In the beginning of the Rio+20 Conference, the expectation of a detailed green growth roadmap was high, but contrasting interpretations of green growth among individual countries made it difficult to establish a roadmap. Colombia and Guatemala jointly proposed the SDGs to spread the green growth initiative. Civil society also proposed a similar initiative, but Colombia and Guatemala's initiative finally became a mainstream.

RIO+20
United Nations
Conference on
Sustainable
Development

From the beginning, the United States, Norway, China and the United Kingdom supported the SDGs and the most of member states reached a consensus on the establishment of SDGs as the outcome of Rio+20. However, there was a slight difference in the understanding behind the support of SDGs among the states. Most of the developed countries conceived of SDGs as an alternative to the existing economic development paradigm and sought to limit the normative and regulative mandates of SDG by stipulating clear objectives, indicators and timeline. On the other hand, the developing countries did not limit the area of SDGs to green growth, instead they saw it as a framework that can pressurize developed countries to pledge more financial and technology transfer to the developing countries in order to achieve SDGs. Therefore, the developing countries appealed to include the issues of assistance for sustainable development, more poverty reduction efforts, and global financial regime change into the agenda of SDGs.

Due to the difference in the understanding of SDGs, both the developed and developing countries made only a general consensus on the principles of Rio+20. It was decided to establish an "inclusive and transparent intergovernmental process open to all stakeholders, with a view to developing global sustainable development goals to be agreed by the General Assembly."[35] In the Rio+20 outcome document, member states agreed that sustainable development goals (SDGs) must:

1) Be based on Agenda 21 and the Johannesburg Plan of Implementation.
2) Fully respect all the Rio Principles.
3) Be consistent with international law.
4) Build upon commitments already made.
5) Contribute to the full implementation of the outcomes of all major summits in the economic, social and environmental fields.
6) Focus on priority areas for the achievement of sustainable development, being guided by the outcome document.
7) Address and incorporate in a balanced way all three dimensions of sustainable development and their interlinkages.
8) Be coherent with and integrated into the United Nations development agenda beyond 2015.
9) Not divert focus or effort from the achievement of the Millennium Development Goals.
10) Include active involvement of all relevant stakeholders, as appropriate, in the process.

It was further agreed that SDGs must be:

- Action-oriented
- Concise
- Easy to communicate
- Limited in number
- Aspirational
- Global in nature
- Universally applicable to all countries while taking into account dif-

35 Future We Want – Outcome Document, The General Assembly, recalling its resolution 64/236 of 24 December 2009, in which it decided to organize the United Nations Conference on Sustainable Development at the highest possible level in 2012, as well as its resolution 66/197 of 22 December 2011.

ferent national realities, capacities and levels of development and respecting national policies and priorities.

The outcome document further specifies that the development of SDGs should:

- Be useful for pursuing focused and coherent action on sustainable development
- Contribute to the achievement of sustainable development
- Serve as a driver for implementation and mainstreaming of sustainable development in the UN system as a whole
- Address and be focused on priority areas for the achievement of sustainable development

The Rio+20 outcome document "The Future We Want" resolved to establish an inclusive and transparent intergovernmental process on SDGs that is open to all stakeholders with a view to developing global sustainable development goals to be agreed by the UNGA. The outcome document mandated the creation of an intergovernmental Open Working Group, which will submit a report to the 68th session of the General Assembly containing a proposal for sustainable development goals for consideration and appropriate action. The outcome document specifies that the process leading to the SDGs needs to be coordinated and coherent with the processes of the post 2015 development agenda and that initial input to the work of the Open Working Group will be provided by the UNSG in consultation with national governments.

SDGs & MDGs

The discussion over the SDGs drew attention to the relationship between SDGs and MDGs. The MDGs acted as a roadmap in development and cooperation by guiding the international community to maintain their priority for development cooperation and had detailed targets and timelines.

In the Rio+20 Output Document negotiation, the member states of Rio+20 agreed that SDGs do not replace MDGs and confirmed the importance of MDGs at the final Output Document by emphasizing that the development of SDGs should not divert focus or effort from the achievement of the MDGs. Moreover, the Rio+20 Output Document emphasized the need for alignment and coordination between SDGs and MDGs as the international community is preparing for the progress Post 2015.[36]

SDGs Proposal

In July 2014, the Open Working Group (OWG) consisting of UN member countries, private sector and civil society representatives agreed to the SDGs which includes seventeen targets and submitted the SDG proposal to the General Assembly of the United Nations. The SDGs covers various issues and agendas that were discussed by various stakeholders and included the recommendations of the Secretary General of the UN. In particular, the SDGs cover issues, such as inequality and peaceful and inclusive societies, which have not received attention from the MDGs. By doing so, the SDG proposal identified the essential agendas for sustainable development by 2030 and sought to protect the differing interests of stakeholders in the implementation of SDG goals.

Box 10.2 Proposal for Sustainable Development Goals (SDGs) by 2030

17 goals and 169 agendas included in SDG proposal cover areas from poverty reduction to food, health, education, gender equality, water, energy, urbanization, inequality, biological diversity and climate change.

There are 17 proposed goals:

Goal 1. End poverty in all its forms everywhere
Goal 2. End hunger, achieve food security and improved nutrition, and promote sustainable agriculture
Goal 3. Ensure healthy lives and promote well-being for all at all ages
Goal 4. Ensure inclusive and equitable quality education and promote life-long learning opportunities for all
Goal 5. Achieve gender equality and empower all women and girls
Goal 6. Ensure availability and sustainable management of water and sanitation for all
Goal 7. Ensure access to affordable, reliable, sustainable, and mod-

36 Sangin Kang et al., "Green Economy in the Context of Rio+20: Issues and Implications for National Strategies," *Journal of Fundamental Research*, vol. 2012 (2012): 1-195.

ern energy for all

Goal 8. Promote sustained, inclusive and sustainable economic growth, full and productive employment and decent work for all

Goal 9. Build resilient infrastructure, promote inclusive and sustainable industrialization and foster innovation

Goal 10. Reduce inequality within and among countries

Goal 11. Make cities and human settlements inclusive, safe, resilient and sustainable

Goal 12. Ensure sustainable consumption and production patterns

Goal 13. Take urgent action to combat climate change and its impacts

Goal 14. Conserve and sustainably use the oceans, seas and marine resources for sustainable development

Goal 15. Protect, restore and promote sustainable use of terrestrial ecosystems, sustainably manage forests, combat desertification, and halt and reverse land degradation and halt biodiversity loss

Goal 16. Promote peaceful and inclusive societies for sustainable development, provide access to justice for all and build effective, accountable and inclusive institutions at all levels

Goal 17. Strengthen the means of implementation and revitalize the global partnership for sustainable development

Source: Open Working Group on Sustainable Development Goals, "Outcome Document: Introduction to the Proposal of The Open Working Group for Sustainable Development Goals," (2014)

As presented in this chapter, the environmental threats that have emerged to challenge the global community are diverse. The costs to protect the environment from degradation are high. The efforts of NGOs and civil societies have assisted the global community to become more aware of the threats to the environment, and today both the North and South are aware of the obstacles that the global community faces. Fortunately, there have been international efforts to alleviate these problems and countries have cooperated and collaborated their efforts to build diverse environmental regimes to address these problems. However, future efforts need to consolidate the current fragmented efforts that are concentrated on direct stakeholders for each environmental issue.

Within the context of development assistance, it is evident that environmental sustainability will contribute towards promoting development. Nonetheless, it is important for donor countries to continue to allocate development aid separately from environmental aid. Environmental aid needs to be provided independently and should not be siphoned away from development aid. Donor countries should be careful when making decisions since reallocation and shifting of limited aid budgets will lead to inefficient utilization and a waste of resources.

Chapter 10. Review Discussion Questions

1. Identify the three pillars of sustainable development and the significance of environmental sustainability in achieving sustainable development.
2. What are some of the major threats to the environment today and how has the international community responded to these threats?
3. Explain the position of the North and South regarding environmental aid. Why does a tension exist between the North and South? How are the concerns of the two comparable?

Chapter 11

Aid for Trade (AfT)

> *"Earning and accumulating surplus resources and profits is a critical precondition for economic and social development. The international community has therefore focused on trade promotion and capacity building in developing countries through aid for trade (AfT). AfT is not dedicated to trade expansion simply for the sake of trade, but as a tool for development. To attain this objective, AfT aims to increase trade and coordination capacities through diverse policies. This trend fits the needs of developing countries, which are insisting on 'trade, not aid.'"*[1]

11.1 Concept and Mechanism of Aid for Trade (AfT)

AfT grew from the efforts of the WTO, and mainly evolved from a joint framework including the OECD and the WTO. The WTO Ministerial Conference of 2001 in Doha tackled the issue of supply-side capacity building and trade-related infrastructure building in order to expand the benefit of the WTO agreement and trade by emphasizing trade-related assistance and capacity building under the multilateral trade regime. This conference finally agreed to recommend the establishment of a task force for AfT, the preparation of a proposal of recommendation for AfT, and requested the IMF, World Bank and other UN agencies to discuss additional financial resources for AfT.

https://issuu.com/logar-trade/docs/logar-trade-potraby-pre-vcelarov-2012-2013

The first official meeting for AfT was at the Sixth WTO Ministerial Conference in Hong Kong

1 Minkyung Choi, "KOICA's Aid Policy for Africa through Aid for Trade(AfT)," *Journal of International Development Cooperation*, vol. 2009, no. 1 (2009): 25.

in December 2005. The conference agreed that the promotion of trade of the less and least developed countries is critical for poverty reduction and economic development. It adopted the Ministerial Declaration for the Promotion and Increase of Effectiveness of Aid for Trade Initiative. In particular, this declaration noted that AfT has to contribute to the expansion of trade-related infrastructure for the less and least developed countries and the spread of the WTO's multilateral trade regime.[2] It further specified the expansion of 'Integrated Framework (IF),' an agreement on the preferential treatment of products from LDCs, such as customs-free and quota exemption, and the financial initiative for AfT by member states including emerging donors.[3] The Hong Kong Ministerial Declaration also provided a venue to discuss the AfT initiative and generated momentum for establishing a joint monitoring system within the OECD.

In February 2006, the WTO launched a Task Force body to operationalize AfT. This task force raised the issue of adjustment costs of developing countries in the process of structural adjustment towards a trade friendly structure. In 2007, the WTO convened 'Regional Review: Mobilizing Aid for Trade' and the 'Global aid for Trade Review.' The latter meeting was the first high level conference on AfT, which included participation from the UNCTAD, World Bank, IMF, UNDP and ministers of trade and treasury. This high level conference reviewed the AfT policies of member states and adopted the implementation principle of AfT. In addition, the conference emphasized the importance of efforts to increase the effectiveness of AfT under the framework of the Paris Declaration on aid effectiveness.[4]

The Concept of AfT

AfT seeks to mobilize resources to address the trade-related constraints identified by developing and least-developed countries.[5] The WTO and the OECD categorize AfT into six areas: trade policy and regulations, trade development, trade-related infrastructure,

2 In-Soo Kang et al., *Major Issues and Policy Implications of Aid for Trade* (Seoul: Korea Institute for International Economic Policy, 2011), 24.

3 WTO, "Doha Work Program: Ministerial Declaration adopted on 18 December 2005," http://www.wto.org/english/thewto_e/minist_e/min05_e/final_text_e.htm, last visited August 2014.

4 Minkyung Choi, 'KOICA's Aid Policy for Africa through Aid for Trade(AfT),' *Journal of International Development Cooperation*, vol. 2009, no. 1 (2009): 12.

5 In-Soo Kang et al. (2011), 24.

building productive capacity, trade-related adjustment, and other trade-related needs.[6]

Table 11.1 Aid for Trade[7]

Trade policy and regulations	Building capacity to formulate trade policy, participate in negotiations and implement agreements
Trade development	To help enterprises engage in trade and improve the business climate, access to trade finance and trade promotion in the productive sectors (agriculture, forestry, fishing, industry, mining, tourism and services)
Trade-related infrastructure	Investing in the infrastructure – roads, ports, telecommunications, energy networks – needed to link products to global markets
Building productive capacity	Strengthening economic sectors – from improved testing laboratories to better supply chains – to increase competitiveness in export markets
Trade-related adjustment	Helping with any transition costs from liberalization – preference erosion, loss of fiscal revenue, or declining terms of trade
Other trade-related Needs	Aid for trade-related priority and activities, including PRSP, in domestic development scheme

In the beginning of the AfT initiative, the term often referred to technical cooperation on trade-related regulations and trade negotiations. It originated from the economic development cooperation approach, which believes that trade assistance can ignite economic development by creating jobs, vitalizing the private sector, and promote technology development. The concept of AfT gradually developed to encompass a supply-side capacity building framework that includes private sector development and trade-related infrastructure development and became embedded in the WTO multilateral trade regime. Finally, the concept of AfT has become understood as a comprehensive approach tackling all issues related to trade.[8] OECD categorized AfT as consisting of three components: ① trade-related technical assistance and capacity building, ② trade-related infrastructure, and ③ building productive capacity.

6 WTO and OECD, *Aid for Trade at a Glance 2007: 1st Global Review* (2007), 19.

7 Minkyung Choi, *KOICA's Aid Policy for Africa through Aid for Trade(AfT)* (Seoul: KOICA, 2008), 67.

8 In-Soo Kang et al., *Major Issues and Policy Implications of Aid for Trade* (Seoul: Korea Institute for International Economic Policy, 2011), 24.

Figure 11.1 Aid for Trade: The Expanding Agenda

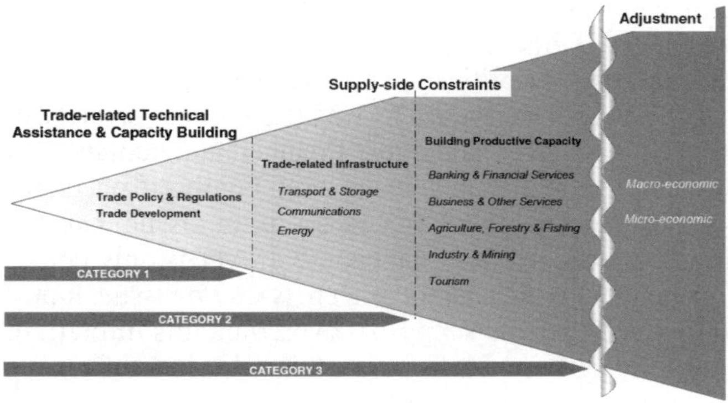

Source: OECD, *Aid for Trade: Making it Effective* (2006), 12.

The Mechanism of AfT[9]

While major donor countries share a consensus on the direction and principles of AfT, they differ on the mechanisms of AfT implementation. There are two main implementation approaches.

Table 11.2 AfT Mechanism

Category	Country	Feature
Type A (Comprehensive)	Germany, Belgium,Canada, etc.	- It is possible to frame AfT as a cross-cutting issue in the major aid areas - but trade issues can be considered as a secondary issue
Type B (Prioritized)	United Kingdom, Japan, United States, etc.	- AfT is the top priority of aid policy, so it is easy to secure the sustainability of projects by raising financial resources and acquiring organizational support - but there is a possibility of the project being reduced more narrowly to trade policy and trade development

The strength of the Type A approach is that all aid activities can incorporate AfT. However, it is clear that this approach treats trade as a secondary issue. To establish AfT as a cross-cutting issue like

9 Hongyul Han et al., "A Study on the Policy Framework of Aid for Trade in Major Donor Countries and Implications for Korea," *The Comparative Economic Review*, vol. 19, no. 1 (2002): 65-66.

other top aid priorities, AfT needs to be stipulated in donors' aid policies in a more rigid way, such as through guidelines, regulations or white papers. If this occurs, AfT can be established as a top priority in the process of prioritization of aid issues and sectors.

The Type B approach puts AfT as the highest priority of aid. Therefore, it is given considerable financial and human resources and can be more effective in the long term. For this to occur, though, AfT needs to be considered as a cross-cutting issue that includes agriculture, private sector, finance, etc. If AfT is only considered as an independent issue and not as a cross-cutting issue, it might be limited to a very narrow scope. To overcome this limitation, AfT needs a working group to incorporate this value into different stakeholders' interests and areas.

11.2 Cases of Successful AfT

AfT by Type

Based on the recognition of the effectiveness of AfT in poverty relief and economic development, this framework has become a major approach of foreign aid. Due to the characteristics of multiyear programs and projects, there are differences between the commitment and pledges of donors, but the overall amount of AfT accounts for 22% of total ODA in the commitment term.

AfT flows have been steadily rising as a percentage of total ODA, reflecting the international community's growing commitment to the idea. From 2006 to 2008, the average of total ODA was $150,099 million in disbursement terms and the volume of AfT was $24,801 million, which was equivalent to 16.5%. In 2010 and 2011, however, the amount of AfT increased to $34,867 million and $33,565 million respectively.

The commitment to AfT by the international community is meaningful. Between 2003 and 2005, AfT commitment was only 21.3%. It then increased to 22.2% between 2006 and 2008, 24.7% in 2009, and reached 27.2% in 2010. In 2011, the share of AfT in total ODA reduced to 25.9% but the share of AfT still counts for a relatively large portion of ODA.

The category of AfT by the OECD is as follow: trade policy and regulations, building productive capacity, economic infrastructure, and trade-related adjustment. Most of AfT flows are focused on eco-

Table 11.3 Aid for Trade: Shares in Total ODA (USD million, 2011 constant)

	Commitments					Disbursements			
	2002-05 avg.	2006-08 avg.	2009	2010	2011	2006-08 avg.	2009	2010	2011
Total Aid for Trade	26,491.7	34,592.5	42,997.4	41,569.6	24,801.0	31,178.5	31,178.5	34,867.5	33,565.9
Total ODA	124,569.7	155,485.6	174,235.8	177,331.0	160,410.9	150,099.7	147,018.0	157,260.1	150,862.9
Share of aid for trade in total ODA	21.3%	22.2%	24.7%	27.2%	25.9%	16.5%	21.2%	22.2%	22.2%

nomic infrastructure and building productive capacity but trade-related adjustment is negligible. In 2011, economic infrastructure counts for 52% of total AfT and building productive capacity was 44%.

Figure 11.2 The Ratio of AfT by Type and Year(Disbursements, USD million, 2011 constant)

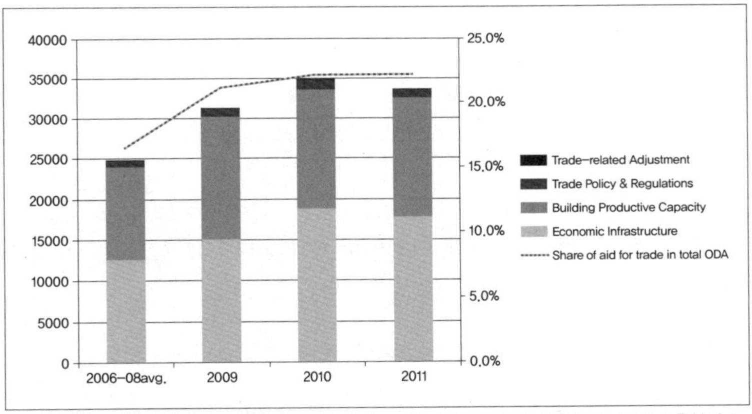

Source: OECD and WTO, *Aid for Trade at a Glance 2013: Connecting to Value Chains* (2013), 351, Annex A, Table A.1 and Table A.15

The largest portion of AfT is focused on economic infrastructure, which consists of transport and storage, communications, energy generation and supply. All assistance reported under the Credit Reporting System on Economic Infrastructure include transport, energy and communications. Although there is inconsistency in individual donors' reporting practices, with some countries attempting to isolate the trade component of each category but others reporting the whole activity as trade-related,[10] it is clear that economic infrastructure is a dominant part. In 2011, the amount of transport and

10 OECD, *Aid for Trade: Making It Effective* (Paris: OECD, 2006), 27-28.

storage in disbursement totaled 57.3%, 39.9% for energy, and 2.9% for communications. The decline in 2011 of $6.4 billion resulted in less support to large economic infrastructure projects, with commitments to the transport and energy sectors falling by $3.5 billion and $3.2 billion respectively.

Figure 11.3 Aid for Economic Infrastructure(USD million, 2011 constant)

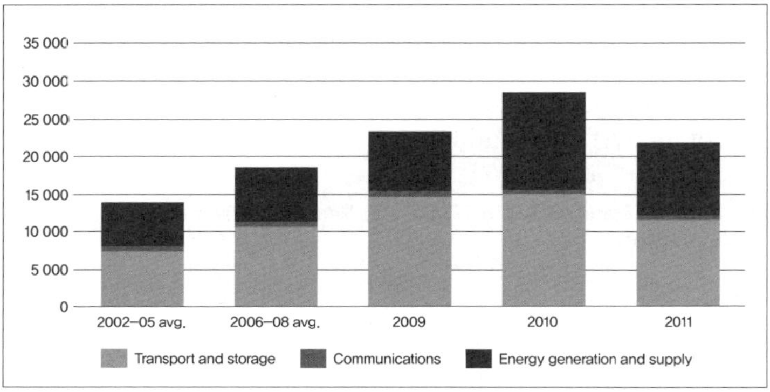

Source: OECD and WTO, *Aid for Trade at a Glance 2013: Connecting to Value Chains* (2013), 66.

Box 11.1 Improving Service Delivery and Reducing Clearing Times at the Chirundu Border, Zimbabwe

The UK's Department for International Development (DFID) launched 'One-Stop Border Posts (OSBP)' in order to reduce border waiting times which are responsible for two-third of the North-South Corridor journey times. In the beginning, the OSBP project was started by Japan on the Zambia side, and later DFID became involved through the Regional Trade Facilitation Programme in 2007. To implement the OSBP there were several issues that needed to be addressed: physical facilities (common control zone with a fenced perimeter and common facilities for scanning, weighbridges and inspection bays); operations and training; and legal framework (extraterritorial jurisdiction).

Based on UK assistance, Chirundu is moving into a phase where it will truly operate as an OSBP. The OSBP operational infrastructure was developed and modified. As a result, waiting times for commercial traffic have been reduced from about four to five days to a maximum of two days and often to a few hours.

There have been challenges but procedures are now established so outstanding issues such as signage, training programs, laying of optical fiber, preparation of a performance charter and final modifications to buildings can now be completed. In addition, the opening of Chirundu as an OSBP has led to significant savings in time taken to cross the border and this has translated into cost savings.

AfT focusing on productive capacity building is gradually increasing. In particular, agriculture, banking, and the finance sector are targeted. Although investments in economic infrastructure have witnessed decreases, commitments to building productive capacities increased to $18 billion in 2011 indicating the growing priority that partner countries and donors attach to developing the private sector. Support for business services, agriculture and industry all rose by 10%.

Figure 11.4 Aid for Building Productive Capacity (USD million, 2011 constant)

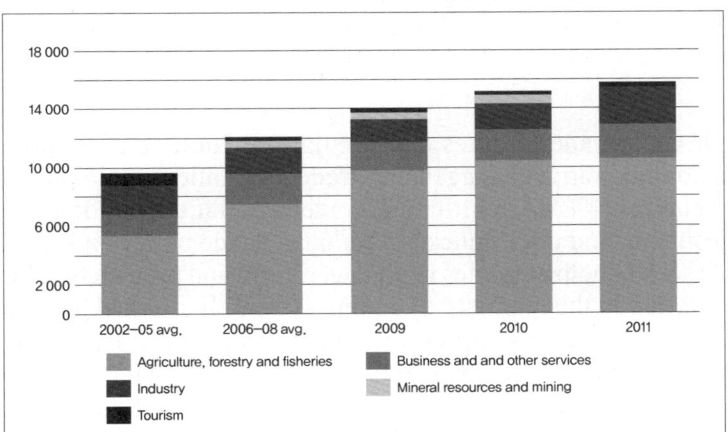

Source: OECD and WTO, *Aid for Trade at a Glance 2013: Connecting to Value Chains* (2013), 64.

Box 11.2 Improving Smallholder Farmers' Access to Cocoa Supply Chain in Indonesia by Australia

Through the Smallholder Agri-business Development Initiative (SADI), AusAID facilitated links between buyers and smallholder cocoa farmers. This helped to address the fragmented supply-chain in cocoa that was leading to poor signaling and a mismatch between producer and buyer expectations. It also contributed to crop storage facility development and sought to create price predictability for cocoa farmers.

This was achieved through working with a major cocoa purchasing companies such as Armajaro, ECOM Cocoa and Mars to establish buying centers, which provided transport and logistical assistance as well as crop storage and consolidation services to farmers. With SADI support, cocoa farmers were organized into farmer groups and extension services were delivered to farmers with direct participation by leading firms. SADI worked with these leading firms to establish buying centers that brought the farmers and farmer groups closer to buyers.

By being linked directly with their buyers, farmers saw increases in productivity and obtained better information about what to produce. This contributed to a 6% increase in cocoa production during SADI's operations in one of the two districts that the project focused on South-East Sulawesi. Ultimately as a result of SADI, farmers were able to receive better prices for their produce.

OECD's trade policies and regulations include trade policy and administrative management, trade facilitation, regional trade agreements (RTAs), multilateral trade negotiations, trade-related adjustment, and trade education/training. Trade policy and regulations seek to help countries negotiate, reform and prepare for closer integration in the multilateral trading system. It also tackles issues such as analysis and implementation of multilateral trade agreements, trade policy mainstreaming and technical standards, trade facilitation including tariff structures and customs regimes, support to regional trade arrangements, and human resources development in trade.[11] Trade policy and regulations only account for 3% of total AfT but it has consistently increased since 2009. Trade policy and administrative management is the largest part of this sector but this

11 *Ibid.*

category has been declining since 2000. Instead, RTAs and trade facilitation have increased in importance.

Figure 11.5 Aid-for-trade Policy and Regulation (USD million, 2011 constant)

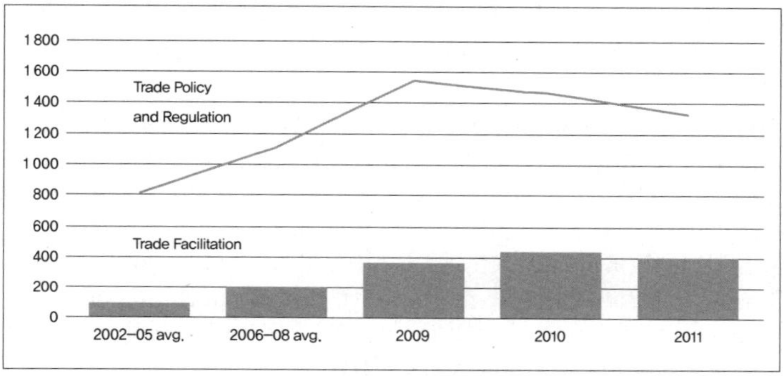

Source: OECD and WTO, *Aid for Trade at a Glance 2013: Connecting to Value Chains* (2013), 68.

11.3 Major Actors in AfT

Major actors in AfT are the government, UN agencies, and the private sector. The donor group of AfT consists of twenty four DAC donors, three Non-DAC donors and twenty multilateral aid agencies.

Figure 11.6 Top Ten Aid-for-Trade Donors (USD million, 2011 constant)

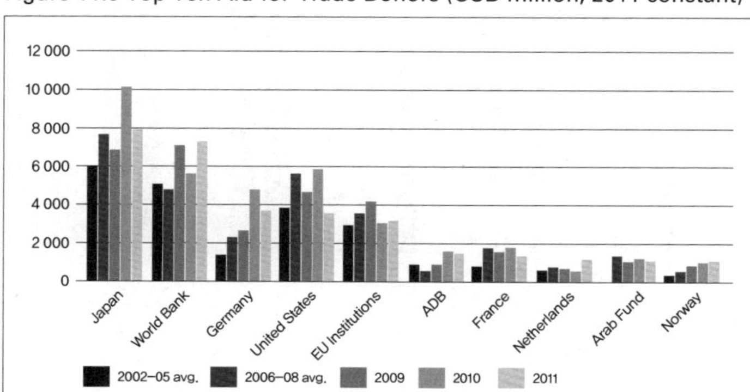

Source: OECD and WTO, *Aid for Trade at a Glance 2013: Connecting to Value Chains* (2013), 75.

Countries

Bilateral donors still provide the majority of aid for trade, accounting for 60% of total support in 2011. However, the total amount they provided in that year fell from 65% in 2010. Twenty-four member countries of DAC provided $28 billion in 2011. The top ten donors are Japan, Germany, United States, France, Netherland, and Norway.

Japan is the largest AfT donor in bilateral and multilateral terms. Japan was the largest donor in 2011 at $7.9 billion. Japan channeled 60% of its ODA to aid for trade. Germany was the second largest bilateral donor at $3.7 billion. The United States' AfT declined from $5.9 billion in 2010 to $3.6 billion in 2011. France provided $1.3 billion, a 29% decline from 2010. The Netherlands doubled its 2010 level of AfT to $1.2 billion. Norway provided just over 1$ billion, maintaining a similar level to 2010.[12]

AfT commitments were made to 146 countries in 2011.[13] The top ten recipients of AfT in 2011 were India, Vietnam, Afghanistan, Morocco, Indonesia, Ghana, Ethiopia, Egypt, Tanzania and Pakistan. In 2011, most AfT recipients were countries in Africa and Asia.

Asia is the largest destination of AfT, with inflows totaling $17 billion. Flows to Africa have declined to $13.1 billion. AfT to European countries declined as well, while other regions continue to re-

Figure 11.7 Aid for Trade by Income Group (USD million, 2011 constant prices)

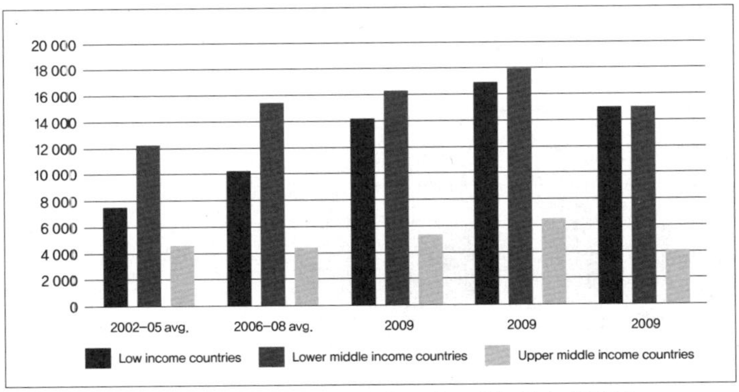

Source: OECD and WTO, *Aid for Trade at a Glance 2013: Connecting to Value Chains* (2013), 73.

---

12 *Ibid.*, 74-75.

13 Hosaeng Rhee et al., *A Study on Priority Areas and Programs for Korea's Aid for Trade* (Seoul: Korea Institute for International Economic Policy, 2012), 84-85.

ceive relatively stable amounts of aid. By income group, the LDCs were least affected by the global financial crisis and low income countries receive the largest share of total AfT.[14]

International Organizations

In 2011 multilateral donors maintained AfT resources at 2010 levels, a total of $16.6 billion. The World Bank is the largest multilateral donor and the second largest donor of AfT overall at $7.3 billion. The Bank increased its provision of aid for trade by 46% compared to the baseline and by 29% ($1.6 billion) compared to 2010. The Asian Development Bank Special Funds committed $1.45 billion in 2011. The increase in aid for trade from the World Bank offset declines from other multilateral donors including the African Development Fund (down $851 million) and Arab donors, specifically the Kuwait Fund For Arab Economic Development (down $540 million) and the OPEC Fund for International Development (down $194 million). The Arab Fund for Economic and Social Development has consistently provided over $1 billion per year since 2008.[15] The EU provided $3.2 billion, with only a 2% decline compared to 2010. This was an 8% increase over the 2002-05 baseline.

Box 11.3 World Bank's Aid-for-Trade Policy Focal Points[16]

- Trade Competitiveness and Diversification
- Trade Facilitation, Transport Logistics and Trade Finance
- Support for Market Access and International Trade Cooperation
- Managing Shocks and Promoting Greater Inclusion

Private Sector

The role of the private sector in implementing AfT is increasing. The private sector participates in the AfT framework through Public-Private Partnerships (PPP). They are an important supplement to government efforts by providing financial resources, creating jobs and transferring technology.[17] For the private sector, the moti-

14 WTO and OECD, *Aid for Trade at a Glance 2013: Connecting to Value Chain* (2013), 72.

15 *Ibid.*, 76.

16 World Bank, *What is the World Bank doing on Aid for Trade?* (2011), 1-3.

17 Minkyung Choi, *KOICA's Aid Policy for Africa through Aid for Trade(AfT)* (Seoul: KOICA,

vation to participate in the AfT framework includes the opportunity to open new markets, securing access to natural resources and logistics and recruiting low-cost labor.[18]

The public sector engages in building infrastructure, providing technical assistance, and improving trade facilitation and trade policy. On the other hand, the private sector focuses more on building trade capacity for developing countries. Participation of the private sector in AfT can be classified as 'business to government' (collaboration with donor government and multilateral agencies for AfT) or 'business to business' (support of local company's production and management, technology transfer and education(R&D), logistic support, etc).

The OECD facilitates MNCs and business associations' efforts to build capacity and facilitate trade in developing countries.[19] The OECD classifies private sector AfT into four types. First, MNCs focus on training and building human capacity. Nespresso, for example, has provided business training to coffee cooperatives in Guatemala. The training included accounting, internal credit management, organizational management and financial planning. As a result of this training, coffee farmers enjoyed improved productivity and profitability and increased exports of coffee.

Second, some MNCs focus on technology, know-how and finance to bolster local productive capacity. In Jachal, Argentina, for instance, Barrick launched a sun-dried tomato exporting initiative to help farmers develop a sustainable livelihood and expand their production and markets. Following a 2005 agreement with the Jachal Farmers Association and the Government of San Juan Province, Barrick offered technical support to help farmers diversify their crops from onions to tomatoes, and constructed a tomato drying facility. This initiative has allowed farmers to improve their productivity and sell their produce on the international markets at competitive prices.

There are also other examples of private sector cooperation in the AfT framework. In partnership with TechnoServe and the Bill & Melinda Gates Foundation, the Coca-Cola Company launched Project Nurture in January 2010 which sought to incorporate producers into global value chains. With regard to trade facilitation,

---

2008), 94.

18 World Bank, *The Role of International Business in Aid for Trade: Building Capacity for Trade in Developing Countries* (2011), 7, 15-16.

19 *Ibid.*, 19-20, 27-33.

the Global Express Association (GEA) has also cooperated with the World Bank to provide customs offices in Latin American countries with software to improve their customs procedures.

11.4 For Better AfT[20]

AfT is a cross-sectoral issue in aid that needs harmonization and alignment among various actors, including different ministries in the donor government, the private sector, civil society and international organizations. In this sense, the mechanism of aid effectiveness that has been adopted by Paris Declaration can be applied to the discussion of the effectiveness of AfT framework.[21] In November 2011, the Global Aid for Trade Review adopted the principle of AfT that can be applied to the AfT projects and programs, which are ongoing or planning by donor countries and multilateral agencies, in order to incorporate aid effectiveness framework by Paris Declaration to the AfT framework.

First, the international community agreed that improving the ownership of partner/recipient countries is important in AfT and recognized that unilateral implementation of AfT by donors or recipients is not effective. Most of all, the needs and priorities of recipient countries should be reflected or emphasized in the planning and implementation of AfT projects or programs. To make trade into a mainstream issue in the recipient country, the recipient country also needs to encourage its public and private sectors to participate in AfT projects or programs and coordinate their activities. In this sense, the commitment of the most powerful policy makers in the recipient countries is critical and a precondition. Their interests in the issue and their strong ownership of AfT projects can help them overcome obstacles encountered by various stakeholders in the implementation stages.

Second, alignment of the donors' and the recipients' objectives is also important to enhance the effectiveness of AfT. The donors' aid should fit the development plan of the recipient such as the PRSP and national development scheme. For this, it is necessary for the donors and the recipients to closely communicate and collaborate during

20 Minkyung Choi, "KOICA's Aid Policy for Africa through Aid for Trade(AfT)," *Journal of International Development Cooperation*, vol. 2009, no. 1 (2009): 12-13.

21 Hosaeng Rhee et al., *A Study on Priority Areas and Programs for Korea's Aid for Trade* (Seoul: Korea Institute for International Economic Policy, 2012), 37.

AfT planning and development stages. Using the public finance management (PFM) system for recipient countries is recommended. While there is a general consensus on the necessity of aid alignment, there are many cases of unilateral AfT driven by the donors' interests.

Third, AfT harmonization among the donors is important. The representative case of harmonization is the Joint Integrated Technical Assistance Program (JITAP). JITAP was established by the WTO, ITC and UNCTAD in 1998 and delivers trade-related technical cooperation and trade capacity development for sixteen countries in Africa. Similar to the Integrated Framework (IF), thirteen donor institutions created a trust fund for JITAP, which is headquartered in Geneva and has coordination offices in Uganda and Cote d'Ivoire. The key role of JITAP is the coordination of donors' aid resources, policies, AfT projects and programs. JITAP does not limit the beneficiaries of its aid to LDCs.[22]

Finally, effective AfT requires careful management of its programs and projects. It is difficult to set clear goals and indicators because AfT covers a wide range of sectors such as infrastructure, trade development, and trade policy and regulation. From the recipient's side, it is difficult to identify the results of specific AfT projects or programs. As a result, there is still a need to develop AfT projects that are measurable and can be comparatively analyzed. Currently, there is no common AfT measurement among the donors, but some countries such as Australia, Belgium, Chile, Finland, Ireland, New Zealand, Netherland, United Kingdom, and World Bank are conducting a joint monitoring of AfT for the purposes of aid harmonization and mutual accountability enforcement.

Chapter 11. Review Discussion Questions

1. Why is the initiative of aid for trade (AfT) important in international development cooperation?
2. What are the six elements of the AfT initiative and how are these elements mutually related?
3. What difficulties does the AfT initiative encounter?
4. How can the AfT initiative be interpreted in the framework of aid effectiveness?

---

22 Minkyung Choi, *KOICA's Aid Policy for Africa through Aid for Trade(AfT)* (Seoul: KOICA, 2008), 84.

Chapter 12
Policy Coherence for Development (PCD)

> *"The 2030 Agenda compels us to look beyond national boundaries and short-term interests and act in solidarity for the long-term. We can no longer afford to think and work in silos."*[1]

> *"The multi-dimensional nature of the SDGs requires linkages across policy areas. The OECD addresses the multidimensional nature of diverse issues through a variety of horizontal projects and international initiatives. Its Policy Coherence for Sustainable Development Framework helps to identify synergies and trade-offs among economic, social and environmental policy areas."*[2]

In today's interdependent world economy, domestic and foreign policies – such as trade, investment, agriculture and fisheries, taxation, security, innovation, migration, climate and environment – can stimulate or hinder growth and development in developing countries. First, development challenges cannot be solved by a single ministry or a single country. In addition, aid alone cannot address the needs of the developing world, which means that development issues extend to areas ranging from agriculture to trade, environment, energy, health, security, investment, tax policies, migration, etc. Second, globalization has increased mutual interaction and reliance, which makes countries more sensitive to other countries' policies. Under the highly interdependent global economy, a country's aid policy can undermine another country's aid efforts; therefore, donors need coherence and coordination among themselves. Last, as US and Western hegemony declined due to economic downturns, Western nations began to pressure new donor countries, such as China, Japan, Russia and South Korea, to contribute to global burden sharing by adopting a new comprehensive approach of PCD for poverty reduction.

Given this operational environment, a donor country's aid to

1 The Secretary-General remarks at summit for the adoption of the post-2015 development agenda (New York, 25 Sept. 2015).

2 OECD PCD Website, http://www.oecd.org/pcd.

boost a developing country's ability to engage in trade makes no sense if the donor blocks imports from that country through trade barriers or trade distorting subsidies. In this context, development cooperation efforts need to be supported by mutually reinforcing policies across a wide range of economic, social and environmental issues to ensure greater results and impact. This entails a comprehensive approach to development and enhanced policy coherence for development.

12.1 Evolution of PCD

PCD, standing for Policy Coherence for Development and introduced by the OECD, is a tool to inform the policymaking process in all countries and regions to achieve inclusive and sustainable development. In this sense, PCD can be understood as an effort to strengthen the capacities of donor governments for more integrated and coherent policies for development in the developing countries.

Although the OECD DAC discussed the framework of PCD in a series of documents since the mid-1990s, there is still no definition of PCD that is commonly accepted. On the basis of these discussions, however, PCD can be understood as progress towards policies that are more coherent and supportive of development and that plays an important part in achieving sustainable and broad-based development of developing countries.[3] PCD aims to exploit positive synergies and spillovers across public policies to foster development. In this sense, a meaningful working definition of PCD goes well beyond minimizing the adverse impact that public policies can have in developing countries; it entails the systematic application of mutually reinforcing policies and integration of development concerns across government departments to achieve development goals along with national policy objectives.[4]

PCD can be categorized into four types and when these types are mutually reinforced, aid effectiveness can be enhanced. The categorization of PCD that is commonly used was introduced by Robert Picciotto.[5]

---

3 DAC, "Declaration on Policy Coherence for Development," 4 June 2008-C/Min(2008)2/final.

4 OECD Office of the Secretary-General Unit for Policy Coherence for Development, Policy Framework for Policy Coherence for Development Working Paper, no. 1, 2012 (2012), 3.

5 Robert Picciotto, "The Evaluation of Policy Coherence for Development," *SAGE journals*, vol. 11, no. 3 (2005): 3, 312.

Table 12.1 Types of Policy Coherence Development

Types	Features
Internal coherence: consistency within aid policies	Integrated development approaches by tackling untied aid, increase of aid scale, private sector, debt relief, good governance
Intra-country coherence: consistency between aid and non-aid policies	coherence between aid and non-aid policies and promotion of aid effectiveness by coordination among government bodies
Inter-donor coherence: aid harmonization	focusing on aid transaction cost among donors through coordination and harmonization
Donor-partner coherence: aid alignment	aid effectiveness focusing on aid conditionality, priority and ownership of the recipient countries, partnership between the recipient and the donor countries

Source: Robert Picciotto, "The Evaluation of Policy Coherence for Development," *Evaluation* 11 (2005): 3, 312.

Among these four types of coherence discourse for development, PCD in general refers to the second category which refers to coherence between aid and non-aid policies.

The OECD has focused on internal coherence, which tackles the issue of consistency within aid policies. This was attributable to the dominance of an integrated development approach in international development cooperation in the 1970s-80s and aid effectiveness discourse later in the 1980s and 1990s which covered the issue of aid conditionality, development partnership, the private sector, debt issues and good governance.

In the beginning of the 1990s, then, the entirety of the government approach had been introduced and became momentum that enabled development actors to consider coherence between aid and non-aid policies. In 1996, the OECD DAC adopted 'Shaping the 21st Century' that envisaged a number of development goals and indicators which should be pursued and could be monitored. Also, this document introduced for the first time the importance of consistency and coordination between aid and non-aid policies to achieve development goals.

With the increase of development actors in the later 1990s, the necessity of aid harmonization to reduce aid transaction costs through the adjustment and proactive coordination among donors' aid policies became evident. Coherence among donors, called aid harmonization, puts emphasis on the problem of aid conditionality and ownership of partner countries from an aid effectiveness approach. Also, the importance of ownership in aid effectiveness drew attention to the alignment between the priorities of the recipient countries and the resources of the donor countries. These issues of aid harmonization and alignment were incorporated into the principles of the Paris Declaration for aid effectiveness.

International PCD Discourse by the OECD DAC and EU

The OECD played an important role steering Policy Coherence for Development discourse in the international community and the EU began to have interest in the policy coherence of its member states' development and aid policies since 2007. In the 2000s, in particular, the OECD DAC contributed to the expansion of the concept of PCD from a focus on coherence in aid policies to a more ambitious focus on the coherence between non-aid as well as aid policies. The OECD DAC also endeavored to incorporate the result-based approach, which tackles more broad and specific targets and goals from the concept of PCD rather than a simple expansion of ODA scale, to the eight goals of MDGs.

Figure 12.1 The Evolution of PCD

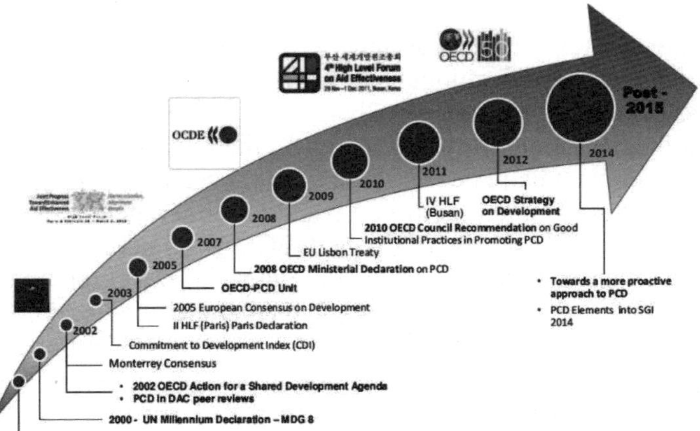

Source: OECD PCD Unit.

In 2001, the DAC emphasized the importance of PCD to reduce poverty through the adoption of 'Poverty Reduction' and advocated the internalization of PCD under the framework of 'OECD Action for a Shared Development Agenda'. With the adoption of 'Policy Coherence for Development: Promoting Institutional Good Practice' in 2005, the DAC introduced the concept of PCD. The implementation mechanism and cases of incoherence were also discussed.[6] For the effective implementation and facilitation of the PCD framework, the OECD established a PCD Unit in 2007. The PCD Unit facilitates analysis, dissemination, and advocacy on policy coherence for development. It aims to strengthen the capacities of governments and other stakeholders to establish more coherent and integrated policies for sustainable development, as well as to foster policy dialogue and knowledge sharing on coherence issues. The Unit is led by the OECD Deputy Secretary-General, who is in charge of development to facilitate mainstreaming and cross-fertilization of expertise relevant for sustainable development across the OECD.

In June 2008, the OECD DAC reconfirmed its willingness to develop a monitoring and assessment tool as well as the implementation of PCD through 'OECD Ministerial Declaration on Policy Coherence for Development.' The Declaration recognized that PCD is essential for the achievement of MDGs and demonstrated the recommendations and direction of PCD to support the development of the countries. In the same year, the OECD DAC issued 'Synthesis Report on Policy Coherence for Development' based on previous DAC Peer Review reports and drew lessons for the internalization and facilitation of PCD through 'Building Blocks for Policy Coherence for Development' the following year. The Ministerial Meeting in 2011 adopted the 'Framework for an OECD Strategy on Development' and it reemphasized the importance of an innovative and sustainable development resource, resource mobilization for development, governance for development, and policy procedures for development. PCD was understood as a strategy that is able to magnify synergy effects of every aspect of development in the Ministerial Meeting document. In the same year, the OECD DAC opened the 'International Platform on Policy Coherence for Development' which was expected to facilitate and disseminate expertise and lessons learned related to PCD.

The European Union also has a strong attachment to PCD. In 1992, Article 178 of the Treaty on European Union (Maastricht Treaty) stipulates that EU member states need to consider develop-

6 OECD, "Framework for an OECD Strategy on Development," at the Meeting of the OECD Council at Ministerial Level (Paris, 25-26 May 2011), 2.

ment goals when they establish policies affecting developing countries. Article 3 refers to coherence between EU policies and external activities and the EU reform treaty (Treaty of Lisbon) in 2005 also reiterated this requirement. Article 21 of the Treaty of Lisbon specifies that the objectives of the EU's external policies should be sustainable development and poverty reduction. It further stipulates that the EU has to pursue such goals and mandates. In addition, the EU showed their recognition of PCD by succeeding to Article 178 of Maastricht.

In 2005, the EU Commission organized 'Communication on Policy Coherence for Development' and issued the 'EU Report on Policy Coherence for Development' in 2007. This report selected 12 thematic issues and analyzed these issues under the framework of PCD. In 2009 the report was updated and the process of revision of the report contributed to the completion of the EU's political framework for PCD. The European Union continues on to cover cross-cutting as well as thematic issues and present progresses made on PCD across various policy areas. All principal EU institutions including the Commission, the European Parliament and the Council are actively taking part as the main PCD actors by proposing legislation, implementing and monitoring EU-level rules in accordance with the PCD principles. The member states also carry responsibility when it comes to ensuring policy coherence for the development in their national policies and also at the EU level and usually have their own coordination mechanisms in place. The efforts at the individual national level are being made by increasing attention to coordination and also by reporting the cause and process.

The roles of civil society organizations also are critical in the EU and the most active and notable movement by the civil groups are that of Confederation for Relief and Development (CONCORD), the principal development NGO umbrella organization and an important interface with the EU institutions on development policy. Made up of 27 national associations, its wide networks and associate members represent over 1,800 NGOs and the CONCORD mainly focuses on monitoring actions towards PCD by the EU and its members.

The EU implement various tools and mechanisms in the field of Policy Coherence for Development. The Commission prepares Impact Assessments for all initiatives that may result in significant economic, social or environmental impacts especially for the developing countries. Trade-specific policies are analyzed through Sustainability Impact Assessments to assess the feasible implications more systematically during the negotiations. Also all initiatives and major programs carried out the European Commission are obliged to go through Inter-Service Consultations to make sure there are not any irregularities and illegal activities involved. Moreover, every PCD related policy initiatives are screened also evaluated once they are implemented under Commission guidelines. PCD reports are being published in every two years and each and every EU delegation receives reports on PCD cases and challenges as well as feedbacks.[7]

Key Issues in PCD

In 2011, the OECD clarified eighteen issues for PCD in 'Better Policies for Development: Recommendation for Policy Coherence.' The issues are categorized according to the four sectors of economic growth, economic governance, environment and natural resource security, and society. The OECD called attention to PCD and the importance of PCD implementation through this document.

Table 12.2 OECD PCD Thematic Issues

Sectors	Issues
Economic growth	Macro-economic policy
	Trade
	Investment
	Financial Regulation
	Science, technology and innovation
Economic Governance	Taxation
	Anti-corruption
	Illicit financial flows
Environment & natural resource security	Climate change
	Food security
	Water security
	Energy security
Society	Conflict and fragility
	Labor
	Education and skills
	Migration
	Health
	Indicators of Progress

Source: OECD, *Better Policies for Development Recommendations for Policy Coherence* (2011).

7 European Commission, Policy Coherence for Development 2015 EU Report, http://ec.europa.eu/europeaid/sites/devco/files/pcd-report-2015_en.pdf.

The EU also selected twelve issues for PCD in 2007 through the 'EU Report on Policy Coherence for Development': trade, environment, climate change, security, agriculture, fisheries, social policy, migration, research, information technology, transport and energy. The EU established a guideline for development assistance in line with coherence and effectiveness. The second report issued in 2009 picked out the five priority issues of trade and finance, climate change, food security, immigration, and security among the twelve issues. Based on these issues, the EU Commission issued 'Policy Coherence for Development Work Programme 2010-2013.' This document aimed to guide the EU Commission's PCD implementation and facilitate PCD in EU member states.[8]

Also, the OECD is actively discussing policy incoherence at the state level. In particular, the OECD is focusing on the identification of policy incoherence in the areas of trade, investment, green growth and finance that can cause negative effects on developing countries. In fact, OECD tackles policy incoherence cases such as suspension of subsides, trade liberalization, anti-corruption, responsible investment, and transparent financing system.[9]

12.2 Mechanism of PCD

The implementation of PCD at the OECD level is delivered through four aspects. The first stage is an establishment of PCD guidelines for OECD member states based on DAC peer review reports. Second, a case study identifies potential and practical impacts of differing development and aid policies at the analytical level. Third, it enables policy makers to disseminate and facilitate PCD at the assessment methodology level. Last, the deepening of PCD through cross-cutting committee meetings is essential at the OECD level. To make good progress towards PCD based on the consideration of the four aspects above, the OECD provides three essential building blocks; Political commitment and policy statements, policy coordination mechanisms and system of monitoring, analysis and reporting.[10]

8 Hyuksang Sohn et al., "Enhancing Policy Coherence for Development in south Korea," *ODA Study*, vol. 24, no. 3 (2012): 33-34.

9 Hyuksang Sohn (2012), 5.

10 OECD, "Building Blocks for Policy Coherence for Development" (Paris: OECD, 2009), 21.

Figure 12.2 The Dynamics of Policy Coherence Cycle

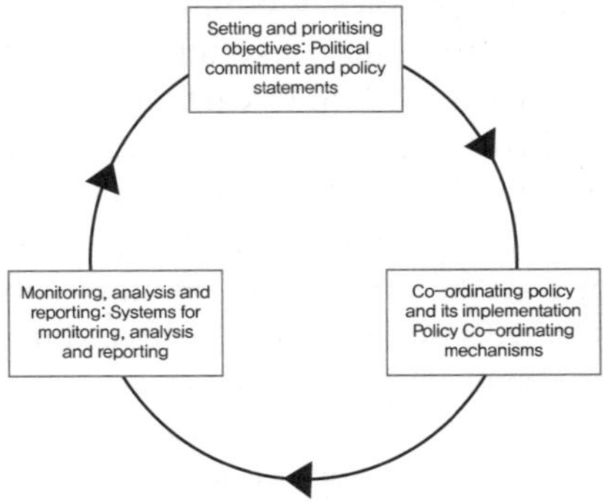

Source: OECD, *Building Blocks for Policy Coherence for Development* (2009), 20.

The cycle of PCD consists of setting and prioritizing objectives, coordinating policy and implementation, and monitoring, analysis and reporting. The stage of objective setting and prioritizing needs political leadership and commitment to development goals at a relatively high level of politics. This is because a proper level of political willingness for PCD can be a starting point of policy coordination between aid and non-aid policies. At this stage, therefore, a policy framework is important because it establishes priorities for making decisions when differing policies confront each other. For a sustainable political commitment to PCD, it requires collaboration among civil society, think tanks, and the recipient country's government to increase awareness on PCD in the long-term perspective.[11] This stage of political commitment requires legal innovations and a sufficiently high level of public support for PCD to be made by policymakers. Especially, it requires legal and institutional support strong enough to influence non-aid policies and cross-cutting issues.

Portugal became the first country among OECD DAC member states to adopt a legal document on PCD in 2010. Germany and Sweden do not have a legal document that solely stipulates PCD itself, but these two are considered to be countries providing a legal basis for the approach.[12] Netherland, Denmark, Belgium, Switzer-

11 Hyuksang Sohn and Youngsun Park, "A Ctirical Study on Policy Coherence for Development in South Korea," *Korean journal of international relations*, vol. 52, no. 3 (2012): 381.

12 OECD, *Better Policy for Development: Recommendation for Policy Coherence* (Paris: OECD,

land, and Ireland specify PCD in white papers or policy documents on development and aid policies. Germany's 'Poverty Reduction a Global Responsibility Program of Action, PA 2015,'[13] Denmark's 'Freedom from Poverty, Freedom to Change,'[14] and Finland's 'Development Policy Programme'[15] are typical examples of strong political support for the PCD concept. These documents emphasize the importance of a whole-of government approach in international development cooperation. Greece, on the other hand, does not expand the PCD framework to its overall policies but it still applies it to specific issue area such as immigrant policy.[16]

At the stage of 'coordinating policy and its implementation,' it is important to maximize the synergy of policy coherence through coordination between aid and non-aid policies based on the objectives prioritized with reducing incoherence among differing policies. Achieving this stage depends on how effectively differing policies are coordinated in the framework of PCD and to what extent development goals are achieved and considered in this policy coordination process. This requires an institutional coordination mechanism at a relatively high level of government policymaking so as to internalize PCD within differing policies and ministries. Some countries establish a PCD unit or official committee tackling this issue under the Prime Minister's Office or the Ministry of Foreign Affairs. Other countries forego an official institutional PCD mechanism but promote the approach through unofficial and informal policy consultation at the working group level.

Eight OECD DAC member states, including Denmark, Spain, Ireland, and Sweden, are known to be operating PCD implementation mechanisms within their governmental structures. The authority and role of PCD implementation mechanisms vary among these countries. For instance, the Coordination Committee under the Prime Minister's Office in Denmark has authority to exert influence on new policymaking initiatives.[17] The German Prime Minister's Office, meanwhile, only plays a role arbitrating policies and

2011).

13 OECD, *DAC Peer Review: Germany* (Paris: OECD, 2006), 47.

14 Ministry of Foreign Affairs of Denmark, *Freedom from Poverty, Freedom to Change* (Copenhagen: Danida, 2010), 25-28.

15 OECD DAC, *DAC Peer Review: Finland* (Paris: OECD, 2007), 25-27.

16 OECD DAC, *DAC Peer Review: Greece* (Paris: OECD, 2006), 38.

17 OECD DAC, *DAC Peer Review: Denmark* (Paris: OECD, 2011), 36.

ministries when they clash with each other.[18] This suggests that the existence of a PCD implementation mechanism itself does not assure a high level of policy coherence. Sometimes political commitment and statements do not lead to the creation of implementation schemes, and sometimes implementation mechanisms do not work as intended. The Development Policy and Coherence Division in Denmark is an example of this. The OECD DAC concluded that this division does not put priority on PCD issues and its mandate is weak as well.[19] However, the leading countries in PCD implementation are operating formal coordination mechanisms at a sufficiently high level of policymaking as well as at the practical level such as working group meetings. Development-related issue areas such as the environment and climate change, immigration, trade, agriculture, and fisheries are dominant in PCD discussions.[20]

The final stage of PCD is 'monitoring, analysis and reporting.' This stage collects and assesses evidence of achievements and progress of policy adjustment and coordination in the framework of PCD. This stage aims to draw feedback on certain policies from the perspective of PCD and this feedback allows policymakers to reset or adjust policy targets and priorities for the further internalization of PCD. This stage also looks at how well each of the relevant ministries incorporated PCD into their policies and evaluates to what extent this assessment was transparently reported to lawmakers and civil society. Because of this, the existence of institutions for PCD monitoring and evaluation is essential for the completion of PCD blocks and the effectiveness of such policy monitoring, analysis, and reporting system is also important. With regard to reporting, whether it is reported to lawmakers, who represent the taxpayers, and whether the report is issued regularly, is important to pressure policymakers to adhere to their commitment to PCD.

Most OECD DAC member states do not have a PCD monitoring and reporting system. Although the countries at the vanguard of international development cooperation are supporting PCD and seeking to implement it, most countries have not established monitoring, analysis and reporting systems yet. Only Germany has established an independent PCD monitoring institution. The German Development Institution aims to evaluate and analyze gov-

18 OECD DAC, *DAC Peer Review: Germany* (Paris: OECD, 2006), 46.

19 OECD DAC, *DAC Peer Review: The Netherlands* (Paris: OECD, 2011), 36.

20 Hyuksang Sohn, "Enhancing Policy Coherence for Development in south Korea," *Development Cooperation and Policy Issue*, vol. 7 (2012): 9.

ernment efforts for PCD and, based on evaluation results, advises government ministries about development and aid policies from the framework of PCD.[21] Without an official institution for PCD monitoring and reporting, Sweden, the United Kingdom, and Ireland are reporting their PCD implementation to their national legislatures and Denmark and Switzerland are reporting PCD progress in the form of regular policy reports. On the other hand, civil societies in Sweden and Ireland are monitoring government policies for PCD. In particular, Swedish NGOs in collaboration with CONCORD, a European NGO confederation for relief and development, have biennially issued a 'Coherence Barometer' since 2008. It evaluates PCD in the areas of Swedish security, trade, immigration, and finance policies.[22] The European Union also issued two reports on PCD progress in their member states in 2007 and 2009 and these reports included the efforts of EU member states' PCD dissemination and facilitation in twelve sectors.

12.3 PCD in Peer Review

The OECD DAC uses 'Peer Review' as a mechanism for PCD evaluation. Peer Reviews are conducted every four or five years to assess the efforts of member states for development cooperation and PCD is one of the evaluation indicators. Between 1996 and 1999, the issue of PCD was included in multiple sections of the Peer Review report, but since 2000 the issue of PCD has been treated as a separate section. There is no consensus on the analytical framework for the analysis of PCD in a Peer Review target country, but PCD in institutional management has been mainly reviewed since 2007.[23] Peer reviews look at policy coherence at country level and within the OECD. The domestic and international policies, whether aid or non-aid, must be coherent and mutually supportive of developing countries' development objectives or at least avoid undermining the aims of the donors.

The OECD's Development Cooperation Directorate (DCD) provides an analytical framework for Peer Reviews. The analytical

21 OECD DAC, *DAC Peer Review: Germany* (Paris: OECD, 2010), 45, 54.

22 OECD DAC, *DAC Peer Review: Sweden* (Paris: OECD, 2009), 35; CONCORD, Coherence Barometer 2008 (Brussels: CONCORD, 2009).

23 *Ibid.*, 18.

framework for Peer Reviews consists of ① strategic orientation, ② development beyond aid, ③ ODA volume, channels and allocations, ④ organization and management of aid, ⑤ effective aid and results, and ⑥ humanitarian assistance. PCD is reviewed in the development beyond aid section. The criteria of Peer Reviews are an internationally agreed standard, the best practices and guidelines of member states, a newly approved standard for DAC membership, and if possible domestically adopted evaluation criteria.[24] Through the Peer Review, the OECD DAC first aims to evaluate whether the targets and policies approved by the OECD DAC are observed by its member states by monitoring their policies of development cooperation. Second, it aims to improve the effectiveness of aid through a mutual learning process. Third, it seeks to facilitate coordination among development policies by drawing lessons from best practices. This process allows donors to reform and adjust their aid and non-aid policies and institutions towards a more sustainable and comprehensive development cooperation mechanism.[25]

Lessons from the Peer Review's Recommendations based on PCD

The OECD DAC drew lessons from each country's Peer Review by analyzing PCD implementation progress. Such lessons provided guidance on how to promote PCD at the domestic level. The OECD DAC issued the 'Synthesis Report on Policy Coherence for Development' in 2008 and 'Building Blocks for Policy Coherence for Development' in 2009 based on the Peer Review reports from 2003 to 2007. These two papers provided a practice-based approach for PCD. In 2011 the OECD DAC issued another policy paper named 'Better Policies for Development: Recommendations for Policy Coherence,' which showcased sectoral recommendations for PCD. However, while these papers showed that the OECD DAC consistently emphasized the importance of development issues and policy coherence for development, state level progress towards PCD did not meet its intended goals.[26]

---

24 Development Assistance Committee. 2010. DAC Peer Review Content Guide. OECD. 2.

25 Hyuksang Sohn, "Enhancing Policy Coherence for Development in south Korea," *Development Cooperation and Policy Issue*, vol. 7 (2012): 9.

26 *Ibid.*, 36.

Box 12.1. Building Blocks for PCD[27]

Building Block A: Political commitment and policy statements

Lesson 1: Educate and engage the public, working with civil society, research organizations and partner countries, to raise awareness and build support for PCD on a long-term basis.

Lesson 2: Make public commitments to PCD, endorsed at the highest political level, with clear links made to poverty reduction and internationally agreed development goals.

Lesson 3: Publish clearly prioritized and time-bound action agendas for making progress on PCD.

Building Block B: Policy co-ordination mechanisms

Lesson 4: Ensure that informal working practices support effective communication between ministries.

Lesson 5: Establish formal mechanisms at sufficiently high levels of government for inter-ministerial coordination and policy arbitration, ensuring that mandates and responsibilities are clear and fully involve ministries beyond development and foreign affairs.

Lesson 6: Encourage and mandate the development agency to play a pro-active role in discussions about policy coordination.

Building Block C: Systems for monitoring, analysis and reporting

Lesson 7: Make use of field-level resources and international partnerships to monitor the real world impacts of putting PCD building blocks in place.

Lesson 8: Devote adequate resources to the analysis of policy coherence issues and progress towards PCD, drawing also on the expertise of civil society and research institutes, both domestically and internationally.

Lesson 9: Report transparently to parliament and the wider public about progress on PCD as part of reporting on development co-operation activities and progress towards meeting the Millennium Development Goals.

27 OECD, *Building Blocks for Policy Coherence for Development* (Paris: OECD, 2009), 23-38.

Figure 12.3 shows the rank of OECD DAC countries in the cycle of PCD.

Figure 12.3 The Evaluation of PCD in Peer Review

1. Political commitment and policy statements

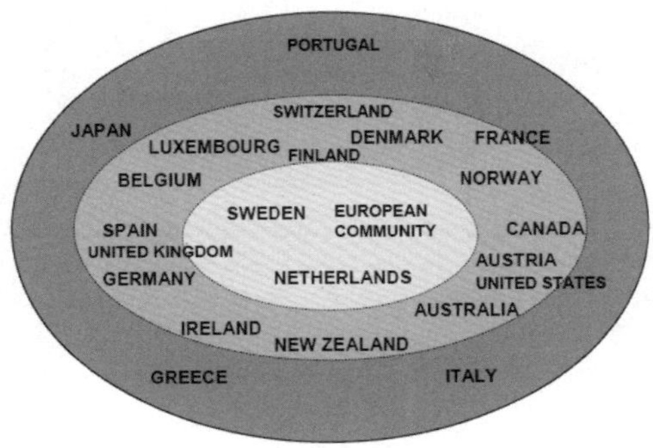

= Substantial political commitment to PCD; clear PCD policy statements

= Moderate political commitment to PCD; some PCD policy statements

= Partial political commitment to PCD; lack of PCD policy statements

2. Policy coordination mechanism

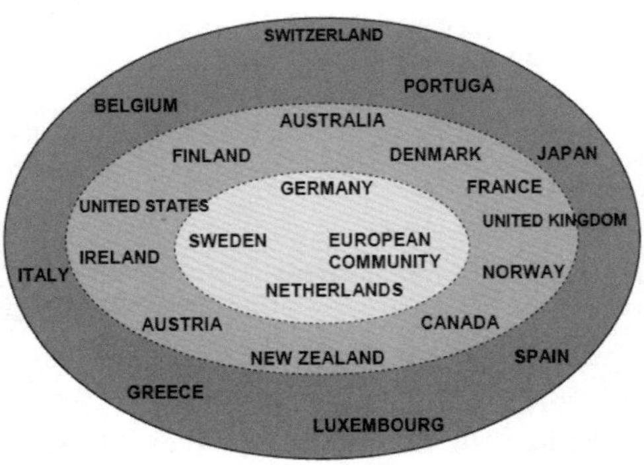

= Substantial success in putting policy co-ordination mechanisms in place

= Moderate success in putting policy co-ordination mechanisms in place

= Partial success in putting policy co-ordination mechanisms in place

3. Monitoring, analysis and reporting systems

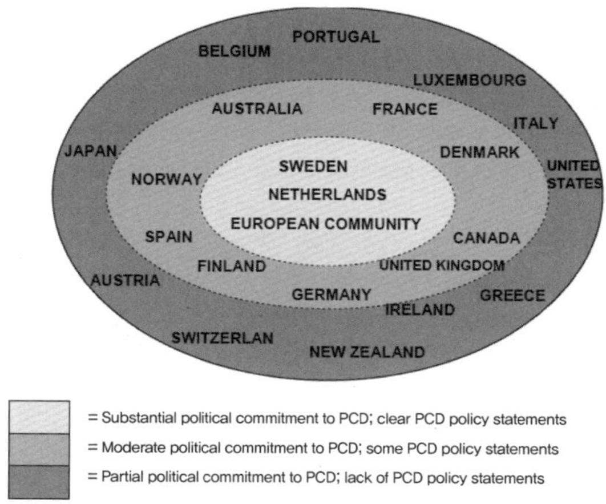

Source: OECD, *Building Blocks for Policy Coherence for Development* (2009), 27, 32, 36.

Through these papers, the OECD concluded that the internalization of PCD issues still has a long way to go before it successfully binds the aid and non-aid policies of donors' development cooperation. Based on this recognition, the OECD DAC decided to review PCD progress, in at least one sector among climate change and environment, trade, and immigration through its next Peer Review. This means that the next Peer Review target countries need to report their efforts to incorporate PCD in at least one of the above sectors.[28]

Chapter 12. Review Discussion Questions

1. How can PCD increase the effectiveness of aid?
2. Why is the cycle of PCD important?
3. Why is it difficult to disseminate and facilitate PCD?
4. What is Picciotto's categorization of PCD and how are the four types of PCD different?
5. How and why has PCD evolved?

28 *Ibid.*, 39.

Chapter 13
Global Aid Architecture

> *"The current global aid architecture represents the wide-ranging and complex challenges that single actors cannot address alone. Key actors at the national, bilateral and multi-lateral levels, including the United Nations system, have been re-examining their roles and ways to make their development assistance more effective in achieving universally accepted goals and standards."*[1]

13.1 A New Global Order

The global order has been transformed in the 21st century. From an economic perspective, globalization refers to the economic integration that has influenced the world economy. In a liberal sense, the term globalization has been defined as a phenomenon by which economic agents in any given part of the world are much more affected by events elsewhere in the world than ever before.[2] Henderson has defined globalization as the free movements of goods, services, labor and capital, thereby creating a single market in inputs and outputs; and full national treatment for foreign investors (and nationals working abroad) so that, economically speaking, there are no foreigners.[3]

There continues to be debates over the nature of globalization. Is it a force for good? Some share the view that globalization has a positive effect on the global economy. By bringing forth an integration of economic, political and cultural systems, this phenomenon will contribute to economic growth, prosperity and democratic freedom. Thus, the proponents of globalization argue that it allows poor countries and their citizens to develop economically and raises their standards of living. Others, however, believe that globaliza-

1 Global Aid Architecture, http://www.educationandtransition.org/guidance/global-aid-architecture/, last visited March 2016.

2 Anne O. Kreuger, "Trading Phobias: Governments, NFOs and the Multilateral System, John Bonython Lecture," (Oct. 10th 2000).

3 David Henderson is a former chief economist of the Organization for Economic Cooperation and Development (OECD). Dvaid Henderson, *The MAI Affair: A Story and its Lessons* (London: Royal Institute of International Affairs, 1999).

tion represents the Americanization of world affairs and is little more than a driving force of environmental degradation and the exploitations of poor countries. In particular, opponents of globalization claim that the creation of an unfettered international free market has benefited multinational corporations in the Western world at the expense of local enterprises, local cultures and the poor. Resistance to globalization has therefore taken shape both at a popular and governmental level as people and governments try to manage the flow of capital, labor, goods and ideas that constitute the current wave of globalization.[4] Opponents of liberal capitalism also emphasize the massive growth in inequality due to globalization. It has been argued that globalization has led to a rise in the ratio of average incomes in the richest countries compared to those in the poorest, and the absolute gap in living standards between today's high-income countries and most developing countries will continue to rise. Thus, globalization is leading to a rise in global inequality among individuals, an increase in the total number of people in extreme poverty and increases in the proportion of people in extreme poverty in the world's population.

According to these critics, market-driven globalization[5]

- destroys the ability of states to regulate their national economies, raise taxes and spend money on public goods and social welfare;
- undermines democracy, imposing in its place the rule of unaccountable bureaucrats, corporations and markets;
- amounts to an abdication of power by benevolent democratic governments in favor of predatory private corporations;
- has increased inequalities within and between states;
- destroys the livelihood of peasant farmers;
- deprives the poor of affordable medicines;
- lowers real wages and labor standards, increasing economic insecurity;
- has destroyed the environment, eliminating species and harming animal welfare; and
- permits global financial markets to generate crises that impose heavy costs particularly on the less advanced economies.

---

4 The LEVIN Institute, "What is Globalization?" http://www.globalization101.org/What_is_Globalization.html?PHPSESSID=cfd52fae9cb40178fef89f0a24682821, last visited March 2009.

5 Martin Wolf, *Why Globalization Works* (London: Yale Nota Bene Book, 2005).

There are both winners and losers of globalization. Some are made worse off because they do not have the capabilities to compete in the global market, while others profit because they retain their comparative advantage. Regardless, there is no denying the fact that the world has become subject to the forces of globalization and that these trends appear irreversible. Therefore, it is important to implement policies that can enhance the potential positive effects of globalization towards alleviating poverty and promote economic growth in the global economy. It has been suggested that when financial globalization is approached with the right set of complementary policies, it is likely to promote growth. Greater financial integration contributes to higher growth by expanding access to capital or new technologies and stimulates domestic financial sector development.[6] Complementary policies have been identified as including the use of flexible exchange rates, macroeconomic stabilization policies and the development of strong institutions. When done right, financial liberalization increases the scope for capital inflows to developing countries, which in theory is able to alleviate poverty.

Ironically, regionalism and nationalism have also emerged as byproducts of globalization. It is difficult to identify the relationship between globalization, regionalism and nationalism. Does globalization promote regionalism and, or nationalism? Or can the relationship be interpreted as mutually beneficial? In order to understand the relationship between these phenomena, it is first necessary to identify the concepts of regionalism and nationalism.

In *International Regionalism*, Joseph Nye defined regionalism as a region of a limited number of states linked by a geographical relationship and by a degree of mutual interdependence. For Nye, regionalism has developed alongside globalization and can be perceived as one of its aspects. Regionalism contributes to bringing the world closer together by bringing forth commonalities that exist on the ground level. On top of this, the world has seen a proliferation of regional institutions and an expansion of their areas of responsibility and agendas. To some extent, these regional financial institutions are miniatures of their global counterparts and their activities overlap with those of global institutions. An advantage of regional institutions is that their governance structures are founded

6 Ann Harrison, "Globalization and Poverty," *National Bureau of Economic Research Working Paper Series* (Cambridge: National Bureau of Economic Research Working Paper Series, 2006).

on ground-level problems, which will contribute to facilitating implementation from below. In particular, these regional bodies, by which rich countries provide financial resources to poor country recipients, function as vehicles of development assistance. Hence, regionalism can be interpreted as promoting or acting as the building blocks of globalization.

Contrary to the idea that regionalism is a driving force of globalization, it is also possible to understand regionalism as a deliberate effort to counteract the forces of globalization. In this regard, regionalism is perceived as a potential stumbling block of globalization. As economic, political, and cultural integration brings the world closer together, it has also given richer countries an opportunity to project their values and ideas to other countries. Thus, smaller states feel threatened and form alliances to counter these forces. Diverse alliances were formed among countries that had similar interests. In many cases countries that were geographically close to each other emphasized these shared interests or values in certain agendas, which can be understood as the core of regionalism.

On a different level of analysis, nationalism has also emerged as a reaction to globalization. Nationalism emphasizes the establishment of separate states and the distinct differences that exist among peoples and cultures. The origins of nationalism date back to the late 18th century. A negative consequence of nationalism has been its role in international conflicts and disputes, particularly in the 19th and early 20th centuries. It was during the First World War that the principle of national self-determination was acknowledged as a universal principle and became the basis of the international order on which the current system of international law was founded. At the cultural level, the concept of nationalism can be interpreted as a response to the impacts of globalization. Although it has existed for centuries, this concept has become a useful tool to encourage a revival of traditional cultures and heritage within the globalizing world under the objective of preserving national values. Hence, states began to defend their national cultures, customs and ideas by strategically using nationalism to distinguish one country from another.

13.2 Fragmented Networks

The changes in the global order and the proliferation of development assistance actors have led to a fragmentation of networks.

It is difficult to identify the roles that different actors are playing in the field of development assistance, and there is much overlap that leads to a waste of valuable resources. The emergence of these new actors is due to the changing structure of the new world order. Nation-state have ceased to dominate international relations and numerous new actors have emerged, including international organizations, non-governmental organizations, private sector actors or even individual persons.

The statistical data provided by the DAC is mostly limited to bilateral and multilateral ODA efforts, and does not cover other official or non-official flows of aid, such as donations made by the private sector. An inspection of bilateral aid flows to developing countries presents an overlap of inconsistent bilateral agreements. The international community currently lacks any organization or institution that is able to monitor the numerous bilateral agreements that exist. Most agreements are based on the decision making process of participating countries. The interests of participating actors often conflict and since countries individually pursue their own interests, it is difficult to organize agreements. Thus, the proliferation of aid agreements contains much inefficiency.

The biggest challenge is to create a database that can be shared by all development actors and that identifies existing projects and programs in progress in order to minimize the overlap of aid allocations. This is directly related to the importance of an effective evaluation mechanism. Currently, most evaluations and monitoring of ODA practices are conducted through peer reviews among DAC member countries. However, the role of NGOs in monitoring ODA efforts needs to be emphasized. Before scrutinizing the potential role of NGOs, identification of the various players in development assistance and the complex networks that exist within this industry should be discussed first.

The emergence of diverse institutions focusing on development has been described as the "dev biz" or the development "industry."[7] The term "dev biz" was first introduced at a conference on NGOs held by the United Nations in 1984 to distinguish between a relatively innocent past, when development work was a calling, and the image-conscious present in which the work was an industry, somewhat like "show-biz."[8] Implicit within these concepts is the idea

7 Thomas W. Dichter, *Despite Good Intentions* (Amherst: University of Massachusetts Press, 2003).
8 *Ibid.*

that various players in the area of development assistance work are comparable to private corporations in other industries, such as the manufacturing or service sectors. This concept is even applicable to NGOs, which are by definition non-profit organizations.

NGOs are difficult to conceptualize, as there is no such thing as a typical NGO. They are scattered throughout the world, varying in every possible feature imaginable, including size, operating style, geographic focus, religious background, or programmatic orientation.[9] Most NGOs are non-profit organizations, but even as such, they are established to achieve certain goals and objectives. Based on voluntary membership, NGOs work for member interests. A remarkable development in the late 20th century was the rise of NGOs that straddle national borders, known as INGOs. According to one source, whereas in 1854 only six INGOs had been founded, by the turn of the century this figure had reached 163, and by 1945 over a thousand INGOs had been established.[10] In 2007 there were over 60,000 INGOs. Across the world, the number of NGOs that operate internationally is around 40,000. The number of national NGO in countries is even higher, with around one to two million NGOs in India and another 277,000 NGOs in Russia alone. Statistics on the number of NGOs worldwide are incomplete, but according to the United Nations Development Program, there are approximately 40,000 non-governmental organizations around the globe in addition to the community-based organizations, which number in the hundreds of thousands.

A distinction needs to be made between Northern and Southern NGOs. The majority of Northern NGOs are an alternative to bilateral or multilateral institutions that provide aid to developing countries. Collectively they have provided more aid to developing countries than the World Bank.[11] In recent years, the proliferation of Southern NGOs has been even greater than that of the North, and most estimates place the number at upwards of a million. Southern NGOs are similar to their Northern counterparts in that they are diverse, but a general commonality within Southern NGOs is their reflection of the culture of the people they aim to assist, which has been perceived as a symbol of new found confidence in defining

9 Paula Hoy, *Players and Issues in International Aid* (West Hartford: Kumarin Press, 1998).

10 Georges P. Speeckaert, *Les 1978 OrganisationsInternationalesFondéesdepuis le Congrès de Vienne* (Brussels: Union of International Associations, 1957).

11 Paula Hoy, *Players and Issues in International Aid* (West Hartford: Kumarin Press, 1998).

their own needs and priorities, and in taking responsibility.[12]

At its core, the work of Southern NGOs is a process of empowerment. They view development as a holistic process, emphasizing the linkages between structural causes of poverty and development work, and they respond to local needs and engage in various activities on multiple levels. It is evident that Northern and Southern NGOs have different characteristics with separate objectives and goals, but it is important to promote cooperation and collaboration among these NGOs. It is difficult to understand the complexities of North-South relations. This will require much effort and work, but strengthening the partnerships between Northern and Southern NGOs will obviously be a starting point essential to organizing the networks among the diverse actors that exist within the realm of development assistance.

Despite their initial good intentions, as institutions NGOs must compete to survive vis-à-vis numerous other organizations, especially to raise funds for their activities. As the development industry evolved, more and more NGOs began to raise funds through private and public means. In this sense, an overflow of NGOs will again lead to unnecessary competition and ultimately a waste of valuable funding and resources. It has been argued that the "dev biz" has taken on a self-perpetuating persona, seeking its own relevance and effectiveness. Similar to the corporate world, the players in the development assistance industry sell what they do as a commodity, making compromises to survive, and at times putting the survival of the institution before the mission.[13]

Thus, it is important for NGOs to recognize the efforts of their counterparts, and strengthen ties among themselves to work towards increased effectiveness. Extreme competition among NGOs will lead to a waste of resources and funds. The idea that aid has become a business, whose main stake is its own survival, is a highly controversial claim. This idea also brings forth an awareness of the side effects of development aid; namely that there are organizational imperatives that exist within the structure of any organization, no matter how humanitarian. Any aid organization, once established, becomes a stakeholder that strives to stay alive and wants to "grow."[14]

12 *Ibid.*

13 Thomas W. Dichter, *Despite Good Intentions* (Boston: University of Massachusetts Press, 2003).

14 *Ibid.*

The globalization of world economies has also witnessed the emergence of multinational corporations, whose operations are not limited to within national boundaries but have expanded to encompass the global arena. Traditionally, the private sector was defined as profit-oriented entities. The ultimate goal of any corporation was perceived as gaining profits, so the private sector's participation in development assistance was limited. Oftentimes private sector involvement with developing countries was even severely criticized as exploiting natural resources and human capital from these less advantaged countries. Furthermore, as individuals have become more aware of human rights issues in developing countries, corporations are also severely criticized for violations of human rights, which has resulted in negative corporate images. Thus, whether they wanted to or not, more corporations have become involved in the debates and thinking about development assistance.

Recent recognition of the significance of sustainable development and growing criticism of corporate practices has led to an increased awareness in the private sector that corporate behaviors should not be guided solely by prospects of short term profits, but must work to increase long-term sustainable growth and development. The concept of Corporate Social Responsibility (CSR) has emerged as the private sector realized the potential benefits of economic growth in developing countries. CSR refers to the recognition by the corporate sector that they must take responsible action. These new norms and values protect the environment and the global community from the effects of irresponsible development or exploitation of human and natural resources. In the past the ultimate goal of any private entity was to increase its profits, which made efficiency and productivity the private sector's central values. The new inclusion of CSR thinking represents a rising corporate awareness of responsibility for the impact of their activities on the environment, consumers, employees, communities and other stakeholders.

Compared to the public sector, private sector efforts at implementing aid projects have proven more efficient. The expertise of private corporations such as management skills, operational flexibility and distribution system has increased the effectiveness of aid. The positive outcome of involvement was the distribution of contraceptives and information on HIV/AIDS to farmers on the remote rural areas using system used to distribute fertilizers.[15] However,

15 Penny Davies, "The Role of the Private Sector in the Context of Aid Effectiveness; Consultative

there are also many concerns over private sectors' involvement in aid projects; The emergence of private sector actors has led to even more complications within the network of development assistance by adding yet another type of actor. Furthermore, a mechanism to monitor and evaluate activities is necessary considering the past experiences of the private sector's exploitation of developing countries. Also, private sector participation should be managed so that large amounts of ODA do not end up flowing back into the donor government economies, for example, by creating domestic employment opportunities.

13.3 Limitations of DAC

The Northern countries possess a stronger bargaining power compared to their Southern counterparts, especially within international organizations. To some extent, this is an inescapable result since international organizations need support and funding to subsist, and most of the capital funding for international organizations to conduct operations is provided by Northern countries. Thus, in most cases, the decision making processes of international organizations reflect the desires of these countries.

The Development Assistance Committee is without doubt a pivotal institution in the field of development assistance, with its members contributing around 80% of the total ODA volume. Throughout the years the DAC has provided the global community with a systematic collection of resource flow statistics, which has been used as the standard data in the arena of development assistance. However, the method of calculating aid volumes is based on the budgets of donor countries. The problem is that the amount of aid that is provided within the budget may not meet the actual need at destination. This again reflects the importance of strengthened partnerships between donor and recipient countries. There is a gap between the amount of aid that is provided by the donor government and the amount that is received by the recipient government. This is due to inefficiencies that exist during the implementation process or aid that flows back into the donor economy during the procurement process. In order to provide accurate statistics of aid, it is important that the gap between aid sent and received is identified.

Findings Document Final report" (2011).

Better statistics will help to enhance the effectiveness of aid.

OECD Global Forum on Development 2014. Photo by: OECD

In an era of increased attention by the international community of the significance of partnership, which emphasizes recipient country participation and empowerment of ODA, the DAC has received criticism that it prohibits the full participation of recipient organizations. As an institution, DAC is largely based on donor values and beliefs and its lack of consistent dialogue with developing countries has resulted in limitations to implementing effective aid practices. At the onset, the DAC was established as a forum for consultations among aid donors, currently comprised of twenty three OECD member countries. This was acceptable at first, since the DAC was meant to act as a forum for consultation, addressing concerns and sharing experiences among donor countries to increase aid effectiveness. Today, however, the DAC has developed into an organization that dominates the field of development assistance, making recommendations for action to both donor and recipient countries. As such, it has become an institution that is instigating fragmentation instead of strengthening partnerships. In this respect, the DAC is now at a critical turning point; it must broaden its perspectives to include the voices and participation of recipient partners on the same level as donor countries. Also with increasing recognition of the importance of partnerships and ownership, the international aid community has been trying to promote involvement of developing countries in development activities. Regional banks have been created to represent the voices of developing countries and counter the predominantly Northern country-oriented perspectives of international organizations.

13.4 Global Governance of Aid

The importance of global partnerships has been widely accepted in the field of development assistance. Most indications of partnerships emphasize the relationship between developed donor countries and developing recipient countries. The strengthening of partnerships has concentrated on empowering recipient countries and reinforcing the value of ownership and responsible use of donor funds. Moreover, responsible implementation of aid from the perspective of the donor countries is also emphasized, especially minimizing donor-oriented interests and increasing effectiveness. However, these partnerships have yet to include the newly emerging actors in development assistance, such as NGOs or the private sector. These actors challenge traditional models of development assistance and are further complicating preexisting networks of aid distribution. In this respect, a more comprehensive framework is necessary to increase synergies in the implementation of aid programs and to incorporate all of these diverse actors into an effective network that promotes cooperation and collaboration.

The concept of global governance emerged as the power of the nation-state began to diminish in international relations. States no longer possess authoritative sovereign power, and international organizations and institutions brought forth new perspectives and an influx of new actors within the scope of international issues. Similarly, the nation-state, or government, is no longer the predominant actor in development assistance and must recognize the participation of other diverse actors working to integrate efforts to increase effectiveness.

Due to the complex nature of governance and the lack of a concrete universal conceptualization of the term, definitions vary among international organizations. In a definition by the World Bank, governance is defined as the manner in which power is exercised in the management of a country's economic and social resources. The UNDP defines governance as the exercise of economic, political and administrative authority to manage a country's affairs at all levels. The OECD defines it as the use of political authority and exercise of control in a society in relation to the management of its resources for social and economic development.[16] The Commission on Global Governance, established under the UN in 1995, defines global governance as "the sum of the many ways individuals and institutions, public and private, manage their common affairs. It is continuing process through which conflicting or diverse interests may be accommodated and cooperative action may be taken."[17] Another definition recognizes global governance as "efforts to bring more orderly and reliable responses to social and political issues that go beyond the capacities of states to address individually."[18]

Thus, within the context of global governance the nation-state no longer possesses dominating power over other actors; there now exists numerous actors co-existing on various levels. They are interconnected into a network system and the objective of governance lies in the effective interaction among the actors in each network system. The realm of development assistance has shown a progression comparable to that occurring in other international areas, so applying the concept of global governance to development assistance will contribute to increased effectiveness in future efforts.[19]

13.5 Aid Mechanisms and Donor-Recipient Relations

As some political scientists have observed, the practice of foreign aid has deep internal implications in the recipient countries. It is a fact that aid-giving states are intervening in the internal affairs of other states.[20] The current way where states cooperate to ensure the development of the underdeveloped world is problematic, mostly leading to failures, and in great need of new solutions. In many cases, donors are involved deeply in the internal affairs of 'future

---

16 Thomas G. Weiss, "Governance, Good Governance, and Global Governance: Conceptual and Actual Challenges," *Third World Quarterly*, vol. 21, no. 5 (2000): 795-814.

17 A Report of Committee on Global Governance, *Our Global Neighborhood* (Oxford: Oxford University Press, 1995).

18 Thomas G. Weiss and Leon Gordenker, "Pluralizing Global Governance: Analytical Approaches and Dimensions," in *NGOs, the UN, and Global Governance*, ed. G. Weiss and Leon Gordenker (New York: Lynne Rienner Publishers, 1999), 17.

19 For a more in depth discussion on global governance, see previous work by the author. Changrok Soh, "Theoretical Approaches to Global Governance," *Korea Review of International Studies*, vol. 5, no. 1 (2002).

20 Arun Agrawal and Tony Fun Lai, *Economics of Development and Planning*, 2 ed. (New Delhi: Vikas Publishing House, 1993).

states' and shaping their internal political environment and culture. One of the better ways to fix this problem is to encourage participation from below, particularly in recipient countries.

Among the many possible incentives of providing aid are commercial benefits for the donor country. By definition, foreign aid refers to aid given to countries in need in order to improve their conditions. However, under problematic means as we have examined above, the incentives of aid are not fully given to recipient countries, and donor countries also consider the possible gains that they can achieve through providing foreign aid, such as political and commercial benefits.

It is, therefore, necessary to understand the economic impact of global development assistance from a dual perspective — the impact of foreign aid on developing country economies and the possible commercial incentives or benefits that are rewarded to donor countries. This duality of perspectives has become more apparent due to the pressures of globalization. As countries have been brought closer together through global trade, finance and a liberalization of markets, it has brought forth a realization that countries have become increasingly dependent on one another.

As Jeffrey Sachs explains, in the economic ladder of development, the countries that are struggling from extreme poverty need assistance to get on the first rung of the ladder. The majority of the extreme poor are caught in a poverty trap; it is impossible for them to escape from their dire condition. They are trapped by disease, physical isolation, climate stress, environmental degradation and extreme poverty.[21] Developed countries must provide aid to these struggling countries to help them on to the ladder of economic development and guide them up the ladder towards sustainable development. These countries have evidently been left behind in the globalization process, and as globalization is bringing developed countries closer together at faster speeds, the gap between those included in globalization and those that have been left behind is growing wider and wider.

From a donor country perspective, it has been identified that providing assistance to developing countries contains long term economic benefits for the global community as a whole. By providing developing countries with foreign aid, donor countries can enlarge the total size of global markets, i.e. a bigger pie for everyone. There

21 Jefferey Sachs, *The End of Poverty* (London: Penguin Books, 2005).

are limitations to competing for a larger portion within a limited sized economic pie, and over-competition by developed countries for a redistribution of gains can lead to a waste of resources and capabilities. On the other hand, by promoting development in poor countries the total size of the economic pie can grow, leading to larger shares for all participating countries.

The potential that developing countries possess is not limited to enlarging market size, but also includes the possibility of access to their natural resources and their human capital, such as cheap labor. The populations in developing countries do not have the buying power necessary for mass consumption. But if development and economic growth takes root in these countries, they will become a lucrative market for sales. Another potential incentive for donor countries in providing aid to developing countries is the abundant natural resources that many developing countries possess. For example, the objectives of China's ODA to Africa are identified in the popular press as primarily motivated by a desire to cultivate access to raw materials and natural resources.

More direct commercial interests for donor countries are seen in the practice of tying aid. Donors of bilateral aid condition their ODA, tying aid to purchases of goods and services from within the donor country. These conditions restrict recipient countries' ownership and empowerment, limiting their bargaining power in securing the necessary goods and services for their own development. Additionally, by conditioning aid directly to donor-associated goods and services, a large proportion of the aid actually flows back into the donor country's economy. Furthermore, since the donor country becomes responsible for providing not only the goods and services for development but also the money with which to purchase them, it gains more influential power, perhaps even creating situations in which recipient countries become highly dependent on specific bilateral donors.

Tied aid can also provide indirect incentives for the donor country in a number of ways. It can provide a variety of trade promotion activities that subsidize export-credit schemes, or it can provide aid to lower the costs of firms in bidding for tenders, or it can put more informal pressures for recipients to purchase from donor-based commercial companies. In all of these cases, aid ends up flowing back into the donor's domestic economy, resulting in diverse economic benefits and commercial advantages.

Lancaster pointed out that a key factor for the increase in priority for the development purposes of aid in advanced countries was the establishment within most donor countries of a political constituency for development aid.[22] This development of a political constituency in donor countries was caused in large part by outside pressure from NGOs supporting aid. While it is true that each donor country has its unique political structure and therefore has different purposes in giving aid, there has been an obvious convergence in the purposes of aid over the past decade and a half among different aid-giving governments.[23] Nowadays the impact of NGOs and international organizations on aid is huge. There have been a growing number of development-oriented NGOs in the 21st century that are networked to government aid agencies in donor countries. They have contributed to promoting an aid-for-development norm in global society.

Criticisms levied at the current lack of aid effectiveness and comprehensive efforts to evaluate aid effectiveness have been driven by new multilateralism. In the past, multilateralism referred to the collaborative efforts of three or more nation-states. New multilateralism is a concept that has emerged to capture the role of new actors in the global arena. Compared to old multilateralism, which concentrated on the efforts of state actors, new multilateralism refers to the collaborative efforts of states and non-state actors. The increases of aid have been justified by the promise that aid will be more effective in the future. Under increased pressure from some elements of civil society and because of the transparency and accountability of these institutions, the 1990s saw the world embark upon a strategy of incremental reform. Furthermore, this reform effort was generated by pressure from civil society actors seeking to foster a more exclusive form of multilateralism that is built from the 'bottom up' and is based upon a participative global civil society.[24]

Today's trend in aid seems to be more focused with "many-to-many" in aid-giving.[25] whereas aid in the past was given from donor governments to recipient governments (one-to-one). Now there are a growing number of actors, not only governments, but internation-

---

22 Carol Lancaster, *Foreign Aid Diplomacy, Development, Domestic Politics* (Chicago, London: University of Chicago Press, 2006), 213.

23 *Ibid.*, 221.

24 Robert O'Brien, Anne Marie Goetz, Jan AartSchote and Marc Williams, *Contesting Global Governance: Multilateral Economic Institutions and Global Social Movements* (New York: Cambridge University Press, 2000), 3-4.

25 Carol Lancaster (2006), 225.

al organizations, NGOs, private enterprises, etc. In this complicated world, the values that the rich should assist the poor will be called for and the bottom up process of norm making will be very critical.

Chapter 13. Review Discussion Questions

1. Who are some of the main actors in global development assistance? How and in what aspects are they different from those in the past?
2. Why has the international community emphasized the importance of global partnerships? What are some of the potential benefits of strengthening global partnerships?
3. Identify some limitations of the Development Assistance Committee (DAC). How has this affected development assistance efforts?
4. What is implied in the term "dev biz"? Do you agree with this perspective regarding development assistance actors? Has development assistance become an "industry"?
5. What measures must be taken to strengthen North-South partnerships?
6. What is global governance? How can global governance be applied to development assistance efforts?

Chapter 14

International Norms and Lessons Learned

"Ensuring respect for humanitarian principles is an essential element of effective coordination of humanitarian action and central to the role of a Humanitarian Coordinator. Humanitarian principles provide the fundamental underpinning for humanitarian action. Operating in accordance with humanitarian principles is the basis for establishing acceptance by all relevant parties for humanitarian activities to be carried out. Humanitarian principles are thus central to establishing and maintaining access to affected populations."[1]

14.1 Building Blocks: 12 Lessons from DAC Peer Review

The OECD DAC issues reports including lessons based on DAC Peer Reviews. In this sense, the DAC Peer Review is a learning process drawing knowledge through the review of operations and policies. In fact, the OECD DAC clarified the objectives of Peer Review as follows: to help improve the quality and quantity of aid; to provide credible analyses based on common principles that can be used by both OECD countries and the wider international community; to enable donors to share experiences, identify good practices and improve coordination.[2]

To improve effectiveness of aid management, donor countries, especially DAC member states, first began issuing thematic reports in 2008. The first report highlighted 12 points that needed special consideration. In 2009, the OECD DAC issued a report focusing on how DAC member states need to manage aid. In 2012, the OECD DAC issued three thematic reports and their reports respectively tackled how donors need to build a partnership with civil society, how to assist the recipient government in the aspect of capacity empowerment, and drew 12 lessons for a better humanitarian donorship. The 2013 report emphasized the importance of evaluation in development cooperation. The two reports issued in 2014 shed light on the necessity of public engagement and the importance of

1 WHO Humanitarian Coordination Group, *International norms and principles* (Geneva: Inter-Agency Standing Committee, 2010), 15.

2 OECD, *Mainstreaming Cross-cutting Issues: 7 Lessons from DAC Peer Reviews* (Paris: OECD, 2014), 5.

mainstreaming cross-cutting issues in development cooperation.

Table 14.1 The List of Reports on Lessons from DAC Peer Reviews

Year	Name
2008	Effective Aid Management: 12 Lessons from DAC Peer Reviews
2009	Managing Aid: Practices of DAC Member Countries
2012	Partnering with Civil Society: 12 Lessons from DAC Peer Reviews
2012	Supporting Partners to Develop their Capacity: 12 Lessons from DAC Peer Reviews
2012	Towards Better Humanitarian Donorship: 12 Lessons from DAC Peer Reviews
2013	Evaluating Development Activities: 12 Lessons from DAC Peer Reviews
2014	Engaging with the public: 12 Lessons from DAC Peer Reviews and the Network of DAC Development Communicators
2014	Mainstreaming Cross-cutting Issues: 7 Lessons from DAC Peer Reviews

In particular, "Towards Better Humanitarian Donorship: 12 Lessons from DAC Peer Reviews" issued in 2012 explains why donors need to pay special care and attention to humanitarian distress and what kinds of efforts are needed to relieve humanitarian suffering. The paper supports the importance and reliability of its lessons by showing examples from Peer Reviews.[3]

Box 14.1 Towards Better Humanitarian Donorship

The strategic framework

- Lesson 1: Provide clear strategic vision
- Lesson 2: Promote recovery and resilience
- Lesson 3: Reduce disaster risks
- Lesson 4: Priorities participation

Delivering effective funding

- Lesson 5: Match your vision with your money
- Lesson 6: Decide how to decide
- Lesson 7: Build strong partnerships
- Lesson 8: Develop rapid response mechanisms

3 OECD, *Towards Better Humanitarian Donorship: 12 Lessons from DAC Peer Reviews* (OECD, 2012), 7-8.

Organization fir for a purpose

Lesson 9: Co-ordinate across government

Lesson 10: Work to clarify the role of the military

Lesson 11: Invest in your staff

Learning and accountability

Lesson 12: Demonstrate value for money and promote learning

The first lesson, 'provide clear strategic vision,' was drawn from the cases of Denmark, Poland, Spain and Switzerland. They have incorporated their humanitarian programs into wider development strategy documents. These countries endeavored to secure their humanitarian budgets by designing their aid policies and strategies realistically in terms of implementation plans and exploiting their comparative advantages. In this lesson, a policy coherence between aid and non-aid policies was also emphasized.

Lesson 2 'promote recovery and resilience' was drawn up to reduce aid recipient's reliance on relief assistance by allowing the beneficiaries of aid to use humanitarian assistance for livelihood assets. The experience of tsunami relief in Sri Lanka gave momentum to the Swiss Agency for Development and Cooperation (SDC) to design cash-based recovery programs. It helps victims in conflict- and disaster-affected communities to recover their normal lives and livelihoods. To do this, it first recommends that donors need to improve coordination between humanitarian and development instruments. Second, donors need to review the bureaucratic and hierarchy procedures, lack of predictability and flexibility, and short funding timeframes which restrict holistic responses in protracted crisis situation. Third, they need to systematically integrate the humanitarian and development operations into their country strategies and support innovative approaches.

Lesson 3, 'reducing the vulnerability of people and protecting economic growth', came from the experiences of Australia, the European Union, Japan, Switzerland, the United Kingdom, and Denmark. It emphasizes that donors need to advocate for risk reduction to be mainstreamed across all development planning and operations. It also recommends the necessity of crisis mitigation in partner country strategies and the adjustment of funding streams to ensure a continuous risk reduction throughout the crisis cycle.

Based on Good Humanitarian Donorship (GHD, refer to section

15.2) principle 7 and some cases of donors such as Denmark, Sweden and the United Kingdom, Lesson 4 emphasizes the importance of promoting beneficiary participation – particularly women - in the humanitarian program cycle. The reason that the participation of crisis survivors is important is that the opportunity of aid recipients to participate in an official aid policy making process is limited and that feedback from aid recipients on relief programs is difficult to gather. Lesson 4 insists that aid beneficiaries need to be considered properly in aid operations.

Lesson 5 focuses on the ratio of humanitarian aid to the overall development cooperation budget. Based on the European Consensus on Humanitarian Aid (2008) and GHD principles, the European Union allows predictability and flexibility in humanitarian funding. For instance, Finland, Denmark and the United Kingdom have a legal basis on the provision of information on humanitarian budgets. Some donors prefer to assist goods and services in kind rather than providing cash to humanitarian NGOs and multilateral agencies. In the provision of commodities in kind, however, donors need to make sure that they carefully evaluate if the provided goods are the best effective way to tackle humanitarian needs in crisis situations.

The basic principle of humanitarian aid is a matching of 'predictable and flexible' assistance with 'needs' in field. However, there is a political challenge that due to the lack of comprehensive definition or measure of humanitarian 'need', it is difficult for donors to objectively compare scale and severity. In this sense, Lesson 6 emphasizes the decision of humanitarian donors on choices about whom, what and where to fund. Lesson 6 was drawn from the cases of Canada, ECHO and Germany that hold regular consultations with partners to support the better application of the principles of neutrality, impartiality, independence and transparency in donor decision-making.

Lesson 7 emphasizes a strong, equal and principled partnership between donors and NGOs and multilateral agencies based on the interdependence of the humanitarian community. Most DAC member states are maintaining a close and sustainable relationship with major multilateral and NGO partners and they give financial assistance to empower the capability of NGOs. France, Australia, and New Zealand are exchanging information through the framework of the FRANZ agreement and collaborating for resource mobilization for disaster relief operations in the Pacific region.

Lesson 8 is on an effective rapid response mechanism in cases of sudden-onset crisis. The OECD evaluated that although donors have achieved substantial progress in this issue, donors need further efforts to align with the international response community in terms of partnership and resource mobilization for communities, families and women, local government, civil society and the local private sector. In this sense, the OECD DAC became known for increasing response capability through the cooperation with Red Cross societies and NGO partners as well as operating an institutional mechanism for rapid funding decisions and the dispatch of technical experts.

Lesson 9 criticizes the fragmentation in humanitarian management structures and advocates the importance of inter-ministerial cooperation. Each country has a different institutional model for a cross-government co-ordination mechanism. Ring-fencing is when one entity (agency or ministry) makes all policy and funding decisions. Split responsibility type is when a Ministry of Foreign Affairs sets policy and sometimes provides core funding to multilaterals, with a separate agency for earmarking funding and partnerships with NGOs. Split objectives type is when two ministries or agencies with mandates for different areas of humanitarian response set policy and provide funding individually. Multiple actors type is when delivery is done through multiple branches of government, and often also through municipal structures. The OECD points out that as each of the current donor humanitarian aid management models has strength and weakness, each model needs to be used so as to maximize useful outputs.

Lesson 10 focuses on the role of the military as one of the counterparts in humanitarian crisis response considering the military's comparative advantage in heavy-lift capacity or specialist engineering for life-saving assistance. It advises that the military should follow humanitarian principles based on partnership with the civil sector. In the case of Australia, inter-ministerial cooperation including military branches is one of the humanitarian response principles.

Lesson 11 emphasizes an investment in personnel on the donor side because the people who design and implement its strategic orientations, advocacy actions and funding decisions affect the success and failure of humanitarian operations. High staff turnover can reduce the impact of institutional experience sharing, restrict the donor's capacity to engage at an international level and limit the scope for staff to add value beyond a basic administration role. In fact, the United States has a system to recruit qualified staff and operates the Disaster Assistance Response Team (DARTs) forum consisting of experts on rapid disaster response.

Lesson 12 emphasizes a humanitarian evaluation framework focusing on the monitoring of overall humanitarian results, criticizing the existing monitoring tendency to simply focus on assistance input. Proper monitoring enables the taxpayers and donors to fulfill their right to know how their taxes are being used and lowers the potential for waste, fraud and corruption.

These 12 lessons cover a wide range of issues and aims to provide adequate guidance to those in the field of development policies so that improved plans are established, implemented and monitored.

14.2 Good Humanitarian Donorship

At the meeting in Stockholm on June 2003, hosted by Sweden, seventeen donors endorsed the Principles and Good Practice of Good Humanitarian Donorship. This emphasizes that donors can more effectively encourage and stimulate principled donor behavior by working together.

GHD aims to enhance the coherence and effectiveness of donor action, as well as their accountability to beneficiaries, with regard to the funding, coordination, follow-up and evaluation of such actions.[4]

http://www.ghdinitiative.org/ghd/gns/about-us/about-ghd.html

4 GHD homepage, http://www.goodhumanitariandonorship.org/gns/about-us/about-ghd.aspx, last visited September 2014.

Through the adoption of the GHD initiative, major donors confirmed that the objectives of humanitarian assistance are to save lives, relieve humanitarian distress, and protect human dignity. It also assured that humanitarian assistance needs to be distributed impartially and neutrally based on need and humanitarian objective itself and delivered independently from political, economic and other strings. As a network expanding knowledge and recognition of lessons learned and best practices in international development cooperation, GHD provides a platform for knowledge sharing among the donor countries.[5]

The GHD secretariat convenes several working level meetings each year. There are currently forty members of the Good Humanitarian Donorship group, who contribute through this forum to the pivotal role of donors in providing effective and accountable humanitarian assistance.

23 Principles of Good Humanitarian Donorship

The 23 Principles and Good Practice defined by the group provide both a framework to guide official humanitarian aid and a mechanism for encouraging greater donor accountability. The key principles of GHD are ① need-based flexible and timely assistance, ② involvement and capacity building for victims and disaster-affected community, ③ linking emergency relief operations and long-term development assistance. These were drawn up to enhance the coherence and effectiveness of donor action, as well as their accountability to beneficiaries, implementing organizations and domestic constituencies, with regard to the funding, co-ordination, follow-up and evaluation of such actions.

Box 14.2 23 Principles of Good Humanitarian Donorship

Objectives and Definition of Humanitarian Action

1. The objectives of humanitarian action are to save lives, alleviate suffering and maintain human dignity during and in the aftermath of man-made crises and natural disasters, as well as to prevent and strengthen preparedness for the occurrence of such situations.

5 Good Humanitarian Donorship Initiative (2011); Myonggeun Lee et al., *A Study of Humanitarian Assistance Policy and Operation: Emergency Relief System* (Sungnam: KOICA, 2012), 48-60.

2. Humanitarian action should be guided by the humanitarian principles of humanity, meaning the centrality of saving human lives and alleviating suffering wherever it is found; impartiality, meaning the implementation of actions solely on the basis of need, without discrimination between or within affected populations; neutrality, meaning that humanitarian action must not favor any side in an armed conflict or other dispute where such action is carried out; and independence, meaning the autonomy of humanitarian objectives from the political, economic, military or other objectives that any actor may hold with regard to areas where humanitarian action is being implemented.
3. Humanitarian action includes the protection of civilians and those no longer taking part in hostilities, and the provision of food, water and sanitation, shelter, health services and other items of assistance, undertaken for the benefit of affected people and to facilitate the return to normal lives and livelihoods.

General Principles

4. Respect and promote the implementation of international humanitarian law, refugee law and human rights.
5. While reaffirming the primary responsibility of states for the victims of humanitarian emergencies within their own borders, strive to ensure flexible and timely funding, on the basis of the collective obligation of striving to meet humanitarian needs.
6. Allocate humanitarian funding in proportion to needs and on the basis of needs assessments.
7. Request implementing humanitarian organizations to ensure, to the greatest possible extent, adequate involvement of beneficiaries in the design, implementation, monitoring and evaluation of humanitarian response.
8. Strengthen the capacity of affected countries and local communities to prevent, prepare for, mitigate and respond to humanitarian crises, with the goal of ensuring that governments and local communities are better able to meet their responsibilities and co-ordinate effectively with humanitarian partners.
9. Provide humanitarian assistance in ways that are supportive of recovery and long-term development, striving to ensure support, where appropriate, to the maintenance and return of sustainable livelihoods and transitions from humanitarian relief to recovery and development activities.
10. Support and promote the central and unique role of the United Nations in providing leadership and co-ordination of international humanitarian action, the special role of the International Commit-

tee of the Red Cross, and the vital role of the United Nations, the International Red Cross and Red Crescent Movement and non-governmental organizations in implementing humanitarian action.

Good Practices in Donor Financing, Management and Accountability

(a) Funding

11. Strive to ensure that funding of humanitarian action in new crises does not adversely affect the meeting of needs in ongoing crises.
12. Recognizing the necessity of dynamic and flexible response to changing needs in humanitarian crises, strive to ensure predictability and flexibility in funding to United Nations agencies, funds and programs and to other key humanitarian organizations
13. While stressing the importance of transparent and strategic priority-setting and financial planning by implementing organizations, explore the possibility of reducing, or enhancing the flexibility of, earmarking, and of introducing longer-term funding arrangements.
14. Contribute responsibly, and on the basis of burden-sharing, to United Nations Consolidated Inter-Agency Appeals and to International Red Cross and Red Crescent Movement appeals, and actively support the formulation of Common Humanitarian Action Plans (CHAP) as the primary instrument for strategic planning, prioritization and co-ordination in complex emergencies.

(b) Promoting standards and enhancing implementation

15. Request that implementing humanitarian organizations fully adhere to good practice and are committed to promoting accountability, efficiency and effectiveness in implementing humanitarian action.
16. Promote the use of Inter-Agency Standing Committee guidelines and principles on humanitarian activities, the Guiding Principles on Internal Displacement and the 1994 Code of Conduct for the International Red Cross and Red Crescent Movement and Non-Governmental Organizations (NGOs) in Disaster Relief.
17. Maintain readiness to offer support to the implementation of humanitarian action, including the facilitation of safe humanitarian access.
18. Support mechanisms for contingency planning by humanitarian organizations, including, as appropriate, allocation of funding, to strengthen capacities for response.
19. Affirm the primary position of civilian organizations in implementing humanitarian action, particularly in areas affected by armed conflict. In situations where military capacity and assets are

used to support the implementation of humanitarian action, ensure that such use is in conformity with international humanitarian law and humanitarian principles, and recognizes the leading role of humanitarian organizations.

20. Support the implementation of the 1994 Guidelines on the Use of Military and Civil Defense Assets in Disaster Relief and the 2003 Guidelines on the Use of Military and Civil Defense Assets to Support United Nations Humanitarian Activities in Complex Emergencies.

(c) Learning and accountability

21. Support learning and accountability initiatives for the effective and efficient implementation of humanitarian action.
22. Encourage regular evaluations of international responses to humanitarian crises, including assessments of donor performance.
23. Ensure a high degree of accuracy, timeliness, and transparency in donor reporting on official humanitarian assistance spending, and encourage the development of standardized formats for such reporting.

Humanitarian Response Index (HRI) of DARA

DARA International, an NGO based in Spain, issues a report on the OECD DAC 23 countries' humanitarian assistance spending, encourages the development of military capacity on the humanitarian domain and uses assets to support the report, which was able to earn its credibility in that it is written by humanitarian agencies such as the Red Cross, UNHCR, and UNOCHA with the support of academia. For the measurement of HRI, DARA re-categorizes 23 principles of GHD into 5 pillars: responding to needs, prevention, risk reduction and recovery, working with humanitarian partners, protection and international law, learning and accountability.

http://reliefweb.int/report/world/humanitarian-response-index-2009-whose-crisis-clarifying-donors-priorities

HRI 2011 was written for 18

OECD DAC countries and the European Commission except for Austria, Greece, New Zealand, and Portugal, which lack sufficient data for evaluation. The report scored the level of GHD compliance and categorized 18 countries into three groups classified as principled partners, learning leaders, and aspiring actors.[6]

Principled Partners are characterized by a high ratio of humanitarian assistance compared to Gross National Income (GNI), a strong commitment to humanitarian principles of neutrality, impartiality and independence, and by flexible funding arrangements with partners. This group includes Denmark, Finland, Netherlands, Norway, Sweden and Switzerland.

Learning Leaders are characterized by their leading role and influence in the humanitarian sector in terms of their capacity to respond, field presence, and commitment to learning and improving performance in sector. However, this group tends to do poorer in the issues of prevention, preparedness and risk reduction efforts, and in perceptions around the neutrality, impartiality and independence of their aid. Canada, the European Commission, France, the United Kingdom, and the United States fall into this group.

Aspiring Actors are characterized by their focus on building strengths in 'niche' areas, such as geographic regions, or thematic areas like preparedness and prevention, and their aspirations to take on a greater role in these sectors. Australia, Belgium, Germany, Ireland, Italy, Luxembourg and Spain make up this group. This group tends to have a more limited capacity to engage with the humanitarian system at the field level and scores below the OECD DAC average in the majority of the HRI pillars and indicators.

14.3 Code of Conduct and Sphere Project

Code of Conduct

With the increase of actors in humanitarian operations, there was demand for the establishment of international standard on cost effectiveness, effectiveness of relief operations, and basic human rights protection. The International Federation of Red Cross and Red Crescent Societies (IFRC) sought to guard humanitarian agencies' standard of behavior when there was no accepted body at professional standards. In 1994, the Code of Conduct was adopted and

6 DARA, HRI 2011. http://daraint.org, last visited January 2015.

439 humanitarian agencies signed it.[7]

Box 14.3 The Principle Commitments of Code of Conduct[8]

1. The humanitarian imperative comes first.
2. Aid is given regardless of the race, creed or nationality of the recipients and without adverse distinction of any kind. Aid priorities are calculated on the basis of needs alone.
3. Aid will not be used to further a particular political or religious standpoint.
4. We shall endeavor not to act as instruments of government foreign policy.
5. We shall respect culture and custom
6. We shall attempt to build disaster response on local capacities.
7. Ways shall be found to involve program beneficiaries in the management of relief aid.
8. Relief aid must strive to reduce future vulnerabilities to disaster as well as meeting basic needs.
9. We hold ourselves accountable to both those who seek to assist and those from whom we accept resources
10. In our information, publicity and advertising activities, we shall recognize disaster victims as dignified human beings, not hopeless objects

As the Code of Conduct clarified in its mandates, it is a voluntary code, enforced by the will of organizations accepting it to maintain the standards laid down in the Code. In the event of armed conflict and disaster, the present Code of Conduct will be interpreted and applied in conformity with international humanitarian law. In the Code of Conduct, there is not only rules for NGOs but also an envisioned working environment that can be applied to donor governments and intergovernmental organizations in order to facilitate the effective delivery of humanitarian assistance.[9]

7 Cheolho Song, *The Study of Government Response Strategy for International Disaster* (Seoul: National Security Council, 2006), 28.

8 International Federation of Red Cross and Red Crescent Societies and the ICRC, "The Code of Conduct for the International Red Cross and Red Crescent Movement and Non-Governmental Organisations (NGOs) in Disaster Relief" (1994).

9 *Ibid.*

The Sphere Project

The Sphere Project – or 'Sphere' – was voluntarily initiated in 1997 by a group of humanitarian NGOs and the International Red Cross and Red Crescent Movement. Sphere, which is not a membership organization and is governed by a board composed of representatives of global networks of humanitarian agencies, brings a wide range of humanitarian agencies together around a common aim. Their aim is to improve the quality of their actions during disaster response and to be held accountable for them.[10] The Sphere Project has published a Handbook offering the humanitarian sector a common language for working together towards quality and accountability in disaster and conflict situations. Sphere's main project activities are: awareness raising, distributing the handbook and other tools, technical revisions of the handbook, training on how to apply the handbook, and support to agencies.

The Sphere Project

Humanitarian Charter and Minimum Standards in Humanitarian Response

http://www.sphereproject.org/press-room/the-sphere-project-logo/

There are multiple reasons why Sphere emerged. In humanitarian response, the issue of quality and accountability were continuously raised. With the increase and complication of disasters and the emergence of multiple actors in humanitarian operations, operation skills and strategies became more diversified.[11] Responding to these demands, the initiative sought to determine and promote standards by which the global community could effectively respond to the plight of people affected by disasters.

10 The Sphere Project, "The Sphere Project in Brief," http://www.sphereproject.org/about/, last visited December 2014; *The Sphere Project, The Sphere Project: Humanitarian Charter and Minimum Standards in Humanitarian Response*, Third edition (2011), 4.

11 Martin Faller, "Briefing on the Code of Conduct for the International Red Cross and Red Crescent Movement and NGOs in Disaster Relief and the Sphere Project" (International Federation of Red Cross and Red Crescent Societies, 2010).

Sphere's philosophy is based on two core beliefs: first, those affected by disaster or conflict have a right to life with dignity and, therefore, a right to assistance; and second, that all possible steps should be taken to alleviate human suffering arising out of disaster or conflict. The Sphere Project framed a Humanitarian Charter and identified a set of minimum standards in key life-saving sectors which are now reflected in the Handbook's four technical chapters: water supply, sanitation and hygiene promotion; food security and nutrition; shelter, settlement and non-food items; and health action. The Core Standards are process standards and apply to all technical chapters.[12]

The Sphere Handbook contains a Humanitarian Charter with legal and moral principles reflecting the rights of disaster-affected populations. These include Protection Principles as well as Core standards and minimum standards in four key life-saving humani-

Figure 14.1 Contents of the Handbook

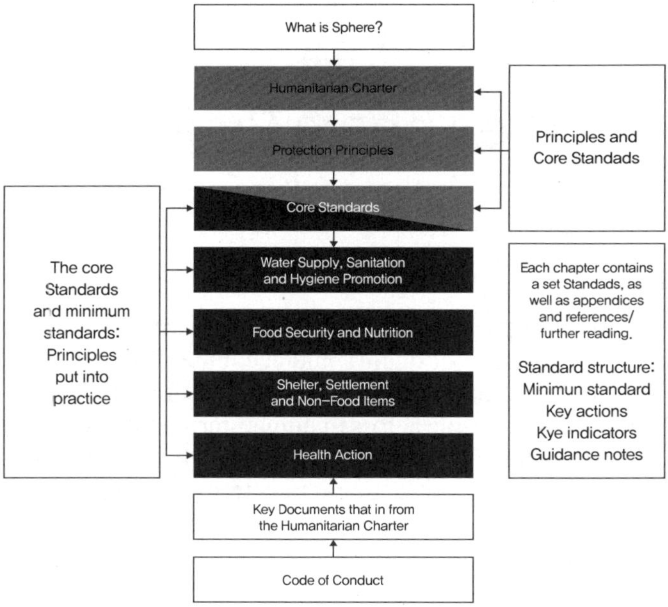

Source: The Sphere Project, *The Sphere Project: Humanitarian Charter and Minimum Standards in Humanitarian Response*, Third edition (2011), 2.

12 The Sphere Project, *The Sphere Project: Humanitarian Charter and Minimum Standards in Humanitarian Response*, Third edition (2011), 4.

tarian sectors: Water supply, sanitation and hygiene (WASH) promotion; food security and nutrition; Shelter, settlement and non-food items; and Health action.

The Sphere Handbook is designed for use during humanitarian responses in a range of situations including natural disasters, conflict, slow- and rapid-onset events, rural and urban environments, and complex political emergencies in all kinds of countries. The term 'disaster' encompasses these situations, and where appropriate, the term 'conflict' is used. 'Population' refers to individuals, families, communities and broader groups. Consequently, the publishers of the handbook commonly use the wording 'disaster-affected population' throughout.[13]

Focusing on the period of humanitarian response, Sphere's minimum standards cover activities that meet the urgent survival needs of disaster-affected populations. This phase can range from a few days or weeks to many months and even years, particularly in contexts involving protracted insecurity and displacement. It is, therefore, impossible to assign a particular timeframe to the usefulness of Sphere's standards. The Handbook does, however, have a specific place within the broader realm of humanitarian action, which goes beyond providing immediate relief and covers a spectrum of activities that start with disaster preparedness. Actors such as governments, humanitarian agencies, local civil society organizations, communities and individuals have the capacities, relationships and knowledge to prepare for and respond effectively to disaster or conflict. It then includes humanitarian response and finally extends into early recovery. This is the period following relief and leading into long-term recovery. As a reference tool, the Handbook is useful for both the disaster preparedness and the early recovery phases that conceptually 'frame' humanitarian response but in reality need to be considered simultaneously.[14]

A number of developments in the humanitarian sector and other relevant areas have arisen over the past few years, encompassing changes in the nature of disasters and conflicts, as well as of humanitarian work.[15]

- a growing conceptual and operational focus on local and national responses with the awareness that affected populations must be consult-

13 *Ibid.*, 8.

14 *Ibid.*, 8-9.

15 *Ibid.*, 10-11.

ed and the response capacities of the crisis-affected state and national agencies and institutions must be reinforced.

- more proactive accountability of humanitarian action, in particular accountability to affected populations, but also more proactive coordination, including within the humanitarian reform process (cluster approach), under the auspices of the Inter-Agency Standing Committee (IASC).
- an increased focus on protection issues and responses.
- increasing awareness of potentially large-scale forced migration due to climate change-induced disasters and an awareness that environmental degradation increases vulnerability.
- the recognition that poor urban populations are growing rapidly and that they have specific vulnerabilities, in particular related to the money economy, social cohesion and physical space.
- new approaches to aid, such as cash and voucher transfers and local purchases replacing in-kind shipments of humanitarian assistance.
- an increased recognition of disaster risk reduction as both a sector and an approach.
- an increased involvement of the military in humanitarian response, a set of actors not primarily driven by the humanitarian imperative, requiring the development of specific guidelines and coordination strategies for humanitarian civil–military dialogue.
- an increased involvement of the private sector in humanitarian response requiring similar guidelines and strategies as the civilian humanitarian response

14.4 Global Commitments to Better Aid

While the first seven goals of the MDGs provide a set of quantitative objectives to alleviate poverty and promote living conditions in developing countries, the final goal, to develop a global partnership for development, identifies the role of donor countries in order to achieve these objectives. The MDGs cannot be achieved without cooperative and collaborative efforts from not only both donor and recipient countries, but also with all non-state actors, including NGOs, IOs and the private sector.

From the perspective of donor countries, the aid that governments provide must concentrate on improving the well-being of recipient countries. To this end, the direct needs and desires of recipient countries must be recognized. The contextual differences within individual countries are unique. In order to create effective measures to implement aid, these unique characteristics must be taken into account. The problem is that these characteristics are not perceivable from the donor perspective. Thus, recipient countries must be able to identify and communicate their needs directly to the participating actors in the development project. This is related to the recognition of the importance of ownership and empowerment.

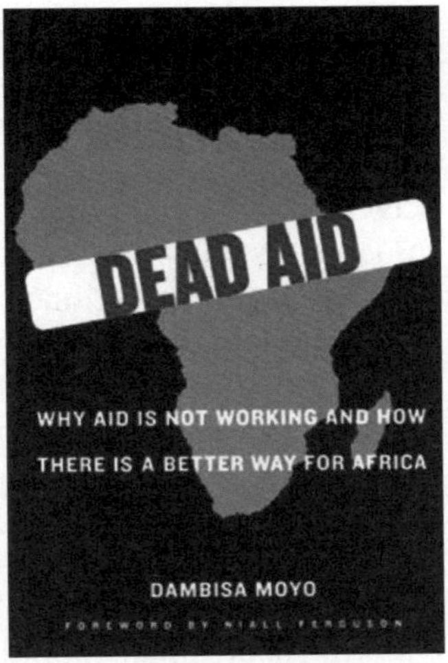

http://www.wsj.com/articles/SB123749211536187585

There are six indicators for actions identified within goal 8 of the MDG. The first is to develop an open, rule-based, predictable, non-discriminatory trading and financial system, which further includes a commitment to good governance, development and poverty reduction on both national and international levels. The second target addresses the special needs of the least developed countries (LDCs), such as tariff- and quota-free access for LDC exports, enhanced programs of debt relief for heavily indebted poor countries (HIPCs), cancellation of official bilateral debt and more ODA to countries committed to poverty reduction. Aid selectivity means that donor countries want to provide aid to countries with better conditions or policy infrastructure, and so it is difficult for LDCs to attract because of their dire state of conditions. Therefore, there have been efforts on the global level to encourage preferential treatment of these countries, which was been specifically identified in the MDG targets. The third target addresses the special needs of landlocked and small island developing states, and target four deals comprehensively with debt problems of developing countries through national and international measures in order to make debt sustainable in the long term. Another target identifies the importance of cooperation with pharmaceutical companies to provide access to affordable essential drugs in developing countries. The final indicator relates to cooperation with the private sector to make available the benefits of new technologies, especially information and communications. In efforts to achieve these targets, separate monitoring standards have been set for LDCs, Africa, landlocked developing countries and small island developing countries. It is necessary to increase the percentage of ODA that is allocated to least developed nations. A larger proportion of bilateral and sectoral ODA that is allocated to basic social services will also contribute to achieving the MDGs. Other indicators set within the MDGs monitor the proportion of the population with access to affordable essential drugs on a sustainable basis as well as the number of telephone lines, cellular subscribers, and Internet users.

It is evident that the international community is aware of the importance of global partnerships in promoting effective aid practices. The role of leadership, in both developed and developing countries, is essential to strengthen global partnerships. It is expected that leaders from the developed world should work to assist in building the capacity of developing countries and to maintain openness in trade policies, allowing market accessibility to poor countries. Other measures that should be undertaken by developed countries include providing agricultural subsidies and boosting resources for developing countries. The role of leadership of the developed countries is important, but we cannot disregard the role that leaders in developing countries must perform in order to increase effectiveness of aid policies.

It is a relatively recent understanding that good, strong leadership is also needed in the context of developing countries. The importance of leadership in recipient countries is related to the significance of empowerment and ownership for effective implementation of aid programs. Leaders of African countries have argued for the necessity of a new partnership for African development that sprouts from both developed and developing countries. All participating parties must engage actively to promote growth, based on strong commitments and responsibility.

Despite these efforts, the continuing emergence of new actors has further complicated the network of actors in development assistance. The fragmented networks have led to increased challenges that must be overcome before global partnerships can be achieved to promote aid effectiveness. Furthermore, it needs to be recognized that the scope of global partnerships does not encompass all of the complexities within multilateral development assistance efforts, and that future considerations must include the possible applicability of a global governance framework to include the intricate networks amongst and between multiple levels of actors.

Chapter 14. Review Discussion Questions

1. Why are norms and ideas difficult to expand or incorporate?
2. What are the lessons DAC Peer Reviews point out? How can these lessons be used to improve current donorship?
3. How does the constructivist explain norm and idea internalization?
4. How does Good Humanitarian Donorship initiative define Humanitarian Action? What are the objectives of it?
5. Which factors affect the proliferation of norms and ideas?
6. What is Humanitarian Response Index (HRI)? What are its pillars?
7. How can Peer Review change policies and behavior of donors?
8. What is Sphere Project? How did it come to be and what does it try to achieve?

References

African Development Bank. "About Us." http://www.afdb.org/en/about-us/profile/who-weare (last visited December 2008).

Agénor, Pierre-Richard, and Joshua Aizenman. "Aid Volatility and Poverty Traps." NBER Working Paper no. 13400, National Bureau of Economic Researchs, September 2007.

Agrawal, Arun, and Tony Fun Lai. *Economics of Development and Planning*. 2 ed. New Delhi:Vikas Publishing House, 1993.

Aldaba, Fernando et al. "NGO Strategies Beyond Aid: Perspectives from Central and South America and the Philippines." *Third World Quarterly*, vol. 21, no. 4 (2000).

Alesina, Alberto, and Beatrice Weder. "Do Corrupt Governments Receive Less Foreign Aid?" *NBER Working Paper series.* Cambridge: National Bureau of Economic Research, 1999.

Amprou, Jacky et al. "Aid Selectivity According to Augmented Criteria." *The World Economy*, vol. 30, no. 5 (2007).

Annan, Kofi. Lecture at the London School of Economics (4 October, 2012).

Arslanap, Serken, and Peter B. Henry. "Helping the poor to help themselves: debt relief or aid." NBER Working Paper no. 10230, National Bureau of Economic Researchs, January 2004.

Asian Development Bank. "Our Vision- an Asia and Pacific Free of Poverty." http://www.adb.org/About/default.asp (last visited December 2008).

______. "PHI: Strategic Private Sector Partnerships for Urban Poverty Reduction in Metro Manila (STEP UP)." http://www.adb.org/sites/default/files/projdocs/2007/36020-PHI-JFPRICM.pdf (last visited July 2014).

AT Kearney. "FDI on the Rebound?" https://www.atkearney.com/gbpc/foreign-direct-investment-confidence-index/publication/-/asset_publisher/lsBVD71WgZDd/content/2016-a-t-kearney-foreign-direct-investment-confidence-index/10192 (last visited August 2016).

______. *New concerns in an uncertain world: The 2007 AT Kearney FDI Confidence Index* (2008).

______. *The 2003 AT Kearney FDI Confidence Index* (2004).

Bae, Jinsoon, and Sungho Kang. "Study of Transnational NGO Network and Activities: Territory Issues and Conflict Resolution." *OUGHTOPIA*, vol. 24, no. 1 (2009).

Bandyopadhyay, Subhayu, and E. Katarina Vermann. "Donor Motives for Foreign Aid." *Federal Reserve Bank of St. Louis REVIEW*, vol. 95, no. 4 (July/August 2013).

Berthélemy, Jean-Claude. "Bilateral Donors' Interest vs. Recipients' Development Motives in Aid Allocation: Do All Donors Behave the Same." *Review of Development Economics*, vol. 10, no. 2 (2006).

BetterAid. "About Better Aid." http://www.betteraid.org/en/about-us/about-better-aid.html (last visited June 2014).

_______. *BetterAid Response to the Busan Outcome Document* (2011).

_______. *CSOs on the Road to Busan: Key Messages and Proposals* (2011).

_______. *Key Demands from Women's Right Organizations and Gender Equality Advocates* (2011).

Boone, Peter. "Politics and the Effectiveness of Foreign Aid." *European Economic Review*, vol. 40, issue 2 (1996).

Browne, Stephen. *Aid and Influence: Do Donors Help or Hinder?* London: Earthscan, 2006.

Brzoska, Michael. "Extending ODA or Creating a New Reporting Instrument for Security Related Expenditures for Development." *Development Policy Review*, vol. 26, no. 2 (2008).

Bulow, Jeremy, and Kenneth Rogoff. "Grants versus Loans for Development Banks." *American Economic Review*, vol. 95, no. 2 (2005).

Burnside, Craig, and David Dollar. "Aid, the Incentive Regime, and Poverty Reduction." Policy Research Working Paper 1937, *Macroeconomics and Growth Group,* The World Bank, June 1998.

_______. "Aid, Policies, and Growth." *NBER Working Paper 9846* (July 2003).

_______. "Aid, Policies and Growth." *American Economic Review*, vol. 90, no. 4 (2008).

Carnegie Council. "Soft Power: The Means to Success in World Politics." http://www.cceia.org/resources/transcripts/4466.html (last visited Mar 2009).

Chatterjee, Santanu, and Stephen Turnovsky. "Tied versus Untied Foreign Aid: Consequences for a growing economy." *Computing in Economics and Finance*, vol. 2004, no. 8 (2004).

Choi, Daeseok, and Seokhyang Kim. "The Characteristics and Dynamics of NGO Networks in Northeast Asia." *Discourse* 201, vol. 10, no. 1 (2007).

Choi, Minkyung. *KOICA's Aid Policy for Africa through Aid for Trade(AfT).* Seoul: KOICA, 2008.

Clark, Ian. *Globalization and International Relations Theory*. Oxford, New York:

Oxford University Press, 1999.

Clay, Edward J., Matthew Geddes, Luisa Natali, and Dirk Willem te Velde. *Thematic Study, the Developmental Effectiveness of Untied Aid: Evaluation of the Implementation of the Paris Declaration and of the 2001 DAC Recommendation on Untying ODA To the LDCs, Phase I Report. Copenhagen, December 2008.* London: Overseas Development Institute (ODI), 2008.

CNN. "Japan unveils $17B Asian aid package." http://edition.cnn.com/2009/BUSINESS/01/31/davos.wef.japan/index.html (last visited March 2009).

Carroll, Ellie. "Twenty-five Years in the Making: Why Sustainable Development has Eluded the UN and How Community Driven Development Offers the Solution." *Houston Journal of International Law*, vol. 32, no. 2 (2010).

Chasek, Pamela et al. *Global Environmental Politics*. Boulder: Westveiw Press, 2006.

Collier, Paul, and David Dollar. "Aid Allocation and Poverty." *European Economic Review*, vol. 46, issue 8 (Sept. 2002).

Commission on Global Governance. *Our Global Neighborhood*. Oxford: Oxford University Press, 1995.

Commission on Human Security. *Human Security Now: Protecting and Empowering People*. New York: United Nations, 2003.

_______. http://www.humansecurity-chs.org (last visited March 2009).

CONCORD. *Coherence Barometer 2008*. Brussels: CONCORD, 2009.

Cordella, Tito, and Giovanni Dell'Ariccia. "Budget Support versus Project Aid." IMF Working Paper no. 03/89, August 14 2003.

Council on Foreign Relations. http://www.cfr.org/botswana/botswana-african-success-story-shows-strains/p15108 (last visited July 2014).

Cox, Robert W. "Critical political economy." In *International Political Economy: Understanding Global Disorder*, ed. Bjorn Hettine. London: Zed Books, 1995.

_______. "Social Forces, States, and World Orders: Beyond International Relations Theory." In *Approaches to World Order*, ed. Robert W. Cox and Timothy J. Sinclair. New York: Cambridge University Press, 1996.

_______, ed. *The New Realism*. London: Macmillan for the UN University Press, 1997.

Dalgaard, Carl-Johan, and Henrik Hansen. "On Aid, Growth and Good Policies." *The Journal of Development Studies*, vol. 37, issue 6 (2001).

Dalgaard, Carl-Johan et al. "On the empirics of foreign aid and growth." *The Economic Journal*, vol. 114, issue 496 (2004).

DARA. HRI 2011. http://daraint.org (last visited January 2015).

Davies, Penny. "The Role of the Private Sector in the Context of Aid Effectiveness." Consultative Findings Document Final report, 2 February 2011. http://www.oecd.org/dac/effectiveness/47088121.pdf.

Degnbol-Martinussen, John, and Poul Engberg-Pedersen. *Aid: Understanding International Development Cooperation*. London: Zed Books Ltd, 2003.

Department for International Development. "Statistics on International Development." 2015. https://www.gov.uk/government/uploads/system/uploads/attachment_data/file/482322/SID2015c.pdf.

Di Leva, Charles E. *Achieving the Millennium Development Goals: World Bank Projects, Partnerships and Policies for Sustainable Development*. American Law Institute, 2005.

Dichter, Thomas W. *Despite Good Intentions*. Amherst: University of Massachusetts Press, 2003.

Dollar, David, and Lant Pritchett. "Assessing Aid — What Works, What Doesn't, and Why." In *World Bank policy research report*. Washington D.C. : The World Bank, 1998.

Dollar, David, and V. Levin. "The Increasing Selectivity of Foreign Aid, 1984-2003." *World Development*, vol. 34, no. 12 (2006).

Dubarry, Ramesh et al. New Evidence on the Impact of Foreign Aid on Economic Growth, Credit Research Paper.

Eifert, Ben, and Alan Gelb. "Coping with Aid Volatility." *IMF Finance & Development*, vol. 42, no. 3 (2005). http://www.imf.org/external/pubs/ft/fandd/2005/09/eifert.htm.

Encyclopedia of the nations. "Economic and Social Development - Second un development decade." http://www.nationsencyclopedia.com/United-Nations/Economic-and-Social-Development-SECOND-UN-DEVELOPMENT-DECADE.html (last visited December 2008).

European Commission. "Policy Coherence for Development : 2015 EU Report." http://ec.europa.eu/europeaid/sites/devco/files/pcd-report-2015_en.pdf.

Export-Import Bank of China. "Infrastructure development in Africa supported by the Export-Import Bank of China." Paper presented at the 3rd annual Meeting of the Infrastructure Consortium for Africa, January 17th, 2007, Berlin.

Faller, Martin. "Briefing on the Code of Conduct for the International Red Cross and Red Crescent Movement and NGOs in Disaster Relief and the Sphere Project." Gayle, Helene, Nafis Sadik, and Naruo Uehara. "The Human Security Impact of AIDS and Other Communicable Disease in Asia." presented in the Human Security Challenge of HIV/AIDS and Other Communicable Disease: Exploring Effective Regional and Global Response hosted by Asia Society and JCIE, on March 22, 2004.

Fengler, M.G., and H. Kharas, *Delivering Aid Differently: Lesson from the Field*. Washington D.C.: Bookings Institutions, 2010.

Feyzioglu, Tarhan, Vinaya Swaroop, and Min Zhu. "A Panel Data Analysis of the Fungibility of Foreign Aid." *The World Bank Economic Review*, vol. 12, no. 1 (1998).

Fitzgerald, Sarah. *International Wildlife Trade: Whose Business is It?* Vaud: World Wildlife Fund, 1989.

Franceys, Richard, and Almud Weitz. "Public-Private Community Partnerships in Infrastructure for the Poor." *Journal of International Development*, vol. 15, no. 8 (2003).

Frankovits, Andre. "Rejoinder: the Rights Way to Development Elsevier Science Ltd." *Food Policy*, vol. 21, no. 1 (1996): 123-128.

French Embassy. "French ODA — Interview given by M. Charles Josselin to the La Croix daily newspaper, Paris 29.04.2001." http://www.ambafrance-uk.org/French-ODA-Interview-given-by-M.html (last visited March 2009).

GHD. "Good Humanitarian Donorship Initiative." http://www.goodhumanitariandonorship.org/gns/about-us/about-ghd.aspx (last visited September 2014).

Global Aid Architecture. http://www.educationandtransition.org/guidance/global-aid-architecture (last visited March 2016).

Global Environment Facility. "What Is the GEF?" http://www.gefweb.org/interior_right.aspx?id=50 (last visited May 2009).

Gonzales, Robert. *A Strategy to Increase Participation of Philippines NGOs in the Policy Formulation and Programming of Official Development Assistance*. Asian Institute of Management, 1998.

Gould, Benjamin, and Lira Lazarus. *Security and Human Rights*. Oxford: Hart Publishing, 2007.

Gulrajani, Nilima. "Bilateral versus multilateral aid channels: Strategic choices for donors." London: ODI Report, 2016, 5.

Gupta, Sanjeev et al., "Are Donor Countries Giving More or Less Aid?" *Review of Development Economics*, vol. 10, no. 3 (2006).

Han, Hongyul et al. "A Study on the Policy Framework of Aid for Trade in Major Donor Countries and Implications for Korea." *The Comparative Economic Review*, vol. 19, no. 1 (2002).

Hansen, Henrik, and Finn Tarp. "Aid and Growth regression." *Journal of Development Economics*, vol. 64, Issue 2 (2001).

Harrison, Ann. "Globalization and Poverty." National Bureau of Economic Research Working Paper Series, Cambridge, 2006.

Hattori, T. "Reconceptualizing Foreign Aid." *Review of International Political Economy*, vol. 8, no. 4 (2002).

Hayter, T. *Aid as Imperialism*. Baltimore: Penguin Books, 1972.

Health GAP. "History of the Global Fund." http://www.healthgap.org/gfatm.

htm (last visited May 2009).

Henderson, David. *The MAI Affair: A Story and its Lessons*. London: Royal Institute of International Affairs, 1999.

Hicks, Robert et al. *Greening Aid? Understanding the Environmental Impact of Development Assistance*. New York: Oxford University Press, 2008.

Hong, Jae-Hwan et al. *A Study on the Evaluation System of the ODA Projects in Korea*. Korea Institute of Public Administration, 2012.

Hoy, Paula. *Players and Issues in International Aid*. West Hartford: Kumarin Press, 1998.

Hudson, John, and Paul Mosley. "Aid politics and growth: in search of the holy grail." *Journal of International Development*, vol. 13, Issue 7 (2001).

Hughes, Barry, and Peter Johnson. "Sustainable Futures: policies for global development." *Futures*, vol. 37, no. 8 (2005).

IDD and Associates. *Evaluation of General Budget Support: Synthesis Report*. Birmingham: International Development Department, University of Birmingham, 2006.

IMF. "Debt Relief under the Heavily Indebted Poor Countries (HIPC) Initiative." http://www.imf.org/external/np/exr/facts/hipc.htm (last visited July 2014).

IMF. "Debt Relief Under the Heavily Indebted Countries (HIPC) Initiative." https://www.imf.org/external/np/exr/facts/hipc.htm (last visited August 2015).

______. "History." http://www.imf.org/external/about/history.htm (last visited December 2008).

______. "Our Work." http://www.imf.org/external/about/ourwork.htm (last visited December 2008).

______. "The Multilateral Debt Relief Initiative." http://www.imf.org/external/np/exr/facts/mdri.htm (last visited May 2009).

Independent Evaluation Group. *Hazards of Nature, Risks to Development: An IEG Evaluation of the World Bank Assistance for Natural Disasters*. Washington D.C.: World Bank, 2006.

International Development Act 2002. http://www.legislation.gov.uk/ukpga/2002/1/contents (last visited July 2014).

International Development Research Centre. "From Pearson to Johannesburg." http://www.idrc.ca/en/ev-114186-201-1-DO_TOPIC.html (last visited December 2008).

International Federation of Red Cross and Red Crescent Societies (IFRC). "Relief, recovery and Root Causes." In *World disasters Report 2001*. Geneva: International Federation of Red Cross and Red Crescent Societies, 2001.

International Federation of Red Cross and Red Crescent Societies and the

ICRC. "The Code of Conduct for the International Red Cross and Red Crescent Movement and Non-Governmental Organisations (NGOs) in Disaster Relief." (1994).

International Financial Group. "What We Do." http://www.ifc.org/ifcext/about.nsf/Content/WhatWeDo (last visited December 2008).

Jain, Sanjay. "Project Assistance versus Budget Support: An Incentive-Theoretic Analysis of Aid Conditionality." *Review of World Economics*, vol. 143, no. 4 (2007).

Japan Bank for International Cooperation. http://www.jbic.go.jp (last visited March 2009).

Jeon, Seung-Hoon et al. "Mid to Long-Term Bilateral Aid Policy of Korea." Seoul: KOICA, 2006.

Johnson, Doug, and Tristan Zajonc, "Can Foreign Aid Create an Incentive for Good Governance? Evidence from the Millennium Challenge Corporation 1." Working paper series, Kennedy School of Government, April 11, 2006.

Jung, Jione et al. *Enhancing the Effectiveness of South Korea's Multilateral Aid.* Seoul: KIEP, 2010.

_______. "Woorinara dajawonjo chujin jeonryakgwa jungchakgwaje *[Enhancing the Effectiveness of South Korea's Multilateral Aid]*." Seoul: KIEP, 2010.

Kang, In-Soo et al. *Major Issues and Policy Implications of Aid for Trade.* Seoul: Korea Institute for International Economic Policy, 2011.

Kang, Sangin et al. "Green Economy in the Context of Rio+20: Issues and Implications for National Strategies." *Journal of Fundamental Research*, vol. 2012 (2012).

Keck, Margaret E., and Kathryn Sikkink. *Activists Beyond Borders: Advocacy Networks in International Politics.* Ithaca: Cornell University Press, 1998.

Keohane, Robert. "International Institutions: Two Approaches." *International Studies Quarterly*, vol. 32, no. 4 (1988).

Kim, Youngrae, Hasoo Lee, and Kiho Lee. "A Comparative Study on the Transnational Network of Non-Governmental Organization (NGO) and the Strengthening Strategy of Civil Society: Korea, Japan and America." *Korean Association of International Relations.* vol. 41, no. 4 (2001).

King, Kenneth. *China's Aid to Africa: A View from China and Japan, lead paper to the JICA seminar on China's Aid to Africa the Beijing Summit and its Follow-up.* Tokyo: Japan International Cooperation Agence (JICA), 2007.

Knack, Stephen. "Aid Dependence and the Quality of Governance: Cross-Country Empirical Tests." *Southern Economic Journal*, vol. 68, no. 2 (2001).

Koh, Dae-Won. "Accountability and Coherence in Global Governance for Development and Poverty Reduction." *Local Development Studies*, vol. 19, no. 2

(2010).

KOICA. *Annual Report* (2008).

______. *Development Cooperation Evaluation Guideline* (2008).

______. *Understanding International Development Cooperation*. Seoul: Hanul, 2008.

KOICA International Development Education Academy. *Understanding KOICA Project* (2012).

Krugman, Paul. *International Economics: Theory and Policy*. Boston: Addison Wesley, 2003.

Kwon, Yool. *A Strategy for Advancing South Korea's ODA: Paradigm Shift in International Development Cooperation and South Korea's ODA Reform*. Seoul: KIEP, 2006.

Kwon, Yul et al. "*Dajawonjoeui hyogwajeok silhangeul wuihan tonghapchujinjeonryak [Korea's Multilateral Aid: Recent Developments and Future Challenges]*." Seoul: KIEP, 2013, 20.

Krumme, Katherine. *International Management of Hazardous Wastes: The Basel Convention and Regulated Legal Rules*. Oxford: Clarendon Press, 1995.

Kreuger, Anne O. "Trading Phobias: Governments, NFOs and the Multilateral System." Annual John Bonython Lecture, The Centre for Independent Studies, Melbourne, Australia, October 10 2000.

Lancaster, Carol. *Foreign Aid: Diplomacy, Development, Domestic Politics*. Chicago: University of Chicago Press, 2006.

Lee, Gye-Woo. "South Korea's policy on international aid market." *Journal of International Development Cooperation*, no. 4 (2009).

Lee, Myonggeun et al. *A Study of Humanitarian Assistance Policy and Operation: Emergency Relief System*. Sungnam: KOICA, 2012.

Lensink, Robert, and Howard White. "Are there negative returns to aid?" *The Journal of Development Studies*, vol. 37, issue 6 (2001).

Lim, Sojin. "A life of dignity for all." [*Development and Issue*], KOICA, no. 12. (2013).

______. "Busan HLF4 Conference Outcome and Challenge of Korean ODA," *Development Cooperation Policy and Issue*, vol. 3, no. 3 (2011).

______. "Post-2015 Development Framework and UN HLP Report." KOICA, vol. 2, no. 10 (2013).

Lumsdaine, David Halloran. *Moral Vision in International Politics: The Foreign Aid Regime, 1949-1989*. Princeton: Princeton University Press, 1993.

MacNaughton, Gillian. "Decent Work, Human Rights and the Millennium Development Goals." *Hastings Race and Poverty Journal*, vol. 7, no. 2 (2010).

Makoba, J. Wagona. "Nongovernmental Organizations (NGOS) and Third World Development: An Alternative Approach to Development." *Journal of Third World Studies*, vol. 19, no. 1 (2002).

McGillivray, Mark. "Aid and Public Sector Behavior in Developing Countries." *Review of Development Economics*, vol. 4, Issue 2 (2000).

______. *Is aid Effective?* OECD, 2004.

Mcgillivray, Mark, and Akhter Ahmed. "Aid, Adjustment and Public Sector Fiscal Behaviour in the Philippines." *Journal of the Asia Pacific Economy*, vol. 4, no. 2 (1999).

McGillivray, Mark, and Bazoumana Ouattara. "Aid, debt burden and government fiscal behaviour in Côte d'Ivoire." *Journal of African Economies*, vol. 14, no. 2 (2005).

McGillivray, Mark, and Oliver Morrissey. "Aid Fungibility in Assessing Aid: red herring or true concern?" *Journal of International Concern*, vol. 12, no. 3 (2000).

Ministry of Finance of the Russian Federation. *The Russian Federation ODA National Report*. 2011.

Ministry of Foreign Affairs of Denmark. *Freedom from Poverty, Freedom to Change*. Copenhagen: Danida, 2010.

Ministry of Foreign Affairs of Japan. "History of Official Development Assistance." http://www.mofa.go.jp/policy/oda/summary/1994/1.html (last visited March 2009).

______. "ODA Evaluations and Recent Trends in Japanese ODA." http://www.mofa.go.jp/policy/oda/evaluation/1998/japanese.html (last visited December 2008).

Moon, Kyungyon. "International Development Cooperation and Development Finance: Discussion and Analysis of Major Actor's Policies on Development Finance." *Journal of East and West Studies*, vol. 26, no. 2 (2014).

______. "The role of humanitarian NGOs: impact on South Korean fod aid policy towards North Korea from 1995 to 2007." Ph.D. Dissertation, Cranfield University, 2011.

Morgenthau, Hans. "A Political Theory of Foreign Aid." *The American Political Science Review*, vol. 50, no. 2 (1962).

Multilateral Investment Guarantee Agency. "About MIGA." http://www.miga.org/about/index_sv.cfm?stid=1588 (last visited December 2008).

Myers, Norman. "Environmental Refugees: A Growing Phenomenon." *Philosophical Transactions: Biological Sciences,* vol. 357, no. 1420 (2002).

Nelson, Paul. "Human Rights, the Millennium Development Goals, and the Future of Development Cooperation." *World Development*, vol. 35, no. 12 (2007).

O'Brien, Robert, Anne Marie Goetz, Jan AartSchote, and Marc Williams. *Contesting Global Governance: Multilateral Economic Institutions and Global Social Movements*. New York: Cambridge University Press, 2000.

OCHA. *OCHA in 2006: Activities and Extra-Budgetary Funding Requirement.* New York: UNOCHA, 2006.

______. "OCHA Mission Statement." http://ochaonline.un.org/AboutOCHA/tabid/1076/Default.aspx (last visited May 2009).

ODA Watch. "UN DCF: the Possibility of Collaboration for Future Development Cooperation?" *Newsletter OWL*, 67 (2012).

OECD. *2008 DAC Report on Multilateral Aid* Paris: OECD, 2009.

______. *2011 DAC Report on Multilateral Aid*. Paris: OECD, 2012.

______. *2012 DAC Report on Multilateral Aid*. Paris: OECD, 2013.

______. *Aid for Trade: Making It Effective*. Paris: OECD, 2006.

______. *Better Aid Managing Aid: Practices of DAC Member Countries*. Paris: OECE Publishing, 2009.

______. *Better Policy for Development: Recommendation for Policy Coherence*. Paris: OECD, 2011.

______. *Building Blocks for Policy Coherence for Development*. Paris: OECD, 2009.

______. *Development Cooperation Report 2007 Statistical Annex* (2008).

______. *Development Co-operation Report 2013: Ending Poverty*. Paris: OECE Publishing, 2013.

______. *Effective Aid Management: Twelve Lessons from DAC Peer Reviews* (2008).

______. *FDI in Figures*. 2014.

______. "Framework for an OECD Strategy on Development." at the Meeting of the OECD Council at Ministerial Level (Paris, 25-26 May 2011).

______. *Mainstreaming Cross-cutting Issues: 7 Lessons from DAC Peer Reviews*. Paris: OECD, 2014.

______. "OECD Development Assistance Committee (DAC) welcomes Korean membership." http://www.oecd.org/dac/oecddevelopmentassistance-committeedacwelcomeskoreanmembership.htm (last visited July 2014).

______. "Official Development Assistance — Definition and Coverage." http://www.oecd.org/investment/stats/officialdevelopmentassistancedefinition-andcoverage.htm (last visited July 2014).

______. "Official development assistance-definition and coverage." http://www.oecd.org/dac/stats/officialdevelopmentassistancedefinitionandcoverage.htm.

______. *Promoting Private Investment for Development: The Role of ODA*. OECD DAC Guidelines and Reference Series, 2003.

______. *Promoting Pro-Poor Growth: Policy Guidance to Donors*. Paris: OECD, 2006.

______. "Rome Declaration on Harmonisation." in *DAC Guidelines and Reference Series: Harmonising Donor Practices for Effective Aid Delivery*. Paris: OECD, 2003, 10-12.

OECD. "The Paris Declaration on Aid Effectiveness and the Accra Agenda for Action." http://www.oecd.org/dac/effectiveness/34428351.pdf.

_______. "The Russian Federation's Official Development Assistance (ODA)." http://www.oecd.org/russia/russiasofficialdevelopmentassistance.htm (last visited July 2014).

_______. *Towards Better Humanitarian Donorship: 12 Lessons from DAC Peer Reviews*. OECD, 2012.

OECD DAC. *Aid Effectiveness 2005-10: Progress in Implementing The Paris Declaration* (2011).

_______. *Busan Partnership for Effective Development Co-operation*. Busan: OECD, 2011, 3.

_______. *DAC Peer Review Content Guide* (2010).

_______. *DAC Peer Review: Denmark*. Paris: OECD, 2011.

_______. *DAC Peer Review: Finland*. Paris: OECD, 2007.

_______. *DAC Peer Review: Germany*. Paris: OECD, 2006.

_______. *DAC Peer Review: Germany*. Paris: OECD, 2010.

_______. *DAC Peer Review: Greece*. Paris: OECD, 2006.

_______. *DAC Peer Review: Sweden*. Paris: OECD, 2009.

_______. *DAC Peer Review: The Netherlands*. Paris: OECD, 2011.

_______. "Data on total use of multilateral system: All DAC members." http://www.oecd.org/dac/aid-architecture/multilateralaid.htm (last visited June 2014).

_______. "Declaration on Policy Coherence for Development." 4 June 2008-C/Min(2008)2/final.

_______. *Glossary of Key Terms in Evaluation and Results Based Management* (2002).

_______. "Lessons from Peer Reviews." http://www.oecd.org/dac/peer-reviews/lessons-peer-reviews.htm.

_______. *Principles for the Evaluation of Development Assistance* (1991).

_______. *The DAC Multilateral Aid Report in 2013-14*. Paris: OECD, 2013.

_______. http://www.oecd.org/dac/aid-architecture/multilateralaid.htm (last visited June 2014).

OHCHR. "Principles and Guidelines for a Human Rights Approach to Poverty Reduction Strategies." New York; Geneva: United Nations, 2002.

One Campaign. "Monitoring the G8 promise to Africa, France – Development Assistance." http://www.one.org/report/2010/en/country/france/oda.html (last visited Jan 2011).

Pagani, Fabrizio. "Peer Review: A Tool for Cooperation and Change." *The OECD Observer*, no. 235 (2002).

Park, Soo-Kyung et al. "Busan segyegaebalwonjo chongheo(HLF-4)eui juyo noneuiwa sunggwa [Busan HLF4 Key Issues and Outcome]." *KIEP jiyuk-*

gyungje Focus [KIEP Regional Economic Focus], vol. 5, no. 48 (2011).

______. "Busan HLF4 Key Issues and Outcome." *KIEP Regional Economic Focus*, vol. 5, no. 48 (2011).

Pessoa, Argentino. "Public Private Partnerships in Developing Countries: Are Infrastructures Responding to the New ODA Strategy." *Journal of International Development*, vol. 20, no. 3 (2008).

Picciotto, Robert. "The Evaluation of Policy Coherence for Development." *SAGE journals*, vol. 11, no. 3 (2005).

Rhee, Hosaeng et al. *A Study on Priority Areas and Programs for Korea's Aid for Trade*. Seoul: Korea Institute for International Economic Policy, 2012.

Riddell, Roger C. *Does Foreign Aid Really Work?* Oxford University Press, 2007. http://ww.house.gov/budget/prezbudget.html (last visited March 2009).

Rogerson, Andrew. "Aid Harmonization and Alignment: Bridging the Gaps between Reality and the Paris Reform Agenda." *Development Policy Review*, vol. 23, no. 5 (2005).

Ruggie, John Gerald. "Multilateralism: The Anatomy of an Institution." In *Multilateralism Matters: The Theory and Praxis of an Institutional Form*, ed. John Gerald Ruggie. New York: Columbia University Press, 1993.

Sachs, Jefferey. *The End of Poverty*. London: Penguin Books, 2005.

Schmidle, Nicholas. "Wanted: A New Home for My Country." *The New York Times*, May 8, 2009.

Sjöberg, Helen. "Restructuring the Global Environmental Facility." Woking Paper 13, Global Environment Facility, September 1999. http://thegef.org/Outreach/outreach-PUblications/WP13-Restructuring_the_GEF.pdf.

Soh, Changrok. "Theoretical Approaches to Global Governance." *Korea Review of International Studies*, vol. 5, no. 1 (2002).

______. "Theoretical Considerations Why Countries Provide Development Aid." *Journal of International Politics*, vol. 15, no. 1 (2010).

Sohn, Hyuksang. "Busan HLF4 and Global Civil Society: Case Study of Better Aid and Open Forum." *Journal of International Development Cooperation*, no. 3 (2011).

Sohn, Hyuk-Sang. "Framing Theory and Discourse Contestation of 'Aid Effectiveness' and 'Development Effectiveness' in International Development Cooperation." *The Korean Journal of International Relationship*, vol. 53, no. 1 (2013).

Sohn, Hyuksang, and Youngsun Park. "A Ctirical Study on Policy Coherence for Development in South Korea." *Korean journal of international relations*, vol. 52, no. 3 (2012).

Sohn, Hyuk-Sang et al. *A Study on Multilateral Aid Strategies of OECD/DAC Members and Policy Implications for South Korea*. Seoul: KIEP, 2013.

Sohn, Hyuksang et al. "Enhancing Policy Coherence for Development in South Korea." *ODA Study*, vol. 24, no. 3 (2012).

Song, Cheolho. *The Study of Government Response Strategy for International Disaster*. Seoul: National Security Council, 2006.

Speeckaert, Georges P. *Les 1978 OrganisationsInternationalesFondéesdepuis le Congrès de Vienne*. Brussels: Union of International Associations, 1957.

Stubbs, Rebecca. "The Millennium Challenge Account: Influencing Governance in Developing Countries through Performance-Based Foreign Aid." *Vanderbilt Journal of Transnational Law*, vol. 42, no. 621 (2009).

Susana, Franco-Rodriguez, and Morrissey Oliver. "Aid and the Public Sector in Pakistan: Evidence with Endogenous Aid." *World Development* vol. 26, no. 7 (1998): 1241-1250.

Swaroop, Vinaya, Shikha Jha and Andrew Sunil Rajkumar. "Fiscal Effects of Foreign Aid in a Federal System of Governance: The Case of India." *Journal of Public Economics*, vol. 77, no. 3 (2000).

The Commission on Global Governance. *Our Global Neighborhood: The Report of the Commission on Global Governance*. Oxford: Oxford University Press, 1995.

The LEVIN Institute. "What is Globalization?" http://www.globalization101.org/What_is_Globalization.html?PHPSESSID=cfd52fae9cb40178fef89f0a24682821 (last visited March 2009).

The Sphere Project. *Humanitarian Charter and Minimum Standards in Humanitarian Response*. Third edition. The Spehre Project, 2011.

______. "The Sphere Project in Brief." http://www.sphereproject.org/about (last visited December 2014).

The World Bank. "Bridging the Gap between Human Rights and Development." Presidential Lecture, December 2001.

______. "FAQs: Global Poverty Line Update." http://www.worldbank.org/en/topic/poverty/brief/global-poverty-line-faq (last visited August 2016).

______. http://data.worldbank.org/indicator/BX.KLT.DINV.CD.WD/countries? display=graph (last visited July 2014).

______. "International Bank for Reconstruction and Development." http://web.worldbank.org/WBSITE/EXTERNAL/EXTABOUTUS/EXTIBRD/0,,menuPK:3046081~pagePK:64168427~piPK:64168435~theSitePK:3046012,00.html (last visited December 2008).

______. "Net Official Development Assistance and Official Aid Received." http://data.worldbank.org/indicator/DT.ODA.ALLD.CD?year_high_desc=false (last visited August 2016).

______. "Overview: Understanding, measuring, and overcoming poverty." http://web.worldbank.org/WBSITE/EXTERNAL/TOPICS/EXTPO

VERTY/0,,contentMDK:20153855~menuPK:373757~pagePK:148956 ~piPK:216618~theSitePK:336992,00.html (last visited December 2014).

The World Bank. *The Role of International Business in Aid for Trade: Building Capacity for Trade in Developing Countries* (2011).

______. *What is the World Bank doing on Aid for Trade?* (2011).

The World Bank and Agenda 21, July 2002.

The World Bank, Development Research Group. "Assessing Aid, What Works, What Doesn't and Why?" *Policy Research Report* (1998).

Thorp, Willard L. "The Objectives of Point Four." *Annals of the American Academy of Political and Social Science*, vol. 268, no. 1 (1950).

Tisch, S., and M.B. Wallace. *Dilemmas of Development Assistance, The What, Why and Who of Foreign Aid*. Boulder: Westview Press, 1994.

UDG. "About the UNDG." http://www.undg.org/index.cfm?P=2 (last visited May 2009).

UN Department of Economic and Social Affairs. "*About the DSD*." http://www.un.org/esa/dsd/dsd/dsd_index.shtml (last visited April 2009).

UN General Assembly. *Triennial Comprehensive Policy Review of Operational Activities for Development of the United Nations System*. A/RES/62/208 (19 December 2007).

UN System Task Team on the Post-2015 UN Development Agenda. "Realizing the Future We Want for All: Report to the Secretary-General." http://www.un.org/millenniumgoals/pdf/Post_2015_UNTTreport.pdf (last visited June 2014).

UNCTAD. *Word Investment Report 1996, Investment, Trade and International Policy Arrangements*. New York & Geneva, 1996.

UNDP. "About the MDGs: UNDP's Role." http://www.undp.org/mdg/undps_role.shtml (last visited March 2009).

______. *Human Development Report*. New York: United Nations Development Programme, 2009.

______. *The Millennium Development Goals Report 2008*. New York: United Nations, 2008.

______. *The Millennium Development Goals Report 2012*. New York: United Nations, 2012.

______. *The Millennium Development Goals Report 2015*. New York: United Nations, 2015.

UNDP Human Development Report 1997.

UNDP. *Human Development Report 2006*. New York: Palgrave McMillan, 2006.

UNESCO Korea. "Principal International Documents Regarding Human Rights." Seoul: UNESCO, 1995.

United Nations. *A New Global Partnership: Eradicate Poverty and Transform Econo-*

mies through Sustainable Development. The Report of the High-Level Panel of Eminent Persons on the Post-2015 Development Agenda. New York: United Nations Publications, 2013.

United Nations. "Accelerating progress towards the Millennium Development Goals: options for sustained and inclusive growth and issues for advancing the United Nations development agenda beyond 2015." *Annual report of the Secretary-General*, A/66/126, August 6 2012.

_______. "Final Outcome of the International Conference on Financing for Development." http://www.un.org/esa/ffd/0302finalMonterreyConsensus.pdf (last visited April 2009).

_______. "Report of the World Commission on Environment and Development." *General Assembly Resolution*, 42/187 (1987).

_______. *Report of the World Summit for Social Development.* Copenhagen: UN, 1995.

_______. *Report on the International Conference on Financing for Development.* New York: United Nations, 2002.

United Nations Development Group. "About the UNDG." http://www.undg.org/content/about_the_undg (last visited June 2014).

United Nations Economic and Social Council. "Background Information." http://www.un.org/ecosoc/about/ (last visited December 2008).

United Nations Environment Program. "Desertification: The Problem that Won't Go Away." (1992).

United Nations Human Rights Office of the High Commssioner. "HIV/AIDS and Human Rights." http://www.ohchr.org/EN/Issues/HIV/Pages/HIVIndex.aspx.

United States Library of Congress. "For European Recovery: The Fiftieth Anniversary of the Marshall Plan." http://www.loc.gov/exhibits/marshall/mars.html (last visited December 2008).

Universal Declaration of Human Rights (1948), Art. 3.

USAID. "General Budget Support and Sector Program Assistance." *PPC Evaluation Working Paper*, no. 19 (2004).

_______. *US Foreign Aid: Meeting the Challenge of the Twenty-first Century* (2004).

WaterAid. "Essential Element: Why International Aid for Water, Sanitation and Hygiene Is Still a Critical Source of Finance for Many Countries." (2015).

Weiss, Thomas G. "Governance, Good Governance, and Global Governance: Conceptual and Actual Challenges." *Third World Quarterly*, vol. 21, no. 5 (2000).

Weiss, Thomas G., and Leon Gordenker. "Pluralizing Global Governance: Analytical Approaches and Dimensions." In G. Weiss and Leon Gordenker, ed. *NGOs, the UN, and Global Governance.* New York: Lynne Rienner Publishers, 1999.

Wendt, Alexander. "Anarchy is What States Make of It." *International Organization*, vol. 46, no. 2 (1992).

WHO Humanitarian Coordination Group. *International norms and principles*. Geneva: Inter-Agency Standing Committee, 2010.

Wolf, Martin. *Why Globalization Works*. London:Yale Nota Bene Book, 2005.

Wood, Robert E. *From Marshall Plan to Debt Crises: Foreign Aid and Development Choices in the World Economy*. Berkeley: University of California Press, 1972.

WTO. "Doha Work Program: Ministerial Declaration adopted on 18 December 2005." http://www.wto.org/english/thewto_e/minist_e/min05_e/final_text_e.htm (last visited August 2014).

WTO and OECD, *Aid for Trade at a Glance 2007: 1st Global Review* (2007).

_______. *Aid for Trade at a Glance 2013: Connecting to Value Chain* (2013).

Yoon, Ji-young. "UN DCF and International Development Cooperation." *Journal of International Development Cooperation*, vol. 2012, no. 4 (2012).

Index

E

R